The Angry Christian

THE ANGRY CHRISTIAN

A Theology for Care
and Counseling

Andrew D. Lester

Westminster John Knox Press
LOUISVILLE • LONDON

Scripture quotations, unless otherwise indicated, are from the New Revised Standard Version of the Bible, copyright © 1989 by the Division of Christian Education of the National Council of the Churches of Christ in the U.S.A. and are used by permission.

Scripture quotations marked JB are from *The Jerusalem Bible*, Copyright © 1966, 1967, 1968 by Darton, Longman & Todd, Ltd., and Doubleday & Co., Inc. Used by permission of the publishers.

Book design by Sharon Adams
Cover design by Night & Day Design

First edition
Published by Westminster John Knox Press
Louisville, Kentucky

This book is printed on acid-free paper that meets the American National Standards Institute Z39.48 standard. ∞

PRINTED IN THE UNITED STATES OF AMERICA

03 04 05 06 07 08 09 10 11 12 — 10 9 8 7 6 5 4 3 2 1

Library of Congress Cataloging-in-Publication Data

Lester, Andrew D.
  The angry Christian : a theology for care and counseling / Andrew D. Lester.
     p. cm.
  Includes bibliographical references and indexes.
  ISBN 0-664-22519-5 (alk. paper)
     1. Anger—Religious aspects—Christianity. 2. Pastoral counseling. 3. Pastoral care. I. Title.

  BV4627.A5 L46 2003
  253.5'2—dc21

                                                              2002038092

Contents

Contents

Acknowledgments

A Henry Luce III Fellows in Theology grant, one program of The Henry Luce Foundation, Inc., made a significant contribution to this research project. I am appreciative of the personal investment of Henry Luce, III, chairman and CEO of the foundation; John W. Cook, president; and Michael F. Gilligan, program director for theology, who are instrumental in the success of this program.

This Luce Fellowship program is administered through The Association of Theological Schools in the United States and Canada. My thanks to Dan Aleshire, executive director, and to Matt Zyniewicz, at that time coordinator of Faculty Grant Programs, for their investment of time and energy in this program.

During my tenure at Brite Divinity School, Texas Christian University, the trustees, administration, and faculty have provided significant support for the faculty's research and writing projects through a generous sabbatical program. Much of this project was finished during a sabbatical graciously granted by the administration and faculty for the academic year 2000–2001. The administration also provided a teaching assistant to assist with research during this leave.

My thanks to Westminster John Knox Press for granting permission to use material taken from my *Coping with Your Anger: A Christian Guide*, published in 1983, in which many of these basic ideas were first conceptualized. They also granted permission to use material from my *Hope in Pastoral Care and Counseling*, published in 1995, and from *It Takes Two: The Joy of Intimate Marriage*, published in 1998 (coauthored with my wife, Judy).

I am grateful for friends and colleagues who have willingly engaged and critiqued this material. Mahan Siler read an entire first draft and provided challenging responses and suggestions. Molly Marshall not only read and critiqued the entire manuscript but graciously and competently served as my presenter/responder at a meeting of Luce Scholars at Princeton. Bill Ratliff, professor at Earlham School of Religion in Richmond, Indiana, used an early draft of this material in a course and offered insightful critique. Dorothy Panelli graciously read several drafts, contributing immeasurably to my conceptualization of the issues and my writing style. I have been in dialogue over the years with many other colleagues, friends, workshop participants, students, and scores of authors who have written on this subject. I am grateful for all they have contributed to my thinking about these ideas.

Katherine Godby served as my research associate during this sabbatical. She worked untold numbers of hours (I'm afraid to ask!), some underwritten by the Luce Foundation, and many more that she graciously gave. Her thorough approach saved me hundreds of hours in the library and on the computer. She intuitively tracked down the most important items and excavated from piles of material that which was germane to the project, and her suggestions about content and style were on target.

Other friends and colleagues were faithful in providing feedback from within their respective disciplines: David Balch, Brad Binau, Jim Duke, Larry Graham, Bill Hendricks, James Hyde, Charles Scalise, Frank Tupper, and Janice Yusk have all read selections of this material. Amy Cooper and Tammerie Spires gave many editorial suggestions to an early draft. Linda Ford and Andy Shelton served as my professor's assistants during the sabbatical year, diligently finding sources and performing other time-saving tasks. Sherry Willis and Suzanne Stone, my administrative assistants during this period of time, were always willing to assist with administrative tasks and procedures.

Stephanie Egnotovich, who has been my editor at Westminster John Knox Press for a number of years, has guided this project from beginning to end (through numerous drafts!) with steadfast affirmation and support. I have greatly appreciated her insightful ideas about the style, structure, and content.

Judy, my wife and partner of forty-three years, never expected this one-year sabbatical project (my goal) to stretch over two years (the reality), but in her usual style she thoughtfully and consistently created the space for both work and play that was necessary to complete this project and stay sane. Furthermore, she read and critiqued this material from her perspective as a marriage and family therapist, offering ideas that resulted from her use of them in her therapeutic work. I am exceedingly grateful for all she gives to our relationship.

The dedication page in my first book on anger, *Coping with Your Anger: A Christian Guide* (Westminster/John Knox Press, 1983), read as follows:

> To Wayne E. Oates
> who first taught me how
> to deal creatively with anger

Wayne was my professor, advisor, friend, pastor, and colleague. His gifts to me and my family are too numerous to recount, but one of them was his witness to effective ways of thinking theologically and ethically about anger. He helped me learn to identify and express more creatively this aspect of my being. He died in 1999 as I was preparing for this project. I remain grateful.

ANDREW D. LESTER
Summer, 2002

Introduction:
The Problem with Anger

I grew up afraid of anger and uncomfortable around conflict. I was carefully taught to "be nice," and in my family and culture being nice clearly meant not expressing anger. Furthermore, I had experienced destructive anger, both my own and that of others, which convinced me anger was dangerous.

When I was in the seventh grade, a boy named Ira transferred into our school. For reasons I never understood, Ira picked on me constantly. His favorite annoyance was to jump on my back when I wasn't looking. I tried to ignore him, be nice, and avoid fighting, but to no avail. One day when Ira jumped on my back, I didn't control my anger. It exploded, and I threw him over my head onto the basketball court and began to beat his head on the asphalt. When the coach finally pulled me off, I was shaking with rage. His tears, cries of pain, and the blood on his head also left me frightened. Guilt piled on immediately. Having trespassed against my moral values about not being angry and not hurting people, I was embarrassed by my behavior. I vowed anew never to get angry.

Ira deserved it, you might think, so why the guilt and embarrassment? Along with the cultural concern to be nice, I had been carefully taught that *good* Christians would not express anger and that the *best* Christians would not even feel it. I was an idealistic teenager and wanted to please both my parents and God by being the best Christian possible, so I kept my anger well camouflaged—even from myself. I was able to deny ever getting angry until young adulthood, but then I married.

My wife Judy and I have shared in many marriage enrichment workshops that the most difficult adjustment we had to make after we married was figuring

1

out what to do with anger. We did not handle conflict effectively or creatively. In the early years of our marriage, Judy was excellent at becoming quiet in a way that captured my attention; I knew she was being silent at me! I retaliated by withdrawing, which I did in socially acceptable ways: going to the library and pretending to study, or going to play basketball, but in either case I would be sure to stay out late enough that she would have gone to bed without me. That was my way of trying to punish her because she hates going to bed by herself. Childishly we would try to make each other feel guilty and make the other one apologize first. By then, however, we had no idea of what caused the anger in the first place, so we didn't resolve the real issues. Our retreat into silence and withdrawal led to emotional distance, and the tension interfered with our growth as a couple, as we have described elsewhere.[1]

Needing to learn new ways of thinking about anger motivated my first journey into the literature on this subject. New insights provided creative new ways of dealing with anger that led to more intimacy for Judy and me. These new perspectives also provided us new ways of functioning as therapists.[2]

Like me, you may desire a better understanding of your own anger and increased wisdom about how to handle it creatively. You may struggle with how to handle anger toward your spouse, children, parents, or in other intimate relationships. Perhaps your anger is hidden behind sarcasm and petty resistance; maybe it is expressed with volatility, and your destructive words and actions leave you embarrassed and guilty, having to accept yourself as one who hurts others. You may have been wounded by and suffered serious consequences from someone's anger, such as having been fired, divorced, abused, or assaulted. Understanding what happened and why the other person was so angry may be difficult. You might find it difficult to understand and resolve anger you feel toward yourself and find the consequences of self-punishment to be destructive to you and your relationships. Like many Christians, you may be angry with God and unsure how to deal with it.

THE CHURCH AND ANGER

Christianity has frequently discounted anger, describing it as part of our "carnal nature" and representative of human depravity. By the Middle Ages anger had become one of the Seven Deadly Sins. Subsequent generations of theologians have compounded the error. Fervent sermons have traced anger back to the "fall," and pastors have suggested that were it not for original sin, human beings would not be plagued by anger at all. Church school teachers have painted Jesus as a passive recipient of all the injustice that came his way (particularly during Holy Week), a model for never becoming angry regardless of the situation. Jesus' words in the Sermon on the Mount, "You have heard that it was said to those of ancient times, 'You shall not murder'; and 'whoever murders shall be liable to judgment.' But I say to you that if you are angry with a brother or sister, you will be liable to judgment" (Matt. 5:21–22), have been misinterpreted to mean that feeling angry is the same as murdering someone.

Many Christians, therefore, have learned that anger, in any shape or form, is sinful. One friend said that he didn't hear this explicit message from the pulpit, "but it is what I heard implicitly, a part of the air I breathed [at church] but never named with words directly"—a common report from the Christians with whom I minister. Many Christians, therefore, assume that being angry is rooted in our sinful nature, has no place in the life of a mature Christian, and, if asked, will explain this as the biblical view.

I believe, in contrast, that our capacity for anger is one of God's good gifts, intentionally rooted in creation and serving important purposes in human life. Though we can certainly sin with it, our anger also contributes to such life experiences as courage, hope, and intimacy. Anger is not necessarily contrary to love and can actually function as an expression of love. In fact, *not* being angry in some circumstances (such as in response to injustice and oppression) is to miss God's claim on our lives. Compassionate anger is often necessary for Christians to "proclaim release to the captives" and "let the oppressed go free" (Luke 4:18).

You might wonder how this anger-is-sin tradition, as I name it, can still be so influential after a century of challenges from psychology, the social sciences, and more recently the neurosciences—not to mention popular culture, which tolerates and promotes expressions of anger. Yet, in the manner of many dominant narratives, this tradition seems entrenched. Pastoral counselors, therapists, chaplains, and other caregivers constantly work with people who either consciously or unconsciously function with this belief about anger[3] and behave, often at unconscious levels, as if anger is always sinful. Therefore, they often deny that they are angry, or when they do experience anger, often suppress it. By the time they finally express their anger, as in my experience with Ira, this emotion has become so intense that it bursts forth in destructive ways, leaving feelings of guilt and shame, and reinforcing the idea that anger is bad.

On the opposite end of the spectrum, many other Christians (and most pastoral care specialists) have adopted modern psychology's idea that anger is simply a "natural" part of being human. They accept anger as a normal, natural, even healthy emotion, something they should be free to experience without guilt or shame—only being concerned with how it is expressed. Though I am in general agreement with this stance, it does run the risk of approaching anger as if it were a morally neutral experience. This stance borrows too much from the older idea that anger is an instinctive response over which we have little control.

In this book I take a different perspective, presenting developments in the neurosciences and the social sciences that confront us with the fact that we have much more control over both *why* we get angry and *how* we express it than previously supposed. Brain research is teaching us that the capacity for anger, which is "wired" into all of us, is not something that is activated randomly. An environmental event or an internal perception must be interpreted as a threat before a person will experience emotional arousal as anger. My definition of anger that emerges from this study is as follows: *Anger is the physical, mental, and emotional arousal pattern that occurs in response to a* perceived threat *to the self characterized by the desire to attack or defend.* The key phrase is "perceived threat"; constructionist narrative theory reminds us that we have significant control over what we perceive as threatening to the values, beliefs, and meanings that are part of our core narratives.

WHAT'S THE PROBLEM?
ANGER CAN BE DESTRUCTIVE

All of us have seen anger cut a destructive path through many lives. Every day, it seems, I work with people who are angry with their children, parents, spouses, friends, partners, employers, and church. Many are angry at themselves for mistakes, weaknesses, and failures, both real and imagined. Many are also angry with and alienated from God. Frequently this anger is expressed in life-destroying ways. I have known people who were badly wounded by abusive anger from powerful others and who suffered significant damage to their sense of worth and their ability to cope with life effectively. The verbal and physical abuse they experienced as children makes intimately relating with significant others difficult. Their patterns of behavior negatively affect their family life, particularly children, who then suffer from the damaging results as the "sins of the parents" are passed through the generations. The church can play an effective role in interrupting this cycle.

Anger is a powerful emotion that has destructive potential. By "destructive anger" I mean anger that destroys our relationship with ourself, others, and God. Instead of moving us toward loving God with all our heart, mind, and soul, and our neighbor as ourself—creating loving relationships, breaking down barriers, promoting peace, and bringing about reconciliation—destructive anger moves us in the opposite direction—toward disunity, estrangement, hostility, and alienation. While creative anger moves us and our community toward spiritual well-being, destructive anger moves us and our community toward spiritual dysfunction:

Instead of love there is hate.

Instead of grace there is punishment.

Instead of reconciliation there is alienation.

Instead of forgiveness there is vengeance.

Instead of healing there is wounding.

Anger that is expressed destructively toward others, ourselves, or God adversely affects our spiritual journey. Anger's power can destroy our health, our relationships, our community, and our sense of God's presence and grace.

A Hazard to Health

Chronically angry people pay a physical price for their unresolved anger. Chronic anger that has become resentment, bitterness, hostility, or hatred negatively effects the immune system—making those persons more vulnerable to disease.[4]

Anger can also be misdirected at one's self. Rather than expressing anger outwardly toward the threat, we turn it back onto ourselves, because of guilt, fear, or embarrassment about being angry. This internalized anger can be expressed in physical symptoms including headaches, high blood pressure, nervous stomach, and irritable bowel syndrome; through mental states such as depression; and in self-mutilating behaviors such as cutting.

A Hazard to Relationships

Anger is often destructive to intimate relationships, creating chaos between spouses, partnerships, parent and child, and extended families. Anger can make relationships painful and shorten their life span. Marital wars (either cold or hot), for example, interrupt intimacy for long periods of time during which a marriage can be "worn and torn" in ways that are difficult to repair.

Another common way to express anger is to dump it on an innocent object or person. A door is kicked, or a child is slapped, or a spouse is chewed out. The injustice felt by spouses, children, and partners who serve as substitute targets contributes to many broken relationships. Untold numbers of children have carried into their adult lives a wounded identity and a deep-seated rage over the injustice of being substitute targets for destructive parental wrath, whether it is expressed physically or through silence and withdrawal.

Destructive anger in relationships can be expressed in many ways, not just in the abuse we hear of most frequently. In addition to silence and withdrawal, other common expressions of anger frequently come to the attention of pastors, marriage and family therapists, pastoral counselors, and other caregivers.

Nagging. Nagging, or "fussing," is an attempt to force people to act in the way we want them to act. Nagging is actually an impotent expression of anger because its very use communicates the nagger's feeling of helplessness at making the other person change behavior. Both the nagger and the "naggee" know that no change is really expected. "I've told you a thousand times . . ." or "How many times have I told you . . . ?" are statements that reveal this sense of powerlessness. Nagging is not effective in the long run because it does not lead to resolution, much less reconciliation.

Passive-Aggressive Behaviors. Passive-aggressive behavior is hostile behavior that is not self-evidently angry. One way to express anger is by making other people upset, frustrated, or mad. Resistance that expresses anger indirectly may be expressed through forgetting, procrastination, being late, or getting "confused." Individuals who use these behaviors often make other people angry by what they *don't* do, or *do contrary to expectations*. Only in the context of their effect on others do we ascertain that such behaviors are indeed expressions of "cool" anger. Passive-aggressive people don't get mad, they get even. Although it may be indirect, their retaliation satisfies their need for revenge or "pay back." Passive-aggressive behavior happens both in family relationships and within larger systems, particularly when a differential in power is being used unilaterally or unfairly. Nagging and fussing frequently occur in response to passive-aggressive behaviors.

Hostile Humor. Hostile humor, whose purpose is not to be humorous but to hurt, punish, or ridicule, is a common disguise for anger.[5] Sarcasm can be quite hurtful. Ridicule makes someone feel stupid or inadequate. Teasing and joking can be fun, but when anger is the motivation, then the "humor" has a "bite" to it and results in "cutting" remarks, with a person being "ripped," "dissed," or "put down." You may have been at a party where one person seems intent on teasing a partner. Though supposedly lighthearted teasing for our entertainment, the words have a hidden venom, and the "victim" is compromised and made to look stupid. Other guests become increasingly quiet—embarrassed for both parties—and look for ways to end this situation. Later, of course, the victim is angry and may be confrontational, but the person using hostile humor will deny that they were angry: "I was only kidding, having a little fun, don't take it so personally!"

Verbal Abuse. Some people express anger through spontaneous bursts of abusive language that cause fear and self-denigrating responses in spouse, children, partners, and coworkers. Expressing hurtful, painful words can be a way of trying to gain control, taking revenge, or salvaging self-esteem. Verbal abuse is often directed at an innocent target because the angry person feels helpless or powerless in other circumstances, such as place of employment, where expressing anger directly would be dangerous.

Violence. Violence is motivated frequently by anger that is not handled creatively. Judges routinely send those accused of domestic violence, for example, to anger management courses to learn how to handle their anger more responsibly. Not all violence, however, results from anger. The basic drive for power and control motivates some violence. Some males behave violently even when not angry in order to maintain fear in women or children they want to dominate, and governments may use violence to enforce laws (drug busts, breaking up a riot) and protect law-abiding citizens even though the police and soldiers may not themselves be angry. Normally, however, anger is a precondition to conflict and violence. Though my focus in this book is not on violence, achieving a more wholistic understanding of anger and learning how to manage this volatile emotion is imperative if we are to reduce violence in our society. The use of physical violence is all too common in our culture.

A Hazard to Community

The experience of anger among members of any institution creates conflict within that system. This situation certainly takes place in the church. Who of us has not endured, or participated in, a congregational conflict with painful consequences for many members? How many people have dropped out of a local church because of a negative experience with church conflict?

The loss of civility, the increase in domestic violence, the rise of intolerance, the surge of ugly hate crimes, and the use of force to settle social differences are obvious concerns. American culture, of course, has always permitted, even encouraged, violence through portrayals in movies, TV (even the cartoons for children!), magazines, sports, and the easy availability of weapons. With the easy availability of powerful weapons, such as assault rifles, rage in response to real or imagined insults can lead to massacres that were hard to imagine several decades ago.

WHY I'M WRITING THIS BOOK

The Apostle Paul reminds us that as the family of God, the Church is called to the "ministry of reconciliation" (2 Cor. 5:18), a task filled with risks. To be ministers of reconciliation means to risk entering into the antagonism, alienation, and animosity that characterize many human relationships. We also know that one of the major dynamics causing this disruption is the hostility that grows out of unresolved anger. How can we minister to people who are angry? How can we effectively present the "message of reconciliation" (2 Cor. 5:19)? As "ambassadors for Christ" (v. 20) we are to live and act in a way which proclaims the good news that Jesus the Christ "is our peace," and "has made both groups into one and has broken down the dividing wall, that is, the hostility between us" (Eph. 2:14). We have the privilege and responsibility to encounter and transform the destructive anger that is eating away at the physical, emotional, and spiritual health of many people and destroying relationships with their parents, children, spouses, partners, friends, and other members of the congregation. Ideally we experience in ourselves and represent to others the unifying power of God's love and the possibility of reconciliation.

I have three purposes in writing this book. My first purpose is to develop a pastoral theology of anger that will inform the church's understanding of the human experience of anger and conflict. The church continues to suffer from the historical theological constructs that led early church theologians to move from the Hebraic tradition's open acceptance of anger to a negative, suppressive stance. The creative, energizing potential of anger was/is too often ignored and, therefore, lost as a source of vitality and healing. Pastors and congregations find it difficult to offer legitimate theological and ethical guidance about anger in educational programs, worship, and caregiving because the historical anger-is-sin tradition, as I name it, still dominates our thinking about this common aspect of life. I want to demonstrate that the anger-is-sin tradition is an inadequate portrayal of both Scripture and alternative theological concepts within the Christian tradition. I have worked with too many Christians who are hampered in creative living by the traditional anger-is-sin doctrine and want Christians to be free from the tyranny of this tradition.

My second purpose in writing is to use this pastoral theology as the context for an ethical perspective that will assist individuals, families, and the church in handling the anger and conflict that regularly surface in our day-to-day process of living in community. We must reevaluate our practice, developing new ways of handling anger that enable Christians to deal with this powerful emotion more lovingly and productively. Facing heightened levels of conflict in families, congregations, denominations, and the public arena, the church must develop a new theological and ethical perspective on the subject.

My third purpose is to provide both theoretical and practical guidance for pastors and other Christian caregivers and counselors who desire to intervene effectively in circumstances marked by anger and the resulting conflict. People entering ministry often do not expect the constant encounter with anger. One colleague who served many years as a pastor wrote:

> I had no idea how much anger I would be facing in congregational leadership, sometimes at me, but more often anger between members and anger with God. I think many of us go into the pastorate believing this will be a loving, intimate, comforting, harmonious experience—surprise, surprise![6]

You probably work with people who need to come to grips with their anger if they are to move forward toward abundant life and are looking for ways to guide them on this journey. Your professional encounters may be pushing you to look for concepts and insights that would guide your caregiving with both individuals and larger systems, such as a congregation—a task for which many pastors do not feel adequately trained. I hope this constructive pastoral theology will serve as a resource for your work as a pastoral caregiver, but also in the preaching and teaching ministries through which you can address anger and conflict in families, congregations, and the larger culture. Of further help, I trust, will be a revised and expanded version of my *Coping with Your Anger: A Christian Guide*, scheduled for release in early 2004.

CONSTRUCTING A PASTORAL THEOLOGY

A central purpose of pastoral theology is to conceptualize a comprehensive theological understanding of the human condition—including physiological functioning, mental processes, involvement in special relationships and community, interaction with culture, and experiences with the *numinous*. Pastoral theology has a specific interest in contributing to theological anthropology, which is a foundational frame of reference for its task.[7] Pastoral theologians are interested in the physical, mental, emotional, and spiritual potential of humans; why things go wrong that inhibit these possibilities; and discovering what processes bring healing and lead to well-being. Such understanding informs not only the ministry of pastoral care and counseling, but also the pastoral functions of preaching, teaching, and leading—a primary goal of pastoral theology.

Pastoral theology works on the boundary between the human sciences and the theological disciplines. Science includes both the physical sciences (such as neurology, biology, chemistry, and physics) and the social sciences (particularly psychology and sociology, but also including philosophy, anthropology, literature, and the rest of the humanities). Theological disciplines include biblical studies (languages, textual critique, and theology), theological studies (historical, philosophical, and systematic), and ethics. Pastoral theology works on the border, placing these two academic worlds in conversation around one of their common subjects of research: the human being.[8]

Pastoral theologians (at least this one!) cannot possibly become experts in all of these various disciplines. Attending to so many fields of inquiry requires dependence on scholars in these other disciplines for cutting-edge theory and research that feeds the work of pastoral theology. Furthermore, giving a complete account of the material from these other disciplines is impossible within the page limits of this book. I have depended on the most notable experts from the neurosciences, such as Jaak Panksepp and Joseph LeDoux, who are widely recognized as scholars in the affective sciences. Theologians who are comfortable with emotion, particularly anger—such as existentialist, feminist, and process theologians—are prominent. Of necessity I have provided only brief summaries that relate to my specific purposes. The notes and bibliography provide more grist for the mill when you are interested in pursuing an issue more thoroughly.

Pastoral theology, as I understand it, recognizes a broad range of epistemologies, validating many ways of knowing what is "real" through both objective and subjective processes. While respecting the scientific method and integrating data from quantifiable research, pastoral theology also considers other sources of knowledge about the "truths" of our existence.[9] In the words of Pauline Marie Rosenau, a postmodern social scientist, we also consider "feelings, personal experience, empathy, emotion, intuition, subjective judgment, [and] imagination" as important data for understanding the human condition.[10]

Pastoral theologians include as important research data both their own experience and the experience of persons to whom they minister. An important question for pastoral theology is "What does our actual participation with real people as they narrate their lived experience teach us about the human condition?" For example, how persons interpret their own experience, a process discounted by some social scientists, is accepted by pastoral theology as a valid way of gaining insight into their reality. The practicing pastoral theologian, therefore, inserts clinical experience into the conversation between the human sciences and the theological disciplines.[11] I am grateful for the students, parishioners, hospital patients, and clients in pastoral counseling relationship who have shared with me their experiences with anger, adding significantly to the concepts in this book. Some of these experiences appear in these pages with their permission. Most stories have been disguised by changing some of the data, but without affecting the dynamics.

Research in both the physical and social sciences on the nature of human beings has changed the nature of theological and philosophical inquiry about humanity. Theologian John Macquarrie proposed over two decades ago that "the doctrine of man is the right starting point for a contemporary theology."[12] To be credible in the face of this scientific evidence, theologians must now demonstrate an anthropological foundation, defendable from a scientific perspective, for understanding the human condition. Wolfhart Pannenberg points out that understanding the human interaction with both the physical and cultural environment is now the foundation for theological reflection on the nature of human existence.[13] Any explanation or defense of the faith must be fought "on the terrain of the interpretation of human existence."[14] Theological anthropology today does not start with dogmatic presuppositions about humankind, says Pannenberg, but rather "turns its attention directly to the phenomena of human existence as investigated in human biology, psychology, cultural anthropology, or sociology and examines the findings of these disciplines with an eye to implications that may be relevant to religion and theology."[15]

I doubt that any theology of personhood can be credible if it does not attend to the revelations provided by the human sciences. To develop a theological understanding of anger, obviously, we must take seriously the physical and social sciences on the one hand and the Christian tradition in Scripture and theology on the other—believing that both offer revelation about the human condition.

A MAP OF THE JOURNEY AHEAD

Though the chapters that follow have a logical sequence, many of them can be read independently for specific information and conclusions about certain topics. The following section briefly introduces the purpose and content of the four parts of the book and its specific chapters.

Anger is an emotion. A pastoral theology of anger, therefore, cannot be adequate if separated from a consideration of this larger topic. In part 1, "Thinking about Emotion," I provide a brief overview of this immense subject. Chapter 1, "The Significance of Emotion," reviews the historical suspicion of, even prejudice against, emotion and then explores the current rebirth of interest in this subject in philosophy, psychology, sociology, and the neurosciences—particularly brain research.

Examining the Christian response to emotion is the focus of chapter 2, "The Christian Tradition and Emotion." Here I review biblical perspectives, giving particular attention to what has been written about emotion as experienced by Jesus and God. Then I briefly explore the philosophical and cultural factors that influenced the early theologians and summarize theological views on emotion expressed by a select few of the most influential theologians from the early period of Christian history through the twentieth century.

In chapter 3, "Theological Reflections on Emotion," I identify some basic concepts that can be gleaned from the neurosciences, social sciences, Scripture, and historical theology for inclusion in a meaningful theology of emotion. I focus on embodiment, creation, mind/body integration, and our responsibility for what we feel and how we express these feelings.

"Where does anger come from?" and "Why do people get angry?" are the questions I wrestle with in part 2, "Understanding Anger." But first, in chapter 4 I explore the difference between anger and aggression because both scientists and theologians continually confuse these terms and often use them interchangeably. Some theological reflections on aggression end the chapter.

What the neurosciences are learning about the human experience of anger is the subject of chapter 5, "Where Does Anger Come From? The Neuroscience Contribution." Brain research indicates that the potential to experience anger is basic to our physiology, that we are "wired" with the capacity for anger. This capacity for anger, however, is only activated when triggered by a situation we consider dangerous or threatening. Neuroscience, however, cannot tell us *why* an environmental event appears dangerous to a particular person.

In chapter 6, "Why Do People Get Angry? A Constructionist Narrative Perspective," therefore, I turn to constructionist narrative theory to address the question, "How do people know, or decide, what is threatening?" Constructionist narrative understandings of the self confirm that anger occurs when persons perceive a threat to their physical survival or their psychosocial identity. Because anger always involves an interpretation of the environment, as well as physiological arousal, I argue that the hermeneutical process is central to the experience of anger. Individuals and communities decide what is threatening as they interpret life situations through the lens of their own narratives—their values, meanings, and beliefs.

Having gathered basic data that the neurosciences and social sciences provide for constructing a pastoral theology of anger, I turn next to the contribution of the Christian tradition. Part 3, "A Constructive Pastoral Theology of Anger," explores the contributions of biblical scholarship and historical theology to the construction of a pastoral theology of anger.

In chapter 7, "Why Is Anger One of the 'Seven Deadly Sins'? The Christian Tradition," I explore the history of the anger-is-sin tradition that has dominated the church. First, I examine three cultural factors that influenced this development in the first centuries of the church: Mediterranean philosophies (particularly Stoicism), the need to defend God's transcendent holiness, and the dualistic perceptions of flesh and spirit. Then I discuss those theologians who contributed to making anger one of the "seven deadly sins." I found that the very theologians who condemned anger also recognized the positive side of anger, but these "alternative stories," as narrative theory calls them, have been largely suppressed by, even subjugated to, the anger-is-sin narratives. These alternative stories will inform our conclusions about anger.

Chapter 8, "Biblical Perspectives: The Alternative Story about Human Anger," explores what we can learn about anger from Scripture. Biblical scholarship challenges the common perception that the Bible has only negative things to say about anger. The Bible, I will demonstrate, though very concerned about the destructive consequences of anger, does not question anger's rightful place in human experience. Scripture does not lobby for the eradication of anger, but is instead concerned about *why* we are angry and *how to express* anger ethically so that we don't behave destructively.

The focus of chapter 9, "The Anger of God and Jesus," is on how the Bible specifically portrays anger as experienced and expressed by both Jesus and God. Did God and Jesus sin by being angry? God's wrath, particularly as expressed in the Hebrew Scripture, has always been problematic for theology, so one section focuses briefly on this issue.

Chapter 10, "Toward a Pastoral Theology of Anger," is the heart of the book. Drawing on all the selected material in previous chapters—neuroscience research, constructionist narrative theory, biblical studies, and theological perspectives from various eras of church history—I construct a pastoral theology of anger. I contend that anger has its origins in creation, not our sinfulness. I discuss how anger is connected to embodiment and is a basic ingredient in the *imago Dei*, actually a gift from God. Furthermore, I contend that we have the freedom to choose which events will activate our capacity for anger as well as how to express it. This conclusion challenges the modern perspective of many pastors, pastoral care specialists, and other therapeutic specialists that anger is a "natural" phenomenon and, therefore, that our only concern is *how* we express our anger. I argue from neuroscience research, the constructionist narrative understanding of anger, and theological wisdom from the past that we also have significant freedom to decide *what* makes us angry.

I turn in part 4, "Dealing with Anger: Christian Care and Counseling," to an exploration of how this pastoral theology of anger informs Christian living. These chapters explore circumstances in which anger is appropriate, identify some ethical parameters and guidelines for handling anger, and describe methodologies and strategies for intervention.

Accordingly, in chapter 11, "Anger as Spiritual Ally," I argue that we should think of anger not as a spiritual enemy, but as a spiritual ally, associated with hope, courage, intimacy, and recovery of self, and functioning as an idol detector and a "diagnostic window" that provides opportunities for emotional and spiritual growth.

Chapter 12, "Compassionate Anger," pursues the central, and perhaps most heretical, ideas that emerge out of this pastoral theology of anger: that anger is sometimes the most loving response and that Christians *should* be angry in certain life situations, such as injustice, radical suffering, and oppression. This anger must not only be in the service of love, but directed by the ethical parameters of love.

Chapter 13, "Handling Anger Creatively," describes a process for responsibly working our way through an experience of anger. The way to transform anger into something positive and creative is to recognize, acknowledge, and accept our anger. Then we have responsibility to identify and evaluate the narratives that are threatened and change the stories that leave us vulnerable.

LIMITED PERSPECTIVES

Writing a book that sets forth a theological position runs the risk of intimating that a definitive understanding of God has been reached. To do so would certainly be an expression of arrogance. Though feeling strongly about the position described, I realize the tentativeness and limitations of all theological discourse and accept that the ideas expressed here cannot be definitive truth about either God or the human condition. A colleague and friend, Carroll Saussy, has expressed what I feel about sharing these ideas:

> While theologies can be dangerous, they can also offer grace-filled, life-giving, albeit limited perspectives, and they must be put forth tentatively and with modesty . . . to recognize that theologies are limited attempts to fathom the unfathomable. No one knows God's experience. Yet for as long as there have been believers in a divine being, people have tried to know God's mind and heart, to see God's face, to hear God's voice, to come to an understanding of God. All attempts are efforts to penetrate mystery to push the limits of human knowing in order to know the ineffable.[16]

With these limitations, therefore, I do think it is my responsibility to call into question the dominant Christian narrative about anger, which has been so destructive to so many. An important task is to clearly identify the alternative stories in Scripture and theology, to establish that these alternative perspectives are supported by current research and theory in both the neurosciences and the social sciences, and to establish a more wholesome theological perspective on this troublesome, but potentially creative, emotion.

My perspectives are also limited by my particular experience of life. I am a middle-aged (OK, late middle-age!), Euro-American, male, pastoral theologian (not trained as a scientist), speaking from within the Protestant tradition. Furthermore, I am the oldest child of six and spent the first ten years of my life in a rural area and the rest of my time in urban areas. These aspects of my identity shape my narrative in ways that are different from you, the reader. I trust that you will translate my ideas into your narrative as informed by your age, gender, ethnic and cultural background, and faith tradition—not to mention family of origin and traumatic experiences.

So, I turn this work over to you, hoping the theoretical and clinical content will clarify, expand, and even challenge your ideas about this normal human experience. I hope, more personally, that these ideas might enable you to make more sense of your own experience with anger. Finally, of course, I hope the material will inform your care of angry souls. Becoming more effective in our care of angry people can both limit anger's destructiveness and capture anger's creative power in the service of Love.

PART 1

Thinking about Emotion

1

The Significance of Emotion

Anger is a human emotion. Like sadness, fear, and joy, it is experienced as a feeling. We cannot begin to develop a pastoral theology of anger without first considering this larger reality: Humans are emotional beings. Emotions, therefore, are a basic category for any study of the human condition. In this chapter, we look at emotion from the viewpoint of philosophy, the social sciences, and the neurosciences. An important consideration is the wider issue of how Western culture and the Christian tradition think about all emotion, because these perceptions necessarily influence beliefs about any specific emotion such as anger.

WHAT IS EMOTION?

Most of us know immediately when we feel an emotion, but philosophers and psychologists argue over a precise definition of the term. Most definitions of emotion are similar to Aristotle's that emotions are "states of feeling—passions . . . conditions in which one's mind or consciousness is affected, moved, or stirred up."[1] Dictionaries describe the same phenomenon with phrases such as "an agitation or disturbance of mind" and "excited mental state." Everyone agrees that emotions are certain kinds of mental states, but disagree about how they may be different from other mental states.

Most definitions and descriptions refer to the bodily sensations that accompany emotions, giving them the sense of "feelings."[2] Jaak Panksepp, a neuroscientist, writes that emotion occurs "when powerful waves of affect overwhelm our sense of ourselves in the world."[3] Emotions, he notes, are rarely expected, often catch us off guard, and threaten to move us to action that may or may not be appropriate. Observers from various disciplines agree with Aristotle that emotion includes being "stirred up" in both mind and body, resulting in strong physical and mental motivation toward action.

This connection between emotion and action is central to most understandings of emotion. Emotions push us toward some particular behavioral reaction or response—anger toward striking out, fear toward hiding, joy toward dancing, sadness toward crying—whether or not the impulse is acted upon. The action sparked by emotion may be helpful, such as when anger gives us strength to resist an assault. But sometimes the immediate physical expression of these impulses is not appropriate, such as when anger leads to domestic violence. This "moves us to action" aspect of emotion is a primary clue in determining why emotions developed in humans. Primitive brain systems evidently developed as part of the survival functions of our evolutionary ancestors, as we will discuss later.

THE PHILOSOPHICAL CASE AGAINST EMOTIONS

The classical philosophical debate among Mediterranean philosophers about the place of emotions in human life has significantly influenced Western culture, including Christian theology. Most classic Greek philosophers, such as Plato and Aristotle, accepted that emotions had a positive role in human life, though adamant that emotions must stay under the control of reason if they were to serve their ordained purposes rather than becoming destructive. Virtuous persons, they argued, use their will to force emotion to function under the rule of reason. Stoics, in contrast, took a more negative stance, arguing that emotion has no place in the virtuous life and "that life has meaning only insofar as we disown . . . our emotions" and respond to life with "detachment, dispassionate contemplation, *apatheia* or apathy."[4]

In modern Western culture, philosophers have tended toward the Stoic position. Emotion has been relegated to the sidelines and treated reductionistically if at all.[5] From the time of French philosopher Rene Descartes's (1596–1650) emphasis on thinking ("I think, therefore, I am"), reason and cognition became the favored traits of the human species. As for the classic Greek philosophers, these characteristics were identified in the modern era as the most defining mark of humans, distinguishing us from the animal world.[6] Furthermore, rationalists could deal with the seemingly obvious dimensions of thought processes easily, while emotions were a complex phenomena that made definitive study difficult.[7] Indeed, one of the defining features of modernity is the dualism between emotion and reason, with reason being by far the more respected.[8]

Most philosophers have been suspicious of emotion, fearful that it had a distorting influence on the process of reasoning and, therefore, had to be neutralized or completely annihilated. Immanuel Kant, the influential eighteenth-century philosopher, set the tone for such negative assessments when he suggested that emotions are "an illness of mind."[9] By using the disease metaphor, Kant not only pathologized emotion but suggested that emotions are intrapsychic events, primarily occurring within a person's private mental functions rather than a result of interaction with the environment. Furthermore, Kant conceptualized emotions as if they had a life of their own: instinctive entities that represent our animal nature and exist apart from interaction with the external world. Many philosophers discounted emotions, writes philosopher Martha Nussbaum, by identifying them as "blind animal reactions, like or identical with bodily feelings, that are in their nature unmixed with thought, undiscriminating, and impervious to reasoning."[10] Only in the last few decades, as discussed below, has it been demonstrated that emotions do not normally occur either biologically or intrapsychically apart from past or present encounters with the social or physical environment.

Kant also perpetuated the belief that emotions are irrational, claiming that "both emotion and passion exclude the sovereignty of reason . . . [E]motion makes one more or less blind."[11] This critique of irrationality has a long history in philosophy. From a historical perspective, notes philosopher Roberto Unger, concern about emotion has focused on the idea that "passion is a threat to reason [and] a risk to society."[12] Emotion has been marginalized by the assumption that judgments made by emotions are based on false premises about life situations that humans can't control.[13] Current research, however, as I discuss below, demonstrates that it is impossible to separate emotions from cognitive processes.

The connection of emotion with irrationality also influenced the field of psychology. Sigmund Freud set the tone by placing passions in the Id and separating them from the reasoning, sense-making Ego. In psychoanalytic theory the rational Ego is always in danger of being overwhelmed by the irrational passions of the Id.

In the twentieth century, emotion was basically ignored, receiving almost no attention in Western philosophy. Philosopher Robert Solomon has critiqued this omission, saying that it leaves the discipline with what he poetically calls "a hole at the heart."[14] He summarizes the modern view of emotions: "The passions have been generally agreed to be primitive and 'natural,' disruptive and irrational, lacking in judgment and purpose or reason, without scruples, and sometimes shockingly short of taste."[15] The perception that emotions reflect immaturity, or even mental illness, and are a threat to our rational decision-making ability causes philosophers to believe they should be tightly controlled, or even eradicated, in order to free humans to function rationally.

Psychology and other social sciences have been slightly better in attending to emotions. During the twentieth century, however, these disciplines worked hard to be recognized as academic fields of study by using hardcore scientific methods. Because emotions are notoriously difficult to quantify, the study of emotions was marginalized in academic research. Furthermore, twentieth-century psychologists were interested in predicting and controlling the behavior of individuals and societies. Understanding thinking and reasoning processes seemed much more suited to that task than emotions, which seem so unpredictable and irrational. Even those courageous enough to study emotions could rarely agree on a definition of the subject, or on acceptable research methods.[16]

Practicing psychologists, psychiatrists, and particularly psychotherapists were more likely to pay close attention to emotions. Though agreeing that emotions were important, they often pronounced conflicting views on the subject. Given that they were most frequently working with people who had mental disturbances, psychotherapists spent more time on the pathology of emotion than on the significance of emotion for healthy human existence.

THE POSTMODERN RECOVERY OF EMOTION

In the twentieth century, existentialism played an important role in bringing emotion back into philosophical discourse. Existentialists such as Martin Heidegger, Jean Paul Sartre, and Rollo May resisted the division of cognition, affect, and volition into separate "faculties" of the self—as if they were activities of the mind and heart that functioned without reference to each other. They "recognized that feeling has its place in the total texture of human existence . . . [and that] any given moment includes intellectual, emotional, and volitional elements . . . [which] belong within a living whole."[17] Today, many philosophers, psychologists, and social scientists are reconsidering the significance of emotion for human well-being and agree that no aspect of our existence (thinking, feeling, willing) can be left out of our understanding of a particular event. Solomon, for example, accuses modernity of developing a "myth" that the emotions are simply "dumb forces beyond our control" and then argues that this myth is collapsing under the weight of current research.[18]

One reason for the postmodern recovery of emotions is their obvious importance for living a full, vital life. As neuroscientist Daniel Goleman says,

"Every feeling has its value and significance. A life without passion would be a dull wasteland of neutrality, cut off and isolated from the richness of life itself."[19] Particularly from existentialist and phenomenological perspectives, emotions are now acknowledged as a central aspect of our humanity, enlivening and energizing all of life: "Emotions are constituted by forces of great power that vitalize and revitalize the lives we live," says philosopher of religion James Gilman.[20] Without emotions, life would be flat, lived out in a perpetual state of robotic numbness. The idea that emotions are left-over ingredients from our biological history, unnecessary in a technological society, has been forcefully refuted. Solomon sums up nicely the positive view of postmodernists about this crucial aspect of human existence: "Emotions are intelligent, cultivated, conceptually rich engagements with the world, not mere reactions or instincts."[21]

The difference between perceptions of emotionality in modernist and postmodernist perspectives can be illustrated by the difference between the original *Star Trek* series and *Star Trek: The Next Generation.* Theologian Stanley Grenz has pointed out that Spock was perceived as a hero in the original *Star Trek* because of his use of reason. Spock's rationality was uncompromised by emotion, thereby making him "a transcendent human ideal" for modernism. He reflected the desire of the modernist to reach a level of "pure reason" that would allow a totally rational existence undisturbed by messy emotions. In the postmodern *The Next Generation*, however, Spock is replaced by Data, an android who is a "more fully realized version of the rational thinker than Spock." Unlike Spock, however, Data thinks of himself as incomplete because he does not have such human qualities as emotion. His curiosity about, even desire for, the human capacity for emotion reflects the postmodern conviction that rationality by itself is not adequate for being fully human.[22]

Emotions and Rationality

A major postmodernist tenet is that our culture's worship of reason as the only viable way of knowing truth and informing behavior is much too narrow. Social scientists from various disciplines are challenging this "modernist" belief that reason is the only trustworthy guide to understanding life. In his book *Emotional Intelligence*, neuroscientist Daniel Goleman summarizes this critique:

> A view of human nature that ignores the power of emotions is sadly shortsighted. [We applaud] the new appreciation and vision of the place of emotions in our lives that science now offers. As we all know from experience, when it comes to shaping our decisions and our actions, feeling counts every bit as much—and often more—than

thought. We have gone too far in emphasizing the value and import of the purely rational.[23]

Furthermore, postmodern thinkers in both psychology and philosophy argue that developing research in the neurosciences makes separating emotion from reason impossible. Rather than being only a raw vestige of our animal heritage, emotions, psychologists argue, are necessarily connected to major aspects of uniquely human nature. Emotions are integrally involved with social experience, cognition, imagery, conceptualization, physiological changes, and behavior.[24]

The historical philosophical belief that emotions are irrational is under attack in many disciplines. Solomon argues that "emotions are themselves rational." Current research, he says, demonstrates that emotions "have conceptual and intelligent form" and are characterized by their own logic.[25] Earlier, Jean Paul Sartre wrote that "emotion is a way of apprehending the world" and argued that emotion is a basic context for "reading" the environment and eliciting the proper response from humans to their world.[26] Solomon agrees, saying that emotions "are ways of seeing and engaging the world, our ways of 'being tuned' into the world."[27] Emotions are an integral factor, along with reason and intuition, for helping us make sense of the world. Today's intellectuals grant emotion a central place in the process of thinking.

Humans experience reason and emotion working in tandem, which also argues against the belief that emotions are irrational. Was it only ideas that led Mother Teresa and her followers to a life of sacrifice? Or does their choice of vocation depend on a commitment that results from emotional responses to poverty and illness and their love of God? When emotion agrees with the conclusions reached by reason, then emotion is an advocate for reason's conclusions, which is easy to illustrate with value systems. Martin Luther King Jr.'s mind and heart were in agreement that segregation was not only a violation of the Bill of Rights, but untenable from a Christian ethical perspective. When we are emotionally bonded to what our thinking process has identified not only as real, but also valuable, then the emotions provide the energy for intense commitment and risky actions that support the cognitive conclusions. The dedication of numerous women and African Americans to the active, and sometimes dangerous, pursuit of cognitively held beliefs about equality is fueled by the emotional intensity that grows from commitment to this belief.

Emotions, Truth, and Reality

Postmodernism challenges the modernist assumption that truth exists in objective realities and is, therefore, known only by reason. Social scientist

Pauline Marie Rosenau, for example, says, "reason and rationality are inconsistent with post-modern confidence in emotion." She points out other aspects of human capability often overlooked by the scientific method, such as "feeling, introspection and intuition, . . . imagination, fantasy, and contemplation."[28] Postmodern thinkers argue that most "truths" are subjective and can be known through these other human attributes, including the emotions. "Postmoderns," summarizes Grenz, "look beyond reason to non-rational ways of knowing, conferring heightened status on the emotions and intuition."[29] Postmodernism promotes emotion to stand alongside cognition at the center of human self-consciousness.

Many people now argue that emotions offer their own perception of reality, which may be different from the reality that reason perceives. This difference in perspective occurs because emotional responses are inclusive of other "information" than presents itself to reason. A team of theologians and scientists writes, "Our emotional reactions inform us (many times unconsciously) of things we know but may not be able to formulate in rational discourse or conscious mental images. Our tacit knowledge is communicated to awareness via our emotional response."[30]

Most postmodernists agree that emotions do not necessarily function in opposition to our reasoning process. They demonstrate that when logic is separated from the "data" revealed by our emotional response to a life situation, then our reasoning process can easily misunderstand the full reality of the situation. When emotional responses are incorporated with rational perceptions into our overall perspectives of a situation, we usually have a more unified picture of reality.[31] To James Hillman, a Jungian analyst, emotions direct us to the reality of situations at least as quickly as reason, and are often more reliable in searching out the truth.[32] Cultural perspectives of what modernists think of as "objective" reality limit our cognitive processes, while emotions are often in touch with more "subjective" realities that transcend a particular society's view of "reality." Hillman reminds us, "A principle intention of an emotion is to connect our animal nature with the world in which it is embedded. Emotions respond immediately to the truth of things. They are the most alert form of attention."[33] Anger, for example, may put us in touch with an experience of injustice, a breach of relationship, or a threat to an important value more quickly than our cognitive interpretations.

Our emotions are more in touch with our existential realities and the deeper meanings of relationships than is reason. Emotions allow us to empathize, so "we can thank emotion for our shared humanity,"[34] says Hillman. From the existentialist perspective, says theologian John Macquarrie, "feelings are not seen as antithetical to reason and thought but as a source of insights."[35] Ontological anxiety in the face of finitude, for example, often reveals and accepts reality in a way that our reason finds difficult.

Emotion and the Self

David Rosenthal, professor of philosophy and cognitive science, argues that emotions serve as an effective organizing structure for understanding the self because "emotions . . . combine in complex patterns that contribute substantially to the makeup of one's character and personality."[36] Furthermore, central lifestyles and belief systems can serve a unifying function for the self only if they are "to a high degree, emotionally charged."[37] Emotions are, says Panksepp, "highly influential processes in our personal lives that affect not only the quality of our other mental states but also our sense of bodily well-being."[38]

An existentialist perspective, which views the human condition as a psychosomatic unity, sees emotion as that aspect of self which unites us to the physical and social world around us. Feelings, existentialists point out, are our most unique way of directly participating in the world. The language of existentialists, such as Paul Ricoeur's use of *atmospheric*, describe how emotion is the process by which we "breathe in the world . . . and are merged into the world as the environment in which we live and move and have our being."[39]

In fact, research in various disciplines has increased understanding of affective disorders. Psychiatrists identify a problem in the development of the self that results when humans don't experience and express emotion. This results in a clinical dynamic, or symptom, called *alexithymia*, which describes a psychological condition in which individuals are overly dependent on cognitive-rational processes for engaging the world and find it difficult to identify, accept, or express emotions. Psychiatrists Graeme Taylor, Michael Bagby, and James Parker argue persuasively that many psychiatric and medical disorders are a result of "affective disregulation."[40] Such a condition in milder form results in personality styles called sociopathic and in extreme form can be psychopathic.[41] Study of this disorder raises our awareness about the important function of affect in healthy humans.

Without emotional attachments to people and ideas, humans find it difficult to make meaning out of life, to find a reason for living. After noting that reason alone cannot answer the question of meaning in life, Solomon identifies the connection:

> But if reason alone cannot answer the question, what about our impassioned (and by no means irrational) engagements in life? Thus I suggest that emotions are the meaning of life. It is because we are moved, because we feel, that life has a meaning. The passionate life, not the dispassionate life of pure reason, is the meaningful life.[42]

Unger writes persuasively about the significance of the "passions" in our entire quest for a full human life, pointing out the importance of emotions for establishing our identity, comprehending our existential experience, and motivating our actions.[43] Sartre similarly says "what an emotion signifies is the totality of the relationships of the human reality to the world."[44] Emotions are necessary for the process of becoming, the existential project of gaining acceptance for our unique self and "being at home in the world."[45]

NEUROSCIENCE AND EMOTION

Neurological research is providing a biological basis for understanding the physiological components of emotion, helping us construct more informed psychological hypotheses.[46] Technological developments have fostered a significant increase in neurological research, particularly of the brain, using noninvasive procedures, and major advances in neuroanatomy, neurochemistry, and neurophysiology make it possible to further understand the intricacies of how the brain works. Brain imaging technologies, for example, allow researchers to observe how brain cells are functioning while a research subject is experiencing emotions such as anger and fear.

Given that psychologists have focused historically on intrapsychic phenomena, perceived to occur only within the mind, they often define emotions in psychological terms that neglect the biological context for mental processes. Current neurological research, however, makes it untenable to portray emotions as purely psychological phenomena, as if they exist separate from our physiology. Brain research demonstrates that complex neurological processes are in operation when we experience an emotion.

Neurological research has led to new understandings of what some call "affective programs,"[47] that is, identifiable activities of the brain related to the experience of emotion. Virtually all scientists studying the emotions, regardless of point of view or type of research, include anger, fear, joy, and sorrow on their short list of primary emotions. Other emotional responses that receive strong support for being primary systems include love, surprise, disgust, and shame.[48] Each primary emotion has a variety of close relatives, and some theorists prefer to speak of emotional "families" rather than single emotions. Not surprisingly, anger and its close associate fear both make everybody's short list of basic emotions.[49]

Researchers used to think that all emotions, from a neurological perspective, were processed in the same brain system, but they now know that different emotions occur within diverse neurological systems. Scientific debate about the level of difference in the biological "signature" of each emotion is still in process, as research demonstrates the difficulty of distinguishing the neurological particularity of specific emotions. Some neuroscientists believe there is significant similarity in the arousal patterns for all emotions, while others maintain that each family of emotions has a cluster of unique biological processes.[50] My impression is that as neuroscience research progresses, more differentiation is being discovered,[51] even as similarities are also identified. In summary, all emotional arousal seems to include universal processes, though physiological arousal specific to such feelings as grief, fear, and anger have their individual biological markers.

How does the body decide to mobilize in response to a particular life situation? The normal manner in which we interpret and respond to our environment seems to occur in the following manner. Our senses, particularly sight and sound, encounter stimuli in the environment. We see, hear, touch, taste, or smell something. Our senses send this raw data to the thalamus, the part of the brain that seems to be responsible for the first stage of collating and organizing data from the senses. Then the thalamus forwards this information through two neurological systems—the amygdala/limbic system and the neocortex/prefrontal lobe system—specifically dedicated to processing and interpreting this information, and initiating an appropriate physiological response that ensures our survival. The amygdala/limbic system is the most primitive, meaning it developed much earlier in our biological history, and includes organs sometimes referred to as the mammalian brain, or even earlier, the reptilian brain. The neocortex/prefrontal lobe system is related to the development of human levels of consciousness and cognitive ability. At this point, neurologists know of at least two pathways by which information from the senses is almost simultaneously processed by the brain in order to ascertain whether the self needs to become aroused in response to some occurrence in the environment. For ease of understanding, we will consider these pathways separately.

The Amygdala and Emotion

Until recently, neuroscientists thought that all emotional responses involved neurotransmission through the neocortex. More recent research, however, indicates that neurological pathways directly connect the thalamus to the amygdala and limbic system. Through these pathways, information is transmitted from our senses to the more primitive amygdala and limbic system, bypassing the neocortex.[52] Evidence now exists that mechanisms for seeing and hearing, and probably the other senses, are directly wired to the amygdala and perhaps other parts of the limbic system, which explains how certain sights and sounds trigger immediate responses.[53] The "emotional brain," as this system is sometimes called, can function without immediate input from the neocortex, or "thinking brain."

The amygdala is interconnected with other parts of the brain, such as the hippocampus, which are involved in the process of memory: recording, storing, and recalling events from the past. When receiving sensory information, the amygdala runs a quick crosscheck within its "files" to see if the message is associated with past events that call for a mobilization of the body, an arousal response of some type.

Many of an individual's specific alternative neural pathways may have developed early in life, before the neocortex was fully formed, but experiences in adulthood also leave impressions in the memory system that can later be activated by sensory data sent directly from thalamus to amygdala. If the new stimulus is recognized as similar to a past event, such as a traumatic accident, then the body is mobilized and takes action before we are consciously aware of what happened. Flashbacks by war veterans offer an example of when a current stimulus, such as the sound of an airplane flying low to the ground, can spark an involuntary reaction.

The Neocortex and Emotion

In the second pathway, information from the thalamus is forwarded to the neocortex, or prefrontal lobe, which is sometimes referred to as the "reasoning" or "thinking" brain. The neocortex is the part of the brain that is much more highly developed in humans and most responsible for consciousness. It is the seat of the advanced cognitive skills developed during our evolutionary history[54] and, therefore, responsible for a different type of interpretation of the sensory data from the thalamus.

Humans have developed the capacity for complex emotions that are usually rooted in psychosocial needs for connection, safety, recognition, and so forth. These emotions developed along with higher brain functions. With extensive neural connections to the regions of the brain that process information from the senses, store memory, and activate physiological responses to sensory information (the amygdala and other parts of the limbic structure),[55] the neocortex is the brain's primary switchboard between sensing, interpreting, and responding to environmental events more clearly connected to psychosocial events. The neocortex enables us to think through our encounters with the environment, make decisions, and tie behavior to needs and desires that go beyond physical survival. This part of the brain produces nuanced responses related to our values, meanings, worldview, and personal identity.

Contrary to earlier assumptions, the neocortex cannot by itself generate emotionality. When stimulated by electrodes it does not produce emotional responses. Emotion is generated in the subcortical structures of the brain ("below" the neocortex), which include the most primitive parts of the brain, commonly called the reptilian and mammalian sections and the limbic system.[56] Thus the neocortex, while the primary instigator of most of our emotion, is dependent on the "lower," more primitive, structures of the brain (developed earlier in our biological history) to produce the physiological arousal so basic to the experience of "feeling."

So when the neocortex sorts through and interprets messages from the thalamus and discovers something in the environment that calls for a specific response, that information goes to the amygdala. The amygdala, whether responding to an immediate interpretation of information from the thalamus or to a warning message sent from the neocortex, organizes the limbic system and sends an instantaneous message throughout the body's neurological system that triggers the sympathetic branch of the autonomic nervous system. The body responds in a manner specific to the interpretation of the neocortex, and this leads to particular emotions such as grief, compassion, erotic arousal, fear, and anger.

The neocortex is the part of the brain involved in the cognitive assessment of exterior events that trigger emotions, but in reciprocal fashion the neocortex is also significantly influenced by emotion. Emotions cue the neocortex to organize the storage of memories that become the basis for later interpretations of the environment that should trigger an emotional response.

The Evolution of Emotions

Evolutionary biologists and neuroscientists are examining the function of emotions in human development and developing theories about the natural history of emotions.[57] Most agree that emotions developed as an energizing process to motivate our earliest ancestors in solving survival problems. Our ancestors had to be physiologically prepared for the hard work of obtaining the necessary ingredients that sustain life: food, water, shelter, safety, social interaction, and procreation.[58] The "rage circuit," for example, to which we return in chapter 4, was necessary to mobilize the body into fighting mode in order to survive the attack of a predator or the dangers of natural phenomena such as fire, flood, and volcanic eruption. Without the development of emotionality, humans would not have had the energizing patterns of physiological arousal that led to behaviors that made physical survival possible.

Many philosophers and behavioral scientists believe that self-interest is the most basic reason for our behaviors and therefore our emotions. Others argue that many positive emotions can be shown to focus on "other-interest," that is, putting the other person's needs as a priority without thought to one's own gains. Robert Frank, however, suggests that the emotions which lead to moral behavior, cooperation, fairness, and even love mutually serve the good of both parties.[59] His conclusion is that even "good" emotions are part of our capacity for survival.

Emotion and Reason

I noted earlier the tendency of philosophy to separate emotion and reason. In reality, of course, emotion and reason are both mental processes based in the physiology of the brain. Thinking and feeling both occur through neurological processes. Neuroscientists have now established the links between cognition and emotion in the operation of the neurological system. Though emotion has its roots in our physiological systems, neuroscience research demonstrates that a triggering event is necessary to provoke a feeling.[60]

Neurological research makes it clear that emotional response originates with a perception of the environment that triggers a neurological response. As described earlier, experiencing a particular emotion begins with an environmental event that our brain appraises in a way that calls for activation of a particular neurological program. In response, the brain sends chemical messages, which activate the physiological responses that provide the "feeling" component of emotions. For example, if your telephone rings in the middle of the night, the neocortex will most likely make the interpretation that something bad has happened. The body, then, is immediately activated into a state of general anxiety as you answer the phone. If your mother is in the coronary care unit at a hospital, then your interpretation is likely to focus on her condition, and the possibility that she has taken a turn for the worse or even died. If the message is, indeed, that your mother has died, the general state of arousal will turn into grief as the neocortex interprets her death as a major loss. All interpretations, of course, come from socialization processes and both past and present life experience.

An emotion does not occur in the brain as an instinct activated by a biological clock. A person's cognitive perception of the environment, whether an external event or an internal mental image, is what actually triggers the physiological response. This interpretation can take place at both conscious and unconscious levels. Because of past experiences, the amygdala/limbic system may react before we have had time to cognitively process our response. Though either emotion or cognition may dominate at any particular moment, they are always linked. In chapter 6 I discuss constructionist narrative concepts that help us understand the interaction between emotion and environment.

The Body/Mind Connection

Though some psychologists have attempted to separate the body and the mind, most recognize the pervasive interaction between them. Emotionality in each person is affected by the constant interaction between perception and memory that influences ongoing interpretations of our environment. Each person's distinct physiology and life experience cause the experience and expression of emotion to be unique for that person.

First, consider the physiological differences that affect our response to external events. Every person's genetic code renders them uniquely neurologically prepared to respond with different degrees of intensity to such circumstances as noise, light, and movement. Neurological differences lead us to speak of a young child's personality with phrases like "laid back," "gets upset easily," "constantly active," "never stops," and so forth. We often use the word "temperament" to describe both the cumulative personality pattern that results from this biological diversity and the neurological disposition or readiness to experience certain families of emotions and moods.[61] Like the famous snowflake and fingerprint analogies, each person is neurologically programmed to experience real-world events in a unique manner. Given the uniqueness of our temperaments, each person also experiences a particular emotion a little differently than anyone else.

Second, reactions to specific external events that have occurred during a person's lifetime have shaped that person's neurological system. Furthermore, a given emotion usually leads to an entire cadre of associated subjective perspectives that create a person's unique moods, which are more muted and last longer than specific feelings. An individual's emotionality is mutually and interactively informed by both original biological disposition and ongoing life experience, particularly in response to trauma. Painful events such as accidents and injuries, frightening occurrences such as thunderstorms, significant losses such as divorce of parents or the death of a family member, and horrific experiences such as rape or incest all affect the shape of our neurological systems.[62] In short, the neurological pathways in our brain literally change as we interact with life situations, particularly traumatic ones, that challenge us. Throughout life, therefore, our brain responds uniquely to events that "remind" the brain of previous experience, as we discuss further in chapter 5.

Both the amygdala/limbic system and the neocortex/prefrontal lobe process sensory information in the context of all the experiences that make up the unique conscious and unconscious memory of each individual. Our life experiences and the culture in which we grow up shape neurological possibilities. In fact, our individual and collective experiences even affect what we used to think of as the "hard-wiring" of our neurological system. Neuroscientists have known for several decades that cognition is normally connected with the activation of emotions, but recent research establishes that the reverse process is also true: emotional experience, in cyclical fashion, informs and influences further cognitive perceptions. As Panksepp notes:

> Emotional circuits achieve their profound influence over the behavior and mental activity of an organism through the widespread effects on the rest of the nervous system. Emotive circuits change sensory, perceptual, and cognitive processing, and initiate a host of physiological changes that are naturally synchronized with the aroused behavioral tendencies characteristic of emotional experience.[63]

Emotions "mold and are molded by experience throughout the life span."[64] The idea that thought and feeling are either separate functions or processes of the brain is difficult to defend in light of current research. Cognition and emotion, thinking and feeling, are mutually interactive, and both develop in the context of the self's interaction with the environment.

Despite the growing awareness of biological diversity as a contributor to the uniqueness of emotionality, two questions remain unanswered by neurobiological research: "*Why* do certain external events, and not others, trigger the neurological system?" and "*Why* do some external events trigger an emotional response in one person and not the other?" Constructionist narrative theories, to which we turn in chapter 6, help us answer this question. We are programmed to experience anger in the face of threat, as I explore in chapter 5, but our individual and cultural stories, including our faith narratives, shape both what we discern as threatening and how we express our anger.

NEUROSCIENCE AND PASTORAL THEOLOGY

We live in a time of significant advances in the field of neurological research, particularly of the brain. Developments in neuroscience and neuropsychology are changing our understanding of many human processes. This neurological information has been pivotal in the postmodern renewal of interest in the emotions, because such research reveals significant data about the biological factors that contribute to the experience of emotionality. These disciplines are necessary conversation partners with pastoral theology as we continuously update our theological anthropology.

The final answers about emotion are not yet known. Davidson reminds us of the current limitations of neuroscience when he says:

> it must be emphasized . . . that the circuit instantiating emotion in the human brain is complex and involves a number of interrelated structures. . . . Therefore, hypotheses about the set of structures that participate in the production of emotion must necessarily be speculative.[65]

Given the constant advances in neuroscience, we can assume that in a few years we will understand even more about the specific ways in which our neurological "wiring" affects our experience of emotion.

A theology of anger, it seems to me, must be connected to—and demonstrate continuity with—a theology of emotion. Theological reflection on emotions from a pastoral theological perspective, however, must include what we can learn from Christian theology. So, in the next chapter I examine both Scripture and theology to see what the Christian tradition has to say about emotions. Then, in chapter 3, I combine these ideas with the new insights of postmodern philosophy and the exciting developments in neuroscience, psychology, and other social sciences to inform my theological reflection about emotion.

2

The Christian
Tradition and Emotion

Neuroscience provides a physiological basis for the current interest among philosophers and social scientists to reclaim the central place of emotion in human existence. This new emphasis on emotion seems antithetical to the common perception that the Christian tradition frowns on emotion, at least the so-called negative emotions—such as anger. Because my goal in this first part of the book is to establish basic theological concepts about emotion, it is necessary to explore this popular idea from the perspective of the Christian tradition. What is the story of the church's response to human emotion?

Theologians James and Evelyn Whitehead have studied the influence of theological ideas on devotional practices and offer a helpful overview when they identify two opposing views of emotion within the tradition of Christian spirituality. The dominant view, as they perceive it, claims that "emotions are unruly instincts erupting with blind and selfish force."[1] This approach paints a theological picture of emotions as dangerous to the life of faith, and even demonic. The response to these problematic emotions is to master them. This tradition, as the Whiteheads describe it, takes the stance that "emotions are like wild animals that must be domesticated and controlled."[2]

The second view recognizes the volatility and danger of emotions, but accepts them as "potential partners in our search for holiness and health."[3] Instead of fighting off emotions, or denying their existence, this positive approach seeks to embrace, tame, and harness their significant energy and potential. The focus is on "befriending" rather than "mastery."[4] This spiritual perspective believes that body and soul are not opposed to one another, but potential partners that can connect us with the Creator. This perspective on spirituality rejects dualism and accepts that body and soul, flesh and spirit are a unity.

We shall see examples of both views when we explore how Christian thinkers have wrestled with this universal marker of human existence. First, however, I explore what can be learned from Scripture that informs a theology of emotion.

EMOTION AND THE BIBLE

Scripture is filled with stories that include emotional responses to life situations, ranging from Cain's jealousy to David's lust and from Peter's fear to Mary's grief. The entire scope of human emotion is on display in its pages. Scripture assumes that emotion is simply part of the human condition, so I now focus on issues subject to debate over the centuries: emotion in the life of Jesus and in the nature of God.

Jesus and Emotion

A close look at the Gospels provides a picture of a fully human Jesus, a real person who was tested and tempted in every way that we are (Heb. 4:15). The Gospel writers are clear that Jesus experienced and expressed the full range of human emotion: sorrow as he overlooked the city of Jerusalem (Luke 19:41), fear in the Garden (Matt. 26:37–44), grief at the tomb of Lazarus (John 11:35), joy in welcoming the children (Mark 10:16), disappointment in the denial of Peter (Luke 22:61), and, of particular interest, anger on numerous occasions— with Peter, with the Pharisees, and in the Temple, to name a few (see chapter 9 for a full discussion).

When Jesus went into Gethsemane to pray, for example, he seemed to be aware of the coming confrontation with the authorities and the possibility of being arrested, convicted, and executed. As you would expect of any person, the possibility of death, and the presumed failure of his mission, created stress for Jesus. Fear seems to be present in his request of God, "Remove this cup from me" (Mark 14:36). His anxiety is clearly described by the Gospel writers. Matthew 26:37 says he was "grieved and agitated." Mark 14:33 notes that he was "distressed and agitated." To show how comfortable the early church was with Jesus' emotions, a scribal addition to the original text in Luke 22:44 describes him in such "anguish" that "his sweat became like great drops of blood falling down on the ground."[5] These descriptive phrases purposefully portray Jesus going through an intense emotional experience. The Gospel writers were unanimous in declaring that Jesus was fully human and took part in every aspect of finite life, including feeling anguish and anxiety in the face of potential loss, suffering, and life-threatening circumstances.

Not everyone in the Christian tradition has been convinced of Jesus' humanity. The Docetic controversy in the early church reflected the church's theological struggle with the dualism of Hellenistic philosophy that drew clear lines between the flesh and the spirit, and emotion and reason. The Docetics adopted the dualistic belief that spirit is good and material things, including the body, are evil. Because Jesus was the Son of God, one expression of the deity, the Docetics felt the need to protect his essence as a spiritual entity. They could not conceive of the Divine participating in our flesh-and-blood existence and argued, therefore, that Jesus didn't really have a human body like ours, but only *appeared* to have a body.[6] This belief led to a number of conclusions about the nature of Jesus' "humanity," one being that Jesus did not experience any real human emotions, certainly not any negative ones such as anger.

Though Doceticism fell into disfavor in the early church, many of its ideas filtered into various Christian traditions. Even today, a common assumption is that people who claim to be transformed into brothers and sisters of Christ ought not experience negative emotions, particularly anger. Despite the careful attempts of church councils and denominational creeds to balance the divinity and the humanity of Jesus, Christian teaching often emphasizes the divinity of Jesus (the Son of God) and discounts the humanness of Jesus (the Son of Humanity), particularly when it comes to emotionality. Some people find it hard to accept that the "humanness" of the carpenter from Nazareth included having emotional reactions to persons and events.

But even people whose Christology accepts that Jesus was fully human may assume that Jesus transcended emotion. Believers who grow up in a community of faith that is suspicious of emotion may view Jesus through that predetermined lens and imagine that he was too "good," or too "perfect," to have emotions. Accepting Jesus as a model for what being a mature Christian means, their assumption may be that those who are Christ-like have overcome any tendencies toward emotionality.

The Docetic tradition would agree that Jesus "loves," of course, but this love is a nice, comforting, thoughtful character trait, rather empty of actual passion, not the love portrayed in the Gospels. The love Jesus expressed was filled with compassion. In English the word "compassion" means "to feel with," referring to our visceral identification with another person's pain and heartache. New Testament scholar Marcus Borg points out that the word "compassion" was used often by the Gospel writers to describe Jesus.[7] The Greek word *splangchnizomai*, which is translated by the phrase "moved with compassion," is used only twelve times in the Gospels and refers exclusively to either Jesus or God. The word *splangchma* identifies that part of our anatomy we refer to as our "guts," the bowels in men and the womb in women, where we feel most intensely the physiological symptoms of emotion.[8] This Greek word, as pastoral theologians Donald McNeill, Douglas Morrison, and Henri Nouwen point out:

> is related to the Hebrew word for compassion, *rachamim*, which refers to the womb of Yahweh. Indeed, compassion is such a deep, central, and powerful emotion in Jesus that it can only be described as a movement of the womb of God. . . . When Jesus was moved to compassion, the source of all life trembled, the ground of all love burst open, and the abyss of God's immense, inexhaustible, and unfathomable tenderness revealed itself.[9]

Jesus' compassion was a deep, powerful feeling, not superficial sympathy.

God and Emotion

To establish that Jesus experienced emotion is one thing, but what about God? While we do not know definitively the mystery of God, the Christian tradition has normally taken seriously those experiences with God recorded in Scripture, which do portray a God who felt emotion. Furthermore, Christians have often reported that the God they encounter in religious experience expresses emotion.[10]

In the Hebrew Scriptures, the Israelites clearly experienced God as a feeling God. At the beginning of the flood narrative the Lord looks on human evil and was "grieved" to the "heart" (Gen. 6:6). In this same story we find the emotion of regret, for the Lord was "sorry" to have created humankind (Gen. 6:6–7). God was "pleased" with Solomon (1 Kgs. 3:10), frustrated with the Israelites (Num. 14:11–12), and self-proclaimed as "a jealous God" (Exod. 20:5). The psalmist indicates that God is "merciful and gracious, slow to anger and abounding in steadfast love" and is "compassionate" like a parent (Ps. 103:8, 13).[11] Are such descriptions of emotionality only the necessary result of using anthropomorphic language? Or merely the projections of human experience onto God? Certainly when considering events in Hebrew Scripture that include violence against innocent people, which is attributed to God's command (a problem I engage in chapter 9), projection is often proposed as an answer. But even if we concur with this interpretation of those specific events, that conclusion does not automatically suggest that all emotions perceived in God are simple human projections.

The New Testament also offers important insight into God's emotional nature. When Christology claims that in some mysterious way Jesus was not only fully human, but also fully divine, then another significant theological truth unfolds. The Christian tradition developed the concept of Trinity to explain the relationship between the Creator God of the Israelites, Jesus of Nazareth sent from God, and the church's unique encounters with the Spirit. Extensive commentary on this idea of Trinity has provided numerous perspectives for understanding this relationship, each one recognizing in some manner that Jesus is part of the Godhead. This approach was troublesome to some of Jesus' contemporaries: "For this reason the Jews were seeking all the more to kill him, because he was not only breaking the sabbath, but was also calling God his own Father, thereby making himself equal to God" (John 5:18). Whatever one's understanding of Trinity, if Jesus, one participant in the Trinity, experiences emotion, then logically the other two participants also experience emotion. After all, Jesus is quoted as saying, "The Father and I are one" (John 10:30).

Not only was Jesus described as compassionate in the Gospels, but Borg argues persuasively that the concept of *compassion* also sums up Jesus' teachings about God. One succinct but powerful saying of Jesus sums up this truth: "Be compassionate as God is compassionate" (Luke 6:36).[12] "For Jesus," Borg says, "compassion was the central quality of God and the central moral quality of a life centered in God."[13] To fully appreciate the theology of Jesus' statement, we must further examine this word "compassion." As noted earlier, the Hebrew and Aramaic word translated as "compassion" means "womb." The ancient Hebrews associated compassion with the lower abdomen, rather than the head, where thinking takes place. This word, *rachamim*, then, refers to the intensity of feelings we find deep within our bodies associated with people who are special to us.[14] Jesus' claim that God is compassionate, therefore, is a foundational theological idea: God feels intensely! God is visceral, affective, and emotional about what happens in God's creation.[15]

Some people argue that claiming that God feels compassion, identified as a "positive" emotion, is different than claiming that God feels anger, perceived as a "negative" emotion. Challenging Christians to be compassionate, they would argue, is qualitatively different than challenging them to be angry, but I show in chapter 12 that anger and compassion are more closely connected than this viewpoint realizes.

Not until a few centuries into the Christian era, as we shall see below, did theologians begin to argue that emotion attributed to God in Scripture was a projection of the human writers, that these attributes should not be taken literally, and that God was in reality immutable and without feeling.[16] Jesus' belief that God is compassionate challenges this idea that God is unmoved and nonemotional. Next, we explore briefly how the Christian tradition has wrestled with the human experience of emotions.

HISTORICAL FACTORS AFFECTING
THE CHRISTIAN TRADITION

Through the centuries, Christian theologians, like their contemporaries in philosophy, have been ambivalent about emotion. The theological, philosophical, and cultural reasons for this ambivalence are not easy to discern. While pinpointing all of the factors that influenced the early church's developing attitude toward emotion is difficult, we can identify three. The first factor was the belief of classical Greek philosophy, and later of Stoicism, that reason was more spiritual than emotion, because reason could guide a person to understanding the Divine more certainly than emotion. The second factor was the need of Christian apologists to defend God as transcendent, holy, and moral in contrast to the popular gods in the Greco-Roman world who were portrayed with humanlike vices and functioned immorally, particularly because of destructive emotions. Popular gods also included powerful, violent humans who were deified, such as Alexander the Great. Their immoral behavior was often the result of anger expressed as jealousy, revenge, and violence. The third factor was the dualistic differentiation between flesh and spirit adopted into the belief and practice of the monastic tradition.

The Influence of Mediterranean Philosophies

A basic concern in the ancient world was the apparent tension, even dichotomy, between reason and emotion. The most famous of classical Greek philosophers, Plato (c. 427–c. 347 B.C.) and Aristotle (384–322 B.C.), differences aside, both recognized the power of emotions to lead humans into self-defeating behaviors and feared that a society in which passions were untamed by reason was in danger of becoming what we would call "dysfunctional." They argued, therefore, that emotion should always be under the control and direction of reason, which, along with will (volition), were the most distinguished parts of the soul. This tension between reason and emotion was communicated in the metaphor that compares emotions to the spirited horses that pulled chariots and reason to the charioteer. When the charioteer (reason) is in command, the horses (emotions) function effectively and accomplish their purpose, but if the charioteer (reason) loses control, the horses (emotions) pull in contrary directions and chaos results. Emotions must be bridled and guided by the firm hand of reason.

Stoic philosophy, which flourished a century later in Greece and then in Rome, viewed emotions less positively. The famous Stoic, Seneca (c. 4 B.C.–65 A.D.), believed that the mind is vulnerable to the passions and loses its rational powers when emotions are felt and expressed.[17] Stoic doctrine held that external concerns should not affect a person's inner life; only reason should. Because emotions were a response to something external that a person either feared or desired, they revealed a defect in reasoning.[18] Furthermore, Stoics believed that emotions were the enemy of the spiritual principle, and, therefore, that reason should not only control emotions but suppress them. As Vernon McCasland summarized, to the Stoics "the emotions are an abnormal, diseased aberration of personality. The goal of Stoic discipline is to annihilate them. The virtuous [person] should . . . never give way to mirth, sorrow, or anger."[19]

The classical Greek view, particularly the more radical Stoic approach, was one of the cultural factors that conditioned the early church's understanding of emotion. Many early Christians admired the Stoics for their ability under stress to control strong emotions, particularly fear and anger. Early monastic authors frequently used Stoic concepts to complement and reinforce their own theological positions, and these ideas are found throughout early Christian writings.[20] One of the main tasks of reason, they agreed, was to control the passions and suppress the appetites. Christian lists of vices and virtues, for example—the forerunners of the seven deadly sins—often referred to parallels between Stoic thought and specific biblical passages. A negative result of this theological emphasis was the gradual adoption of the Stoic distaste for emotions and suspicion that they interfered with the process of seeking unity with God.

Christian Apologetics: Defending God's Holiness

Early Christian apologists had to demonstrate that the Creator God of the Judeo-Christian faith was different from the "pagan" gods of popular Greek culture. How could they argue that the Christian God was not guilty of, or even tempted by, the same passion-driven excesses and immoral behavior (jealousy, lust, greed, rape, murder, and so forth) of the all-too-human gods of the Greeks? One approach to separate God from any taint of human vice was to claim that God did not even possess the capacity for humanlike passions, so obviously God couldn't express them destructively. This Christian defense of God was shaped by the perception both of the Greeks and early Christians that the emotions were one of the main motivational culprits behind destructive, sinful behaviors. If God doesn't have any emotions, then God can't sin. Christian theologians thus began to argue that God was impassive and immutable—unmoved by emotion either toward or from the world.

Augustine (354–430), one of the most influential theologians in the early church, argued that despite biblical passages to the contrary, God and angels do not feel any emotion. He attributed the use of emotive words to describe

God in the Bible to the limitations of human language for describing God's behavior: "Ordinary language ascribes to [God and angels] also these mental emotions, because, though they have none of our weakness, their acts resemble the actions to which these emotions move us."[21] John Cassian (360–430), whose work and writings significantly influenced the monastic tradition, also believed that God is free from all emotion[22] and argued on the basis of "the authority of Holy Scripture" that God is "invisible, ineffable, incomprehensible, inestimable, simple, and uncomposite."[23]

The impact of this theology has been long-standing. Thomas Aquinas (c. 1224–1274) was clear that God acts out of volition, not emotion: "When [emotions] are attributed to God or the angels . . . they refer simply to acts of will which produce indeed the same sort of result as does action prompted by emotion, but are not in fact accompanied by emotion."[24] Some theologians continued to shape theology around an immutable God who was unmoved by passions. John Calvin (1509–1564), for example, who studied and wrote about the Stoics, wrote in his commentary on various psalms that God's decrees "cannot be changed," that God "remains unmoved," and that "nothing could ever affect the immutability of God."[25]

Flesh/Spirit Dualism

Many of the early church theologians belonged to, or were significantly influenced by, the monastic tradition, which made a distinction between things of the flesh and things of the spirit. The monastics strove to achieve purity of heart, to be united with God, and to be perfected in their ability to love like Christ. Their dualistic theology held that the flesh is corrupt and antithetical to spirituality, and interferes with one's ability to unite with God. Flesh, therefore, must be completely overcome to attain salvation. Spirit, in contrast, is pure, the arena in which we meet God. Because the monastics recognized the limitations of both reason and emotion, this flesh-versus-spirit dualism is larger than the "head"-versus-"heart" language that popularly describes the difference between actions resulting from emotions and those resulting from logic.

The strong physical reactions that accompany emotion make it easy to understand how emotions became assigned to the flesh; the body rather than the heart served up emotions. Furthermore, many early monastic writers suspected that emotions usually served selfish purposes, another reason to link them with bodily desires. The monastics, however, in contrast to the Mediterranean philosophers who elevated reason into the realm of the spiritual and a guide toward the divine, believed that reason, like emotions, was part of the flesh and could also lead a person away from God. Both emotion and reason, therfore, were part of the flesh and had to be conquered in order to "put on the mind of Christ."[26]

The monastic path toward being Christ-like included poverty, which one could achieve through renunciation of material possessions, and humility, which one could attain by subduing reason and emotion—either of which could push a person toward pride and arrogance. This flesh-versus-spirit theology also created a strong ascetic emphasis within the monastic community. Some early monastics went to extremes to "deny the flesh" as represented by the body: wearing hair shirts, depriving themselves of sleep, lashing themselves with whips, starving themselves, isolating themselves from others, hoping to conquer the flesh and the desires of the body for food (the problem of gluttony) and sex (the problem with lust). Their positive purpose in subduing the body, including the emotions, was to allow freedom for their spirit to find God.

A WORD FROM THE THEOLOGIANS

Before the twentieth century, Christian theologians carefully and thoughtfully discussed the emotions, though usually within the context of their thinking about the "passions" and the "affections." As a result of their own life-changing religious experience, they rarely separated theological reflection from their concern about spiritual life and morality. Theological thinking was their attempt not only to understand God, but also to reflect on how to be faithful Christian disciples. They felt it necessary, therefore, to analyze and understand emotion because they recognized experientially and existentially that the emotions were a focus of constant concern for those struggling to know God and to follow God's desire. So they sought, within the context of their times, to reconcile the cultural perceptions of emotion and Christian belief in a way that allowed them to most faithfully live what they perceived to be "the life of Christ."[27]

Like the classical Greek philosophers, early theologians gave prominence to the human ability to reason, but they did not separate cognitive from emotional processes. Even as they considered reason superior to emotion, they acknowledged both of these basic components of consciousness. In other words, they were more followers of Plato and Aristotle than of Stoicism and normally resisted the complete negation of emotion. They accepted emotions as part of what God had created and understood that emotions contributed to abundant life, even though they had significant potential for harm. From the Reformers to the twentieth century, theologians wrestled with the reason-versus-emotion dynamic. They had ambivalent feelings about emotions and warned about the dangers they posed to Christian living, but in light of their understanding of faith and religious experience, theologians accepted emotions as an important aspect of the human condition. Consider now the perspectives of seven prominent theologians from Augustine through Jonathan Edwards, and then a short summary and critique of twentieth-century theology's approach to emotions.

St. Augustine (354–430)

Augustine, like the Stoics, had a high regard for our ability to reason, although he differed from them in his belief that the ability to reason and to focus our wills had been compromised because of original sin. In Augustine's theology, human beings became subject to a divided will when they disobeyed God's command and fell from paradise. Therefore, although we want to obey God and to do good, we find ourselves making sinful choices, including allowing emotions to lead us astray.

However, Augustine did not want to eliminate emotions, but to direct them toward God through the appropriate use of reason.[28] In *The City of God*, he compared the Stoic view of emotions with that of Plato and Aristotle and decided against the Stoics' desire to do away with emotions, taking the position that "the sum of Christian knowledge" directs us to subject the passions to God so that God can help us "moderate and bridle them, and turn them to righteous uses."[29] Augustine clearly acknowledged that emotions come from God and have a potentially important role in the Christian life.

Saint Macrina (327–379)

Saint Macrina, the older sister of both Gregory of Nyssa and Saint Basil, believed that emotions were part of God's intentional creation of human beings and part of the "desiring and spirited faculties" that are "joined to the [soul], but they are not what constitutes the essence of the soul."[30] Interestingly, she thought of creation as a process by which the sensuality necessary to life and survival were first implanted in plants and animals and then, later in the creation saga, into humans, who as the crown of creation were imbued with a mix of sensual appetites and intelligent reasoning. Macrina taught Gregory that these "[emotions] have not been allotted to human life for an evil purpose," but are necessary in order for the soul to "choose good or evil."[31] If emotions had been created for an evil purpose, she reasoned, God would be responsible for evil—and she plainly dismissed that possibility. Like other theologians (and the philosophers), Macrina believed that emotions became problematic only when they escaped control by our power to reason.[32] Emotions do not serve evil when reason is in control, but in fact they enable the accomplishment of virtue: "when emotions govern the mind, man goes from the intellectual and the godlike to the irrational and the foolish, and he is ruined by the onrush of such affections."[33]

Thomas Aquinas (c. 1224–1274)

Aquinas, who filled three volumes of his *Summa Theologiae* with theological reflections on the emotions,[34] placed emotions in the context of physiology. He believed that emotions are a feature of existence that we share with the animal kingdom, and he intentionally included the emotions in his chapters that describe characteristics common to both humans and animals, rather than his chapters discussing uniquely human behavior. Though ultimately rooted in the soul, emotions, Aquinas believed, are finitely based in our physical senses,[35] and are part of the created order, an aspect of our finitude planned by the Creator.

Martin Luther (1483–1546)

Luther was convinced that emotionality is based in God's intentional creation and criticized the Stoics, and monks who adopted Stoic philosophy, for their negative perspectives about emotion. In a sermon after the death of a friend, Luther challenged the idea of a "heathen" who considered it a "virtue not to be affected by the death of a good and dear friend or to weep at his bier."[36] He identified the Stoic idea that "we must entirely shed all human emotions" as an "artificial virtue . . . which God has not created and which does not please Him at all."[37] The Christian response to Stoic philosophy was clear: "we condemn it and call it wrong."[38] God did not create humans to be like stones, said Luther, but purposively gave us five senses and a heart so that we can love, be angry, and feel grief.[39] Not to be moved by "affections," he argued in another lecture, "would be altogether contrary to nature, which was created by God to have such inclinations."[40]

Luther accepted emotion as a significant aspect of the human condition, necessary for the faith by which we are saved. He believed that emotion was more important to the Christian life than reason, and in his commentary on Romans argued that faith is a feeling.[41] While discussing Psalm 119, Luther expressed a strong preference for emotion, saying that "faith needs affection, not understanding." He described how faith illuminates our emotions, but emphasized that faith "does not illumine the understanding; indeed, it blinds it!"[42] Luther obviously takes a strong stance about the foundational, perhaps primary, place of emotion in a dynamic faith.[43]

John Calvin (1509–1564)

Calvin believed reason was the mark of human nature that distinguished us from "irrational animals." In fact, at several points he seems to identify rationality as the aspect of the self that represents the image of God.[44] In contrast, he argued, emotions operated in excess, rebelled against God, resisted control by the intellect and reason, and endangered the soul.[45] Influenced by the traditional flesh-versus-spirit dualism and by his own life experiences, Calvin identified the body as a sinful entity, the prison of the soul, and described it as "dirt and corruption" and "a stinking infection."[46] This negative view of embodiment colored his view of the passions. Because he felt that emotions, when unaccompanied by reason, were so dangerous, Calvin, like the classic philosophers and theologians before him, wanted emotions to be under reason's strict control: "God has given us reason and judgment to combat our passions."[47]

Nevertheless, Calvin attacked the Stoics for their insistence that wise and mature persons should completely suppress all emotion, noting that the Stoics "must have been devoid of common sense in taking away all feeling from a man."[48] Starting with the biblical narratives which clearly demonstrate that Jesus had an emotional life, Calvin argued that Jesus' emotions were part of his essential humanity: "Those who claim that the son of God was immune from human passions do not seriously acknowledge him as a man."[49] He illustrated this assertion by pointing out that Jesus was "struck with fright and afflicted with anxiety." Emotions were foundational to Jesus' humanity and therefore, Calvin concluded, are appropriate for Christians, "implanted in us by God; we cannot find fault with them without insulting God himself."[50]

Calvin also recognized the important role of emotions in experiencing dynamic faith and a saving knowledge of God and suspected that reason, for all of its good qualities, was not necessarily helpful to faith. In the *Institutes*, Calvin indicated that "knowledge of God" is rooted in the heart, not the head.[51] "Heart" for Calvin, when put beside the "mind," refers clearly to "the seat of the emotions,"[52] and he actually reprimands those scholastics who identified faith with "simple assent arising out of knowledge" and who "do not have regard to that firm and steadfast constancy of heart, which is the chief part of faith."[53] Discussing the dependence of faith on illumination by the Holy Spirit, Calvin noted that this illumination must not only be of the mind but also of the "heart." He instructed that "faith is much higher than human understanding" and argued that the essence of faith is something that we cannot grasp primarily with the intellect.[54] To comprehend the fullness of faith, we must use other aspects of our being, including the emotions.

John Wesley (1703–1791)

In a sermon titled "What Is Man?" Wesley differentiated soul from body. He believed that within the body is an "inward principle" that not only thinks, judges, and reasons but is capable "of love, hatred, joy, sorrow, desire, fear, hope, etc., and a whole train of other inward emotions, which are commonly called passions and affections."[55] These essential aspects of our existence he called "soul," and he describes it as "this self-moving, thinking principle, with all its passions and affections."[56] For Wesley, emotion is part of God's intentional creation, integral to what makes us "fearfully and wonderfully made."[57]

Jonathan Edwards (1703–1758)

In America, Jonathan Edwards followed the Reformers' lead by including the emotions in his theological anthropology. Edwards wrote his famous *Religious Affections* in part to defend the importance of emotion in religious experience.[58] He observed that the "affections" were the primary motivator of human behavior, and although suspicious of the exaggerated enthusiasm and "intemperate zeal" he saw in the revivalism of the Great Awakening, he argued theologically against people who used such excess to denounce the place of emotion in religious experience. While very careful not to separate the "affections" from "understanding" and "will," the other two aspects of selfhood, Edwards was adamant that emotion brings a foundational ingredient to religious experience.[59] He argued that the valid work of the Spirit in an individual soul is marked by warmth, joy, and zeal. Genuine religious experience "in great part, consists in holy affections."[60] His theology definitely supports the idea that emotions are part of God's planned creation.[61]

Twentieth-Century Theologians

One of the big surprises of this project was discovering that not many twentieth-century theologians, at least not the influential "giants," chose to engage the subject of emotionality in a scholarly, systematic fashion. Little in the work of major theologians can inform a theology of emotions, much less contribute to a pastoral theology of anger. Some scholars seemed to neglect the subject; others purposefully ignored it.

In *Church Dogmatics*, for example, Karl Barth was concerned with revealed truth from a sovereign God revealed in Jesus Christ, and he was challenging the idea of subjective religious experience as a substantial window into truth. Unlike Friedrich Schleiermacher, Barth rejected the affections as a "point of contact"[62] and did not believe that theology should attend to affections and

passions as significant vehicles for knowing God or discerning our relationship with the Divine. In *Ethics*, he pointedly declared, "Psychological analysis
cannot serve as a means to reveal in man not only his sin and not only his
protest against himself but beyond that his saving openness to the will of
God."[63] Barth, moreover, held that human sinfulness significantly scarred our
capacity as humans to know ourselves. This approach added to his suspicion
of emotions: "There is a way from Christology to anthropology. There is no
way from anthropology to Christology."[64]

Emil Brunner, Barth's contemporary, did not deal with emotion in his *Revelation and Reason: The Christian Doctrine of Faith and Knowledge*,[65] choosing not
to elaborate on the tension between these two aspects of consciousness in the
same way that the classic philosophers had pursued. Though focused on revelation and "knowledge," this book does not consider the role of emotion in
knowing about God. In his *Dogmatics*, Brunner's approach to anthropology is
limited by the perception that "the Bible understands man as a whole, as an
entity consisting of 'soul' or 'spirit' and 'body.'"[66] Though he addresses the
subject of embodiment with positive attitudes, he does not include the emotions, passions, or affections—leaving his readers with the idea that these are
irrelevant to understanding the human condition.[67]

In Reinhold Niebuhr's central treatise, *The Nature and Destiny of Man: A
Christian Interpretation*, the concept of emotion is not included in the index.[68]
Though dealing briefly with anxiety, and trying to develop a full theological
anthropology, emotion does not receive categorical treatment as a significant
aspect of the human condition. Niebuhr also examines the nature of human
being in his *The Self and the Dramas of History*, but the subject of emotions does
not appear as a particular aspect of the human equation.[69] His brother,
Richard, was more inclusive of emotions, particularly in his *Experiential Religion*. There he explores the many meanings of affections and passions and then
says:

> Even with all these ways of describing affection, the corrective implied
> by all this nomenclature remains clear: it is not sufficient to conceive
> of faithful man as a rational soul, nor even as a rational being whose
> dignity lies in choosing or willing. He is also an affectional being. To
> ignore this is to commit a psychological reductionism.[70]

Existentialist theologian Paul Tillich, though not addressing emotion as a
specific category, does include the subject when discussing reason. In the first
volume of *Systematic Theology*, he includes the role of emotion in reasoning
processes. He claims, for example, "that an emotional element is present in
every rational act" and defends a positive role for emotions when he says, "the
fact that in some [rational acts] the emotional element is more decisive than in

others does not make them less rational."[71] Tillich even suggests the primacy of emotion, noting that "Emotion is the vehicle for receiving cognition" and claiming that "No union of subject and object is possible without emotional participation."[72] Specifically talking about revelation, Tillich declares that emotion and reason are equal partners, even though he also warns of "emotional distortions."[73]

Interestingly, volumes 2 and 3 of *Systematic Theology*, where Tillich also deals with anthropological themes, do not return to emotion except in a marginal manner. When he addresses existential concerns, his positive view of our existential existence implies a positive place for emotion, though it may also play a part in estrangement and evil.[74] Moreover, when he discusses "self-actualization" and the effect of "the spiritual presence" on our finitude, emotion is only tangentially an issue.[75] Although his *The Courage to Be*[76] made an influential contribution to theological anthropology, it does not specifically analyze emotionality. In dealing with anxiety in this work, including fear and guilt, Tillich does, however, bring attention to that which goes beyond the rational. He makes clear in this work that because we are finite creatures, a "natural anxiety" regarding the threat of "nonbeing"[77] permeates our existence. This anxiety manifests itself in questions about our ultimate fate, in threats to our sense of meaning, and in the ambiguity and guilt involved in our attempts to live a moral life. In the midst of this ubiquitous and natural anxiety, which could be thought of as including emotionality, Tillich is inquiring about the role of courage.[78]

In Hans Küng's major work, *On Being a Christian*, he does not deal with emotion as a theological category, though he does mention its importance to love:

> When *eros* is depreciated, however, *agape* is overvalued and dehumanized. . . . Vitality, emotion, affectivity are forcibly excluded, leaving a love that is totally unattractive. When love is merely a decision of the will and not also a venture of the heart, it lacks genuine humanity.[79]

Furthermore, when talking about our responsibility to become "fully human," Küng says, "Must we not strive for the best possible development of the individual: a humanization of the whole person in all his dimensions, including instinct and feeling?"[80] Given the stated significance of emotion in full human existence, full treatment would seem to be forthcoming, but is not.

Wolfhart Pannenberg includes emotion in his theological anthropology, addressing affections in a chapter in his *Anthropology in Theological Perspective*.[81] Pannenberg discusses the affective life in the context of the problem of identity and selfhood, and views feeling as a "horizon of original familiarity,"[82] in which we are aware of our lives as individuals in relationship. This awareness comes through to us in feelings, characterized by pleasure and displeasure.

Furthermore, this view of feeling as the backdrop of "original familiarity" means that Pannenberg is writing about the affective life in a "comprehensive sense";[83] he believes that the "original familiarity" of feeling relates to the way in which we begin to differentiate ourselves from caregivers and from the world during the first few years of life. Feeling provides the "symbiotic existential certainty"[84] out of which this differentiation occurs. Another important point in this regard is that, for Pannenberg, "Every feeling . . . is related to the whole of the individual's life."[85] This wholeness provides a further backdrop for his discussion of alienation through guilt and the "judgment of conscience,"[86] in which we sense ourselves separated from this wholeness and authentic relationship. Alienation is what "keeps us imprisoned in nonidentity," the freeing of which can only come through community."[87]

Another current German theologian, Jürgen Moltmann, does not attend systematically to theological anthropology in his work and, therefore, no treatment of emotions as a significant part of human existence or in faith experience is found in his writings.

After the rich exploration of emotion in the writers of the early centuries of the Christian era, the lack of attention to emotion (with the exception of Tillich and Pannenberg) in the systematic writings of these theological giants is both surprising and frustrating. How can this absence be explained? They were males of European origins, mostly Germanic, reared in a culture that prized the intellect over the emotions, and perhaps they feared that to deal with the emotions would make their work suspect. As in every period of history, these theologians were influenced by philosophy, and from Descartes through the middle of the twentieth century most Western philosophers tended toward body/mind dualism.[88] Perhaps these theologians are more dualistic than they imagined. Richard Niebuhr describes this problem: "Rarely has the theologian broadened his view (beyond volition and cognition) to take account of the affections, with the result that Protestant representation of faith still suffers from an excessive rationalism."[89] These theologians spent most of their careers in academic environments, which in the modernist era emphasized objectivity, logic, and scientific method, as discussed in chapter 1. Personal experience was not accepted as valid epistemological data. They also wrote at a time when disciplines were carefully categorized and jealously guarded, so they may have felt inadequate to consider emotions academically without specific training in the physical and social sciences.

Whatever the reasons, that these influential theologians did not deal with this central aspect of the human predicament is disappointing. We know intense passion for their faith and work guided their lives, as can be seen in their sermons, but the omission of emotions from their systematic writings conveys the idea that they discount the emotional life, implying that emotional responses are intellectually inferior or irrelevant. Their failure to deal systematically with emotion in their doctrine of personhood leaves the impression that they concur with the modernists' decision to set emotion at the margins of the intellectual life, perceiving that emotion interferes with the process of logical thinking.[90] The silence, whether intended or not, suggests that emotions are second-class citizens within the created order, unimportant to the life of faith.

The astute reader might wonder if this sample of theologians working in the twentieth century is too small to draw my conclusions. Certainly delimitation was necessary because of time and space constraints. Many modern theologians doubtlessly have given serious attention to emotion. I hope that theologians will do more thorough research, and if my findings are accurate, make a more scholarly attempt to understand the reasons—both theological and psychological—for this omission.

In the later decades of the century, feminist and process theologians did accept emotionality as a significant aspect of the human condition. They became concerned with the absence of emotion from the work of contemporary theology. Patricia Beattie Jung sums up my own experience in reading the influential theologians of the twentieth century, and she gives a strong description of the differences between feminist theology and these more dominant theologies:

> The full spectrum of feelings, including not only joy but also sorrow, anger, and fear, is seen as integral to human wholeness within feminist theologies. In contrast, patriarchal theologies are highly suspicious of "emotionalism" in general and condemn the "negative" emotions in particular. . . . [M]ost traditional theologies have denigrated the affections and advocated the Stoic ideal of emotional detachment. They commended the restraint, if not the elimination, of the disturbing power of the affections. . . . The importance of the affections has been grossly underestimated within such theologies.[91]

Recovering the significance of emotion is particularly necessary when considering morality and the spiritual life. Social scientists and theologians who study the development of morality are both recovering the significant role that emotions play in the decisions that people make, particularly early in life, about what to value and how to act.[92] Feminist moral theologians are demonstrating the significance of emotion both for the pilgrimage of faith and for ethical choice. Ellen Charry, for example, challenges the perception that humans are basically cognitive minds "bereft or fearful of emotions," and wants to "encourage theology to reclaim the emotions."[93] "If we are not perceptive in discerning our feelings, or if we do not know what we feel," says

Beverly Wildung Harrison, "we cannot be effective moral agents."[94] Sidney Callahan has written extensively on the importance of emotions for the development of conscience.[95] From a constructionist perspective (see chapter 6), she thoughtfully discusses the importance of both emotion and reason in the construction of moral values.[96] In summary, these theologians argue that a theological understanding of the emotions is essential to integrating Christian faith and behavior.

Process theologians are also a notable exception to the lack of attention given to emotions in the twentieth century. Feeling is a metaphysical category in process thought. Feelings are a central component of Alfred North Whitehead's philosophy, because through feelings everything in the universe is linked and is continually relating to everything else. An emotional tone underlines all relationships, and relationality itself is an "ability both to affect and to be affected."[97]

For process thinkers, the entire universe is composed of "entities that feel," and that reality itself can be thought of as "an ocean of feeling."[98] Process theologians make the point that virtually everything we experience in life is experienced in some fashion as a feeling. Interestingly, Charles Hartshorne, another influential early process thinker, has used Whitehead's work to help him understand an experience he had in 1917 or 1918. As a young man looking out at a beautiful ocean scene from a cliff in France, he "suddenly saw 'into the life of things' and at that moment gained a sense of all nature being alive and expressing feelings."[99]

Furthermore, for process theologians, feeling plays an important role in their conception of God as completely relational and open to all emotions. Whitehead held that God "is the lure for feeling, the eternal urge of desire."[100] From this assertion, we may understand that God is constantly touching or calling us—in each "drop of experience,"[101] which comes to us through feeling—toward that which is best for us in each situation. L. Bryant Keeling writes that Hartshorne believed God was "Perfect Being, [including] all reality within himself . . . and [God] feels the feelings of every individual in the universe and preserves forever the values inherent in these experiences."[102]

An understanding of "self" that dismisses the emotional life as a foundational aspect of personhood, I would argue, cannot produce a valid theological anthropology. Theology must realize that humans without emotion would be entirely different creatures. Constructing a theological anthropology without attending to the affective life is like trying to understand an automobile without addressing the role of the motor. In short, emotion is a necessary ingredient in any theological consideration of the human condition, imperative for a theological anthropology.

Now we have before us from chapter 1 a brief overview of what philosophy, neuroscience, psychology, and the social sciences are discovering about emotion, and from this chapter a selective history of the theological struggle with emotion in the Christian tradition. With this information in mind, the following chapter discusses some theological perspectives on emotion.

3

Theological Reflections
on Emotion

Because anger is an emotion, establishing some basic components of a theology of emotion is important as a context for my primary purpose: constructing a pastoral theology of anger. A theological exploration of anger is dependent on, rooted in, and congruent with valid theological perspectives on emotion in general. In this chapter, I reflect theologically on the new discoveries and theories about emotion gleaned from the philosophical, psychological, neurological, biblical, and theological sources explored in the previous two chapters.

Emotions frequently have been denied and demeaned throughout the history of Western culture, not only in philosophy and science, but also in religion. Theology, with some ambivalence, has usually been suspicious of emotions, assigning them a subversive role in human nature. Over the centuries, some Christians have consistently attempted to discount, even suppress, the emotional aspects of personhood, including grief, ecstasy, sexual passion, and anger, as part of our fallen carnal nature—our depravity—and relegate them to the "demonic" side of life. All emotions have at one time or another been viewed as inimical to spirituality. The negative result of this approach can be illustrated from the journal of Yena, who is in her late thirties and working as a minister in a local church.

> I grew up in a family that subscribed to Western culture's emphasis on thinking, reason and rationality. Emotions were seen as a threat to rational decision-making ability and were to be tightly controlled or even eradicated. A Stoic position was adopted in which emotions were thought to have no place in a virtuous life. The Church played into this conclusion, communicating that "Christians shouldn't be emotional." Emotions were not valued, or seen as useful, or able to change a situation, and thus were discouraged. . . . I recall my parents telling

me to stop crying or "moping around." I got the distinct impression from these words and others that they not only did not want to see my emotions, but that I should not be having these emotions. The message was that emotions were somehow not called for, were unnecessary, and not useful. How one felt was not relevant. Feeling negative feelings such as sadness, loneliness, or anger I felt were a result of something I was doing wrong. . . . Thus, on top of experiencing a "negative" feeling, I also felt guilty about it! I, along with many other Christians, felt that good people didn't feel this way.

Only in recent times, in existential and postmodern thinking, has emotion been acknowledged as a way of knowing in its own right. Not until the last third of the twentieth century, particularly in the work of feminist and process theologians, do we find emotion embraced as friend and gift to the human spirit. They recognize emotion as an integral part of theological reflection and, therefore, of Christian ethics.

Though Christian care specialists have found support in Scripture and theology for their perspectives on emotion, finding systematic theological attention to emotion in the care and counseling literature is difficult. To inform their ministries, caregivers deserve a carefully thought-through pastoral theology of emotion, not to mention anger, informed by recent developments in neurology and the social sciences. Psychologist Archibald Hart, who calls for "a stronger bridge" between clinical practice and theology, expresses this need:

> Christian counseling has sometimes run ahead of its biblical and theological foundations. We have tried to develop a Christian understand-ing of the emotions, for instance, but do not have a theology of emotion. . . . [W]e have borrowed extensively from secular models . . . . [W]e have had to rely heavily on what is already known in the secular field of psychology, and sometimes our borrowing has not been discerning enough. . . . Furthermore, we have had little or no help from our theological colleagues. . . . [We need] greater dialogue between counselors and prestigious theologians and biblical scholars with a view to re-examining many of our present counseling ideas.[1]

The following discussion might add some ideas to that dialogue and offer some contribution to the establishment of a more coherent pastoral theology of emotion.

EMOTION AND EMBODIMENT

The first conclusion we can draw from the sciences is that the capacity for experiencing emotion is rooted in our physiology, rather than in a disembodied psyche. From a scientific standpoint, emotions are not an instinct in the technical sense, because they don't arise within us on the basis of an innate biological need. We are neurologically "wired" with the *capacity* for emotional response, but this capacity only springs into operation as we encounter life situations. Only when one part of our brain (either the amygdala or the neocortex) interprets a life situation as deserving of a physiologically aroused response is this capacity to feel emotion activated. A theological discussion of emotion, therefore, must acknowledge that emotions are part of our embodiment, rather than a nonphysical entity. This perspective is not new; over thirty years ago, existentialist theologian John Macquarrie said that "feelings, affects, moods, or emotions . . . belong so intrinsically to man's constitution that they cannot be overlooked in any attempt to give an account of who man is."[2] More recently, theologian Patricia Beattie Jung concurs, "Emotions are an integral part of what it means to be embodied."[3]

The concept of incarnation can contribute to our ideas about human emotions. The incarnation, God's coming in the flesh, suggests a second blessing of our embodiment (the first being at creation). Emotionality is part of the human experience as described throughout Scripture. In its stories, people are constantly grieving, joyful, anxious, compassionate, fearful, and angry. As was obvious when we explored Jesus' various feeling responses, this coming in the flesh included the capacity for emotions. Jesus did not represent some higher level of humanness by being "above" emotions, but rather confirmed through his own experience of grief, anger, and so forth that both the experience and the expression of emotion are basic to being fully human.

Those Christians who wish they could do away with emotions ignore the fact that this capacity is deeply engrained in our brain and neurological system, a foundational aspect of our embodiment. To eliminate emotions is impossible (short of radical surgery or certain types of disease processes). As Jaak Panksepp writes, "the ability of the human cortex [our cognitive ability] to think and to fantasize, and thereby to pursue many unique paths of human cultural evolution, can dilute, mold, modify, and focus the dictates of these [emotional] systems, but it cannot eliminate them."[4]

The capacity for emotional experience is a neurological given, and attempts to suppress emotions leave a person less than fully human. Theological discourse that separates emotion from embodiment makes it difficult to achieve a wholistic theological epistemology. Feminist theologians have been quick to realize this truth. As Beverly Wildung Harrison says, "If we begin, as feminists must, with 'our bodies, ourselves,' we recognize that all our knowledge, including our moral knowledge, is body-mediated knowledge. All knowledge is rooted in our sensuality."[5] Integrating emotion into our selfhood is imperative for the psychosomatic unity that is basic to wholistic human functioning.

IN THE BEGINNING—EMOTION

A second conclusion that can be drawn from the sciences is that this neurological capacity for emotional arousal has developed over our entire biological history. Neurological research demonstrates that the human capacity for emotion has been building on primitive brain systems for millions of years, rather than suddenly appearing as if by a mutation. All emotion, both "positive" and "negative," is central to our development—our "becoming" as human beings. From a theological perspective, we can conclude that our capacity for emotion is part of the creation, an integral aspect of embodied humanity from the beginning.

Scripture contributes to the same conclusion. The Bible is filled with stories that fully attend to the emotional aspects of finitude. While concerned with how emotions are expressed, and critical of destructive behavior motivated by emotion, Scripture does not question the phenomenological observation that emotion is part of human nature. Furthermore, Scripture cannot be interpreted to suggest that the capacity for emotion is contradictory to God's intentional creation, or that godly people should strive to be emotionless, unless the interpreter brings a specific theological agenda to the process. The biblical narratives *assume* that human emotions are part of the created order, an important aspect of our finitude.

Certainly the Bible is concerned when emotion leads to pain and suffering. The letter to the Ephesians, for example, asks readers to put away all expressions of anger that are destructive of relationships (4:31). Scripture is clear, I would argue, that when emotion does lead to suffering, which is all too common in day-to-day living, it is not because emotion itself is by nature destructive, but because the emotion has expressed the dark side of human possibility and been ethically mishandled. Concern about the destructive expression of an emotion is appropriate, but the destructive potential of emotions (as is true with other aspects of our finitude) does not offer support for people who argue that the *capacity* for emotion is evil and should be eradicated.

CREATED IN GOD'S IMAGE

Another conclusion connected to Christian beliefs about creation has to do with the *imago Dei*, that is, the creation of humans in God's image as expressed in Genesis 1:26, where the creation story quotes God: "Let us make humankind in our image, according to our likeness." This central aspect of our theological anthropology argues that in some mysterious way we contain or reflect aspects of God's being.

In chapter 2 I note that, in both Scripture and many strands of Judeo-Christian theology, God is perceived as possessing the capacity for emotion. Concluding from biblical and theological perspectives that emotion is an aspect of God's being, part of God's nature, one can argue that experiencing and expressing emotion is part of what it means to be created in God's image *(imago Dei)*. In some mysterious way emotion is part of the Creator's original plan for human selfhood. We are created with the capacity for compassion and other emotions that are part of God's nature—including anger, as we shall see later. Because we are created in God's image, then to suppress emotion, or to try and eradicate it from our lives, is to deny the *imago Dei*.

A significant point in Jesus' exclamation "Be compassionate as God is compassionate" (Luke 6:36) is his assumption that *God feels—and feels intensely*. Furthermore, Jesus invites his hearers, perhaps even challenges them, to be emotional and compassionate like God. Jesus obviously believed that we are created with the capacity to feel emotion as God feels emotion. Because God is emotional, we can be emotional.

Furthermore, in chapter 2 we saw that Jesus was obviously an emotional person, feeling the entire range of human feelings from sadness to anger. It makes sense, then, to argue that as a participant in the Trinity (however your theology describes this mystery), Jesus reflects the idea that emotion is part of the character of the Godhead.

THE GIFT OF EMOTION

Research in the neurosciences, along with postmodern philosophical and social science perspectives, establishes that emotions have developed in the biological history of humans to serve a positive purpose. Sartre argued for the importance of emotions when he wrote that "an emotion signifies the totality of the relationships of the human reality to the world."[6] Emotions, as Harrison reminds us, enable us to establish and maintain our connections to the world around us.[7] Without emotions there could be no love, nor would joy or suffering be possible. We could not be in meaningful relationships with others, our environment, or even God.

Furthermore, as noted in chapter 2, emotions play a central role in our search for meaning. As philosopher Robert Solomon says, "Our passions constitute our lives. It is our passions, and our passions alone, that provide our lives with meaning."[8] Emotions combine with our cognitive process to provide the motivation for acting on our ideas and values, providing evidence that emotions are crucial for meaning-making. Roberto Unger, a philosopher, has written persuasively about the significance of the passions in our entire "quest for freedom" and "being at home in the world."[9] He praises the contribution of emotion to a full human life, pointing out the importance of emotions for establishing our identity, comprehending our existential experience, and motivating our actions.[10] Emotions are necessary for the process of becoming, the existential project of gaining acceptance for our unique self.[11]

Because the capacity for emotion is part of embodiment, present within the process of God's creation of humankind, emotions were clearly included when God looked upon creation and proclaimed that it was good (Gen. 1:31). Emotions are unequivocally part of God's intentional creation, a blessed aspect of our "imageness." Theologians have identified emotions as a basic ingredient in faith and, therefore, a significant contributor to our relationship with God. Furthermore, emotions are integrally involved in creating our faith narratives and motivating ethical behavior. Given all of the potential for good that exists in our capacity for emotionality, one can argue that emotions are a gift present in the creation and necessary for physical, mental, and spiritual wholeness. Emotions are foundational to the full experience of God's grace and the divine invitation to wholistic life.

Yes, emotions can be problematic, but their existence as an aspect of our finitude is positive. Emotions can contribute creatively to abundant life if we take them seriously, appreciate them, and learn from them. The temptation to divide emotions into "good" and "bad" overlooks both scientific theory and the experiential reality that all emotions have as their basic purpose the promotion of life, not its destruction.[12] While recognizing the potential for destructive behavior, a valid theological anthropology must not only recognize the significance of all emotions, but argue for their basic goodness. As theologians James and Evelyn Whitehead suggest, "emotions may come as gift instead of affliction, sources of grace rather than disgrace."[13] A theology that argues for "fixing" humans so they won't feel emotions is not defendable scientifically or biblically. We have the privilege and responsibility to claim this gift of emotion and to muster the courage to direct it through ethical behaviors.

Psychological research has concluded that humans who can't or won't access their emotions are in some way compromised in their ability to become fully human. Generations of psychotherapists have argued that emotions are necessary to the well-being of people, confirming the theological position that emotions are part of God's intentional creation. Emotions such as grief, joy, and sadness serve as sources of self-awareness and revelation about ourselves and our relationships that can move us toward transformation. Jung says succinctly, "Feelings are gracious, life-enhancing sources of interconnection with others, the world, and God."[14] This comment is specifically true of anger, one of the more maligned emotions, as is shown in chapter 11. In fact, the experience of anger can serve as a "diagnostic window" through which we can gain insight about ourselves that might not come in any other context.

Theologies that decry emotions are, in fact, denigrating humanness rather than confirming God's blessed creation. They contribute to the repression and suppression of emotion that is destructive to abundant life, as is discussed with reference to anger in part 4. Using current research and theory in both the neurosciences and the social sciences, confirmed by reclaiming the positive understanding of emotion both in Scripture and the work of many respected theologians across the centuries, a theological anthropology should recognize and celebrate the central place of emotions in the process of becoming fully human, and strive to defend the basic goodness of our capacity for emotion.

HEAD *AND* HEART: A WHOLISTIC APPROACH

In order to explain behaviors that differed depending on whether passion or reason seemed to be dominant at the moment, Christian writers over the centuries have described emotions as coming from the "heart," while logic or reason has been assigned to the "head." Accepting without question these perceptions of phenomenological differences, however, can lead to dualistic concepts that consider emotion and reason as separate entities—set over against each other, rather than working in tandem on our behalf. Recent research in philosophy, the neurosciences, psychology, and the social sciences demonstrate that emotions are tied to cognitive interpretations of our environment. The various disciplines conclude that emotion and reason mutually inform each other, rather than functioning as separate entities within our mental apparatus. The data support the theological view that our potential as God's creatures is fulfilled when we function as a unified psychosomatic whole, integrating every component of our being.

Theological dualism, which suggests that emotion and reason can be separated (even when both are assigned to the "flesh"), is no longer defensible, given what we now know about the brain. Appropriately, current work in theological anthropology by both biblical scholars and theologians is slowly rooting out dualism. They are recognizing the interconnectedness of emotion and cognition and understanding that both are foundational aspects of selfhood. More recent understandings of Paul concur that his various anthropological words refer to the whole person, not to some specific part of our anatomy.[15]

One team of scientists, theologians, and philosophers who are studying human nature in light of recent scientific discoveries has rejected dualistic thinking and formed a consensus supporting what they call "nonreductive physicalism."[16] This phrase conveys their conclusion that the idea of "soul" best describes something that is not separate from the body, but a higher level of complex functioning that results from human relationships and interactions with both society and God.[17] This higher level of complex functioning definitely includes emotional responses, so we can conclude that "soul" includes our capacity for emotion. These scholars argue that meaningful religious experience does not necessitate a dualistic conception of human nature because "religious experiences do not depend on any special faculties over and above humans' ordinary emotional and cognitive faculties."[18]

Our discussion leads to one conclusion: We cannot explore the vital life force that motivates humans unless we embrace the connection between emotion and reason. This truth is captured by Harrison: "All power, including intellectual power, is rooted in feeling. If feeling is damaged or cut off, our power to image the world and act into it is destroyed and our rationality is impaired."[19] As we saw in chapter 1, philosophers and psychologists have established that emotions work with cognitive ability to enhance our understanding of reality. Emphasizing the importance of the reasoning brain in human life is theologically appropriate, but equally important is recognizing the role that emotions play in cognition. In fact, from the perspective of evolutionary biology, theology needs to accept the primacy of emotion in the historical development of our cognitive capacity.

Søren Kierkegaard long ago called for a unification of thought and feeling in the pursuit of "purity of heart."[20] Parker Palmer, writing about spirituality and education, gives poetic voice to this concern. After speaking of our overdependence on "the eye of the mind," he recommends "opening the other eye, the eye of the heart, looking for realities to which the mind's eye is blind. Either eye alone is not enough. We need 'wholesight,' a vision of the world in which mind and heart unite."[21] Christians, Palmer suggests, have both the desire and the responsibility to pursue not only knowledge, which is what interests the mind, but also truth, which can only be found when we look through "wholesight."[22] Using Paul's metaphor of the importance of each part of the body, we could say that both emotion and reason serve the whole self. The desert monastics saw this connection from the reverse perspective, knowing that to reach the level of devotion to Christ and unity with God they passionately sought, they must subdue *both* reason *and* emotion.

Separating emotion and cognition contradicts science, our understanding of creation, embodiment, and incarnation, so such a separation no longer makes theological sense. Along with postmodernists of all disciplines, theology can argue that God intentionally placed emotion alongside of, and integrally related to, reason at the center of human life. Descartes's basic premise—"I think, therefore I am"—must be joined by the equally valid truth, "I feel, therefore I am." Both are theologically true. A better summary statement from a theological perspective might be, "I think and feel, therefore I am, and continue to become."

WE ARE RESPONSIBLE FOR OUR EMOTIONS

In chapter 1, I presented current arguments from philosophy, psychology, and the neurosciences in support of the centrality of emotion in human existence, demonstrating the positive contributions that emotion makes to the fabric of our lives. Many psychotherapists, pastors, and pastoral care specialists have accepted these arguments because their clinical experience confirms these perspectives. They use social science perspectives about the "naturalness" of emotion as the guiding directive for their theory and practice. They work to help people adopt the idea that emotions are a natural phenomenon, an important aspect of life they should be free to experience without having to assess any aspect of the emotional experience except *how it is expressed*.

This approach tends to perceive an experience of emotion as morally neutral. The fact that emotions occur in response to our interpretation of the environment, however, suggests that we bear some responsibility for our values and beliefs, the narratives which trigger the emotional response. Recent developments in both neurology and the social sciences cause us to revisit this modern notion of moral neutrality.

I turn now to consider the "myth of passivity" that suggests we are helplessly co-opted by emotions. This myth draws on the observation that emotions often seem to overpower us with their intensity. Language about emotions both reflects and promotes this sense that passions rule: they "sweep over us," or we are "carried away," or "blinded by," or "couldn't help" ourselves. We know that a person can become the slave of an emotion, such as anger, but from a biological perspective the giving away of control is rarely necessary.

Emotions occur as responses to our environment that are shaped by our experiences and the narratives we have developed to explain the way things should be in life, as chapter 6 shows. We have the freedom to change these narratives, and therefore we control to a significant extent which events in our environment elicit our emotions. Being responsible for our lives includes being accountable for both what shapes our emotions and how they are expressed,[23] a concept I return to in part 4.

Emotions, of course, can lead to harmful actions and behaviors, not because emotions are intrinsically evil, but because they have become vehicles for the misuse or abuse of human freedom. We must remember that *reason* also leads people to evil behavior and serves purposes other than the good for which the Creator originally intended.

We must challenge the idea that emotions have a life of their own, separated from our cognitive processes and free to take over our actions without our endorsement. Such a stance contradicts both current scientific perceptions[24] and the theological concepts of creation and freedom. Humans (with a few exceptions related to physical injury, major chemical imbalance, some brain diseases, and various forms of dementia) have the ability to control emotions and to use them either creatively or destructively. The use of either emotion or reason for evil purposes is the result of the corrupt expression of freedom, certainly contrary to the basic purposes for which emotion and reason were placed at the heart of our being. A pastoral theology of emotion must recognize our responsibility, within the limitations mentioned above, for choosing when and what to feel emotionally and how we express these emotions.

Now we turn in parts 2 and 3 to understanding the specific emotion of anger. I follow the same methodology of exploring the neuroscience and social science perspectives first, then examining Scripture and the Christian tradition for theological perspectives. Using all of these insights, I construct a pastoral theology of anger in chapter 10.

PART 2

Understanding Anger

4

Anger or Aggression?

Before we turn to the specific emotion of anger, we must consider the important relationship between anger and aggression. These two terms are frequently but incorrectly used interchangeably both in the social science research literature and in popular usage. In this chapter, I argue that "anger" should refer only to an emotion, as defined in chapter 1, while the word "aggression" should be reserved for describing behavior.[1] Anger and aggression are two different dynamics, with aggression referring to a variety of behaviors that express distinct underlying neurological processes. Many aggressive behaviors are *not* motivated by anger, and anger *does not* always lead to aggression. They are linked only in those instances where anger is the emotional motivator of a particular aggressive behavior. I distinguish between the two so that you will not misinterpret my use of the word "anger" in this book to refer to aggressive action. I also describe some of the positive meanings of aggression and offer some theological reflections.

SCIENCE AND AGGRESSION

The cultural revolution in America in the 1960s and 1970s featured a level of aggression and violence not faced since the unionization movement earlier in the century. After the relative calm of the post–World War II era came the Vietnam War protests, urban riots, civil rights marches, bombings, police dogs, and assassinations. This aggression and violence called for a response from social scientists. There followed, with mixed results, a rash of studies on aggression and violence by psychoanalysts, psychologists, and sociologists of all persuasions. In retrospect, much of this research was flawed because conclusions that were valid for specific types of aggression in certain situations were generalized to apply to all aggressive behavior, and competing theories contradicted each other.[2] Furthermore, the terms "anger" and "aggression" were used as synonyms, confusing emotion and behavior.

Use of the Term "Aggression"

Scientists who study animal behavior have historically used the word "aggression," rather than "anger," because they are hesitant to use any word that suggests that animals have emotions, or are motivated by anything beyond biological needs. This caution is appropriate because emotions are usually considered a feature of self-transcendent consciousness, though recent research has allowed ethologists to raise new questions about the level of consciousness animals experience.[3]

But this caution does not explain why social scientists, including psychologists, avoid the term "anger." Their reasons are varied, but they center on the difficulty of quantifying or measuring emotions. In contrast, they consider aggression a definable and measurable behavior. In reality, however, social scientists have often studied not only aggressive behavior but the emotion of anger, even when they chose not to identify anger as the emotional content of the behavior they observed. Furthermore, they sometimes use the word "anger" to describe conclusions about research focused on aggressive behaviors when, in fact, the aggressive behavior might not be rooted in the emotion of anger. The unfortunate result is that many conclusions about aggression are assumed to speak to the problem of anger, but in fact they overlook the unique neurology of anger as compared to the neurological foundations for other expressions of aggression, as we see below. Using the word "aggression" to refer to both emotion and behavior is a mistake that continues to create confusion.

Another problem in making distinctions between anger and aggression is that the concept of aggression has multiple, contradictory meanings. The word "aggression" is used to describe both positive and negative behaviors. We say, with positive implications, that a salesperson was aggressively trying to make a sale. When a medical team treats a disease aggressively, we applaud. But we also use the word "aggressive" to describe the actions of a playground bully and a fast-growing cancer, both with negative implications. Both the purse-snatcher and the woman who fights him off can be said to be acting aggressively. Both the rioters and the police may act aggressively. Aggression is inherently neither good or bad, and moral valuation depends on the context, including the code of ethics to which the evaluator is committed. However, when speaking of negative aggression, we often assume angry aggression. When someone behaves destructively we often use the word "aggression" to describe the motivating emotion of anger as well as the behavior, a connection which contributes to the idea that anger is always bad and, in fact, supports the equally false idea that all aggression is negative.

Noted psychoanalyst Erich Fromm, for example, in his landmark study of aggression, *The Anatomy of Human Destructiveness*, distinguished between "benign" (positive) and "malignant" (negative) aggression.[4] However, nowhere did he distinguish aggression from anger. In fact, anger does not even appear in the index. The result of this oversight is that Fromm makes little distinction between benign aggressive behavior that is either motivated by anger expressed creatively or not motivated by anger at all, and malignant aggression that is usually motivated by anger that has become hatred, jealousy, or hostility.

Aggression in Animals

Almost all vertebrates, and certainly all mammals, exhibit aggression. Animal research has provided neuroscientists with basic knowledge of how the "mammalian" brain works. Detailed neurological maps now reveal the process by which various neural systems of the mammalian brain send messages that activate various aggressive behaviors. Brain circuitry for three types of aggression in animals has been identified: predatory (killing for food), intermale (competition for territory and females), and "affective attack" (also called the "rage circuit").[5] Neither predatory or intermale aggression features the type of physical and mental response that humans associate with anger. These neurological arousal patterns simply provide the physiological readiness for effective involvement in biological necessities, such as catching food and maintaining (or challenging for) procreational access to females.

The type of aggressive behavior called affective attack or rage circuit, however, includes physical features (teeth bared, nose flared) and behaviors (snarling) which seem to mimic the arousal pattern that in humans we call anger or rage. The affective attack type of aggressive response is activated when an animal is trapped or wounded, or its food supply or offspring is threatened. Observing such a "cornered" animal leads us to label an enraged person as being "like a wild animal." This capacity for "rage," and the resultant physical mobilization, is basic to animal survival. As psychiatrist Theodore Lidz says about both fear and anger,

> These built-in automatic defenses against danger, which arose early in the evolutionary process to implement the capacity to fight enemies,

flee danger, and mobilize resources in emergencies, are only slightly
less important to the preservation of the animal than the drives arising from tissue need [such as hunger and sexual drive].[6]

Because of neurological similarities with human anger, animal studies that
provide physiological data on the particular arousal pattern called "affective
attack" or "rage circuit"[7] are providing fundamental insight into the human
brain circuitry that underlies arousal patterns which are the source of our primal anger.[8]

We know that in animals certain environmental stimuli trigger the neurological rage circuit that leads to aggressive behavior. Note, however, that animals also possess many other survival needs that motivate aggressive behavior:
hunger, sexual arousal, nesting instincts, and social bonding being the most
common.[9] These other aggressive behaviors, however, are quite different
from the aggressive arousal pattern (rage circuit) that appears to be like human
anger. Given that only one type of aggression in animals is neurologically similar to rage in humans, then labeling all aggression in animals as anger, and
applying these observations to humans, is misleading and distorts our understanding of human anger.

Animal Research Applied to Human Aggression

Scientists who have been overly zealous in their attempt to apply findings in
research on aggression in animals to the human condition have been strongly
critiqued by social scientists. In a thorough review of the early literature, psychologist Dolf Zillman surveyed these correlations and was quite dissatisfied
with the "obvious overextension of models . . . most obtrusively manifest in
the inferential leaps from animals to humans, that are at the core of some of
the most popular theories of aggression."[10] He was also concerned that in
response to the cultural concern about violence, outbursts of destructive
behavior were frequently tied to the idea of aggression with little attention
given to research on the emotions that motivated the aggressive behavior.[11]

Research on aggression that does not differentiate between aggression and
emotion results in questionable application of scientific work. Konrad Lorenz,
for example, is a noted ethologist who became well known in academic circles
for his ideas about aggression and violence in humans through his book *On
Aggression*.[12] His actual research, however, was with geese and other animals
rather than humans. Lorenz demonstrated that aggression was an innate evolutionary development that served the survival needs of animal species. This
aspect of his work is widely applauded. At the end of his book, however,
Lorenz steps out of his area of expertise into the field of social psychology and

attempts to apply his studies to the behavior of human beings, which led to several problems.[13] He makes clear that aggressive behavior in animals has a positive evolutionary purpose, but when he applies his conclusions to human behavior, he narrows his working definition of aggression to negative behaviors that are cruel, painful, and destructive. This delimitation ignores the many positive motivational contributions of human aggression to such activities as exploring new worlds and resisting exploitation.

During this same period, Robert Ardrey examined the roots of aggressive behavior in our evolutionary history. In his first book, *African Genesis*, Ardrey argues that the earliest humans were "killers" and posits that humans from their earliest days developed tools as weapons for the purpose of killing fellow humans. He concludes that "man is a predator whose natural instinct is to kill with a weapon."[14] In *The Territorial Imperative*, Ardrey argues that humans are biologically programmed to defend territory and that aggression is the evolutionary instinct that produces the necessary behavior to accomplish this goal.[15] Desmond Morris popularized these ideas in *The Naked Ape* and *The Human Zoo*.[16]

All of these studies make several mistakes. First, they clearly base their definition of aggression in animals on observable behavioral patterns and make no attempt to assign emotion as the motivation behind this aggressive behavior. But when they move to describe human behavior, aggression is connected with behaviors that are obviously motivated not by survival needs but by angry emotion. They rarely recognize that anger is an emotional dynamic that is uniquely developed in humans.

Second, by connecting destructive aggression with what many observers would call the emotion of anger, they conclude that anger, like aggression, is innate. This connection leads readers to believe that anger in humans is instinctive in the same way that these authors think aggression is instinctive in animals. The conclusion, of course, is that anger cannot be controlled by humans who are, because of some biological determinism, its unwilling prisoners.

Third, because anger is tied to a definition of aggression in humans that is limited to destructive behavior, they end up with a narrow, negative view of anger. All anger becomes identified as problematic to civilization, with the implication that we would be more advanced without it. This conclusion is the psychological equivalent of the anger-is-sin tradition in Christianity.

In short, these authors have led many people in our culture to assume that scientific studies prove conclusively that anger is an innate, instinctive characteristic of the human condition. It is imperative, therefore, to point out that recent neurological research (and the constructionist narrative theories discussed in chapter 6) contradicts this notion, establishing that anger as an emotion is distinct from many basic aggressive drives that are normally emotionally neutral. As Lorenz's original research with animals demonstrates, aggression is not, of necessity, negative and destructive, but is often productive and life-enhancing.

Incentive-Motivated and Annoyance-Motivated Aggression

Social scientists have highlighted the same diversity in human aggression, noting that a variety of goals and objectives—such as the desires to succeed, to accomplish a task, to protect a child, or to win a game—lead to aggressive behavior. None of the behaviors necessary to accomplish these goals would normally be motivated by feelings of anger.

Social science researchers distinguish between "incentive-motivated" and "annoyance-motivated" aggression.[17] Incentive-motivated aggression is the instinctive human desire to act in ways that meet basic needs for food, water, shelter, companionship, and procreation. The normal desire to achieve goals that we have rationally decided to pursue leads to behaviors that can be labeled as aggressive, but are not normally motivated by anger. Incentive-motivated aggression refers to actions that are contemplated and performed without the body being in a reactive, arousal mode. This type of aggression is *not* related to anger, because it does not involve a physiological arousal connected to a desire to fight or hurt another. It is not a reaction to a threat, as the next chapter describes, but a response to a need.

Annoyance-motivated aggression, on the other hand, occurs not as action toward attaining a goal or satisfying a basic need, but in response to noxious external stimuli. This type of aggression is called "angry aggression,"[18] because it describes behavior that is motivated by the emotional experience of anger. The goal of the person experiencing annoyance-motivated aggression is to confront the source of the aggravation and reduce or remove it. This type of aggressive behavior is often not premeditated, but occurs spontaneously in response to the stimulus. Unlike incentive-motivated aggression, there is significant involvement of the body. The noxious stimuli has triggered a physical arousal pattern similar to the rage circuit in animals, preparing the body for confrontation.

Certainly when incentive-motivated aggression toward meeting a basic need or a chosen goal is thwarted, then anger may result. That is, if somebody or some organization is blocking our efforts toward success in an endeavor, we might feel threatened by our failure to achieve success and become angry with the person or group that stands in the way. If the frustration of failure triggered the capacity for anger, the resulting physiological arousal would involve a different neurological process than that which supported the original goal-focused aggression.[19] This anger may lead to aggressive behavior against the person blocking our endeavors. Nevertheless, the first expression of aggression (toward meeting a basic need or chosen goal) is *not* connected to anger, though the second aggression (toward punishing the offending party) *is* an expression of anger. Though anger can be the motivator of a particular aggressive behavior, anger and aggression are not always the same neurological dynamic. Again, aggression describes behavior and anger identifies an emotion.

AGGRESSION AS LIFE FORCE

Another understanding of aggression connects it with the assertive behaviors necessary to sustain life both at physical and psychological levels. This kind of aggression has many names: initiative, assertion, drive, desire, motivation. Kathleen Greider, a pastoral theologian, defines aggression as "one primary expression of the life force, of the drive to survive and thrive, embodied in positive and negative movement toward and engagement with goals, persons, objects, and obstacles."[20] The Chinese word *ch'i* also captures this sense of life force, conveying the idea of "spirit, energy, and arousal." Lee Yearly, a philosopher, says that *ch'i* refers to "the physiological and spiritual energy that stimulates us toward vital self-expression."[21] This life force is part of our biological "givenness," the motivational energy for living. The *ch'i* or "life force" has many expressions, one of which can be conceived as the intense physiological and mental readiness to fight for survival; in this guise the *ch'i* may serve the emotion of anger and may, either concomitantly or independently, manifest as aggressive behavior. In summary, anger may express itself in aggressive behavior, but angry aggression is only one of the aggressive modalities that the life force may express.

While anger often leads to aggressive behavior, this result is not always the case. Anger, as an emotion, can be suppressed rather than expressed, or it can be disguised and expressed in passive ways that are not normally viewed as aggression. Anger can also create aggressive mental images, such as daydreaming about revenge, but these images don't necessarily lead to aggressive behavior. In defining anger in the following chapter, I suggest that anger results in "the desire to defend or attack," but this desire may not be expressed in aggressive behavior. In summary, many aggressive behaviors are not motivated by anger and anger does not always lead to aggression. Therefore, because I am interested primarily in the emotion we commonly call "anger," I do not use the word "aggression" in this book unless it clearly refers to behavior.

Aggression as a primary expression of life force certainly has biological roots and motivates our pursuit of both basic survival needs and achieving psycho/social/spiritual goals that we consciously adopt. This physiological pattern, however, is not the same as the neurological arousal pattern of anger I describe in chapter 5. While anger may express itself in aggressive behavior, the word "aggression" may appropriately describe many other benign behaviors that are in the service of this life force. "Aggression," therefore, when used to describe the emotion of anger itself, only contributes to the confusion.

In summary, keep in mind the main points of this contrast between anger and aggression. In animals, "aggression" refers to a variety of intense activities that promote survival, only one of which approximates what in humans is called "rage." In humans the term "aggression" also refers to numerous types of behaviors that may have either positive and ethical outcomes, or negative and destructive ones. In humans, aggressive behavior may be the outcome of anger, but it may also be unrelated to anger and simply refer to intense activity toward achieving certain goals. But even aggression expressing anger need not be destructive; it may be an appropriate and effective response that ensures positive purposes such as safety and survival. Aggression can be a fundamental expression of the life force, ensuring survival and relationality. Yet in everyday usage the concept of aggression is often viewed negatively, and in social science usage aggression has frequently been confused with anger, and used interchangeably to describe that emotion.

THEOLOGICAL REFLECTIONS

Aggression, defined above as a primary expression of the life force, is part of our endowment as human creatures. This aggression, which is expressed through initiative, activity, searching, exploring, testing, working, and so forth, is deeply rooted in our physiology and has been developing during our entire biological history. Without this motivating life force, our ancestors would not have survived. Furthermore, in order for humans to have developed art, language, architecture, government, and other aspects of civilization, an aggressive component had to be part of our basic nature. As Jean Blomquist says, "The yearning to create—to generate, cultivate, restore, renew—lodges deep in the human heart."[22] Greider says of the purposes for this capability, "the living creation as a whole is endowed by its creator with such a drive to survive and thrive."[23] The capability for aggression is part of what God intended to include in our embodied existence.

Greider thinks aggression is so basic that she identifies aggression and love as the "two primary forces" that are necessary for the fulfillment of our potential, equal aspects of the human condition. She recognizes the basic life-promoting nature of both and thinks of them ideally as "fused" and "braided."[24] Greider recognizes, however, that aggression can function over against love.[25] As with other human traits and potentials, we have the freedom to use aggression for destructive purposes, rather than in the service of love. Like all of our given characteristics, we can express aggression negatively and destructively, or we can express it creatively as a way of promoting life and love among the human community. When it serves its original purpose as an instrument for life-giving behavior, says Greider, then "aggression is an expression of a biological and psychospiritual drive to survive and thrive."[26]

The Judeo-Christian narratives are certainly filled with stories of God being aggressive. The creation accounts in the first two chapters of Genesis picture God actively speaking the world into being, forming order out of the primeval chaos, and breathing life into the first creatures. Throughout Hebrew Scripture, God actively influences and guides the Israelites and directs the nations. Jesus takes initiative during his life through word and deed to accomplish his mission. Process theologian Marjorie Suchocki understands God to be intimately involved with bringing novelty into the world through the process of "continuous interaction—both actively and responsively,"[27] which suggests that God chooses an aggressive stance toward the world as well as a receptive stance.[28] She points out that "openness to both possibility and actuality is a prime characteristic of God."[29] Direct persuasion, she believes, is a constant dynamic in the way God interacts with the world.[30] My understanding that God is love would lead me to view these various types of "continuous interaction" with the world as expressions of love.[31]

I identify the feeling tone and the activity of aggression Greider describes as being like the compassion of God discussed in chapter 2. The statement in 1 John 4:8, "God is love," is for me a foundational description of God's constant character,[32] and because I define aggression as behavior, I think of aggression as being God's intense activity in the service of love. Because God's aggression is a behavioral expression of love, I can't imagine it acting in some destructive manner that places it beyond, or over against, the love out of which it springs. I can easily imagine God's love acting compassionately through aggressive behavior, but not God's aggressiveness moving in acts that contradict the love on behalf of which it is activated. I offer a similar perspective on the relationship between love and anger in chapter 10, arguing that God's anger is an expression of love, not a separate character trait.

Is this capacity an aspect of our being created in the image of God? If this capacity for aggression, as an expression of life force, is one way God's love expresses itself in the world, then it should be no surprise to find it in our humanness, part of the *imago Dei*. Because aggression, along with the capacity to love, is an important part of our basic equipment as human beings bestowed upon us by the Creator, then including this capacity in our understanding of "imageness" is appropriate. This aggressive capacity is implanted within us by the Creator as a basic ingredient of our potential to become what God has made possible, part of the genetic package entrusted at conception to each generation.

5

Where Does Anger Come From?
The Neuroscience Contribution

Now that we have established the overall crucial significance of emotion in human life, explored a theological perspective on emotion, and examined the differences between anger and aggression, I turn attention to the specific emotion of anger. A pastoral theology of anger must tackle the question "Where does anger come from?" To pursue the answer to this question, I begin by describing what the neurosciences contribute to our specific knowledge of the origins of anger. Neurological research on the rage circuit in animals, as documented in the previous chapter, is teaching us much about those parts of our brain that have been evolving for eons and are basic to our experience of anger, although understanding human anger requires research at a different level. I discuss memory, which is crucial for the neurological process, and the connection between anger and fear, which are the two primary emotional systems most closely linked in our experience of danger. This information leads to an understanding of what I call the "threat model" of anger,[1] an explanation of why anger occurs, and finally to some theological reflections.

THE BRAIN AND ANGER

What happens in the human brain when anger occurs?[2] Anger normally originates when the brain interprets data from the senses that signals danger. Information from sensory organs, in the form of electrochemical messages sent by neurotransmitters, is received by the thalamus, the part of the brain that seems to be responsible for the first stage of collating and organizing data from the senses. Then the thalamus forwards this information through two neurological systems specifically dedicated to processing and interpreting sensory information, and initiating a physiological response that ensures our survival: the amygdala/limbic system and the neocortex/prefrontal lobe system. So the brain uses two pathways to process information from the senses in order to ascertain whether any danger to the self exists in the environment. For ease of understanding we consider these paths separately.

The Amygdala, or "Feeling Brain"

One pathway directly connects the thalamus to the amygdala and limbic system, which is sometimes referred to as the "emotional" brain. Until recently, neuroscientists thought that all emotional responses involved neurotransmission through the neocortex. More recent research, however, indicates that information carrying danger signals is transmitted directly from our senses to the amygdala and limbic system, bypassing the neocortex.[3] Evidence now indicates that mechanisms for seeing and hearing are directly wired to the limbic system, which explains how certain sights and sounds trigger instantaneous response from the anger circuit, and how we can suddenly become extremely fearful or enraged without a clear idea of why the fear or anger is so intense.[4]

Both the hippocampus and the amygdala are connected to the process of memory: recording, storing, and recalling events from the past that were painful and traumatic, and therefore experienced as dangerous.[5] Research suggests that this sensory data travels through neural pathways that probably were established as a result of traumatic experience. Many of these alternative neural pathways may have developed early in a person's life, before the neocortex was fully formed, but experiences in adulthood also leave impressions in the memory system that can later be activated by sensory data sent directly from thalamus to amygdala. When information from the senses is received, the amygdala runs a quick crosscheck within its files to see if the message is associated with dangerous past events. If the new stimulus is recognized or interpreted as being similar to a past traumatic event, then the amygdala alerts the entire limbic system. In these instances, the thinking brain (the conscious mind) is bypassed, the limbic system is alerted instantaneously to the dangerous situation, and the body is mobilized and takes action before we are consciously aware of what has happened. Not only is there a physical reaction in defense of the self, but an emotional burst of anger at the object or person that seemed to endanger us usually accompanies the reaction. This research sheds new light on post-traumatic stress disorder and specific mental occurrences such as "flashbacks."

The Neocortex, or "Thinking Brain"

In the second pathway, information from the thalamus is forwarded to the neocortex or prefrontal lobe, sometimes referred to as the "reasoning" or "thinking" brain. The neocortex is highly developed in humans and is the part of the brain most responsible for consciousness and cognitive processes. Within the neocortex, therefore, a different type of interpretation of data from the senses is taking place. With extensive neural connections both to the regions of the brain that process information from the senses and to those regions of the brain that activate physiological responses to sensory information,[6] the neocortex plays the role of primary neural switchboard between sensing, interpreting, and responding to the environment.

The nature of the data processed by the thinking brain, however, is different than that to which the emotional brain responds. Rather than immediate physical dangers, the neocortex usually identifies dangers related to more complicated threats to the self. As humans we are not only threatened physically by dangerous events or circumstances but also threatened psychologically and psychosocially—including threats to our values, meanings, worldview, special relationships, and plans for the future, all of which contribute to our sense of self and personal identity. Within the experience of threat to these aspects of our being, whether from external happenings or internal mental images, we experience fear and anger.

The threat may indeed be to physical survival, but the nature of the danger is not of the sort that the amygdala can pick up simply from sense data. Rather the circumstances must be interpreted by our cognitive processes, which occur primarily within the prefrontal lobe. A doctor's report of a malignant tumor in the liver, for example, is information that only the neorcortex can interpret as dangerous. When such information is interpreted as representing a threat to the self, then the neocortex transmits an immediate message to the amygdala: "Danger ahead!"

Though the limbic system is the section of our brain that regulates this affective neurological defense network, the neocortex, or "the thinking brain," explains some of the unique development of anger in humans. As Panksepp summarizes:

> Higher cerebral abilities must be taken into account in any comprehensive explanation of angry behavior, and it is incorrect to believe that a study of animals will fully explain why humans exhibit and inhibit aggression. Many cognitive aspects of anger are undoubtedly unique to the human. . . .[7]

Humans have developed the capacity for secondary and more complex emotions that are rooted in psychosocial threats and grow exponentially from the resulting anger. We have developed a rich vocabulary for distinguishing the various nuances of anger that are unknown in the animal world. Our words convey negative, destructive descriptions such as jealousy, revenge, spite, sarcasm, hostility, vindictiveness, and hate, but also positive descriptions such as compassion, resistance to injustice, protest, advocacy, and fighting for liberation. These emotions developed in humans along with higher brain functions. The neocortex interacts with the more basic systems that were established earlier in our evolutionary process to produce nuanced responses to threats, particularly within relationships.[8]

The neocortex, therefore, is responsible not only for the constructive uses of anger for psychosocial survival, but also for destructive human behavior against other humans. Biological inhibitors seem to be in place within the animal world that make it unusual for animals to kill others of the same species. In contrast, by misusing the freedom that comes with having a reasoning brain that can transcend our biological heritage, humans cause terrible destruction to each other and the planet. Humans seem to have evolved beyond such inhibitions and regularly engage in behaviors motivated by desires or purposes that are more destructive than anything known in the animal world.

The "Call to Arms"

The amygdala, whether responding to its own interpretation of information from the thalamus to represent danger or to a warning message from the neocortex, immediately sends a message throughout the limbic system, triggering the body's internal alarm system. Various parts of the brain respond to this "call to arms" by mobilizing the body for flight or fight. The sympathetic branch of the autonomic nervous system immediately activates changes in the body: blood chemistry changes (epinephrine and norepinephrine are released), blood pressure rises (the face flushes), heartbeat increases (the heart "pounds"), muscles tense (nostrils flare, teeth clench), and body temperature rises (feeling hot). The body becomes primed for defense, escape, or counterattack.[9]

Flight or fight action, however, may be preceded by a period of "freezing," what we commonly call "being paralyzed" or "tonic immobility." This response is common in animals and leads to our metaphor about a startled person having that "deer in the headlights" look. Biologists interpret this reaction to be an instinctive attempt to avoid detection by predators whose visual cues are focused on movement. Furthermore, many animals have skin color that blends into the environment when they are immobile, further reducing the chances of detection. We can identify with many of these physical changes that occur when we experience anger or fear. Our body instantly achieves a state of heightened awareness prepared to receive all possible incoming information: our pupils dilate (we are literally wide-eyed), nostrils flare in order to take in smells, hearing is heightened, and even the hairs on our arms stand erect in order to detect movement or touch.

THE SIGNIFICANCE OF MEMORY

Consider for a moment those occasions when anger seems to happen so spontaneously that there does not seem to be time for a conscious decision to be angry. Remember situations in which your body had an "instinctive" reaction to something happening around you. Perhaps you "instinctively" dodged an object that suddenly appeared in your vision or "instinctively" hit the brakes and swerved to avoid an accident. We use the word "instinctively" in these circumstances because we appeared to duck more quickly than the brain could say, "Something is flying at me that could hurt. I'd better duck." Or we hit the brakes before we could cognitively process the data and make a reasoned decision that a car was going to run a stop sign and we had better take evasive action. Frequently these "instinctive" moves are accompanied by a quick burst of anger at the situation because the amygdala perceives the situation as dangerous.

What actually happens is that—on the basis of previous experiences that were recorded and stored in the brain as dangerous—we made an "instinctive" response. Both the amygdala and the neocortex are connected to the areas of the brain that process memory: recording, storing, and recalling events from the past that were painful or traumatic, therefore experienced as dangerous.[10] Before we could become consciously aware of what was happening, those areas of the brain "sensed," or interpreted, an event to be dangerous because it reminded the brain of a previous dangerous experience.[11] Data from the senses goes directly to the amygdala, bypassing the neocortex, and elicits a response before the reasoning brain has time to make an interpretation.

How do these instinctive reflexes come about? How do we "know" what signals danger to our brain? How have we developed these sudden, seemingly involuntary reflex responses—the so-called "knee-jerk" response? Part of the explanation comes from biologist Joseph LeDoux, who argues that the primitive brain is equipped with ancient memories that serve as warning signals that lead to aggressive or evasive action.[12] He believes that over eons of time we have developed archetypal memories that act as radar, sensing potential dangers and triggering our basic involuntary responses such as "blinking" and "ducking."

In addition to these ancient memories lodged in the brain, this type of reaction can emerge out of an individual's unique life experience. At some time in our history, we all learned to associate certain situations with danger. This association explains experiences of fear and anger that seem to be separated from our reasoning process, but which are clearly linked with visual and auditory awareness, such as a child who becomes frightened upon seeing the doctor's office because of associating the locale with painful injections. In these situations, the senses send the alarm directly to the amygdala and its memory-based interpretation supersedes the interpretation of the neocortex, which may perceive the situation to be nonthreatening. The conscious self may not understand why, but the primitive regions of the brain have sent out an SOS and initiated an emergency alert status.

Our memory includes traumatic events that the conscious mind has pushed to the back pockets of our mental apparatus as a way of protecting us from the emotional pain of continuing conscious awareness of the event(s). Early in life a person can experience traumas that leave neurological markers and messages in the limbic system. These messages become part of our memory bank and can be quickly triggered when a present circumstance appears similar. Memories, not anger, are stored.

In summary, neural pathways established by past traumatic events can be activated by stimuli that the brain recognizes even when the conscious mind is not immediately aware of the circumstances. Some experiences of anger, therefore, are quick and intense because they are connected in our memory to threatening experiences. When we experience anger that seems to be an overreaction to the present moment, then the wise response is to consider its possible linkage with past trauma(s).

ANGER AND FEAR

Survival is an important motivator in our evolutionary history, as established in chapter 1. Fear and anger are the primary emotional responses that have survival as their main purpose. Arousal of these two emotions is one of the neurological underpinnings of our desire to stay alive. Fear and anger, therefore, are often present in the same circumstances.

We often experience fear and anger simultaneously. Something that frightens us may also make us angry, and something that makes us angry can be terrifying. Being downsized out of a job can spark fear of financial ruin at the same time that it generates anger at the people who made the seemingly impersonal decision. This frequent association of fear and anger calls for a closer look.

Neuroscientists have shown that among the four primary emotional systems (anger, fear, joy, sorrow) considerable overlap occurs among the neurological systems.[13] Physiological connections between the "fight" (anger) and "flight" (fear) responses are continually being discovered: "one can enrage both animals and humans by stimulating very specific parts of the brain, which parallel the trajectory of the FEAR system,"[14] and that the neural pathways for anger and fear overlap in many sections of the brain is becoming clearer.[15] Anger and fear are likely so closely related because of their connection to triggering events that we perceive as threatening.

Some neuroscientists divide emotion into two basic circuits: a positive circuit that motivates "moving toward" responses such as smiling and hugging, and a negative circuit, that motivates "moving away from" or "moving against" responses such as avoiding or hitting. The negative circuit by definition includes both fear and anger.[16] Panksepp's research leads him to assume that anger that expresses itself in defensive aggressive behavior emerges from a dynamic mixture of the rage and fear systems.[17]

A key factor that determines whether we feel either fear or anger is our perception of the environmental circumstances. When our interpretation of the threatening environment is characterized by the sense of being overwhelmed and is marked by the desire to escape the threatening situation (hearing gunshots), we are more likely to name that emotion "fear." When our interpretation is characterized by the desire to move against or defend against the threatening situation (seeing someone hit a child), we usually call that arousal pattern "anger." Often, of course, we feel both.

Identifying arousal patterns as either fear or anger depends on other factors, such as gender socialization, that influence our interpretation. Often socialized to be wary of being angry, women are frequently taught that anger is unfeminine and is, in fact, dangerous because of the potential for male reprisals. A woman in a particular situation, therefore, may be more aware of her fear than her anger. Many males, on the other hand, are socialized to be afraid of fear. They have been taught that fear is unmanly and cowardly. A man may find it difficult to identify the fear aroused in response to a specific triggering event and be more comfortable identifying only his anger.

When a person labels an aroused physical state (a "feeling") as either fear or anger, a further assessment of the emotional response will probably reveal the presence of other feelings as well. Furthermore, an experience of either anger or fear may often be followed by the other. For example, a parent who nervously paces the floor when a fourteen-year-old is an hour late returning from a party may be fearful that some tragedy has occurred. When the car door slams, however, and the daughter nonchalantly walks in safely, the dominant emotion may quickly become anger that she didn't arrive on time or call to communicate that she would be late.

A CAPACITY, NOT AN INSTINCT

One popular idea is that anger is a "thing" that accumulates somewhere in our body. Psychotherapists influenced either by the classical psychoanalytic tradition or by instinct theory often convey that people have a "reservoir" of anger that can explode. Some still speak of the hydraulic model, which suggests that anger builds up steam until it "blows" the gasket off our emotional pressure cooker.

These theories have led, erroneously we now know, to the view that anger is an instinct over which we have little control. Anger, according to this theory, is activated for innate biochemical reasons by a biological body clock, something that happens according to its own rhythm, like hunger or sexual arousal. With or without external stimuli, our bodies become hungry because the body must have fuel. Biochemical changes in the body indicate when the cellular need for food is internally aroused. However, internal biological changes that are precursors to anger have not been identified. The lack of biochemical precursors offers more evidence that anger is *not* an instinct that erupts at unpredictable intervals, but a neurological capacity that depends on external triggers for activation. The classical Freudian idea that anger is constantly seething inside of the Id, constantly attempting to overpower the Ego in order to cause destruction, is not substantiated by neurological research. Neuroscientists have learned that anger doesn't exist somewhere inside us ready to pounce or explode at a given moment. Anger does not have a life of its own separate from the brain's interpretation that the self is being threatened.

Furthermore, anger differs from hunger and sexual arousal because anger is not a biological necessity. Hunger and sexual arousal are biologically determined. Anger, however, is not automatically activated by a biological mechanism. A person must eat to stay alive, but does not have to get angry to live. Many types of aggression, as we pointed out in the previous chapter, are necessary for the procurement of food, shelter, and sexual partners and in that sense are "instinctual"—triggered by biological necessities. As I have demonstrated, however, anger is an emotion that is only activated in response to an environmental event perceived as a threat. Theoretically speaking, if all threats could magically be removed from the environment, one could go through life without experiencing anger.

THE THREAT MODEL OF ANGER

In response to our question, "Why do people get angry?" neuroscience provides the answer: *we get angry when we feel threatened.* Dolf Zillman, a social psychologist who also participates in psychophysiological research, sums up the neurological perspective when he says, "it is the recognition of endangerment that gives rise to feelings of anger."[18] Given this research, I arrive at my working definition of anger:

> Anger is the physical, mental, and emotional arousal pattern that occurs in response to a *perceived threat* to the self, characterized by the desire to attack or defend.

The key to this definition is the phrase *perceived threat*. An event triggers the arousal patterns we call "anger" only if our brain interprets the event as a threat to some aspect of our selfhood. An experience of anger, therefore, is primarily rooted in a hermeneutical event. The physiological arousal does not occur until *after* we have interpreted the environment. Interpretation actually precedes the arousal, if only by a minuscule fraction of time. The precipitating event is usually an exterior occurrence, but a mental image of something past or future can also represent a threat—which is why we can awake thinking about event from last week or anticipating an event in the next week that generates anger. This capacity also speaks to the place of memory in anger, as well as our ability to project our imagination into the future.[19]

The desire to attack or defend describes our cognitive thought process, which may or may not be acted out. Our mental imagery is saturated with an internal monologue of accusation, scorn, and disrespect against the source of the threat, and images of striking out against the adversary. Indeed, Aristotle's definition of anger includes the desire to inflict pain on the person responsible for belittlement or disrespect.[20] We can more easily inhibit our external behavior, choosing not to strike out, than we can inhibit these internal images and monologues.

To understand the uniqueness of anger in humans, we must understand why we become angry in circumstances in which our physical survival is not at stake. Why do people become angry at different life situations? How do people decide what is threatening? The neurosciences cannot answer these questions without help from the social sciences. I discuss constructionist narrative theory in the next chapter, in order to understand the context in which the brain recognizes an event as threatening.

THE FLEXIBLE BRAIN

Our knowledge of the brain confirms that change at the neurobiological level is possible. One of the amazing facts about our brain, particularly the neocortex, is its flexibility and malleability. Brain research continues to demonstrate the dynamic interaction between environmental events and physiological development in the brain.[21] Significant and intense new experience, such as traumatic accidents, can change neurological pathways.[22] Many neurobiologists now argue that certain kinds of life experiences, such as constant abuse or significant early losses, affect the neurological structures of a child, and perhaps also adults who have experienced horrific events over which they have no control (such as witnessing a massacre, or a homicide in the home).

Neurobiologists have demonstrated that our reasoning brain can change the arousal patterns in emotionality. Primary emotional systems "can be modulated by cognitive input."[23] When an individual's perception of external circumstances is modified, change occurs in the emotional sensitivity of the brain systems. In short, the neural programming that produces our emotions physically adapts as experience and perception change. An example is classical conditioning, in which an emotionally neutral stimulus can be programmed with emotional meaning by repeated connection with a threatening event. The interpretive process in the neocortex "reads" threat when that previously neutral stimulus appears and activates a primary emotional system.[24] In the face of neurological research, arguing that a person is helpless or powerless to change current patterns of anger is difficult. Reminding ourselves of the emotional brain's dependence on the interpretations of a life situation by the neocortex is the context for discussing how people can change their experience of anger.

SCIENCE IN PROCESS

The final answers about anger from a scientific perspective are not yet known. When thinking specifically about anger, Panksepp says:

> we must remember that the actual brain mechanisms that control anger are complex, are under multiple physiological, neuroanatomical, and neurochemical controls, and are only roughly understood. Many details of this emotional system remain to be revealed, and many surprises are bound to emerge from future research.[25]

In a few years, the rapid developments in the neurosciences and psychology will teach us even more about the manner in which our neurological "wiring" affects our experience of fear and anger.

With all of the current emphasis on the significant role played by genes in human behavior, assessing what these scientific discoveries teach us about the human condition is important. Our privilege is to examine how we are "wonderfully made" by the Creator and to be grateful for the marvelous complexity of our embodiment. Our theology of anger must remain open-ended as developments emerge in the human sciences, but the following suggestions come from what we now know.

CONTRIBUTIONS TO A
PASTORAL THEOLOGY OF ANGER

We now confront the traditional theological answer to the question, "Where does anger come from?" The anger-is-sin tradition, as pointed out in chapter 2, usually assumes that the origins of anger are located in our sinfulness, rather than in our finitude. Somehow, the traditionalists suggest, this bent toward anger resulted from a weakness in our nature that occurred after an original "fall from grace." The neurological research on emotion in general, and anger in particular, however, leads to a different answer—which, as I discuss in part 3, confirms what I call "alternative stories" in Scripture and traditional theology. Theological anthropology must take seriously the discoveries of brain research in developing a credible understanding of anger. We pursue this statement in chapter 10, but a few preliminary ideas follow.

Embodiment

The emotion of anger has its roots in our physiology, embedded in our brain and neurological system. We cannot seriously think about anger without acknowledging how firmly this capacity is ingrained in our embodied self. This capacity for anger has been in process during our entire biological history, particularly during the development of the neocortex. We must consider this capacity as an essential aspect of our created existence. A pastoral theology of anger acknowledges that part of our "self," our personhood, is a neurological package that includes being "wired" with this capacity to experience anger, a capacity that has been developing throughout our evolutionary history.

We don't have a choice, therefore, about whether or not to possess this capacity (unless there are brain abnormalities, injuries, or disease that inhibit normal neurological functioning). Some people in the Christian tradition have suggested that the most mature response to anger is eradication. But what we learn from the neurosciences about this capacity's neurological rootedness communicates the reality that anger can't be removed from our physiology. People who attempt to eradicate the experience of anger by repression or suppression become mentally or spiritually truncated.

Creation

Anger's rootedness in our neurological system connects it with how we were brought into being: "the emotion of anger is a human birthright, arising from our ancestral heritage."[26] Since embodiment is part of God's intentional creation, so is this capacity for anger. The capacity for anger can be included in what God blessed and called good according to the first creation story in Genesis 1:28, 31. Some Christians have assigned the existence of anger to the "fall" and connect it with evil and sin, but this outlook can only apply to the destructive ways in which we express anger, not to the neurological capacity itself. Given this connection of emotion with our physiology, a pastoral theology of anger must anchor itself in the doctrine of creation, not the doctrine of sin. It can be argued that this capacity has been purposefully molded into our neurological development by the Creator.

If this capacity is part of God's intentional shaping of our finitude, then for what purpose? Chapter 1 demonstrated that all emotion plays an important role in human life. Every emotion, even those labeled as negative, contributes to the fulfillment of human potential. Early in our existence as a species, anger was specifically related to protecting our physical existence, a primary survival mechanism. Anger is part of the body's most primitive response to danger or threat, mobilizing effective physiological responses that allow instantaneous fight or flight reactions (perhaps preceded by the "freezing" response). Our ancestors needed to be physiologically mobilized for strength and stamina in the face of threats from nature or they would not have survived. This biological capacity for anger is part of our finitude, a protective warning system built into our embodied existence.

Responsibility

As culture advanced and civilizations developed, however, the types of behaviors for which this long-standing capacity for mobilization toward survival has prepared us are often inappropriate. Paul Ekman, who conducts research in affective responses, says:

> Anger is the most dangerous emotion; some of the main problems destroying society these days involve anger run amok. It's the least adaptive emotion now because it mobilizes us to fight. Our emotions evolved when we didn't have the technology to act so powerfully on them. In prehistoric times, when you had an instantaneous rage and for a second wanted to kill someone, you couldn't do it very easily— but now you can.[27]

Because of the intensity of the arousal patterns that occur as the body prepares for physical action, and the potential for destructive action while aroused, it is important that we take responsibility for demobilizing our body when physical response to threat is not necessary, which I address in chapter 13.

In day-to-day living, our psychosocial survival is often threatened. While protecting the integrity of the self and the self's special relationships is necessary for our emotional, physical, and spiritual health, unfortunately we often allow selfish, immature interpretations of events to trigger angry responses that are destructive. A pastoral theology of anger can address the responsibility we bear in this regard.

We know that the brain is flexible and that the neurological systems which respond to our perception of threat are open to change. We shall see in chapter 6 that we have much control over what we perceive as threatening and, therefore, what triggers our experiences of anger. Our theologically valid choice about managing anger has to do with taking responsibility for what triggers our anger as well as for the behaviors by which we express our anger. Because an anger event always begins with an interpretation of a life situation, we have responsibility for having created the interpretations that leave us threatened. I use constructionist narrative theories in the following chapter to continue answering the question, "Why do people get angry?"

6

Why Do People Get Angry?
A Constructionist Narrative Perspective

We have established that our embodied self includes the capacity to experience anger and that this neurological response is only activated when we perceive that we are endangered or threatened. We do not get angry, say the
neuroscientists, unless the brain registers some particular sensory input as
dangerous, which leads to the question: How does a person recognize a dangerous situation or decide that a life situation is threatening?

The most basic answer has to do with our biological preparedness to recognize that certain objects and circumstances in the environment are physically dangerous. This preparedness includes the ability to recognize shapes
(That might be a snake!), sounds (That sound comes from an animal or
machine that is dangerous!), smells (That smells like smoke!), and so forth.
Preparedness includes immediate recognition of alarm in a voice. If someone
yells, "Fire!" or "Look out!" we usually experience immediate physical mobilization. The screech of brakes, a siren, an explosion, a gunshot, or a child's
scream quickly arouse the body for survival responses that include the emotions of fear and anger.

As humans, of course, we get angry at much more than physical threats.
Often we are angry at people or situations in which we are not at risk of physical harm. We become angry at criticism from a parent, rejection by someone
we love, poor decisions by a coworker, and so forth when no physical threat is
present. An hour ago, the fourth telemarketer of the day interrupted my writing, and I got angry at their uninvited invasion of my private world! I'm obviously not in any physical danger, so what is going on? Why am I threatened
and physiologically aroused as if I had to fight? You can easily recall situations
in which you have been criticized, downsized, laughed at, or left out. Some-

times such events are no problem, while at other times we feel threatened by the event and are angry. Why? Even more amazing is the anger we feel toward ourselves for perceived mistakes and failures. I recently participated in a committee meeting in ways that I thought were not helpful and, though unintended, discounted an idea valued by another committee member. While driving home, I was angry at myself for being insensitive. The threat in these examples is not to our embodied existence, but to our sense of self, self-worth, values, or self-integrity. These threats are psychological and sociological, rather than physical, which again raises the question, "What makes some social situations threatening and others not?"

Neuroscientists know that when we are angry in response to a social interaction the neocortex/"thinking brain" has sent a message to the amygdala/"feeling brain" that something in the environment is dangerous, but neuroscience is limited in its ability to explain *why* a psychosocial event is interpreted to be threatening. After summarizing the significant contributions made by neuroscience to our knowledge of the physical processes of anger, Jaak Panksepp acknowledges:

> [Neuroscience] cannot explicate the cultural, environmental, and cognitive causes of aggression. In humans, it is usually the appraisal of events that triggers anger; obviously, many values upon which appraisals are premised are culturally learned in humans. For instance, presently many humans are angry at others for the views they hold about abortion, capital punishment, and innumerable other sociopolitical issues.[1]

What process leads our cognitive processes to identify a circumstance as threatening? The causes of these experiences of anger are unique to the human species. To understand why we perceive some life situations as threatening and become angry at them, I turn to constructionist understandings of the self, particularly as expressed in narrative theory.

CONSTRUCTIVIST AND CONSTRUCTIONIST THEORY

To explain what I call the constructionist narrative perspective,[2] I must describe both constructivism and social constructionism. Constructionist thought in general is a postmodern development with roots in a diverse group of disciplines including philosophy; literary analysis and textual criticism; social, philosophical, and experimental psychology; the neurosciences; and various theories and methodologies of psychotherapy. The common denominator among researchers in these various disciplines is the search for new ways to understand the nature of the self and how the self comes to know things, develop ideas, make decisions, and choose to act—the epistemological and cognitive process questions.

In Western culture we have assumed the existence of objective realities that our theories and perceptions can accurately reflect. In the last half of the twentieth century, however, researchers have become increasingly aware that reality is not as objective as imagined. Scientists discovered that fewer universal norms can be uncovered and identified by quantitative research than was originally believed, which contributed to the postmodern perspective that there are multiple truths, that much knowledge is relative, and that many significant aspects of the human condition cannot be grasped through the scientific method. One theory that accounts for these new discoveries is constructivism.

Constructivist theory posits that the ideas we have about the world are not exact replicas, pictures, or maps of the "real" world, but are constructs, or perceptions, of the world that we build in our minds as we encounter the world.[3] "Reality" for each of us is actually our subjective interpretation of our experience with external things (nature, movies, media), social structures (workplace, institutions, church, government), and relational interaction (marriage, parent/child, friendships, significant others). From a constructivist perspective the narratives that make up our worldview reflect only our unique interpretations of the world and are not to be confused with the real world. In this sense, persons must be responsible for their thoughts, feelings, and actions in response to the world as they perceive it.

Constructivist theory, which evolved not only from psychological research but from research in the physical sciences,[4] has demonstrated that even the sensory data which the brain receives and reviews is selected by our unique physiological (particularly neurological) givens.[5] We are embodied selves, a bundle of fluids encased in skin, bone, and muscle, all directed by a network of nerves that serve as the transmitters, the switchboard, the computer (name your own metaphor here). As embodied selves, we encounter the environment through our senses: what we see, hear, touch, taste, and smell. But our unique configurations of neurological wiring result in discernable differences in the way we interpret and respond to our environment. From conception we are neurologically wired to respond at different levels to stimulation from light, noise, pain, hunger and so forth. Because of our individually unique physicality, we are predisposed to interpret our environment differently. For example, a friend e-mailed a birth announcement with a description of the difference between his first and second daughters. After describing Erica's birth, he said:

> And how different [Erica] entered this place called "world" than Lydia
> did. While Lydia screamed at the top of her lungs for the first hour

and never has stopped . . . Erica grunted and whined a little bit, and then she settled . . . comfortably on her mother's belly and seems quite content ever since.

Erica simply has a different physiological context from which to engage sensual stimuli and, therefore, will interpret her experiences with the environment differently than Lydia.

Some proponents of constructionist theories have concluded that no reality exists outside of our perceptions, a radical constructivist position. One still can, however, hold to the existence of an objective world while still recognizing the truths of constructivist theory.[6] My purpose here is not to debate the philosophical question, "Is there an absolute truth?" because constructivist concepts are not necessarily tied to that question. Even people who believe in external truths that transcend human science have difficulty denying that the way individuals shape their perceptions of these objective truths is significantly affected by their unique experience with their environment and the cultural context in which this experience takes place. Bebe Speed, for example, describes a position that takes both objective reality and subjective construction seriously.[7] His perception of this connection between the constructing knower and the reality that must be known is called "co-constructivism."

Social constructionism is more specifically interested in understanding the relational processes by which people come to describe and explain the world in which they live.[8] This emphasis in constructionist theory is based on the assumption that individuals do not create meaning in a vacuum. Proponents show that meaning is created in the social presence of at least one other self, one other worldview to engage.[9] Though each person brings individuality to the creation of personal stories, these stories are not created in isolation. The mind never works completely free of existing perspectives, but is constantly influenced by our social context and personal history.[10]

As we grow up, our families bombard us with their stories, values, and beliefs. We often accept and integrate their understandings of the world with the larger perspectives provided by the extended family, the school system, the socioeconomic group, the religious tradition, and the meanings that are attached to life by gender, politics, and ethnic heritage. As our experience widens in adulthood, so does the barrage of various belief systems from every corner of our culture and around the globe. We must recognize that even persons who seem to grow up in the same family and environment do not create the same values, beliefs, and meanings. Individual members understand family and culture from a different perspective. We interpret the family and community stories, add the unique perspectives that represent our own individual mix of physiology and interpretation (temperament, personality), and develop our particular worldview. Additional experience beyond the family and unique experiences with the environment, along with our varied physiology, explain why siblings do not have the same perspectives. My theoretical and clinical certainty about this was confirmed by personal experience with my own siblings. I am the oldest of six, with eighteen years and four sisters separating me and my brother, the youngest. Many years ago, after my father's death, all six of us met at a sister's home to spend four days talking about growing up together. I was amazed at the diverse perspectives on the basic events in our family of origin, depending on gender, age, birth order, and cultural experience. In this sense every individual perspective is both limited by and explained in some ways by the larger constructions of reality in which that individual's viewpoint has taken shape.

How do we construct our unique interpretations of our environment and make meaning out of the world we encounter? Most social construction theorists believe that language is the key.[11] Language "is a necessary mark of being human, i.e., being capable of having a history."[12] Social constructionist thought focuses on language as foundational to the construction of reality. Because we must describe and interpret our experience through communication, language is the central process through which reality is constructed.

Language is not only "representational," meaning that it describes our world, but is also "creational," because it works to express our mental perceptions to create our realities: "Language as creational includes more than interpretation and framing. Language *creates* the experience. . . . Language does not represent experience—it is inseparable from it."[13] By describing language as creational, constructionist theorists are describing the mutual interaction between meaning and language. As we develop cognitive abilities, we begin to assign words to our various experiences and then use our newfound language to describe and interpret life events. By naming or describing events, humans are not only constructing their ideas about reality, but are also constructing the meanings that they assign to their realities.

The whole event of "languaging" or "storying" our encounters with the environment, both external interactions with people and internal mental processes, is often called "discourse," which indicates that language happens in relationship with the world around us and shapes our own interior thoughts and images. This discourse results in narratives that shape the worldview of participants, giving substance to their vision of reality.

The "current" edition of our narrative is called "local knowledge" by many constructionist theorists, referring to the limitations that these larger worldviews have on our ability to understand, or to speak definitively, about the perceptions of "truth" held by persons from different cultural environments who have quite different understandings of many aspects of the human condition.

NARRATIVE THEORY: LIFE AS STORY

The concept of *narrative* has gained the right to function as a new metaphor for interpreting and explaining the human condition.[14] Stephen Crites was one of the first to conceptualize that human life occurs in narrative form, writing that "the formal quality of experience through time is inherently narrative."[15] Research in narrative theory and narrative psychology has confirmed that human personality is storied and is providing fresh ways of understanding both thought and action.[16] The "narratory principle," as theoretical psychologist Theodore Sarbin calls it, posits "that human beings think, perceive, imagine, and make moral choices according to narrative structures."[17]

Narrative theory provides an alternative way of comprehending how selfhood and personal identity are formed, including the idea that this process does not occur in isolation but in relationship with our world and with others. Our individual stories do not develop in isolation, but are embedded in other narratives. John Navone says that "life stories interpenetrate" and that much of our story develops through appropriating the stories of other persons with whom we interact. These stories have a profound influence on the shape of our stories. In fact, Navone says, "The story of a self cannot be told without the stories of other selves."[18] Each of us is constantly evolving a set of meanings about life that reflect the stories of the individuals and institutions in our environment.

As we humans encounter the world, we organize and make sense out of our experience by means of "narrative structuring,"[19] which refers to the mental process by which the raw data from the senses is organized into story form. When encountering the environment, the embodied self makes sense of life through its capacity for collecting and organizing data into stories. Our mental processes look for a plot line or a story line to explain information. Young children are constantly asking "Why?" and as adults, though we may no longer ask verbally, we are constantly asking this question of our environment: "What is that?" or "Why did that happen?" Our mind works with the data, sorting out how one event is related to another event until we can conclude, "Oh, now I understand." Each new sensation, stimulus, and interpersonal transaction is shaped by our mental processes into a story, by which our experiences are given their individual distinctiveness as *our* story.[20]

From the constructionist narrative perspective, then, the principal function of the mind is to shape our experiences into an organized structure that gives coherence to life.[21] This narrative process provides the continuity, the connecting links, that enable a person to make sense out of life. Human beings do not simply tell stories and illustrate their lives with story-telling, but as Mair explains:

> We live in and through stories. They conjure worlds. We do not know
> the world other than as story world. Stories inform life. They hold us
> together and keep us apart. We inhabit great stories of our culture. We
> live through stories. We are *lived* by the stories of our race and place.[22]

Our stories set the parameters for understanding and interpreting life, and
invest our lives with particular meaning.

Social psychologists Kenneth and Mary Gergen contend that a basic task
of narrative structuring is to establish connectedness and coherence within a
person's identity.[23] We construct our sense of identity out of stories, both conscious stories and those we suppress. That is, our sense of self, our identity, is
built piece by piece as we form our experiences into stories and then integrate
these stories into our ongoing core narratives. These stories establish our
identity. They shape our values, our beliefs, and our understandings of the
world, and provide us with meaning.

A core narrative is the central interpretive theme that provides an individual (or system) with an overarching structure (composed of numerous smaller
stories) that organizes and makes sense out of a particular aspect of our human
condition. Individuals have core narratives that structure their understandings
and values around concepts such as marriage, money, sex, discipline, work, and
so forth. Within a person's religious faith, core narratives explain such concepts as suffering, church, and prayer. As we shall see later, a threat to a core
narrative makes one vulnerable to anger.

How does our capacity for making stories develop? How do humans
become story-makers? Constructionist narrative theorists follow the lead of
neuroscientists and believe that this mental process of narrative structuring is
a neurological given which is grounded in our humanness, part of the natural
way our mental processes have evolved. This natural and automatic process of
narrative structuring constantly organizes our perceptions into stories, though
we pay little conscious attention to this process. As adults we already have millions of storied encounters with life, stories that influence how we "hear" and
interpret any new encounter. When the telephone rings in the middle of the
night, for example, we quickly process possible stories before we even reach
the receiver. The ringing is only a noise, but because of our past stories we
know it is a telephone and that someone wants to tell us something. Both cultural stories and personal history suggest that when phones ring in the middle
of the night the news is not good. Depending on our other stories at the time,
we interpret (story) the event in certain ways. Imagine how you would story
the ringing of the phone if your mother was in the hospital, or your son was
driving home from college, or your daughter was nine months pregnant.

We are not only informed by stories in our past, but we project our stories
into the future. Our narratives are temporal, meaning that we have past sto-

ries, present stories, and future stories.[24] For example, a child sees a colorful box, her hand is put on a crank, and she is helped to turn it. Eureka! She watches the top pop open and a clown emerge. She is surprised, but learns to close the top and turn the crank again for a repeat performance. Through her experience she develops a story that captures cause and effect, which enables her to gain knowledge that she can project into the future. She knows that if she turns that crank, the clown will jump out.

We have little choice but to form our initial perceptions of any current event, any environmental stimulus, through the lens of our own story. Given the uniqueness of our physical, psychological, and experiential history, each of us interprets a life situation differently. Every professor, therapist, and pastor has experienced encounters with people they taught or counseled who refer to content presented in a lecture, class discussion, therapy session, or sermon that they experienced as life-changing. Yet we know that we never communicated the content they "heard." This happens because what they actually "heard" was filtered through their personal narratives before being interpreted in the way they now report it. While we deplore the "spin" that political handlers use to purposefully distort the truth, in our own way our existing narratives put a spin on our interpretation of any event. One way of increasing self-awareness is by being willing to understand the way we are putting spin on our encounters with the world.

Not only does narrative theory explain how we structure experience into stories, but also how these stories then structure our realities and, consequently, our understandings of life events. This further explains the hermeneutical event that is at the core of an anger experience (see chapter 5). Our interpretations, the spin we put on life events, set us up to be threatened and experience anger, as described below.

A CONSTRUCTIONIST
NARRATIVE UNDERSTANDING OF ANGER

So why do people get angry? Information from the physical and social sciences suggests that the potential to experience anger is quite basic to human nature, one of our biological givens. Neuroscience research clearly indicates that we are neurologically "wired" with the capacity for anger (see chapter 5). Furthermore, the social sciences, through constructionist theories and narrative understandings of the self, expand our knowledge of how this capacity for anger is activated.[25]

The constructionist narrative perspective explains that anger occurs when the self, as shaped by a particular person's narratives, perceives that something in the environment is threatening. From a narrative perspective, we get angry when the actions of another person, group, institution, or nation seem threatening. Or we could say that becoming angry means that a particular life situation has been "perceived" through one of our core narratives as a threat to the self's values, beliefs, and meanings (see definition in chapter 5). The neocortex/prefrontal lobe has stored these core narratives that are now being threatened by some person or system. After checking the event against its memory bank, the neocortex registers this situation as a threat and sends a message to the amygdala to mobilize us for defense or attack.

I mentioned the telemarketers who were interrupting my day and at whom I became angry. What narratives were being threatened? First, I have a narrative that "home" is a place where others come when invited, rather than coming any time they want. Telemarketers treat my home as if it were a public place they can visit any time they choose, making me feel violated. Second, I have a core narrative that manipulation is not the normative, ethical way in which to relate to other people. Telemarketers, by and large, are manipulative—in fact, they have been trained to speak fast and attempt to keep me from any meaningful interaction. They also misrepresent facts, which threatens a third narrative, namely that lying is wrong. There are certainly others, but you see the picture.

This idea of threat is not an entirely new idea. According to Aristotle, anger requires "the belief that one (or someone dear to one) has been slighted or wronged or insulted in some serious way, through someone else's voluntary action."[26] Whether the wrong actually occurred is not important; the *belief* that it occurred sparks the anger. If the angered person finds out that the wrong did not actually occur or was not intentional, the anger disappears.[27] Notice that the word "belief" refers to what we are calling our interpretations of events that occur in the context of our narratives. In response to any event, we construct a story about the meaning of the behavior of other persons or systems—a story that may or may not threaten one of our core narratives.

Narrative theorists build an anthropology that stresses both the unity and the context of human experience. They also argue that fully understanding a particular human behavior calls for comprehending the whole context in which that behavior is embedded.[28] Stanley Hauerwas writes that knowing the larger, contextual narrative is basic to our knowledge of a situation because "it is only through narrative that we can catch the connections between actions."[29] Furthermore, following postmodern assumptions, narrative theorists demonstrate that human action is only understandable when attention is given to subjective issues such as motivations, purposes, values, and beliefs that transcend individual actions.[30] This context can only be known if we know that person's full narrative history, because actions flow "intelligibly from a human agent's intentions, motives, passions and purposes."[31] Hauerwas puts it this way: "A story, thus, is a narrative account that binds events and agents together in an intelligible pattern."[32] To understand any particular experience of anger, we must know the larger narrative. Grasping the meaning of a specific anger event is impossible without learning of the narrative that was threatened.

Not long ago I was driving north on I-35 out of Temple, Texas, toward Waco on my way back to Fort Worth. I was in a line of cars in the left lane passing a group of eighteen-wheelers. In my rearview mirror I suddenly noticed a red Jeep Cherokee swerve into the right lane between two trucks and then charge back in front of the woman in the minivan that had been behind me. He was now right on my bumper, and it became immediately clear that his next move would be to try and pass me on the right in between trucks and swing back in front of me before running up on the next truck. I instantaneously became angry.

Why did I get angry? It was not only the physical danger that threatened me. Remember that the neocortex, my thinking brain, was also receiving messages from the thalamus about what was happening behind me. It used a different set of memories that have to do with psychosocial values and my narratives about beliefs and meanings in life. I can identify three other personal narratives that had been threatened. First, my personal construction of reality includes the value of waiting your turn, staying in line. I connect crashing a line to insensitivity, cheating, and placing yourself above others, ideas that are contradictory to my narratives that value humility, fairness, equality, and respect for others. Second, I perceive reckless drivers as immature narcissists who put innocent people in danger. A third value is related to the larger masculine narrative of competitiveness. That driver was trying to beat me to Waco, and I wasn't going to let that challenge go unanswered!

We are often surprised at what makes other people angry. Within families, we often hear one family member expressing complete surprise that another family member is angry about a particular event or circumstance. "I don't understand," "She just blew up for no reason," and "What in the world got into him?" are common refrains in marital, family, and relationship therapy. Furthermore, the intensity of anger is often unexpected. Richard Davidson writes,

> Among the most striking features of human emotion is the variability that is apparent across individuals in the quality and intensity of dispositional mood and emotional reactions to similar incentives and challenges.[33]

Several reasons exist for this variability. One is that we are "wired" differently, as we said earlier. The second reason is that our narratives are different.

For example, whether you consider my responses (my narratives) to the red Jeep Cherokee understandable or immature will depend on *your* narratives.

The environmental events that people perceive to be threatening, and the level of threat, are quite different depending on their history and learning experiences. Knowing a person's full narrative is imperative when trying to make sense of any person's experience of anger. The uniqueness of interpretation is why the same situation sparks anger in one person and not in another. Again, we are angry only if our interpretation of a situation identifies it as threatening.

In summary, we can see that narrative theory helps us understand where anger comes from and why people get angry. When the particular stories we have about life, expectations, values, beliefs, ideas, and meanings lead us to interpret a life situation as threatening, we respond with anger. Because we can't go through life without being threatened, a narrative perspective explains why anger is a universal experience even though the construction of psychosocial realities in various cultures affects the perception of what life situations are threatening. Though aware of its dangers, the social sciences recognize and give significance to the place of anger in survival and development.

THE FREEDOM TO CHANGE NARRATIVES

Social scientists often ask the formidable question, "How do people change?" From the constructionist narrative perspective, change occurs only when a person's stories are reconfigured, reframed, or reauthored. If change is to occur in a person's experience of anger, some transformation must take place in the story through which he or she interprets a life situation to be threatening. According to Stephen Crites, "It therefore becomes evident that a conversion . . . that actually transforms consciousness requires a traumatic change in a [person's] story."[34] Hans-Georg Gadamer points out that effective therapy relies on our ability to change, our capacity to develop new themes, metaphors, and narratives.[35] The only way to change is to change our narrative.

The phrase "affective style" identifies the individual differences in the way people experience and express emotion. Neuropsychologists refer to one aspect of affective style as "emotion regulation"—the ability of people to control their emotional response to situations. Richard Davidson describes our "capacity for self-generated imagery to replace emotions that are unwanted with more desirable imagery scripts."[36] The parallels with constructive narrative theory are evident. We have the capacity to develop new images—that is, new narratives—to replace those that produce undesirable "scripts" (stories) which make us vulnerable to anger. To reduce threats and the resulting angry responses, we can construct new narratives that change our interpretation of events.

We have the capacity and the freedom, to "reauthor" our stories—both past and present—in a way that makes more sense to us in light of new data. This capacity to change contributes to both steady development and more radical transformation as our self moves forward in the process of "becoming." Kierkegaard emphasized that in the present moment we have the freedom to actualize our potential by choosing our "future stories."[37]

As we move through life, new experiences are not only integrated into our developing narratives, but bring change into these narratives. Change is going on all the time. Accidents, new vocation, divorce, death of a loved one, religious conversions, aging, and so forth are constantly affecting our narratives. New experience is interpreted through the lens of our existing narratives, but at the same time new experience modifies the narrative. In some ways each new experience adds to our narratives by confirming, modifying, or sometimes thoroughly constructing them. A current encounter with the environment can change the direction of a core narrative, or what narrative theorists call a dominant story, causing us to adopt new perspectives and purposes. Our environment, for example, is filled with information about food, diet, and nutrition related to health. Chances are that your story about food has changed—and that the way you eat is different now than it was ten years ago. Though change is not easy, we are witnesses to the fact that change does occur in people's stories.

In Scripture, for example, Saul's dominant story established his identity as a zealous Pharisee whose priority was law and who was committed to persecuting, maybe even killing, Christians. Then a mystical experience challenged his core narrative about God and during a long retreat he *re-storied* his life, transforming his whole identity. He became Paul, whose dominant story was centered on being a Christian missionary and whose priority was not law but grace. Theologically we call the change in personal narratives deliverance, conversion, transformation, salvation, rebirth, reconciliation, or becoming a new creation. We pursue this idea in chapter 13 when we talk about transforming our stories to reduce anger.

Sometimes narratives are flexible and easy to change, but many become hardened in our identities and are not easy to change, particularly when they have the power of some authority behind them—such as family tradition, Scripture, or theology. The self is amazingly fluid, but many parts of ourselves seem impervious or at least are difficult to change, such as habits, traits, and personality characteristics that seem to stay the same over time.[38] At other times people use the idea that our stories are unchangeable as an excuse to maintain certain behaviors that they don't want to give up. Temper tantrums are an example. Perhaps you have known someone who defended heated angry responses by blaming a temper—"I'm sorry, but I've got a temper"—as if anger was some uncontrollable thing roaming around inside them that might at any point explode. Some families treat one member like a military land mine, worrying that the temper might "go off" at any time.

Some parts of our story are buried in our unconscious, and narrative theory recognizes that not all of a person's stories are conscious. Many stories are not conscious, but they do linger in the background and may influence the ongoing narrative. Some stories are suppressed because they contradict the preferred stories of important people in our lives, or of the culture in which we live, and would cause both internal and external tension if allowed into consciousness. Other stories are suppressed because they run counter to the dominant story in our own life and, therefore, would create internal tension if admitted to conscious awareness. They become what narrative therapists call alternative stories, many of which can be recovered through therapeutic processes.

These unremembered stories can make us vulnerable to threats that we don't recognize until a sudden experience of anger takes us by surprise and we wonder, "Where did that anger come from?" Often an unconscious narrative of importance to us has been threatened. In chapter 13, I describe one way that anger can be a spiritual ally is when it invites us to understand something about ourselves that has been hidden from consciousness.

Changing narratives, what I call re-storying, occurs when we intentionally use education, insight, self-awareness, and volition to make changes in our ongoing story. We can confront the dominant stories and core narratives of our history and transform them into new stories that accomplish different purposes. Over time, after being intentionally changed, a new story becomes so rooted in one's character—and therefore within the neurology of our brains, particularly the neocortex—that we respond differently to a particular stimulus without being conscious of our decision.[39]

IDENTIFYING AND CHANGING DOMINANT NARRATIVES FROM THE PAST

Though ethical responsibility for our anger is discussed more thoroughly in chapters 12 and 13, one of our first tasks in handling anger effectively is to identify our past narratives about anger that continue to shape how we handle this emotion in the present. Individual narratives, as said earlier, are encased in the larger narratives of family, neighborhood, gender, and culture. We all have ideas about anger—what it is, what it means, how it should be expressed, who can be angry and why, and how God feels about it—that are rooted in these larger narratives, but particularly in our family history. Uncovering these core narratives can teach us much about the way we experience and express anger in the present. Therefore, taking responsibility for our anger includes identifying these narratives and assessing what impact they have on our current functioning. It takes some detective work to gather as much information as possible, looking for clues that put the pieces of the puzzle together in a discernable pattern. I described a little of my story in the introduction. Here are a few more examples of people learning about how past narratives have influenced them.

Ted is a male in his early forties who grew up in a small southern town where his father was a public figure and his mother served as his father's secretary. He described his family as appearing to the outside world as "a picture of perfect calmness and sensibility," but inside "a different story was true":

> My father was an angry man who controlled behaviors by an oak board that stayed on top of the refrigerator. We had what appeared to be the perfect family on the outside, but an inside view revealed the truth. My parents' marriage was not a good model of communication, conflict resolution, or love. My father brought tension and hatred from work, and my mother . . . lived in a constant state of anger and depression, with martyr tattooed on her forehead. . . . I saw my father display his anger at many situations. He, like me, had a tendency to keep his emotions inside until something caused them to erupt. We always knew when he was getting angry. He would first be quiet for a few hours or days, and then move to sarcastic remarks. If the sarcasm did not accomplish compliance, you knew he would blow up. My mother, on the other hand, usually did not express her anger in loud or physical ways. Her method was to manipulate and verbally assassinate. . . . She always seemed to complain, but never took action to change things. My mother keeps a scorecard for transgressions committed against her. Payback is hell. . . . Part of my experience of dealing with anger obviously comes from my parents. . . . I have the volatility of my father, but . . . also my mother's martyr spirit.

Unresolved anger between Ted and his wife had led them to the brink of divorce. They entered therapy and began to uncover how their core narratives about anger were creating major problems. Ted is working hard now at understanding how the specific stories of his family have affected the way he relates to his wife. He realizes that he copies his father's volatility, but is now aware that he also tends to suffer in silence like his mother, allowing his anger to leak out in complaints and accusations. These recent revelations have guided him in changing both his narratives and his behavior toward the family.

Janet, a woman in her thirties, wrote about the influence of her experiences with anger in her family of origin:

> Both of my parents had a problem with anger. . . . My mother lashed out at us verbally and physically, often spanking us, shaking us by the shoulders until our heads flopped, or slapping us in a fit of rage. . . . My father was a "rageaholic" who emotionally abused [us]. . . . Although he never hit any of us, his words hurt far more than any spanking my mother ever gave me.

She described a specific encounter with her father's anger that gave shape to one of her dominant narratives about anger:

> I remember an incident which occurred when I was about five years old while I was helping [my dad] wash the car. I was feeling all happy inside because the tire I was working on was getting really clean, and I was thinking about how proud my father would be. What a good helper I was! Then all of a sudden out of nowhere and for no apparent reason he was standing beside me yelling at me. "Why are you washing the tire? Don't you know you always start at the top of the car and work down? The tires are the last things you clean!" I was devastated. From that incident I learned how unpredictable and frightening anger can be. I learned to be wary around my father and to always try to do things "right" so I would not get yelled at. Today I am a recovering perfectionist who is sometimes afraid of other people's anger.

After describing another incident of her father's rage, she described yet another strong narrative about anger, though one she tried to keep subdued because it was in conflict with the dominant one above.

> I thought that the way to deal with angry feelings was to lash out with angry words, to say mean things to hurt the other person, or to hit somebody (not necessarily the person you were mad at). I learned that it does not matter what you are mad at, a good way to release your anger is to yell at the closest, weakest person in sight, to blame others for your problems, to not take responsibility for your own anger.

After describing how she was slapped by her mother for "sassing" and how her father became even more angry when she protested his unfairness, Janet says:

> I learned that my anger exacerbated my parent's anger. Because it was often not safe to show my anger, I began holding it in—until I could contain it no longer and it came bursting out.

Janet chose to take responsibility for explosive expressions of anger by changing the dominant narrative that she shouldn't be angry, but also by modifying the destructive behaviors that occurred when her anger came "bursting out." She began to identify anger more quickly, and to communicate with her husband and children more carefully and directly. She identified that one of her strong narratives was the need to be recognized and respected by her husband and children as a person in her own right and that much of her anger was generated when they seemed to treat her as if she was the "servant, not wife and mother." She began to communicate her needs and desires so that she wouldn't feel so threatened when they went unheeded. Perhaps most significantly, Janet began to adopt the Christian narrative about anger that is established in chapter 10, viewing anger as part of creation blessed by God and an acceptable experience in many situations.

Helen was trying to understand her fear of expressing anger when she wrote the following story in her journal:

> The main feelings I remember about anger growing up were fear and avoidance. Dad would slap or swat when provoked, and sometimes use a belt. I'd watch him carefully to avoid making him mad.

Then her father had a debilitating heart attack when she was nine years old, and her memories expand to how the family was constantly concerned for her father's health. Helen wrote:

> I complied by doing my best not to make him mad. I was terrified that I'd make him mad and kill him. My self-appointed task was to keep things running smoothly around home.

This story of compliance in relating to angry people became her dominant narrative about anger—that if she became angry, terrible things, like people dying, were going to happen. Needless to say, her choice was for denial and suppression. Now, in her mid-thirties, she is known for making sure that things run smoothly and that no one is upset. Helen is super-vigilant not to let her anger show, because in her words, "I feared that tons of rage would flood out." At another point she said, "I've been afraid of unleashing the anger monster, so [I] have stuffed it inside." She is convinced that this suppressed anger is physically destructive, but because her fear is so strong she is finding it hard to change this story.

Yena is the thirty-year-old minister whom we met in chapter 3. In conversation with me over a period of months, she explored both experientially and theoretically the concepts in this book. The following are excerpts from the journal in which she summarized her personal discoveries related to her own struggle with anger. She begins by examining her dominant stories about anger.

> Although the message I received was, "don't get angry," the model I witnessed in my biological family, specifically from my primary care-giver, added additional information about anger. My mother dealt with anger by raising her voice and using tones and language that made her displeasure clear. Afterwards, she emotionally withdrew. In looking back, I can see now that she expressed her anger indirectly through nagging and silence and withdrawal.

Yena became aware of the effect that her parent's choices about dealing with anger had on her narrative about self-worth. After speaking of her mother's nagging and withdrawal, she writes:

> However, this pattern was true in the home only. Outside the home, even to strangers that called on the phone, she acted nice and polite. At the time, this didn't make sense to me. I wondered how she could act so caring to others, while to her own children she was cold and silent. I interpreted her behavior as a lack of love.

She worked to understand more about her mother's anger, particularly trying to understand the narratives that caused her mother to be so threatened by Yena's behavior.

> The events that angered mother were often about being neat and tidy. She became angry when the house wasn't clean or we didn't put something away in its proper place. She used anger as a policing function, to get us to do things she wanted us to do in the way she wanted them done. However, mother's interpretation of our behavior was that we were being thoughtless. If we loved her, we would do these small things around the house. For her, behavioral expressions of thoughtfulness were signs of love. I believe she felt justified not only in her feelings of anger but in her expressions of it as well.

As Yena continued her exploration of the responses she had to her mother's manner of handling anger (both what threatened her mother and how the anger was expressed), she became more conscious of what she learned from her early experience with her mother's anger.

> From this pattern, I learned several things. I learned that behavioral expressions of thoughtfulness were required expressions of love. I learned that anger in the absence of such behavior, and expressions of this anger, even unhealthy expressions, were justified. And, I

learned that anger was a way to get people to do what you wanted them to do.

As a child, my response to the way anger was handled in my home was multifaceted. While I believed anger was something I as a good Christian should not feel, I did express it in a way similar to my mother. I pouted, changed my tone of voice, and used other non-verbal and verbal forms of communication to express my feelings that something was wrong for me. Although the response I received was [being ordered] to go to my room, I persisted in this pattern I had seen demonstrated.

Like my mother, who believed the anger-is-sin model, when I did experience anger at others that I felt was justified, I admitted [my anger] but blamed others for it, allowing myself to rationalize and excuse myself for having this negative emotion.

Anger, sadness, loneliness, and other "negative" emotions all felt the same to me. My stomach hurt, I felt misunderstood, I wanted to not feel that way, and I wanted someone to show me love. I believed my mother's accusation that thoughtful behavior was a sign of love, and I felt guilty for not showing my love to my mother through thoughtful behavior. I learned to anticipate the behaviors she desired and to try to perform them perfectly, believing that was what a good Christian person did. Looking back now, I realize I felt anger myself at her withdrawal from us. However, feeling anger, and anger at one's parent, was definitely not acceptable. Thus, I denied this anger at my mother and was unable to learn from the recurrent experiences I had of it.

These insights formed the context in which Yena made significant changes in her narratives about anger, which are discussed further in chapter 13.

You might find it helpful to pause and identify your dominant story about anger. What were the specific anger events that became part of your experience? How did you "story" the experiences you had with the anger of others in your family of origin, neighborhood, ethnic group, and both genders? Which did you adopt or reject? What did you learn about who can be angry, when to feel angry, whether or not anger is permissible, how to express it, and how God feels about it? You may want to pursue information by talking with other family members, to see how they remember their history. Parents, siblings, and grandparents may have interesting stories that expand your memories and your understanding of the narratives of other family members that were threatened.

You can compare the theology, either implicitly or explicitly informing these narratives, with the theology of anger constructed in chapter 10. Then you can choose to challenge those narratives from your past that don't measure up to your understanding of the Christian faith. You can choose to stand with the alternative stories in Scripture (chapter 8 and 9) and in the Christian tradition (chapter 7) and accept that our capacity for anger is a gift from the Creator and activate its many positive contributions to fulfilling your potential as a human being. Though certain core narratives are difficult to change, we are capable in the present of reconstructing past stories so that they reflect a consciously chosen theology to carry into the future. Hopefully the new narratives will make you less vulnerable to unnecessary threats, and sensitize you to those situations (based on the ethics discussed in chapter 12) that *should* threaten our Christian commitments and lead us to compassionate anger.

Yena's final reflections focused on the larger picture of how she progressed with her thinking and feeling about anger, and the need for a reconstructed narrative. She connects this need with her spiritual pilgrimage and makes a commitment to construct a new understanding of anger and a new way of behaving with anger.

> I think the thing I have learned that will have the most profound effect on the way I deal with anger and help others to deal with anger is the way I view anger itself. I had never thought of anger as a "spiritual ally" or a "call to action." Deconstructing my narrative of anger and reconstructing it is necessary. Seeing anger as an indication that something is amiss is, I think, warranted. Anger dictates taking the time to hear the call, discerning God's lure, and strategizing a response. In this way, anger, instead of being something to dread, avoid, or pray away, is transformed into a positive partner in our growth and development, in our maturity as people who are committed to being Christian disciples. This reconstruction requires discipline, not unlike other spiritual disciplines. Having a history of practicing spiritual disciplines, this notion of disciplined reconstruction resonates with me and helps me to put anger into a completely different category—usefulness instead of vice. I believe this reconstruction will be the key to my finally learning to deal with anger in a healthy and constructive way in my life and thereby be able to assist others in doing the same.

Yena illustrates how important it is for us as caregivers to attend to our own narratives about anger if we are to be effective in helping other people with theirs.

CONTRIBUTIONS TO A
PASTORAL THEOLOGY OF ANGER

Constructionist narrative theory, as with the neurosciences in chapter 5, makes an important contribution to theological anthropology, which in turn informs a pastoral theology of anger.

Embodiment

The mental process of narrative structuring is based in the neurological capacities of our brain. Like the processes that activate the arousal patterns described in the last chapter, our ability to make stories out of sensory data is lodged in biological processes and, therefore, part of our finitude. This interpretive ability is crucial in understanding anger and includes the integral connections between the physical and the mental aspects of personhood. Constructionist narrative theorists make the same conclusions about body/mind interaction reached by neurological researchers, namely that humans are psychosomatic units. The automatic mental process of constructing narrative interpretations of life events is based in our complex brain functions, part of our embodiment. Yet both religious and nonreligious philosophers have, over the centuries, tried to push physicality out of the human equation when discussing self-transcendence. As Kierkegaard insisted, however, one task of being human is to bring body and soul together into a synthesis.[40]

A theological anthropology that did not take seriously our cognitive and self-transcendent capabilities, as well as our other biological capacities, would fail as a theological context for understanding anger. I agree with those who argue that we must consider both these perspectives if we are to understand the universal aspects, as well as the more unique and idiosyncratic aspects, of anger in human experience.[41] A pastoral theology of anger insists that humans experience anger as a psychosomatic unity. I contend that our capacity for narrative structuring is part of our embodiment that God, as Creator, intentionally brought into being as part of the human condition.

Created in God's Image

Constructionist and narrative theories have sparked the development of fresh approaches to biblical and theological studies. The gospel is identified as a sacred story, the narrative account of God's revelation in Jesus Christ. God as Storyteller is one of the metaphors used by theologians who are influenced by constructionist narrative perspectives. Consider the Genesis account of God's activity as Creator:

> In the beginning when God began to create the heavens and the earth, the earth was a formless void and darkness covered the face of the deep, while the spirit of God swept over the face of the waters. Then God said, "Let there be light"; and there was light. (Gen. 1:1–3, with NRSV alternative readings)

At first, formlessness and darkness covered everything so that nothing could be seen. But God's spirit swept over this chaos and *spoke* the various parts of the universe into being. "Then God *said*" and things began to happen, and God used language to name these things, "God *called* the light Day." God narrates the world into existence. God's creative activity can be metaphorically understood as the construction of a story or the development of a narrative. As the process theologians have conceptualized so well, God is always taking initiative toward us, creating new stories in response to our choices.

In light of this metaphor, it makes sense to recognize our neurological capacity for narrative structuring as a reflection of God as Storyteller, part of what it means to be created in the image of God. God has the capacity for creating through narrative structure, and we join God as cocreators through our capacity for "storying" the events in our lives into a cohesive, meaningful whole. And, as we said about the physiological capacity for anger, this ability for narrative structuring was part of our finitude, which God blessed (Gen. 1:28) and called "good" (Gen. 1:31).

Freedom

The existentialists understood that the reality of human freedom means we are responsible for, in Sartre's words, "being the incontestable author of an event." We are the ones "by whom it happens that *there is* a world."[42] This "world" is the one we create by our narrative constructions and will not be identical to how others have constructed, and are in process of constructing, their world.

Constructionist narrative understandings of the self provide another window into the understanding of human freedom. God chose to create us with this capacity for narrative structuring so that we can participate in the creation of our own self. We have the freedom, and the privilege, to cocreate our own identity, without which we would find it difficult to change, grow, develop, or have the motivation to express anger when our ethical commitments call for action, as discussed in chapter 12.

Most versions of the Christian faith understand this freedom to choose change, to re-create ourselves differently, to be transformed, as one of the Creator's intentional gifts. The freedom brought to us in Jesus the Christ, which the apostle Paul warned us never to give up (Gal. 5:1, 13), includes the freedom to change those stories that make us unnecessarily vulnerable to anger or lead us to destructive behaviors. Within the limits of the life situation into which we are thrown, we have been given freedom by God to cocreate our own story, to plan our own journey. Certainly many people and events participate in the construction of our original narratives, as we said earlier, but as people of faith we have both the opportunity and the potential to re-author our stories. From a theological stance, we believe that God has given us the freedom and the power to significantly change our past and present stories in order to pursue new stories in the future (becoming "new creations" or "new beings").[43] From this theological position comes the working hypothesis that Christian caregiving includes inviting, even challenging, people to change narratives, to author a new edition of those stories that make them vulnerable to anger, at least anger that is not ethically appropriate.

Responsibility

From the constructionist narrative perspective, there is a considerable amount of choice in whether or not a particular event triggers in us an experience of anger. Remember, we respond to an event through the lens of our narratives, interpreting and giving meaning to that event. These narratives are largely self-constructed, though heavily influenced by our physiological dispositions, our family history, and the larger culture. Yet they are ours and we can imagine God calling us, pursuing us, inviting us, challenging us to reconstruct those stories that make us unnecessarily vulnerable to threats. God's desire would be that we so fully accept and adopt the sacred story that we would only be threatened when values informed by our faith narratives are threatened, as I describe in chapter 12.

We ourselves decide (excluding situations in which normal brain functioning has been disturbed by disease or accident) *what* makes us angry, *why* we get angry, and *when* we get angry. Furthermore, we decide how, when, and where to express our anger. This accountability includes the responsibility to uncover unconscious narratives that may be making us vulnerable to unnecessary anger. We now know that anger is not a biological instinct that functions unilaterally and chaotically as if it were the proverbial "loose cannon" inside our psyche, but that our anger occurs within the mix of neurological interactions with the environment. Bringing these narratives into consciousness where they can be assessed and changed if necessary is our responsibility.

The narratives we constructed in our growing-up experiences also influence our interpretations and behaviors. Persons who are reared in an environment where physical abuse is common, for example, are more likely to express physical abuse than someone who is reared in an environment where physical abuse is uncommon. Our upbringing does not free us, however, from the responsibility of choosing whether to copy these early experiences. In a religious context, transforming narratives can be one of our ongoing goals as we seek to bring ourselves closer to the sacred story—what we believe to be mature Christian living. Caregiving and counseling often have this goal.

Because we are responsible for our anger, both the "feeling" of it and the actions that follow, a pastoral theology of anger must speak to the issue of accountability. I return to this issue in both chapter 10, when discussing a pastoral theology of anger, and in part 4, when describing our ethical responsibility for anger.

PART 3

A Constructive Pastoral
Theology of Anger

Why Is Anger One of the "Seven Deadly Sins"? The Christian Tradition

The dominant belief about anger in the Christian tradition is that all anger is sinful. This anger-is-sin tradition declares that anger was not present in humans at creation, but has its roots in the original sin of pride and disobedience that set us over against God. Anger, therefore, is associated with evil—unbecoming to the Christian and leading to estrangement from God. The exception has been those who defended "righteous indignation."

Many voices in the church have taught (from the pulpit, devotional material, and theological treatises) that good Christians subdue this terrible emotion and never express anger by word or action. As Herbert Hohenstein summarized, "Almost from infancy one is taught to believe that angry thoughts [and] feelings are incompatible with the presence of the Spirit in one's heart."[1] Reminiscent of Stoic thought, the church often suggests that the most spiritually mature people so completely eradicate anger from their lives that they do not even experience this emotion.

As a number of feminist theologians have noted, women are more likely to be victimized by this belief. Rosemary Radford Ruether writes, "For Christian women, particularly in more conservative traditions, one of the most difficult barriers to feminist consciousness is the identification of sin with anger and pride."[2] Rita Nakashima Brock agrees, saying that "all anger has been condemned as sin, especially for women."[3]

DOMINANT NARRATIVES AND THE FORMATION OF TRADITION

The terms "dominant story" and "dominant narrative" are used in narrative theory to denote a specific point of view or belief that is regarded as the valid perspective. In becoming a dominant narrative, a particular understanding of reality becomes the accepted dogma. Whether a dominant story belongs solely to an individual, or is adopted by a whole community, organization, or institution (such as the church), that story gains status as the "way things are" and becomes so powerful to the individual or community that it appears to be "the incontrovertible truth." The anger-is-sin tradition gained prominence and became one of the church's dominant stories.

As a dominant story gains status as truth, those voices that doubt, differ, or dissent find it difficult to be heard. Contrary perceptions of reality are marginalized and ignored, becoming what narrative theorists call "alternative stories." The proponents of the dominant story perceive these alternative stories as false. As defenders of the dominant story take on the role of guardians and protectors of the truth, they often gain considerable power to weed out dangerous, heretical stories that differ from their espoused view of truth. An alternative story that is labeled heretical or untrue is frequently suppressed, and may even be oppressed, becoming, in narrative theory terminology, a "subjugated" story. A story may be subjugated by active oppression (the Inquisition, for example) or simply by being ignored and criticized.

A necessary task in constructing a pastoral theology of anger is to investigate the Christian tradition for the existence of alternative stories about anger in Scripture and theology. My approach to uncovering these alternative stories is as follows. I begin in this chapter by searching the writings of a few prominent theologians from across the centuries in order to understand how the traditional Christian position on anger came into existence, but also to explore alternative ideas. I document that alternative stories to the anger-is-sin tradition did exist. In fact, these stories are often found in the writings of the same theologians and scholars whose ideas are used to uphold the traditional anger-is-sin view. However, as is typical in the formation of dominant narratives, these alternative voices are frequently overlooked and often absent from the teachings that the church passed on. In chapter 8, I examine the alternative stories in Scripture that have been overlooked. In chapter 9, I explore what the Bible reveals about God's anger, often known as God's wrath, and the anger that Jesus experienced. Finally, I summarize a constructive pastoral theology of anger in chapter 10.

Historical Factors

The ancient Israelites had a ten-point guide to morality—the Ten Commandments—but it does not include anger (though it does prohibit killing, which often results from anger). In the ancient Mediterranean world, numerous lists of virtues and vices are found in Jewish, Christian, Greek, and Latin literature.[4] Differing in form and content, these lists include both concrete behaviors and mental dispositions. The New Testament includes a number of such lists[5] that often use material from these other sources and from Near Eastern and Jewish wisdom traditions. Their purpose is to offer moral guidance and exhortation toward Christian "perfection."

Centuries later, the medieval church developed one of the most famous lists of moral vices, which became known as "The Seven Deadly Sins":[6] pride, covetousness, lust, envy, gluttony, anger, and sloth. Even when contemporary church members find it difficult to name all seven of these deadly sins, they usually assume anger is among them. The fact that anger was included in the Seven Deadly Sins was a major contributor to the negative view of anger that so many Christians have been taught. Most people heard the message growing up that anger is not simply one among numerous vices, but one of those in the forbidden zone: a deadly sin.

Why was anger included in this list? How did anger become such a problem for the church? Where did the anger-is-sin tradition originate? The answer is not easy to discern, but we can gain some understanding by revisiting the cultural context that contributed to the ambivalence about emotion (discussed in chapter 2) and examine their effect on the church's view of anger: (1) the Mediterranean philosophies, (2) the need to defend God's holiness and morality, and (3) the dualistic differentiation between flesh and spirit.

The Influence of Mediterranean Philosophies

Classical Greek philosophy prioritized reason over emotion; anger was always to be under the rule of reason. Both Plato and Aristotle believed that emotion, including anger, is appropriate when it is the most reasonable reaction to a certain circumstance. Aristotle said in *The Nicomachean Ethics:*

> Anyone can become angry—that is easy. But to be angry with the right person, to the right degree, at the right time, for the right purpose, and in the right way—that is not easy.[7]

Aristotle further observed that persons are not judged because they experience anger, but on the basis of what the anger does to and through them.[8] Nonetheless, Aristotle and Plato both viewed anger as an emotion that constantly sought to break away from the constraints of reason and would then lead to irrational and chaotic behavior.[9] They wrote thoughtfully of their observations that anger was often destructive when expressed as punishment, vengeance, or retaliation.[10]

Anger was one of the emotions that most concerned the Stoics, and anger in Stoic thought was discussed in exclusively negative terms. Seneca, perhaps the best-known Stoic philosopher and a contemporary of Jesus, wrote that anger is "the most hideous and frenzied of all the emotions . . . the greatest of all ills."[11] In contrast to Aristotle and Plato, Seneca was unwilling to consider the possibility that reason could effectively control anger:

> Anger is that which overleaps the reason and sweeps it away.[12]

> Anger, I say, has this great fault—it refuses to be ruled.[13]

> If anger suffers any limitation to be imposed upon it, it must be called by some other name—it has ceased to be anger; for I understand this to be unbridled and ungovernable.[14]

His definition of anger seems to be more like our current definition of uncontrollable rage, rather than the broader human experience of anger. Seneca believed that anger and reasonable behavior were so irreconcilable that "If anger listens to reason and follows where reason leads, it is no longer anger."[15] The ideas of the Stoics about anger were based on their observations that anger always seemed to become excessive, turning into rage that was acted out in revenge, thereby harming the cohesive fabric of society. Seneca, writing within the political context of Rome, knew firsthand of the murderous results of anger expressed by those in power. In his role within Nero's administration, Seneca witnessed the persecution of Rome's enemies and the burning of Rome, perhaps influencing his perception that anger is always destructive.[16]

Stoics believed that all feelings—and certainly anger—could be slowly erased from a person's life by the development of the attitude called "apatheia," an indifference to external events that could be threatening. Seneca argued that wise people should eradicate anger: "Let us not try to regulate our anger, but be rid of it altogether—for what regulation can there be of any evil thing?"[17] Persons who get angry have turned their back upon reason, contradicting Stoic belief. The worldview of Stoicism provided the philosophical context for the aesthetic emphasis that developed several centuries later in the monastic tradition. The Stoic stance toward emotion was adopted by many of the early Christian monastics and often influenced how the monks read Scripture concerning anger, contributing to the development of flesh/spirit dualism and the anger-is-sin tradition.

Christian Apologetics: Defending God's Holiness

Early Christian apologists, as discussed in chapter 2, wanted to demonstrate the difference between their God and the Greco-Roman gods: The God who sent Jesus did not behave in deceitful, destructive ways as did the passion-driven gods of the Greeks and Romans. Some, such as St. Augustine and John Cassian, made this distinction by preaching and teaching that God was impassive and immutable, completely free from humanlike passions such as anger.

St. Augustine (354–430), one of the most influential early theologians, argued in *The City of God* that God and angels do not feel anger:

> For the holy angels feel no anger while they punish those whom the eternal law of God consigns to punishment . . . ; and yet ordinary language ascribes to them also these mental emotions, because, though they have none of our weakness, their acts resemble the actions to which these emotions move us; and thus even God Himself is said in Scripture to be angry, and yet without any perturbation. For this word is used of the effect of His vengeance, not of the disturbing mental affection.[18]

Augustine believed that emotions were a weaker, less important aspect of human mental processes. Because he also believed in a holy God without any "weakness," he concluded that neither God nor God's angels could feel anger. Augustine argued that references in Scripture to an angry God are the result of flawed attempts by the biblical writers, within the limits of human language, to describe God's motivations and actions. He believed the biblical writers mistakenly assigned anger to God simply because God acted in ways that humans associate with anger. In this way Augustine protected God from any association with anger and, therefore, from emotional "weakness."

John Cassian (360–430), whose writings significantly influenced the monastic tradition, also believed that God is free from passions such as anger.[19] He contended with those in the early church who argued that human anger directed at "wrongdoing brothers" was acceptable because "God himself is said to be enraged and angry."[20] This argument disturbed Cassian not only because he thought it provided "an excuse for a most pestilent sin," but in a blasphemous manner his antagonists were "ascribing to the Divine Infinity and Fountain of all Purity a taint of human passion."[21]

This argument, Cassian countered, not only provided an excuse for sin (since he believed all anger was sinful), but was also blasphemous when it ascribed "the injustice of fleshly passion into the divine limitlessness and the source of all purity."[22] After quoting several Scripture passages that describe God as angry, he attacked this "detestable interpretation" of the anthropomorphic language used by biblical authors. According to Cassian, Scripture that suggests God is angry cannot be "literally understood" without committing a "horrible sacrilege," because the "disturbance of anger (not to mention wrath)" cannot be attributed to God without "monstrous blasphemy."[23] His belief in God's immutability directly informed his ideas about the human experience of anger, as we see later.

From his writings, we know that Cassian's theological opponents considered anger important in combating sin and in the quest for justice. We don't know much about those who disagreed with Cassian, however, or about the rest of their theological discourse, because the idea that anger was sinful became the dominant narrative. In fact, as we see later, even Augustine and Cassian themselves identified a positive place for anger in human life, but their alternative stories were marginalized as the anger-is-sin tradition became dominant.

In the work of these two prominent theologians, we see the early church's need to keep God completely free from any taint of humanness, particularly the dreadful emotion of anger. Both Neoplatonic and Stoic philosophy affected their theological reasoning and led to their inability to accept a God of passion. As a result, a view of God significantly different than that found in biblical stories became established in early Christian thought.[24] The theology of Augustine and Cassian is representative of the aesthetic theology that influenced monastic practice and contributed significantly to the dominant anger-is-sin tradition.

Flesh/Spirit Dualism

Recall from chapter 2 that in the dualistic perspectives of the early Christian (monastic) period the flesh was set against the spirit. Everything associated with the flesh was viewed with disdain, as inimical to the truly spiritual life, a perspective that became a theological basis for asceticism. Anger (along with other emotions), reason, and the body were all relegated to the flesh and became aspects of selfhood to be overcome by those striving toward spiritual maturity. With anger thus assigned to the flesh, the flesh-versus-spirit tension contributed to the theological soil in which the anger-is-sin assumption took root.

The goal of the monastic tradition is to attain unity with God and to live a life reflecting this unity based on Jesus' example. Monastics desired to empty themselves of all that would keep them from being unified with God—thus the ascetic emphasis on denying the body, renouncing the world's desires, and putting away selfishness and obsession with material possessions. The flesh/spirit dualism moved the monastic theologians away from "be slow to anger" to "avoid all anger."

The influence of Stoic thought, flesh/spirit dualism, and the theological idea of an immutable and passionless God become clear as we trace the development of the anger-is-sin tradition in the work of influential theologians from the early centuries into the twentieth century.

ANGER IN CHRISTIAN THEOLOGY:
THE EARLY CHURCH

The traditional anger-is-sin theology portrays anger in such a negative light that there seems to be little room for a positive word about anger. Moreover, influential Christian thinkers seem to have been so adamant that anger is sinful that this issue could be marked "case closed." Putting anger in the list of "Seven Deadly Sins" seems conclusive, but we will see that this approach was (1) unfair to the alternative stories about anger also described by these theologians and (2) misrepresented alternative stories in Scripture, as discussed in the next chapter.

A careful inspection of early theological writing reveals an alternative view, a perspective that accepts anger as an integral and potentially positive aspect of the human condition. Even while warning us of the possibilities for anger to become destructive, these theologians accepted anger as part of the human condition—in fact, one with many positive attributes. We have not heard much about these alternative perspectives because of the dominance of the anger-is-sin narrative, but when identified, these alternative stories bring balance to the perspectives on anger that these theologians held. We see below that their wisdom, gleaned from their thoughtful consideration of the human experience of anger, confirms the recent findings of both the neurosciences and social sciences. Furthermore, their alternative stories are closer to the position of Scripture than to the anger-is-sin tradition. These alternative stories offer important materials for the construction of a pastoral theology of anger.

From the writings of the theologians below, I present separately the dominant story, which contributed to the anger-is-sin tradition, and the alternative story, which offers a positive perspective on where anger comes from and when we should be angry. This presentation allows us to clearly distinguish the two separate stories about anger in each theologian—one that says anger is bad, and another that, while recognizing problems with destructive anger, acknowledges anger's positive properties and useful roles.

Saint Basil the Great (330–379)

Basil was born into a family of distinction within the church. His grandmother, mother, father, sister, and two brothers also distinguished themselves in ways that led to official sainthood.[25] Well educated, Basil was known for keeping his theology in respectful dialogue with the best of secular thought. After a sojourn as a monk in Syria and Egypt, he became a hermit near Caesarea. His most significant contributions to the church came in the last decade of his life while he was bishop of Caesarea. Basil's influence on Eastern monasticism continues to this day, as the monks and nuns of the Greek Orthodox Church continue to use his "rule" to guide their day-to-day expression of vocation.

Dominant Story. St. Basil called anger a "vice" that "makes a man wholly bestial."[26] His experience with angry people led him to identify them with poisonous animals: "The effect of anger upon persons aroused by this passion is like that of the poison in animals who carry venom. They become rabid, like mad dogs; they dart about, like scorpions; they bite, like serpents."[27] Basil compared the frenzy of wrathful persons who have set out to "inflict some hurt upon their tormentor" with "persons possessed by the Devil" both in "appearance and state of soul."[28] At another point, his comment that "Anger is a kind of temporary madness"[29] is a precursor to some later philosophers' perspectives on anger as a mental illness (see chapter 1).

Alternative Story. Basil made it clear that his comparison of angry people with poisonous animals or the devil, and association of anger with mental illness, referred to anger that had become destructive rather than to every experience of anger. In his negative metaphors, anger is clearly separated from reason. Later, he linked reason to the positive role of anger: "We should keep it curbed, as we would a horse, and obedient to our reason,"[30] and he warned that such regulation can occur only if anger "follows closely the guidance of reason" like a shepherd's dog, and "is obedient to the call of reason."[31]

Anger properly evaluated and transformed, Basil wrote, "is serviceable to us in many acts of virtue. . . . Anger is the sinew of the soul, which provides it with vigor for the accomplishment of good works."[32] Therefore, Basil argued that Christians should activate anger in their war against evil:

> Unless your anger has been aroused against the Evil One, it is impossible for you to hate him as fiercely as he deserves. For, our hatred of sin should be as intense, I believe, as our love of virtue; and anger is very useful for bringing this about. . . .[33]

Another positive contribution of anger, says Basil, is its potential to "harden [the soul] with a tincture of iron." He recognized anger's positive and negative possibilities, and emphasized our freedom to choose how to express it:

> Let us not, therefore, make the faculties which were given us by the Creator for our salvation an occasion of sin for ourselves. To illustrate again: anger, aroused at the proper time and in the proper manner, produces courage, endurance, and continency; acting contrary to right reason, however, it becomes a madness.[34]

Basil specifically imagined that God would bless certain experiences of anger. He quotes Psalm 4:5, a possible source for the words "Be angry but do not sin" in Ephesians 4:26, as his foundation for saying that our Christian faith "does not forbid that anger be directed against its proper objects, as a medicinal device so to speak."[35]

Evagrius Ponticus (c. 345–399)

Also known as Evagrius the Solitary, Evagrius was a disciple of the Cappadocian fathers. His writings on the spiritual life, particularly *The Praktikos*, influenced the thought of succeeding generations in the development of categories of vices and virtues. He attended the Second Ecumenical Council in Constantinople in 381 with Gregory of Nazianzus, later went to Egypt, and spent his last years in a remote region with the first generation of desert fathers.[36]

Dominant Story. In *The Praktikos*, Evagrius identified "eight kinds of evil thoughts," one of which is anger. Anger, he said, was "the most fierce passion" with the capacity to "darken the soul."[37] Evagrius imagined that "demons . . . are servants of anger and hatred"[38] and warned that they can seek to prevent a virtuous person from praying by "kindling" the person's anger.[39] His negative feelings toward anger are expressed in his instructions about prayer: "Anger is calculated to cloud the eye of your spirit and destroy your state of prayer."[40] While praying, ideas will come to mind that seem "to justify your getting angry," he warned. "But anger is completely unjustified against your neighbor."[41]

Alternative Story. Despite his concerns about the destructive dangers of anger, Evagrius was also certain that anger is a natural part of the human condition. Even as he identified anger as one of the eight evil thoughts, he warned his readers, "It is not in our power to determine whether we are disturbed by these thoughts, but it is up to us to decide if they are to linger within us or not and whether or not they are to stir up our passions."[42] Though he recognized the possible negative consequence of anger, Evagrius did not believe that Christians could choose to rid their hearts and minds of anger. Rather, he was concerned that we not allow angry thoughts to control our actions in ways that would be harmful to others or to our own spiritual maturation. Our ethical option, according to Evagrius, is to take responsibility for anger so that it does not lead us into sin.

But Evagrius went further, acknowledging that anger has a positive purpose: "Anger is given to us so that we might fight against the demons and strive against every pleasure."[43] This supposed sinful part of us is, in fact, a chief motivator in our struggle against sin. Evagrius imagined anger as the first line of defense against temptation, and, he wrote, that when tempted the first response should be not to pray, but "first utter some angry words against the one who afflicts you" because the anger will confuse "the devices of the enemy."[44] Uttering angry words can be creative in freeing us to pray![45] Furthermore, Evagrius believed that the angels "encourage us to turn our anger against the demons," which seems to place the origin of anger with God.

Saint Augustine (354–430)

The "most influential of the fathers of the Western Church,"[46] Augustine of Hippo was born in Tagaste, a small town in Numidia, a Roman province in what is now Algeria. His pagan father, Patricius, held a post in municipal administration. Monica, his mother and herself a saint of the church, was a devout Christian who exerted considerable influence on her son as he searched and struggled spiritually during his first thirty years of life. In 384, upon his move to Milan to teach rhetoric, Augustine came under the influence of Ambrose, the bishop of Milan. The depth of Ambrose's thoughts, as exhibited in his sermons, as well as his integrity, contributed greatly to Augustine's conversion to Christianity in 386. Ordained as a priest in 391 and as bishop of Hippo in 396, Augustine's voluminous writings have "probably been more influential in the history of thought than any Christian writer since St. Paul."[47]

Dominant Story. As we noted earlier, Augustine believed that neither God nor angels feel anger and he argued that the biblical writers used emotive language because they were describing behavior that humans would call anger. Anger, like other emotions, was a sign of weakness. In *The City of God*, Augustine wrote about anger as a "lust for revenge" that may wrongly direct our will toward disobedience.[48]

Alternative Story. Though aware of anger's destructive possibilities, Augustine also described its potential for good. In chapter 2, we noted that in *The City of God* he directed us to subject our passions to God so that God can assist us in turning them toward righteousness.[49] We must carefully attend to our anger, he advised, not only to keep it from becoming destructive, but also to direct it into positive, constructive uses. Augustine understood that it is important to discern the reason for anger:

> In our ethics, we do not so much inquire whether a pious soul is angry, as why he is angry; . . . For I am not aware that any right thinking person would find fault with anger at a wrongdoer. . . .[50]

Discerning why anger has occurred is to take responsibility for identifying both the threat and why we were vulnerable to that threat. Augustine obviously thought that we would be threatened by the actions of a "wrongdoer," a point to which I return in chapter 12.

John Cassian (c. 360–c. 430–435)

As a young man, Cassian lived in a monastery in Bethlehem. From there he joined the desert fathers in the wilderness of Egypt, an isolated, ascetic life that significantly shaped his later writings. In about 399, he was ordained by Pope Innocent I in Rome. He established two monasteries in Marseilles and continued there as abbot for many years.[51] Cassian wrote two of the most influential texts for guiding the practice of monastic communities, *The Institutes* and *The Conferences*. His instructions on the disciplines of discipleship served as a primary spiritual guide in the Western church for many centuries.

Dominant Story. On the basis of how much attention he gave to the subject, one would assume that Cassian saw anger as the most powerful of the passions. He labeled it a "pernicious vice"[52] that harms our relationship with God, precludes our having immortal life, keeps us from participating in wisdom, and prevents us from securing the power of righteousness.[53] This negativity was rooted in Cassian's belief that God was without emotion, as we described in chapter 2. Because humans are created in the image of this passionless God, our true nature cannot include the emotion of anger. Cassian summarized how this belief should affect the spiritual life by quoting his translation of Ephesians 4:31, "All anger . . . should be removed from you," and sternly warned the monks that these words allowed no exceptions. *All* anger must be eradicated.[54]

According to Cassian, a monk's goal was to bring the passions under control. By dealing successfully with the passions, a monk would gain purity of heart, "so the monk who is on the way to perfection and who wishes to engage lawfully in the spiritual struggle must in every respect be free of the vice of anger and wrath."[55] This intense struggle was the equivalent of warfare, and in the fourth "combat" Cassian describes "the deadly poison of anger that must be totally uprooted from the depths of our soul."[56]

Cassian obviously played an important role in strengthening the theological conviction that anger is sin. By the end of the fifth century, the anger-is-sin stance was in place throughout Western monasticism, and these monastic teachings spread through the church. Suppressing anger became a major goal of the most dedicated, spiritual persons.

Alternative Story. Despite his seeming certainty that anger should be eradicated from the Christian life, Cassian later declares the other side of this dialectic. Two chapters after he lambasted anger in *The Institutes* as a terrible sin, he took another tack and described "a function for anger placed quite appropriately within us, and . . . it is useful and beneficial for us to take it up." Anger had a positive role because "When we wax indignant against the wanton movements of our own heart and are angered at things that we are ashamed to do,"[57] we are using anger in a positive manner. We can be angry at those other desires, Cassian allowed, that lurk in our hearts and try to sabotage our efforts toward spiritual maturity. He uses King David's anger at himself as an example of this acceptable experience and expression of anger and concludes, "And so we are commanded to get angry in a healthy way, at ourselves and at the evil suggestions that make an appearance."[58] The good purpose of anger and the command to get angry both originate in God.

Gregory the Great (c. 540–604)

Gregory the Great strongly supported the monastic tradition. Not only did he convert his family home into a monastery, he wrote the only biographical details we have of St. Benedict of Nursia, whose Rule (the Rule of St. Benedict) continues as a guiding wisdom for monastic communities worldwide. Gregory became the papal ambassador to Constantinople, later returning to Rome to serve the pope, and was elected to the papacy himself in 590.[59] Historians applaud him for strengthening the papacy at a critical time in both Christianity and Western culture. His writings were translated from Latin into English, French, Italian, and Spanish. Gregory's writings and work as pope are widely credited with encouraging the development of moral discipline among the faithful and accelerating the spread of monastic life. As the most influential writer bridging the Latin fathers and the medieval scholastics, Gregory's writings established norms for Christian behavior that remained valid for many centuries both for the monastic tradition and among ordinary Christians.[60]

Dominant Story. Gregory wrote prolifically, particularly about faith and morality, including the concept of virtues and vices. His work on what were called the primary, or "capital," sins resulted in the idea of "deadly sins." Gregory developed Cassian's ideas on the moral life, and though he did not follow Cassian's list of capital sins exactly, he also included anger.[61] Gregory made many harsh statements about anger, obviously believing that this emotion was one of the most dangerous sins.

Under Gregory's influence, the church hardened its negative attitude against anger. In talks to his monastic community in Constantinople, later published as the *Moralia*, Gregory discusses the common vices. He begins his section on anger with a clear indictment: "Therefore let us consider how great is the sin of anger." His key concept is that anger breaks us away from the "likeness of our Creator," and when we are angry "the likeness of the supernal image is spoiled."[62] Gregory frequently emphasized the destructiveness of anger to the spiritual life: "By anger wisdom is forsaken," "righteousness is abandoned," "harmony is disrupted," "the light of truth is lost," and "the brightness of the Holy Spirit is banished."[63]

Alternative Story. Though clearly establishing that anger is one of the worst sins, Gregory also acknowledges the presence of both bad anger and good anger: "The anger caused by hastiness of temper differs from anger prompted by zeal. The first springs from evil, the second from good."[64] This description of the origins of anger differs significantly from Gregory's earlier contention that anger is totally sinful.

Gregory, moreover, expressed concern for people who are *not* angry at evil behavior. In these sections of his work, Gregory implies that *not* being angry at sin and evil is a sin in itself (which we pursue in chapter 12). Like Cassian, he argues that we should be angry at sin when we find it in ourselves. Furthermore, he contends, because we have been "commanded to love our neighbors as ourselves it follows that we should be as angry with their faults as with our own evil ways."[65] Here we have a theologian who believed that certain experiences of anger are the result of Christian values based in love rather than sin. Some anger, therefore, is an expression of love, rather than its opposite.

But, Gregory warned, even this righteous anger must be carefully monitored so that it doesn't "gain dominion over the mind" or "escape control by the mind."[66] The influence of classical Greek philosophy is seen in Gregory's concern that anger be under the direction of reason. Anger on behalf of virtuous causes, he wrote, must "with acute analysis rein in the rising agitation of mind, restrain ardor, and subject impetuous emotions to calmness," in order that anger not move from virtue to vice.[67] Anger under the control of reason is acceptable and creative, but when it moves outside of the control of reason, anger "destroys fools." As Gregory summarized, "Anger due to zeal . . . is kept under the control of reason, [but] anger due to sin . . . dominates the vanquished mind in opposition to reason."[68]

John Climacus (early seventh century)

John Climacus was the abbot of the monastery at Mt. Sinai in the early seventh century.[69] His major work, *The Ladder of Divine Ascent,* is the most widely read book on spiritual life in the Eastern church.[70] Climacus used the metaphor of ascending rungs on a ladder to describe the potential pilgrimage from earthbound existence to spiritual wholeness for the Christian disciple. Anger was addressed on the ladder's eighth step, which addressed "placidity and meekness."

Dominant Story. Climacus takes a dim view of anger as "an indication of concealed hatred" and "a disfigurement of the soul." Because the Holy Spirit is identified with "peace of soul," and anger is a "disturbance of the heart," he says, "there is no greater obstacle to the presence of the Spirit in us than anger."[71] Progress toward attaining meekness is best assessed by evaluating our success in controlling anger: "The absence of a tendency to anger . . . among the perfect [means that] anger has been mortified by mastery of the passions, like a snake killed by a sword."[72] In fact, he says, "On the eighth step the crown is freedom from anger"[73]—strong testimony to his belief that anger is the most problematic of the emotions.

Climacus recognized the various causes of anger. He compares anger to a fever that "is a single symptom but has many causes" and recommends that the first step in the healing process is for each person to "very carefully look for his own particular cure, and the first step here is the diagnosis of the cause of the disease [anger]."[74] Once identified, we must work hard to conquer this passion: "So, then, anger the oppressor must be restrained by the chains of meekness, beaten by patience, hauled away by blessed love."[75] In contrast to Gregory, Climacus separates anger and love, saying, "the man who claims to love the Lord but is angry with his neighbor" is having a dreamlike illusion.

Alternative Story. Despite this negative evaluation, Climacus also believed that anger is part of human nature, given to us by God, with an important role to play in our lives. To understand Climacus we must attend to his distinction between our created nature and our fallen nature. He argues:

> God neither caused nor created evil and, therefore, those who assert that certain passions come naturally to the soul are quite wrong. What they fail to realize is that we have taken natural attributes of our own and turned them into passions [which are evil].[76]

Climacus then illustrated how this is true for anger: "Nature has provided us with anger as something to be turned against the serpent, but we have used it against our neighbor."[77] Being angry at a snake is appropriate, he said, because it can be dangerous. Notice his perception that one purpose of anger is to motivate our response to danger, a connection to its role in survival as described in chapter 5. Our problem with anger, he says, occurs when we use this natural, God-given alarm system against our neighbor rather than nature's dangers. Today, of course, we recognize that some humans are more dangerous than snakes.

Thomas Aquinas (c. 1224–1274)

Thomas Aquinas was born near Naples to an aristocratic family who had high expectations for him within the ecclesiastical structures of the church. When he decided to become a Dominican, his family was so disturbed that his brothers imprisoned him in the family castle for a year while they attempted to dissuade him of this choice. He finally escaped, joined the Dominicans, went to

Cologne to study, and became a professor and writer, first in Paris and then back in Naples.[78] His most famous work is *Summa Theologiae*, a masterful sixty-volume synthesis of theology drawn from Scripture, church fathers, and Aristotelian philosophical thought. It has been called "the most successful and influential synthesis of Catholic theology ever composed. . . . there is no book of comparable theological significance."[79] The views of Aquinas are significant contributions to the church's understanding of anger.

Dominant Story. Aquinas was significantly influenced by the writings of St. Augustine and Gregory the Great. He picked up Gregory's ideas about vices and virtues, though he amended the list. Aquinas referred to Gregory frequently as "the highest authority" on the subject of capital sins. When he discussed morality, therefore, he retained anger as one of the capital sins.[80]

Aquinas wrote that anger is an embodied "movement of resistance or attack"[81] and is mostly caused when we are unjustly injured in some way, that is, when we are "slighted" or regarded with contempt.[82] Aquinas believed that over time anger causes hatred, and he equates the effects of anger with hatred in that they both "seek to injure another."[83]

Alternative Story. Aquinas attends to the relationship between anger and reason, referring to Aristotle when noting that "anger involves reason not as commanding but as revealing an injury."[84] By this comment, Aquinas meant that the presence of anger often reveals that someone has treated us unfairly. He believed that anger craves revenge and desires to right a wrong, which can relate anger to justice. In this way anger is associated with reason, because true justice, Aquinas believed, is always rational. Although revenge can be evil when undertaken out of hatred, Aquinas thought that "mercy is more likely in anger than in hatred."[85]

Aquinas was aware of the importance of interpretation in the experience of anger, noting that "if we think the injury was done out of ignorance or emotion we are not angry with them, or at least not violently so."[86] Furthermore, Aquinas understood the place of empathy, noting that we can feel angry on behalf of others. In this sense, he understood the connection between anger and love.

ANGER IN CHRISTIAN THEOLOGY: THE REFORMERS AND BEYOND

Such a brief space does not allow a survey of all that was written about anger during the Reformation and beyond, so I will concentrate on the three persons most associated with the theology of Lutheranism, the Reformed tradition, and Methodism.

Martin Luther (1483–1546)

Born in Eisleben, Germany, Martin Luther was the son of a miner who wanted him to become a lawyer, and a mother who provided her son with an excellent early education.[87] Luther attended the university at Erfurt in 1501 and then, after his terrified conversion during a thunderstorm, entered Erfurt's Augustinian monastery. He took vows in 1506 and celebrated his first mass in 1507. While teaching Romans, Luther rediscovered Paul and the theology of the cross. On October 31, 1517, Luther ignited a controversy over indulgences when he posted his famous Ninety-five Theses on the front door of the Castle Church in Wittenberg, which led to the German Reformation. Condemned in the following years by both Pope Leo X and Emperor Charles V, Luther refused to recant. Steadfast in his resistance to the Roman church, his work as a reform theologian gave us the foundational Protestant emphases on scriptural authority, preaching, justification by faith alone through grace, and the priesthood of all believers.

Dominant Story. Luther did not speak as vehemently against anger as did Calvin, but he did warn his followers that "the root of anger, the spirit that wants to kill, lies hidden within you."[88] Even when a person has a valid reason to be angry, he warned that we "should keep a close watch over [ourselves] and not give way to anger but should either endure and overcome injustice with patience or seek satisfaction."[89] Rather than respond angrily to social conflict, Luther taught that people should use the legal processes of local government to resolve disputes, provide protection, and make decisions about punishment. Even if the government fails in this responsibility, then the Christian's "only recourse is to suffer the injustice patiently and beware of private revenge."[90] To openly express the anger "would turn your right into wrong before God and man."[91]

Alternative Story. Though Luther talked about the need to be careful with anger, he did not suggest that Christians should root out all anger. In his sermons he acknowledged the fact that "anger is sometimes necessary and proper." To be "proper," anger must be "an anger of love, one that wishes nobody any evil, one that is friendly to the person but hostile to the sin."[92] We are commanded to get angry not on our own behalf, Luther said, but on behalf of God. This action is not easy, he warned, because our emotions "have been corrupted by original sin." We can only use anger correctly when we allow "the Holy Spirit to govern these affections."[93] In summary, wrote Luther, "If anger is moderate and stays within the right and legitimate area of its use, it is a natural affection implanted in man's nature by God."[94] Again, we see a theologian focusing on the reason for feeling anger as the major ethical criterion in assessing whether or not anger is sinful. Furthermore, Luther assigns the origins of anger to God's creative activity and purpose, rather than human sinfulness, and points out that anger can be experienced as an expression of love.

In *Table Talk*, Luther offered a self-analysis that informs us of what he thought about anger. After listing those human sins from which he felt free (including avarice, sensual desire, and envy), he confessed, "Up to now only anger remains in me, and for the most part this is necessary and just. But I have other sins that are greater."[95] In fact, Luther said that anger served as an important motivator for him personally: "I have no better remedy than anger. If I want to write, pray, preach well, then I must be angry. Then my entire blood supply refreshes itself, my mind is made keen and all temptations depart."[96]

John Calvin (1509–1564)

Known as the Reformer of Geneva, John Calvin was born in Noyon, France.[97] Educated in the humanities, law, and theology, Calvin did not think of himself as a reformer until 1536 when, during a detour on his way from Paris to Strasbourg, William Farel argued with him to stay and help in the reforms he had begun in Geneva. Calvin's work there was all-consuming and controversial, yet he managed to establish the influential Geneva Academy for the training of pastors, and to produce new editions of his systematic theology, the *Institutes of the Christian Religion*. Scholars note that Calvin's thought focused on the "distance between the transcendent Creator and the sinful creature, a distance overcome only by the revelation communicated in Scripture and certified by the inner witness of the Holy Spirit."[98]

Dominant Story. Calvin contended, as had Augustine and Cassian before him, that the biblical writers had been limited in their ability to describe God's behavior by the inadequacy of language, so they had to be anthropomorphic in their descriptions. He explained away biblical references to God's anger as a "convention of Scripture" to describe God's retribution.[99] In his commentary on Romans, for example, Calvin explained that "when God punishes, he has, as we imagine, the appearance of anger. Thus the word does not signify feeling in God."[100]

Calvin did not view the "affections," or "passions" as he called the emotions, positively, convinced that Christians must "bridle our affections before they become ungovernable." His fear of emotion moved him to recommend that passions be "repressed, bridled, and chained up; we must make every effort to beat down the impetuous frenzy in them."[101] Calvin applied these ideas to anger, contributing to the anger-is-sin tradition.

Calvin saw anger as a sin, and was aware that his own battle with anger was a problem. Calvin wrote of himself, Bouswma tells us, that he was "inclined when seething with anger . . . to lose control and eat too greedily."[102] His response to this fear of his own anger, says Bouswma, was to put much energy into self-control.[103]

Alternative Story. Calvin, who wrote his first scholarly work on Seneca, recognized that anger is part of the human condition. In contrast to the Stoics who disavowed all the passions, Calvin realized that emotions are

> by no means repugnant to reason, nor [do they] interfere with tranquility and moderation of mind; it is only excess or intemperance which corrupts what would else be pure. And surely grief, anger, desire, hope, fear, are affections of our unfallen nature, implanted in us by God, and such as we may not find fault with, without insulting God Himself.[104]

Despite the fact that anger usually "exceeds due bounds" and is often "not aim[ed] at a proper object," Calvin believed that "anger is not in itself or absolutely to be condemned."[105]

John Wesley (1703–1791)

John Wesley was born in Lincolnshire, England, to highly educated and religious parents. His father was an Anglican priest, and his mother, the daughter of a nonconformist minister, was widely known as a saintly woman. After being educated at Oxford and returning to England from his failed mission to Georgia, Wesley had a life-changing religious conversion and dedicated his life to living out the basic principles of Christian love. The small groups he and his brother Charles formed at Oxford for disciplined Bible study and prayer were ridiculed for their methodical structure—hence the name Methodists.[106]

Dominant Story. Wesley believed that anger arises from the "inbred corruption of the heart."[107] In a sermon titled "The Duty of Reproving Our Neighbour," he contrasted anger with meekness. After quoting from the book of James that "the wrath of men worketh not the righteousness of God" (1:20 KJV), he said:

> Anger, though it be adorned with the name of zeal, begets anger, not love or holiness. We should therefore avoid, with all possible care, the very appearance of it. Let there be no trace of it, either in the eyes, the gesture, or the tone of your voice. . . .[108]

The supporting theology is found in his sermon "On Sin in Believers," where Wesley clarifies his belief that our expressions of anger constitute sin: a Christian could experience anger, but should not express anger. A Christian "may have *anger* in him, yea, and a strong propensity to furious anger, without *giving way* to it." Even in a person's heart "where there is much humility and meekness" there may be "*some* anger."[109] Thus, in Wesley's view, a person can experience anger and still be free of sin if the anger is not expressed. Wesley admitted that he personally had felt anger as resentment "a thousand times," but had not sinned because "if the resentment I feel is not yielded to for even a moment, there is no guilt at all, no condemnation from God upon that account."[110] The *expression* of anger is sinful and shows that a person is still immature in the faith. Wesley's ideas contributed to the pietistic notion that good Christians should not express any anger.

Wesley's stronger contribution to the anger-is-sin tradition comes when he pushes his thoughts to their logical conclusion: "in that heart where *only* meekness and humility are felt" there is no room for anger.[111] "Sanctification" and "perfecting holiness in the fear of God" call for being "purified from . . . anger."[112] This Wesleyan understanding of sanctification believes that when people reach a level of perfection in their faith, they will not experience any anger, much less express it.

Alternative Story. Despite these negative thoughts about anger and his concerns about its close connection with sin, Wesley realized that anger was one of "the passions which God has for wise ends implanted in man's nature."[113] The Christian, he believed, is to master the passions and "employ them only in subservience to those ends" that serve God's purposes:

> And thus even the harsher and more unpleasing passions are applicable to the noblest purposes; even hatred, and anger, and fear, when engaged against sin, and regulated by faith and love, are as walls and bulwarks to the soul, so that the wicked one cannot approach to hurt it.[114]

Wesley recognized that some people wished that the phrase "without a cause" were not included in Jesus' words about anger in the Sermon on the Mount, but he defended the phrase as necessary because it supported the fact that some anger is appropriate. Even Jesus was purified from anger only "in the common sense of the word" (meaning when it described destructive expressions of anger), says Wesley, because "all anger is not evil."[115] After referring to Jesus' anger recorded in Mark 3:5, he concluded, "Anger at sin we allow."[116]

TWENTIETH-CENTURY THEOLOGIANS

As noted in chapter 2, few theologians in the modern era chose to deal systematically with human emotion. The same is true, as one would imagine, for the specific emotion of anger. Each of the theologians examined in that chapter have been investigated for some analysis of the human experience of anger, but to no avail, though some mention aggression with the mixed meanings described in chapter 4. Their theological anthropology rarely includes any response to the human experience of anger. Anger has similarly been ignored in the field of theological ethics, and finding more than scattered comments on the subject is difficult. Neither Karl Barth or Dietrich Bonhoeffer, for example, reference the subject of anger in their major works on ethics.[117] African American theologians mention the anger that often permeates people who are victimized by racism, and even express their own, but they do not seem to offer a systematic theological analysis of this anger.[118]

Feminist theologians have been more willing to deal with the subject of anger. They are particularly interested in the connections between anger and personal and social relationships. One of Marjorie Suchocki's contributions to theological anthropology is that anxiety and trust are both "founded in the contextual relationality of the human condition."[119] In the necessary tension between the two lies the dynamic of rage, and she goes on to discuss from this perspective the relational significance of handling anger wisely. Beverly Wildung Harrison's summarizes feminist perspectives on anger:

> All agree that anger is not only a disposition but a relational dynamic and in no way the deadly sin of classical tradition. Feminist theologies all but unanimously reject the patriarchal definition of the Christian life as involving "sacrifice" of self and refuse the notion that the self-assertions involved in the expression of our passions, including anger, are "wrong."[120]

Finding a feminist who would concur with the anger-is-sin theology is hard. As Harrison says, "Happily, no feminist analysis [of evil] could perpetuate the notion that anger, per se, is evil."[121] Indeed, Harrison's article "The Power of Anger in the Work of Love" provides a seminal view of anger's role in love and in justice. She believes:

> we Christians have come very close to killing love precisely because we have understood anger to be a deadly sin. Anger is not the opposite of love. It is better understood as a feeling-signal that all is not well in our relation to other persons or groups or to the world around us. . . . [This] is a critical first step in understanding the power of anger in the work of love. Where anger arises, there the energy to act is present. . . . We must never lose touch with the fact that all serious human moral activity, especially action for social change, takes its bearings from the rising power of human anger.[122]

More is said about the relationship between anger, love, and justice in subsequent chapters. For now, note that feminist theologians have long recognized that anger did *not* originate in sin and evil, but in the Creator's blessed creation—a gift with significant positive potential for assisting with our well-being. They have contributed much to countering the anger-is-sin tradition in the church, and I use them as a rich resource in part 4.

Except for feminist theologians, when anger is mentioned in the twentieth-century works I examined (whether systematic, biblical, or ethical), the assessments and understandings are frequently based more on philosophical or psychological concepts rather than biblical or theological analysis. Again, I realize that some theologians and ethicists whom I did not read may systematically deal with the issue of anger, but the need for systematic analysis from theologians and ethicists is, at least to me, obvious.

CONTRIBUTIONS TO A PASTORAL THEOLOGY OF ANGER

We have traced the development of theological thought about anger and explored the roots of the anger-is-sin tradition. This history itself reflects the process of narrative construction presented in chapter 6. The theology constructed by the early church theologians did not, of course, include information from postmodern psychology or neuroscience, yet their phenomenological observations astutely noted the paradox of anger's power for both good and evil. They wrestled with the concept of anger in the context of their own time, including their understandings of Scripture, Mediterranean philosophies, the larger stories that were passed down in the church, their own religious experience, their desire to live a holy and humble life before God, and their need to proclaim the differences between their God and the Greco-Roman gods.

Anger was often perceived as the most dangerous of all emotions and was, therefore, a particular target for expulsion from the Christian life. Anger was frequently identified as a vice, a work of the flesh that is a detriment to attaining spiritual maturity. Anger has the power to separate us from God, make us function destructively like a poisonous animal, or make us act temporarily insane.

According to the alternative stories, however, anger is not inherently evil. Rather, these theologians believed that anger was a natural part of the human condition and, therefore, most of them claimed that it was part of creation as God ordained it. These alternate stories acknowledge anger's positive role. These theologians mention important purposes for anger: survival (Climacus pointed out that anger is a warning sign of danger), confronting injustice (Gregory was concerned about people who were not angry at evil), and resisting those human desires that seek to destroy us (Evagrius thought anger at those human desires that threatened our virtue was necessary).

Augustine described the importance of understanding why we are angry so we can make ethical choices, and certainly we can choose to sin with our anger. But we can also choose to let anger function in the service of love, as we discuss in chapter 12. Basil pointed out how important anger is to acting virtuously, its contribution to strengthening the soul, and its role in motivating good works. He was clear that we must be willing to become angry at sin. Anger was normally viewed as a useful emotion that could further the work of God as we combat injustice, wrongdoing, and evil. These positive purposes can be achieved if anger is kept under the direction of reason, which was considered to be a superior attribute of the human condition.

In hearing these alternative stories we learn that anger, though considered dangerous, was also assumed to be something over which we have power, freedom of choice, and control—a part of God's creation over which we have responsibility. If these alternative stories had been heard and valued by the church, perhaps anger would not have been placed on the list of Seven Deadly Sins—a placement quite at odds, of course, with our current knowledge gained from the neurosciences. I hope this chapter has shown that the challenge issuing forth from our theological ancestors in the faith is a positive one concerning anger. We're called to manage anger intelligently, that is, to bring our reason, our will, our values, and our faith into the role of directing this emotion so that it does not become life-destroying, but instead serves its original purpose to be life-enhancing.

8

Biblical Perspectives: The Alternative Story about Human Anger

Once anger achieved "deadly sin" status, the church had a hard time "hearing" Scripture in any way that challenged this traditional doctrine. Alternative viewpoints were overlooked because of the blinders this dominant story put in place. The church often "spoke" as if all Scripture was judgmental about anger and ignored or misinterpreted those verses of the Bible that contradicted this position.

From pulpits and devotional books the people of God have heard over the centuries those verses that seemed to support the view that anger is always destructive: implying that anger separates one from God ("the dividing wall, that is, the hostility between us"—Eph. 2:14), leads to judgment ("if you are angry with a brother or sister, you will be liable to judgment"—Matt. 5:22), does not contribute to the kingdom of God ("your anger does not produce God's righteousness"—Jas. 1:20), and interferes with prayer (we should pray "without anger"—1 Tim. 2:8). Such passages, along with numerous lists of vices that include anger, were presented and interpreted as if they convey a definitive truth: "Good Christians should not feel angry." Many Christians, influenced by these proof texts and by the idea that anger is a deadly sin, assume that the Bible is uniformly against any experience or expression of anger.

Scripture has an alternative story, and a reader may be surprised that it is so obvious. For the most part, we do not have to use technical grammatical arguments or employ a hermeneutic of suspicion to see this alternative story. These passages of Scripture, as we shall see below, reveal even to a casual reader that something is amiss in the traditional understanding of Scripture's perspective on anger. The passages provide a different angle of vision on the subject of anger, assuming that to experience the emotion of anger is a normal aspect of being human. Scripture's concern is not with the capacity for anger, but with the destructive potential that anger can unleash.

Hebrew and Greek words for anger, or that refer to anger, are used without reference to whether the anger is seen as positive or negative. The same root is used to describe both Jesus' anger at the Pharisees in Mark 3:5 (ὀργή) and the selfish anger of the elder brother in the "prodigal son" story in Luke 15:28 (ὠργίσθη). Perhaps this is further evidence that the Bible sees anger as a basic capacity of human nature. That the words themselves don't necessarily convey the moral quality of an angry event provides support for the constructionist narrative understanding of why people get angry. We have to make an ethical assessment on the basis of *why* the anger occurred and *how* the anger was expressed.

To be a bit more specific about biblical terminology for anger, at least eight Hebrew words are translated as some form of anger (including wrath, fury, indignation, rage, vexation, etc.).[1] In the New Testament, two words are generally used to indicate anger: ὀργή and θυμός. For the most part these words are used interchangeably, although some translators indicate that θυμός may portray a more sudden, unthinking outburst of anger than does ὀργή.[2] Between four hundred and five hundred references to anger (including both divine and human anger) appear in the Bible.[3] Thoroughly considering even a majority of these verses is not possible. The ones explored below, therefore, are chosen because they most clearly reveal the alternative perspective on anger and are frequently overlooked or misrepresented by those expressing a traditional anger-is-sin theology. The texts in this chapter refer to anger as experienced and expressed by human beings, and the next chapter considers texts that refer to anger experienced and expressed by Jesus and God.

STORIES IN HEBREW SCRIPTURE

Stories in Hebrew Scripture are filled with emotion, and anger is one of the most common of these emotions, including anger expressed destructively. Many stories in the Hebrew Bible, however, describe appropriate expressions of anger. When Rachel, who was jealous of her sister, blamed Jacob for her inability to have children, Jacob became angry, but his angry response was wisely expressed (Gen. 30:1–2). Moses became very angry when Pharaoh refused to allow the Israelites to leave Egypt, but the text says that Moses retreated without taking any immediate action (Exod. 11:8). Numerous examples of anger directed toward injustice and oppression are reported in the

Psalms (Pss. 59:11; 69:28). The common thread through these stories is to keep anger under control and give a measured response.[4]

The Cain and Abel story and the wisdom teachings in the Hebrew Bible specifically challenge the dominant story about anger in the Christian tradition.

Cain and Abel

Consider the Genesis story about Abel's murder at the hands of his brother, Cain.[5] In a sermon I preached as a young minister, my main point was that Cain's anger killed his brother, and therefore all anger is bad, a sin in God's eyes. This understanding is not atypical, but examine the story more closely. For reasons which are not clear (though various scholars have their opinions), Abel's offering was acceptable to God, but Cain's was not. Then the story reads:

> So Cain was very angry, and his countenance fell. The Lord said to Cain, "Why are you angry, and why has your countenance fallen? If you do well, will you not be accepted? And if you do not do well, sin is lurking at the door; its desire is for you, but you must master it." (Gen. 4:5–7)

Notice that Cain "was very angry" before God spoke to him, and yet God did not accuse him of sinning because he was angry. God did not say, "Because you are angry, you have sinned against me."

Walter Brueggemann thinks the questions God asks Cain "suggest Yahweh is not quite acting in good faith, for Yahweh himself is the cause of Cain's anger."[6] Why would he assign the cause of Cain's anger to God? Because God did the rejecting. Looking at this story through the lens of constructionist narrative theory suggests another possible scenario. Maybe the narrative that Cain had constructed about the reason and the meaning of God's rejection caused him to feel threatened. God's first response, in fact, was to be concerned about why Cain was angry. And when God asks Cain, "Why are you angry?" he could have been providing Cain with an opportunity to examine his constructed reality about the situation and learn from his anger. God even suggested ways in which Cain could change his story so that he would be accepted: "If you do well, will you not be accepted?" God did not explain why Cain's offering was rejected, but God was clear that Cain's behavior, not his offering, could lead to acceptance. If Cain changed his narrative, he would not have to feel rejected, would not be threatened, and, of course, would not be angry. So God held Cain accountable for *why* he was angry, not for having the capacity for anger.

Finally, God warns Cain that "sin is lurking at the door; its desire is for you." Sin, obviously, was not in Cain's anger but was hanging around outside licking its chops in anticipation. God knew that Cain was more vulnerable to sin because he was angry. Cain had a choice about whether or not to let sin capture him while he was angry. Though he chose to sin with his anger and murdered Abel, he did not have to. In this early emphasis in Scripture on human freedom, Cain clearly was not predestined to kill. Brueggemann says that Cain "can choose and act for the good" and confirms that, in this story, "Cain is free and capable of faithful living."[7] God let him know that he had the option of mastering the temptation, of choosing a nondestructive way of dealing with this anger. Cain's experience of anger did not create the sin, but what he allowed to threaten him and his choice of behavior did.

The Wisdom Literature

The Wisdom literature in Hebrew Scripture, particularly Proverbs and Ecclesiastes, also provides alternative stories to the traditional understanding about anger. Influenced by the anger-is-sin tradition, many Christians assume that these wisdom sayings identify the wise person as one who does not get angry. But look at these verses:

> One who is quick-tempered acts foolishly. . . . (Prov. 14:17)

> Whoever is slow to anger has great understanding, but one who has a hasty temper exalts folly. (Prov. 14:29)

> One who is slow to anger is better than the mighty, and one whose temper is controlled than one who captures a city. (Prov. 16:32)

> Those with good sense are slow to anger, and it is their glory to overlook an offense. (Prov. 19:11)

> Do not be quick to anger, for anger lodges in the bosom of fools. (Eccl. 7:9)

Does this wisdom literature paint a picture of good humans as those who never feel or experience any anger? No, wise people are those who *are slow* to anger. These verses address the destructive possibilities that exist when people are quick-tempered; they are likely to do foolish things. These verses speak against temper tantrums, explosive hostility, and other immature expressions of anger, but do not forbid God's people from ever experiencing anger. Rather they challenge us to be careful with our anger and to take responsibility for evaluating when to get angry, what to get angry at, and how to express the anger.[8] We explore how to take such responsibility in part 4.

Anger at God

The Israelites even felt free to be angry with God. The Psalms of lament are well known for the amount of anger that was expressed toward God for the suffering and travails of the people of Israel. Addressing God in Psalm 44, the psalmist writes:

> You have rejected us and abased us. . . . You have made us like sheep for slaughter, and have scattered us among the nations. You have sold your people for a trifle, demanding no high price for them. You have made us the taunt of our neighbors, the derision and scorn of those around us. . . . All this has come upon us, yet we have not forgotten you, or been false to your covenant. Our heart has not turned back, nor have our steps departed from your way, yet you have broken us in the haunt of jackals, and covered us with deep darkness. (Ps. 44:9–19)

The psalmist here is calling God to account, an important theme in Israel's relationship with God. Psalms 77:6–9 and 90:7–12 are among many others that also express anger at God. Old Testament scholar James Crenshaw has studied five biblical passages in which human anger at God is justified by the text because God is experienced as abandoning relationships, trivializing the deepest of human concerns, and deceiving people who have committed their lives to God's purposes.[9] When anger at God is claimed and spoken, according to Brueggemann, it seems to evoke a change in the psalmist. Toward the end of the psalm, she or he is then able to once again claim the promises of God.[10] Furthermore, such angry speech is also an important act of faith:

> The lament-complaint . . . introduces us to a "spirituality of protest." That is, Israel boldly recognizes that all is not right in the world. . . . Such speech is against our *docility* before God. Our Western propensity is to imagine God well beyond such strictures and such implicatedness. Israel, however, thinks its way through trouble with realism, and it speaks its truth without stammering. . . . Israel knows its hurt to be unwarranted and unfair. . . . This utterance is a freighted theological act upon the Holy Powers of Heaven, anticipating that such speech works new reality.[11]

Expressing anger toward God may indeed be an act of honesty that restores authentic relationship with the divine. I have more to say about anger as a spiritual ally in chapter 11.

NEW TESTAMENT STORIES

The New Testament also makes many references to anger, and many of the stories are used to support the dominant anger-is-sin position. Some biblical scholars still suggest that the Bible always portrays anger as a negative, destructive emotion that should not be part of the mature Christian's life. After surveying passages in the New Testament that refer to anger, Dwight Sullivan draws the conclusion that anger, though part of the human condition, is connected to "the flesh which is opposed to the way of the Spirit . . . a trait of unregenerated nature, it works against the righteousness of God."[12] But the New Testament also includes passages that directly challenge this tradition, as discussed below.

The Sermon on the Mount

The biblical passage most often quoted by people who defend the position that Christians shouldn't get angry is from the Sermon on the Mount. In a commentary on Matthew, for example, Robert Gundry interprets the words of Jesus in Matthew 5:21–22 as follows: "This is nothing less than a total prohibition of anger. . . . If we are to obey Jesus, all anger must be banished from life, and especially that anger that lingers too long."[13] I suggest a different interpretation, but first read these verses again:

> "You have heard that it was said to those of ancient times, 'You shall not murder'; and 'whoever murders shall be liable to judgment.' But I say to you that if you are angry (ὀργιζόμενος) with a brother or sister, you will be liable to judgment; and if you insult a brother or sister, you will be liable to the council; and if you say, 'You fool,' you will be liable to the hell of fire."

When first read, this passage seems to communicate that having any feeling of anger is the same as committing murder. Indeed, this verse has been used in teaching and preaching throughout Christian history to make people think that being angry is the same in God's sight as killing someone. But the three phrases that follow are not a literal escalating scale of punishments from local judicatories to God's throne, but a command to recognize God's desire that there be no killing and no hostility.[14] This passage is not a more strict legalism, but a call to make sure that all of our anger, like Jesus', is in the service of loving neighbor and not bringing about alienation.

Closer examination of the Greek text reveals a more accurate understanding of the specific phrase about anger. The Greek verb ὀργίζω, translated "are angry," is a present participle, ὀργιζόμενος, and refers to continuous action.

A more exact translation would be "everyone who is continuously angry" or "everyone who keeps on being angry."[15] Unfortunately the New Revised Standard Version, which I quote above, does not reflect this grammatical reality, but many translators are more precise. Long ago Williams translated this phrase as "everyone who harbors malice against"[16] a brother or sister, and the New English Bible reads, "anyone who nurses anger against"[17] a brother or sister.

Matthew's Gospel is concerned to represent Jesus' teachings as a new authority. This saying, and those that follow, are more than insightful moral teachings:

> Jesus does more than give a better interpretation of the old authority; he relocates authority from the written text of Scripture [the Torah] to himself—i.e., to God's presence in his life. . . . [T]he point is that Jesus' teaching is not transgression of the Law, but its transcendence.[18]

What Jesus says about anger, along with his own actions (see the next chapter), becomes quite authoritative for Christians. Jesus is specifically concerned about anger that lies unresolved in the heart, festering until it bursts forth in destructive behavior, but if asked to interpret this passage, many Christians respond as if Jesus had said, "If you ever have the slightest feeling of anger in your heart, you are a terrible person and will be judged harshly!" Jesus, however, is not talking about every internal experience of anger. Remember, Jesus himself had experienced anger, when looking around at the Pharisees with anger (Mark 3:5) and during what is often called "the cleansing of the temple," as we explore in chapter 9. Jesus is not concerned about the fact that our capacity for anger gets activated. He is concerned about why the anger is triggered. In this Sermon on the Mount passage he seems to be referring to attitudes toward other people that are not loving, but judgmental. In fact, he illustrates in v. 22 two such judgmental behaviors: insulting others and calling them fools. Like the author of Ecclesiastes, who said that anger lodges (makes a home in) the bosom of fools, Jesus points out that anger allowed to simmer inside us will poison our interpersonal relationships and destroy our inner peace, which certainly is distasteful to God.

If you memorized this passage in the Sermon on the Mount from the King James Version, you will remember the phrase "without a cause." You may recall hearing persons excuse some destructive form of anger (such as revenge, jealousy, bitterness, or a long-standing resentment) because somebody had given them "cause," a reason to be angry. The oldest manuscripts of the Bible, however, do not include this phrase, and present-day translations of the Bible include it only in the margins.[19] I have often wondered if this phrase was added by a scribe who knew personally that all people get angry and wanted to provide some escape from the seemingly harsh words of Jesus. Correctly translating the verb, however, allows us to realize that Jesus was calling attention to the devastating results of unreconciled anger, not the experience of anger itself.[20]

The Letter to the Ephesians

What was the early church thinking about anger? Note these words written in Ephesians:

> Be angry (ὀργίζεσθε) but do not sin; do not let the sun go down on your anger, and do not make room for the devil. (Eph. 4:26–27)

Most scholars interpret the first Greek word in this sentence, ὀργίζεσθε, as some form of anger. Furthermore, they concur that the words translated "be angry" and "do not sin" are both imperatives.[21] Most New Testament scholars believe the phrase "be angry" is a strong imperative, even a command, as translated by the NRSV above. Others choose to see this word as a conditional imperative—such as the New English Bible, which translates the verse "If you are angry, do not let anger lead you into sin."[22] Whether this phrase is a command imperative or a conditional/permissive imperative is debated, but the answer is irrelevant to the major point that anger is not automatically sinful.[23] Pauline theology here recognizes and assumes that Christians, like all human beings, are bound to experience anger. Ephesians makes no judgment on the actual experience of anger, certainly not on our capacity for feeling anger.

The second imperative, "do not sin," however, makes it clear that the author is concerned about what we do with our anger. The writer knows that trying to ignore anger, pretending we don't have any, or harboring it in our hearts (as warned against in Prov. 14:29 and Matt. 5:21) are choices that almost always lead us to sin with our anger. He warns his listeners, therefore, not to "let the sun go down" before they deal with their anger in some creative way. Allowing anger to go unattended is to run the risk of denying or suppressing it later. Such avoidance is dangerous because it ignores anger's potential harmfulness. The author considers it imperative to deal with anger promptly and "make no room for the devil," thus avoiding any collusion with anger's "dark" side. Notice how closely this parallels God's admonition to Cain, "Sin is lurking at the door, its desire is for you, but you can master it."

Let's look at Ephesians 4:31:

> Put away from you all bitterness and wrath (θυμός) and anger (ὀργή) and wrangling and slander, together with all malice.

These words have been used to bolster the anger-is-sin tradition. But look at the words surrounding the word "anger."[24] From the context the author is obviously describing anger that has "gone bad" and is being handled destructively. The problem was not that the people in the churches were angry, but that they were sinning with their anger—which the author had warned them against in the earlier verse ("Be angry but do not sin").

The Lists of Vices

We mentioned in chapter 7 that many lists of virtues and vices appear in Mediterranean literature and also in the New Testament (though not found in the Old Testament).[25] Paul's list of vices, notes Victor Paul Furnish, borrows from these many other sources and then contextualizes them for the specific Christian communities to whom he is writing.[26] Relating to both the community of faith and the world around them in a manner that was informed by the new ethic of love sparked interest in the positive characteristics (virtues), such as the fruits of the Spirit in Galatians, and negative characteristics (vices).[27]

Applying the new life experienced in Jesus Christ to day-to-day behavior was the focus of many New Testament passages.[28] These lists of virtues and vices are part of what has been called "The Two Ways" tradition. Jack Suggs writes, "The genius of Christianity is its strongly ethical character [and] The Two Ways tradition serves as a witness to the place of obedience in the early church's message."[29] Furnish points out that the lists created by Paul in Galatians and 2 Corinthians are specifically focused on the "social vices" that can disrupt the community of faith.[30]

Of interest to our study is that anger appears in many of these New Testament lists of vices:

> Now the works of the flesh are obvious: fornication, impurity, licentiousness, idolatry, sorcery, enmities, strife, jealousy, anger (θυμοί), quarrels, dissensions, factions, envy, drunkenness, carousing, and things like these. (Gal. 5:19–21a)

> For I fear that when I come, I may find you not as I wish, and that you may find me not as you wish; I fear that there may perhaps be quarreling, jealousy, anger (θυμοί), selfishness, slander, gossip, conceit, and disorder. (2 Cor. 12:20)

> But now you must get rid of all such things—anger (ὀργήν), wrath (θυμόν), malice, slander, and abusive language from your mouth. (Col. 3:8)

When one reads enough of these lists, it would be easy to conclude that anger is always negative. The casual reader could easily assume that all anger is destructive, like the conflictual, alienating ways of behaving with which it is listed. However, that very context is our clue that the anger being described here is anger that is expressed in ways that are life-destroying to both individuals and the community.

Qualification for Bishops

One concern of the letter to Titus is the qualifications to consider when choosing elders and bishops. A bishop, the author states in 1:7–8,

> must not be arrogant or quick-tempered (ὀργίλον) or addicted to wine or violent or greedy for gain; but he must be . . . self-controlled.

As with the Wisdom literature mentioned earlier, this description is not of a person who is never angry, but a person who is not "quick-tempered," but "self-controlled." Arrogant people often get angry when their worldview is challenged and people who are out of control can become "violent," so the qualifications are for mature persons who are not easily threatened and don't lose control. Other descriptive words such as "a lover of goodness" and "prudent" (v. 8) suggest that a person qualified for leadership in the church is insightful about when to be threatened, what to be angry about, and how to behave when angry.

James

Another New Testament verse interpreted to mean that anger is always a bad thing, inappropriate for Christian living, is James 1:19–20:

> You must understand this, my beloved: let everyone be quick to listen, slow to speak, slow to anger (ὀργήν); for your anger (ὀργὴ) does not produce God's righteousness.

To interpret this verse as suggesting that all anger is negative misses the context of these words. The admonition to be "slow to anger" obviously does not prohibit all experiences or expressions of anger. Like those passages in Proverbs mentioned earlier, James's concern is focused on *why* we get angry and *how* we express it. Second, we must remember that James is persuading his readers to endure the testing of their faith in order to "be mature and complete" (1:4). They are to ask God for wisdom and to "endure temptation" in order to receive the "crown of life" that God has promised (1:12). He reminds them that each "is tempted by one's own desire, being lured and enticed by it" (1:14). When James addresses "your anger," therefore, he is concerned about anger that is triggered in response to our own immaturity and selfish desires, for that kind of anger does not accomplish God's purposes.

James, then, does not support the anger-is-sin position.[31] These words, rather, are a warning about allowing our own selfish, immature narratives to become threatened, resulting in anger that is motivated by the wrong concerns and, therefore, not in the service of love. James was alluding to a kind of human anger that "bursts forth" thoughtlessly and contributes to alienation rather than reconciliation. This is another way of saying with the author of Ephesians, "Be angry, but do not sin."

Though obviously not an exhaustive study of Scripture, I have demonstrated with key passages that Scripture offers numerous alternative stories to the idea that anger is a "deadly sin." Let me summarize what these passages contribute to a pastoral theology of anger.

CONTRIBUTIONS TO A
PASTORAL THEOLOGY OF ANGER

Are the stories and sayings in Scripture concerned about anger? Definitely. These biblical texts are quite aware of the destructive potential of anger. The story of Cain's murder of Abel is only the first in a long line of stories in both the Hebrew Scripture and the New Testament that chronicle the destructive powers of anger, all of which have been used over the centuries to illustrate the anger-is-sin theology. These stories confirm our own suspicions of and negative experience with anger, yet we must resist the temptation to conclude that anger is a "deadly sin." The biblical stories and observations discussed above challenge the traditional anger-is-sin position when they suggest the following:

Biblical stories and sayings assume that people experience anger, that this is part of the human condition. Hebrew Scripture does not suggest that the capacity for anger is either an aberration within God's original creation or a contradiction of God's intention for human well-being. Cain's anger was not a problem to God. The Bible contains no story in which either God or Jesus suggests that the best people never feel anger. The Ten Commandments contain no prohibition of anger, only of behavior that expresses anger destructively. The Wisdom literature does not argue that the capacity for anger is in itself a problem for persons trying to live a godly life, but only anger that is quick, foolish, and destructive. Jesus himself gets angry, as we see in the next chapter. Ephesians does not argue that the capacity for anger, or that being angry, is a problem, but in fact commands (or at least permits) the believers to whom it was addressed to be angry—though New Testament scholars debate at whom and why.

Certainly the Bible is concerned when anger leads to pain and suffering. Thus the letter to the Ephesians asks readers to put away all expressions of anger that are destructive of relationships (4:31). Scripture is clear that when anger does lead to suffering, it is not because anger itself is automatically destructive, but because the anger has been experienced unnecessarily or expressed harmfully. Concern about the destructive expression of anger is appropriate, but does not offer support for those who argue that the *capacity* for anger is evil and should be eradicated.

Handling anger ethically is the major concern of the biblical stories and sayings. Rather than trying to rid the human condition of anger, Scripture wants to keep anger from being destructive. The biblical authors spend their energy warning us about the dangers of being angry and the potential for evil when anger goes bad. Furthermore, the biblical material focuses on the ethics of being accountable for why we are angry and the responsibility for creatively expressing anger. All of us know how easy sinning is when we are angry. The basic concern of Scripture is not with being angry, but with angry feelings that are expressed with abusive, destructive behavior.

"Am I responsible for my brothers and sisters?" is a key question in the Cain and Abel narrative. The story's answer is "yes," illustrating that being responsible with our anger is necessary for this task. As an example of personal choice, which is at the heart of the "fall from grace" narrative in Genesis 3, Cain had the choice to "master" sin, which was seeking to take advantage of the vulnerability that comes with being angry. Cain, however, allowed sin to "master" him and killed his brother, obviously not a caring response. Another option for anger is using it to protect and defend our sisters and brothers. To suppress all anger keeps us from using our anger in responsible ways, as explored in chapter 12.

Jesus warns us not to let anger become destructive to relationships and, in fact, is himself an example that fully human persons experience anger. As New Testament scholar Luke Johnson says, "Jesus did not condemn our physical beings as created by God, but the diseases of our freedom."[32] Ephesians is clear in its command of Christians that they "do not sin" with their anger. In short, Scripture accepts anger as part of our embodied existence, part of what God brought into being, rather than some aspect of our existence that was somehow added by the Adversary. I cannot find a Scripture passage that considers anger to be a part of the human condition that should be, or could be, completely eliminated in order for us to become more like God intended.

A summary of the passages examined in this chapter could state that the

Bible is not focused on eradicating the internal *experience* of anger, our capacity for anger, but on *why* we get angry and how to creatively handle the *expression* of anger. The basic concern is not with our capacity for anger, but with allowing anger to become destructive rather than using it for creative purposes. Now we move to a discussion of anger as experienced by Jesus and by God.

9

The Anger of God and Jesus

The inclusion of anger in the list of Seven Deadly Sins seems particularly odd, given the fact that both God and Jesus are described in the Bible as being angry. What does that mean about the character and activity of God and Jesus? Does that mean they sinned? It would be difficult to find a theologian who would argue for that conclusion, but the implication seems obvious. We have three basic choices on the subject. First, we could conclude that the Bible is inaccurate and misleading in its depiction of both God and Jesus experiencing and expressing anger—and choose to believe that God, if not Jesus, is impassive and immutable. Second, we could take Scripture literally and draw one of two conclusions: (1) that God's anger was/is always justified because God is Holy and righteous, or (2) that God was an abuser, a perpetrator of injustice. Third, the position for which I argue, we can accept that God and Jesus, who are loving, compassionate, and committed to justice, actually did feel and express anger, but only in the service of love.

Understanding the anger of God and Jesus as described in Scripture is integral to any attempt to construct a pastoral theology of anger for the Christian community. In this chapter, therefore, I explore the scriptural references to anger in the life experience of Jesus and the activity of God, reflect on the nature of threat in these experiences, discuss the relationship of anger and love, and draw conclusions about how this discussion informs the pastoral theology of anger that I construct in chapter 10.

WAS GOD ANGRY?

We established in chapter 2 that the sacred texts of the Judeo-Christian tradition portray a God who experiences emotion. Though later theologians argued that God was immovable, both the ancient Hebrews and the early Christians experienced God as Person and assigned to God personal characteristics, including emotions. In Scripture, God is often pictured as a passionate Being, characterized primarily by compassion for the poor, the dispossessed, the displaced, and those victimized by the rich and powerful. Scripture clearly and frequently describes God as having the capacity for experiencing anger and the willingness to express it.

References to God's anger in the Old Testament are numerous, and the circumstances in which God is angry are quite diverse. Even a quick reading of the Hebrew Bible makes it clear that the Hebrew people knew a God who could be angered. Their sacred texts (our Old Testament) frequently refer to God's potential for anger and are filled with specific instances of God's anger. In many stories, to disobey and break the covenant brings the wrath of God. In Judges "the anger of the LORD was kindled against Israel" (Judg. 2:14). Jeremiah hears God discuss the idolatry of the people and say that these actions "provoke me to anger" (7:18), and then God says "My anger and my wrath shall be poured out on this place, on human beings and animals . . . ; it will burn and not be quenched" (7:20). Jeremiah asked God to "correct me" but "not in your anger" (Jer. 10:24).

The Israelites describe in a variety of ways their relationship to a God who has the capacity for anger. They are afraid when God's anger is directed at them and ask for mercy: "O LORD, do not rebuke me in your anger, or discipline me in your wrath" (Ps. 6:1). At other times, they lobby God to direct anger at their enemies: "Rise up, O LORD, in your anger . . ." (Ps. 7:6). They can enjoy picturing God toying with their oppressors before expressing anger: "He who sits in the heavens laughs. . . . Then he will speak to them in his wrath, and terrify them in his fury . . ." (Ps. 2:4–5). In Hebrew Scripture, God's nature certainly includes the capacity for anger, and this anger is expressed on numerous occasions.

References to God's anger in the New Testament are less numerous and less obvious. The author of Ephesians writes, "And do not grieve the Holy Spirit of God" (Eph. 4:30), which is usually understood to mean, don't make the Holy Spirit sad or sorrowful. However, the Greek translated "do not grieve" (μὴ λυπεῖτε) has many shades of meaning—sadness, disappointment, frustration, or irritation—that are present in such an experience.[1] We know from our own experience, as well as psychological research, how frequently we experience both sadness and anger toward the same event or circumstance. A person whose partner is dying of lung cancer can be both sad about the coming death and angry at him for continuing to smoke two packs a day. Thus this phrase can also be interpreted "do not provoke" or "do not irritate" and could mean "do not anger the Holy Spirit of God." If the author of Ephesians intended this translation of the word, this passage would suggest that the Holy Spirit of God can experience anger. The fact that translators are hesitant to make such a choice might be one of the ways the dominant anger-is-sin narrative has subjugated an alternative story.

The author of Hebrews reminds readers that God had said, "Therefore I was angry with that generation" (3:10), and identifies the Israelites who followed Moses out of Egypt as the culprits (3:16). To demonstrate the intensity of this anger the author quotes God, who says, "As in my anger I swore, 'They will not enter my rest'" (3:11; 4:3). Then the author urges the brothers and sisters not to "have an evil, unbelieving heart that turns away from the living God" (3:12) in order to avoid landing in the same situation as the Israelites "with whom [God] was . . . angry forty years" (3:17). God apparently can be provoked to anger by "disobedience" (4:6, 11), "an evil, unbelieving heart" (3:12), "the deceitfulness of sin" (3:13), hardened hearts (3:15), and rebelliousness (3:16).

New Testament Christology also speaks indirectly of God's potential to be angry. When Philip asks Jesus, "Lord, show us the Father," the answer from Jesus is, "Whoever has seen me has seen the Father" (John 14:8–9). The image of God's nature is reflected in Jesus. Given that Jesus felt anger, as we will establish below, then God must also feel anger.

So, what about God's anger? Most Christians are familiar with the term "God's wrath" or "the wrath of God."[2] Because of the intensity of the word "wrath," and the images of barely controlled rage or uncontrolled fury the word brings to mind, many think of it as contradictory to images of a loving God. I discuss in chapter 2 that many theologians have argued that God was impassible, immutable, and passionless—one reason being that a wrathful God seemed so contradictory to their basic experience of God's love. Through the ages, however, many theologians have taken the scriptural descriptions as accurate portrayals and tried to address the issue of "the wrath of God."[3] Some viewed God's wrath as a basic aspect of God's nature and, therefore, equal to love. Chambers, for example, argues that, "God is a wrathful God of love and jealousy,"[4] a description that seems to make wrath a more basic characteristic of God than love. Others have imagined that anger and love are "twin passions"[5] that exist simultaneously in God's nature.

Indeed, says Paul Tillich, some theologians have suggested what appears to be a schizophrenic split in the nature of God.[6] On the one hand, he argues, they say God is love, and on the other hand they say that God is wrathful. In some theories of atonement, Christ's death on the cross is seen as necessary to appease God's wrath, which has been provoked by humanity's sinfulness. According to this scenario, somebody has to be sacrificed to "satisfy" God's wrath. Thus Jesus is viewed as the substitute for all humanity, sacrificed to pay the penalty and allow God's love to be victorious over God's wrath. The perception of love and wrath as somewhat equal but opposing attributes of God's nature establishes the need for this sacrificial view of atonement, as if God's love must constantly work to overcome God's wrath.

I do *not* believe that wrath is an attribute of God's nature equal to, and in opposition to, God's love. The statement "God is love" (1 John 4:8) seems to be a description of a characteristic, foundational aspect of God's being. There is no equivalent "God is wrath." I agree that the *capacity* for anger is part of God's nature, but I believe that it is secondary to love and rooted in compassion. God's wrath is *not equal* to God's love, but is *an expression* of God's love. I agree with Tillich when he describes God's anger as "the emotional symbol for the work of love," rather than some affect of God that exists "alongside his love" or as "a motive for action alongside providence."[7] Literal interpretation of some Scripture leads some to think of God as violent and abusive. I believe, however, that God's anger is always expressed in ultimately constructive ways that serve God's primary attribute of love. Anger and love are not opposites in God's nature, nor in ours as beings created in God's image.

WAS GOD ABUSIVE?

We must acknowledge that the expression of God's anger as occasionally interpreted by the ancient Hebrews and recorded in their Scripture is a theological problem. Some of these narratives contain horrific stories about God's anger that have been interpreted to portray God as an abuser,[8] ordering the murder of innocent women and children, for example. I need to explore briefly how these stories reflect on our inquiry about God's anger. Let's look at the complex and disturbing picture of God's anger that emerges from a few of these narratives.

Sometimes God's wrath is manifested in severe and what can only be termed *excessive* punishment. In 2 Samuel 24, for example, an already angry God incites David to take a census of the people, an act of disobedience to the law that will demand punishment. David obeys, but is later heartbroken that he has sinned in such a way. The penalty God imposes for an act that *God* incited David to commit in the first place is indeed great: "So the LORD sent a pestilence on Israel . . . and seventy thousand of the people died" (v. 15). Even if this number is not accurate, it surely indicates a punishment out of all proportion to the sin committed. Furthermore, God is pictured as trapping David into acting in such a manner that he has to be punished.

In Numbers 16, when the people were in rebellion, the Lord made it clear to Moses and Aaron that the "whole congregation" was about to be "consumed in a moment" for its disobedience. Moses quickly ordered Aaron to make an atoning action because "wrath has gone out from the LORD" (v. 46). Because Aaron obeyed quickly, the Lord killed *only* fourteen thousand seven hundred people, including women and children. These stories about God's wrath may have influenced the early church's interpretation of the death of Ananias and Sapphira in Acts 5. There Luke, after describing how the early community of believers shared their possessions, reports that when Ananias and Sapphira are confronted by Peter for holding back a portion for themselves, they immediately fall down and die. Whatever the rest of the story, some early Christians drew the conclusion that, in response to their deceit, God had enacted the most severe judgment.

In the prophetic literature, God is at times portrayed as an angry, abusive husband, with Israel as what we would call the battered wife.[9] In one particularly violent passage in Ezekiel, God gathers Israel's enemies against her to sexually abuse and beat her violently:

> Thus says the Lord GOD, Because your lust was poured out and your nakedness uncovered in your whoring with your lovers, and because of all your abominable idols . . . I will gather all your lovers . . . against you from all around, and will uncover your nakedness to them, so that they may see all your nakedness. I will judge you as women who commit adultery and shed blood are judged, and bring blood upon you in wrath and jealousy. I will deliver you into their hands, and they shall throw down your platform and break down your lofty places; they shall strip you of your clothes and take your beautiful objects and leave you naked and bare. They shall bring up a mob against you, and they shall stone you and cut you to pieces with their swords. . . . So I will satisfy my fury on you. . . . (Ezek. 16:36–42)

What are we to do with these stories that depict God in such a disturbing way?[10] Many nuanced approaches to understanding these stories are available, but for my purposes here I put them into two categories: (1) the stories are misunderstood and inaccurate and (2) the stories are literally true. Then I offer my own understanding.

The Narratives Are Misunderstood

Many theologians through the centuries have doubted that these narratives are accurate portrayals of either God's character or activity. We saw in chapter 2 that many theologians have rejected the idea of a God who experiences any emotion, especially anger. Saint Augustine, John Cassian, and other early theologians believed that God is immutable, holding that God remains transcendent and unchangeable. Cassian, as you remember from chapter 7, held that it was blasphemous to believe that God felt anger. Irenaeus maintained that God "needs nothing and is self-sufficient."[11] Indeed, historical theologian J. K. Mozley asserts, "It never occurred to Irenaeus to look for any archetype of human possibility in the divine nature."[12] Clement of Alexandria agreed, several times describing "God's freedom from everything emotional" and maintaining that in every instance when anger is ascribed to God, its meaning is allegorical.[13] Origen held that "the wrath of God is an expression which ought not to be taken as implying the presence of any passion in God."[14] In fact, he believed that God is "wholly impassible" and "altogether separated from every affection of passion and change, and remains unmoved and unshaken forever on that peak of blessedness."[15] Twentieth-century thinkers have taken similar positions. Though not based in notions of God's complete immutability, they do suggest that negative emotions such as anger are too irrational or too anthropomorphic to be believed about God.[16]

Other scholars maintain that what we call God's anger is a projection of our own unacceptable rage. This perspective argues that in order to rationalize their own anger the Israelites, as expressed by the Old Testament writers, chose to believe that God ordered the massacres, the slaughter of tens of thousands of innocent persons. Separating "national interests" from God's directives is difficult, and history is full of horrific events in which tribes and nations assume that what they do out of self-interest must be blessed by God. I am writing this book during the post–September 11 war against terrorism and under the constant gaze of "God Bless America" signs, which express for many the idea that our war effort is supported by God. On the other side, Muslim extremists in Afghanistan and Palestinian suicide bombers believe that their God blesses, and even demands, such behavior.

Other theologians have argued that projections of wrathful behavior onto God represent human attempts to come to terms with inexplicable evil and suffering. When confronted with tragedy that cannot be rationally explained, some people have assumed that the reasons lie in the activity of their gods. Certainly in the Judeo-Christian tradition one answer to the question, "Why did this happen to me?" has been to blame "it" on an angry God who is meting out punishment for some sin or presenting a "test of faith."[17]

The Literalist Response

A second category of response is from those who take the stories to be literally true. These scholars observe that interpreting these biblical stories as simple human projection of our own angry feelings onto God, or our anxiety surrounding the issues of suffering and evil, discounts the biblical witness. Because Scripture speaks of God's anger or wrath so frequently, they believe that such a perspective psychologizes faith and denies a major source of our authority for speaking of God at all. David Blumenthal, for example, argues:

> [We] cannot understand God (or ourselves) if we censor out what we do not like, or what we would like not to see. The texts on God's abusiveness are there. To censor them out because they are not "ethical" is to limit our understanding of the complexity of human and divine existence.[18]

People who take the narratives seriously as sources of revelation often choose to think that God's anger is always a response to sin. These interpreters suggest that people who suffered as a result of God's wrath deserved it, whether the reason is apparent or not. Job's friends considered this interpretation as the primary reason for Job's suffering (Job 4:7; 8:5–6; 11:6). The disciples assumed this theology when asking Jesus whose sin caused the man's blindness (John 9:2).

Such literal interpretations of God's wrath put a positive spin on the excessive punishment, but Blumenthal maintains that these scriptural accounts of God's wrath, when combined with the fact that profound evil continues to occur in a world under the providence of God, lead him to conclude that God is often an abuser. Blumenthal is obviously correct that these stories, as included in the canon of our sacred texts, indicate by our standards that the wrath of God is at times out of all proportion to the offenses committed. He is also accurate in pointing out the problem inherent in holding *both* to the providence of God—the idea that God is omnipotent and willing to use that power—*and* to the reality of evil in the world. If God is loving and powerful, why doesn't God move against evil and, for example, stop genocide and child abuse (both of which he explores at length)? These questions are disturbing, but Blumenthal's conclusion that God must be an abuser is only one interpretive option. Before exploring other alternatives, let me very briefly present his arguments.

Blumenthal begins by asserting that God is personal, meaning that we can rightly assign personality and character traits to God. God is neither impassible nor immutable. Against those who argue that any language we use for God is inadequate to the task—at most allowing us to say simply that "God is"—Blumenthal maintains that Scripture, tradition, and our own religious experience all support the use of personalist language about God. He further asserts that one aspect of personality that we can attribute to God is the capacity for anger: God does get angry. God's anger, according to Blumenthal, occurs at two times: when humans break the covenant with God and when humans sin. Blumenthal is in line with the tradition, based in large measure on the testimony of Scripture, that God cannot be indifferent to wrongdoing. Some theologies say that God permits the consequences of sin to overwhelm us, while others maintain that God actively punishes us for our sins. Either way, he says, God is angry because we have broken our covenant with God.

Blumenthal's main concern, however, is not that God becomes understandably angry at our sin (a righteous anger), but that God also experiences an anger born of bitterness—an anger that moves toward vengeance, so malicious that it is out of all proportion to the sin committed. Such anger is abusive, and we do not deserve it. Blumenthal maintains that because God loves passionately and expects great things from humanity, this kind of anger is also understandable, even appropriate.[19] His argument rests on three points. First, to assume that believing God is Person enables us to believe logically that the extremes of emotion and personality traits in humanity also exist in God.[20] Second, the experience of the Holocaust and of child abuse in families, in tandem with taking the doctrine of God's providence seriously, opens the way for us to conceive of God as abuser.[21] Third, the texts support this idea.[22]

Though agreeing with Blumenthal that God loves passionately, I disagree that God's love functions destructively, even demonically. My disagreement is based on my belief that God's anger is rooted in God's perfect love, a love that always expresses itself in ethical behavior, not in destructive reaction. One reason God's anger is not violent is that God loves the perpetrator and oppressor as well as the victim. The excessive violence noted in some biblical stories is by our own ethical criteria a nonloving action. If ethical concern at the human level can choose to act out anger nonviolently (see Mahatma Gandhi and Martin Luther King Jr.), then arguing that God could not control anger, letting it become murderous rage, is hard to imagine. Beyond these examples is the life and work of Jesus, the brief record of which does not record expressions of anger that were destructive to innocent life, despite the many opportunities Jesus had to let anger turn into rage, vengeance, and violence.

Now I turn to another alternative, one arising from the conviction that, while something about human behavior evokes God's anger, that anger is grounded in, and in the service of, God's love.

WHY WAS GOD ANGRY? AN EXPRESSION OF LOVE!

Starting with the ideas from chapter 2 that God is personal and that God does feel and express what anthropomorphic language calls anger, the next question is, "Why does God get angry?" As I noted in chapter 5, anger is an arousal

pattern that occurs in response to a perceived threat to the self and is characterized by the desire to attack or defend. Does the "threat model" of understanding anger offer any understanding of God's anger?

Can God Be Threatened?

I have argued that God gets angry, which according to the threat model suggests that God can feel threatened. To some people this statement can make
God seem weak. Popular concepts that reflect our own (largely masculine) ideology describe God as all-knowing and all-powerful, which makes thinking of
a threatened God difficult, because we don't like to consider God as vulnerable. In our androcentric society viewing fear as a weakness is common, so our
projecting this perspective onto God is hardly surprising. But love by its very
nature is vulnerable to hurt, to rejection, to ridicule, to being ignored. Thinking of God as love allows us to realize that God is vulnerable and, therefore,
can be threatened by human actions.

In chapter 6 I used constructionist narrative concepts to describe how a person decides what is threatening. To know why a person becomes threatened,
we need to understand the values, meanings, and commitments incorporated
into that person's narratives. To say that God has narratives may sound too
anthropomorphic, but the Judeo-Christian tradition has believed from the
beginning that God has values and desires to which God is committed. These
values are expressed in covenants that direct God's desires, plans, and hopes
for the creation and explain God's actions. One way the early Christian apologists distinguished their Creator God from the popular gods of Greek culture was to argue that the God of Jesus Christ had consistent covenants,
grounded in steadfast love for the creation. They argued, furthermore, that
God's covenants were constant, both informing and reflected in God's actions,
responses, and relationships.

God's Anger Rooted in Love

Why would God get angry? From a faith perspective, the answer begins in the
context of love, God's most fundamental character trait. Steadfast love is a
basic aspect of God's character in the Hebrew Scripture:

> But the steadfast love of the LORD is from everlasting to everlasting
> on those who fear him.
>
> (Ps. 103:17)

> As a father has compassion for his children,
> so the LORD has compassion for those who fear him.
>
> (Ps. 103:13)

God's desire to be in relationship with the creation, particularly with humans who are created in God's very image, is expressed as desire for our well-being. God is quoted by Jeremiah as saying,

> For surely I know the plans I have for you, says the LORD, plans for
> your welfare and not for harm, to give you a future with hope.
> (Jer. 29:11)

Because God loves the creation, God gets angry "on behalf of" the victims, the poor, and the downtrodden. God expresses anger by advocating for the oppressed. After describing God's love as seeking, restorative, tender, and empowering, Ezekiel is clear about God's anger at those who had the resources to help, but instead betrayed others by neglecting or exploiting them:

> I will seek the lost, and I will bring back the strayed, and I will bind up
> the injured, and I will strengthen the weak, but the fat and the strong
> I will destroy. I will feed them with justice. (Ezek. 34:16)

I am reminded by this of the shepherd image for God in Psalm 23. This shepherd metaphor for God includes the capacity for being angry "in defense of."[23] Shepherds were not passive in their care of flocks. When the flocks were threatened by wild animals or human poachers, we can assume that the shepherds were threatened on behalf of the sheep. They would have become angry at those who would try to harm the flock, and would have been energized to protect them.

The psalmist notes that both gentleness and compassion are two characteristics of love that guide God's anger. Love keeps God's anger from being either spontaneously violent or chronically bitter. Love is the dominant characteristic of God's nature:

> Yahweh is tender and compassionate,
> slow to anger, most loving;
> his indignation does not last for ever,
> his resentment exists a short time only.
> (Ps. 103:8–9, JB)

Similarly the New Testament identifies love as God's most basic characteristic: "God is love" (1 John 4:8). This foundational, all-encompassing aspect of God's nature is the basis for God's emotional and behavioral responses toward creation. John's perception that it was because "God so loved the world that he gave his only Son" (3:16) has been central to the church's understanding of the Christ event. The incarnation, God's coming to be with us in Jesus Christ, demonstrated how deeply God cares for us.

Because God's love is heavily invested in the creation, that love becomes threatened when an aspect of the creation is being hurt or when God's desires for the creation are neglected. Thus we may conceptualize God's anger as a response to threats to those in whom God is invested, and for whom he desires abundant life. Scripture is clear, for example, that God becomes particularly angry in response to injustice against the helpless: widows, orphans, and other needy and oppressed persons. So when humans relate to other humans in ways that are abusive, oppressive, and painful, then God's fully invested and committed love is threatened, and God gets angry. The psalmist says, "The LORD works vindication and justice for all who are oppressed" (Ps. 103:6). When individuals or systems violate and victimize any aspect of creation, then God's love is threatened by that behavior and reacts in anger. This is nowhere more powerfully or poetically summarized than in the words of C. S. Lewis, "Anger is the fluid that love bleeds when you cut it."[24] In summary, God's anger is not the opposite of God's love, but results as an expression of God's love.

I maintain that love is God's primary attribute. But what does this really mean? I mentioned above that for many people, the idea of a God-Who-Is-Love must be protected from anything negative, convinced that love excludes anger. Paul Tillich has written that God's love is always a movement toward wholeness and unity, including the process of reuniting that which is separated within us and between us.[25] God's anger at that which causes the brokenness is an expression of anger in the service of love, even as that love is mending our fragmented lives and the life of the world itself.

From our personal experiences of loving we know that love always carries within it a certain vulnerability. We are heavily invested in those we love and may feel acutely threatened when either a person or a relationship is endangered in some way. Given God's passionate commitment to us, perhaps we can say that God also feels threatened and responds in anger when we behave in ways that perpetrate injustice against God's people or trivialize our relationship with the Creator. We see this in the life of Jesus, and to that expression of anger we now turn.

JESUS' ANGER

Basic to the Christian tradition is the belief that Jesus was fully human. In the last century debate about the nature of Jesus' divinity has taken place, but little question about his humanity—though the specifics of what we can know about it are uncertain.[26] I demonstrated in chapter 2 that Jesus' early followers experienced him as fully capable of emotion, including anger. As with God's anger, given my definition that anger occurs when we perceive that some event or circumstance is threatening to the values and meanings embedded in our narratives, then I need to offer an understanding of how Jesus was threatened. The Gospel narratives present Jesus as a person alive with vibrant feelings, capable of reacting strongly to pain, injustice, hypocrisy, the death of a friend, and "sin" in his world; perhaps these values are the ones contained in his faith narratives. Now I want to explore more specifically what Scripture can teach us about Jesus and anger.

First, however, I want to point out evidence in the Gospel stories of the early church's emerging ambivalence about Jesus' anger, reminding us of the influence of Stoic philosophy and ascetic theology (flesh vs. spirit) on the early church (see chapters 2 and 7). Even though the Gospel writers allow us to see Jesus feeling emotion, the suspicion of emotions—particularly of negative emotions such as anger—had surfaced in the church by the time the Gospels of Matthew and Luke were written. This development in the theology of the church is illustrated in the decisions of Matthew and Luke not to acknowledge Jesus' emotions. We can see in two examples how Jesus' anger as portrayed by Mark, which is accepted by most scholars as the earliest Gospel, was deleted by the time Matthew and Luke were written.

The first example is the healing of the man with the withered hand, an event in which Jesus challenged the Pharisees' perceptions of the sabbath. Jesus asks them, "Is it lawful to do good . . . on the sabbath . . . " (Mark 3:4; see also Matt. 12:12–14; Luke 6:9–11). Receiving no answer, Jesus makes a request of the man, "Stretch out your hand," and when the man does so his hand is healed. All three Gospels record this incident, but only Mark's Gospel records Jesus' feelings: "He looked around at them with anger; he was grieved at their hardness of heart" (Mark 3:5). Matthew 12:12–14 and Luke 6:9–11 leave out the description of anger so that the story reads as if Jesus had no emotional response to this situation.

A second example is seen in the story of the disciples keeping the children from Jesus (Matt. 19:13–14; Mark 10:14; Luke 18:15–16). Again, all three Synoptic Gospels tell of the children being brought to Jesus so that he might touch them. All describe the disciples rebuking the adults who were presenting the children and record Jesus' response, "Let the little children come to me; do not stop them . . ." (Mark 10:14). Only Mark, however, prefaces these words by describing Jesus' feelings: "But when Jesus saw this, he was indignant" (Mark 10:14). Matthew 19:13–14 and Luke 18:15–16 leave out these emotionally charged words.

Perhaps the choice of Matthew and Luke to leave out the angry words is another example of how the dominant anger-is-sin tradition subjugated the alternative narrative.[27] It may also have reflected the growing influence of Stoicism, as described in chapter 7, which did not think of anger as a virtue. For a Stoic to portray Jesus as angry, as Mark does, would have been to deny his heroic qualities. As John Fitzgerald says, "If a Stoic such as Seneca had read Mark, he would not think Jesus sinless."[28] Having noted this evolution in the early church's acceptance of emotions, I now return to these and other stories seeking what we may learn of Jesus' experience of anger, the reasons he became angry, and the way he expressed this anger.

Anger at the Legalists

As I described above, the Gospel of Mark reports that Jesus was angry when he confronted the Pharisees concerning whether or not it was appropriate to heal on the Sabbath:

> Again he entered the synagogue, and a man was there who had a withered hand. They watched him to see whether he would cure him on the sabbath, so that they might accuse him. And he said to the man who had the withered hand, "Come forward." Then he said to them, "Is it lawful to do good or to do harm on the sabbath, to save life or to kill?" But they were silent. He looked around at them with anger; he was grieved at their hardness of heart and said to the man, "Stretch out your hand." He stretched it out, and his hand was restored. (Mark 3:1–5)

There is no question here about what was going on inside Jesus as he looked around at the Pharisees, for when Mark describes the emotion Jesus was feeling, he uses the Greek word ὀργή—the word for anger most commonly used in the New Testament. It cannot be translated in any other way than as anger. Note the connection of grief with anger, as discussed earlier in this chapter (Eph. 4:30). In Mark 3:5, the Greek word is συλλυπούμενος, meaning to be grieved, pained, distressed, and sad, but also annoyed.

How was Jesus threatened? We imagine that his narratives about religious leaders would include the expectation that they would have deeper insight into the tradition they represented, and more wisdom about the foundational desires of God for how believers should function. Perhaps he had the unambiguous descriptions of what God desired written by Amos and Micah as they informed his own narratives about righteousness and justice. Perhaps these religious leaders were concerned with legalistic rules and regulations that seemed to prevent appropriate response to human need, and such priorities were a threat to Jesus' values. Perhaps their failure to raise love and grace over law, despite their supposed study of the Scriptures, triggered his anger.

Indignation on Behalf of the Children

Mark's story that tells of Jesus' frustration with the disciples when they tried to keep parents from bringing children into his presence was also mentioned above.

> People were bringing little children to him in order that he might touch them; and the disciples spoke sternly to them. But when Jesus saw this, he was indignant and said to them, "Let the little children come to me; do not stop them; for it is to such as these that the kingdom of God belongs." (Mark 10:13–14)

When I think of this story, I imagine Jesus sitting on a rock, resting against a small tree. He has just concluded a time of teaching and children have gathered around, standing by his shoulder, sitting on his knee and asking the kind of questions children ask. As was the custom of the day, small children and infants are being handed to him in order to receive his blessing. Suddenly, out of the corner of his eye, Jesus becomes aware of a cluster of people speaking with raised voices. Paying closer attention, he hears his disciples rebuking the adults, ordering them to keep the children away. When he became aware of their behavior, he became "indignant." The Greek word ἠγανάκτησεν translated as "indignant" means to feel irritated and annoyed, discontented, a word that clearly conveys Jesus' anger at his disciples.

What was the threat Jesus experienced? I can imagine that he had a story about the value of the children and appreciation for those adults who had recognized the validity of his message and were thoughtfully attending to their children's religious instruction. Perhaps he was threatened that the disciples evidently had not grasped the value he placed on "the little ones" and the insightful adults. I can also imagine that Jesus hoped that by this point in time his disciples would have understood his values and mission. Perhaps that they continued to misunderstand who he was and what he was about was threatening.

Anger in the Temple

The story of Jesus confronting the money-changers and "cleansing the temple" also challenged the Gospel writers' concept of emotions. Compare the brief, bland accounts in the Synoptic Gospels (Matt. 21:12–13; Mark 11:15–17; Luke 19:45–46) with the intensity and detail in the Gospel of John. Of the four accounts of this event, John's Gospel, the last one written,[29] uses the most emotionally charged language to describe the turmoil, including the evident aggression of Jesus' actions:

> The Passover of the Jews was near, and Jesus went up to Jerusalem. In the temple he found people selling cattle, sheep, and doves, and the money changers seated at their tables. Making a whip of cords, he drove all of them out of the temple, both the sheep and the cattle. He also poured out the coins of the money changers and overturned their tables. He told those who were selling the doves, "Take these things out of here! Stop making my Father's house a marketplace!" (John 2:13–16)

The fury of his words and the obvious force of his physical presence were burned into the disciples' minds. The disciples, amazed at his intensity, were reminded of the psalmist (69:9) who wrote, "Zeal for your house will consume me" (John 2:17).

Can anyone read this account and doubt that Jesus was angry? Jesus' narratives probably included the value his tradition placed on worship in the Temple and of worshipers being treated with fairness as they expressed their devotion. Why should we be surprised that Jesus would be threatened by the money-changers who were making a mockery of worship, insulting God, and profiting from the law? Jesus was indignant at the injustice and acted prophetically, challenging the way in which worship had turned into a money-making endeavor. The Bible often describes God's anger in the face of human injustice, but many biblical interpreters seem shocked by Jesus' behavior. Christian ethicist Arthur Gossip has described the result of their discomfort:

> Desperate attempts have been made by some who feel uncomfortable over it to tone it down and edge out this incident . . . because they feel unhappily that it will not fit into their preconceived idea of what Christ should do and be; that here somehow he acted for once out of character, and fell inexplicably below himself, forgot his own law of life, lost his head and his temper.[30]

As I noted earlier, even the writers of the Synoptic Gospels may have been uncomfortable with Jesus' emotion and action. None of the emotion and passion behind the story is revealed in their accounts. In their words Jesus simply entered the temple, overturned tables and seats, and drove out those who bought and sold, reminding the people that God's house was a house of prayer. Yet it is hard to imagine the tables and seats of profit-makers being overturned and buyers and sellers being driven out without impassioned, forceful action.

Garden of Gethsemane

I describe in chapter 2 how the Gospel writers pictured Jesus' anxiety when he went out to pray before his arrest, but I think he also expressed anger toward the disciples who accompanied him. Jesus invited several of the disciples to go with him further into the garden in this critical and stressful time. Then he asked them to keep watch while he went alone to pray, but, insensitive to Jesus' anxiety and probably oblivious of the events that were about to unfold, they fell asleep. When Jesus returned several times and found them napping he confronted their unfaithfulness: "Simon, are you asleep? Could you not keep awake one hour?" (Mark 14:37).

I can imagine that, being fully human, Jesus' stories about friendship included their willingness to be steadfast in their support during a crisis. Imagine how disappointing and frustrating for Jesus to need the sustaining presence of close friends as he faced hard, life-threatening political realities—then three times to find that they were unable to stand with him. They had bragged that they would be with him whatever happened, but failed in their promise. Perhaps he was grieved and angry, as with the Pharisees in the earlier story about the man with the withered hand, and expressed this angry disappointment to the disciples.

Words from the Cross

Finally, we look at Jesus' experience on the cross. In the garden he had asked God to "remove this cup" (Mark 14:36). He had already suffered the lashes and the crown of thorns at the hands of the Roman soldiers. He had been nailed cruelly to the cross. Perhaps he was doubting the entire purpose and meaning of his life, wondering whether his whole mission had failed. The excruciating physical pain, perhaps reinforcing his sense of failure, is difficult for most of us to imagine in any depth.

And where was God? We can imagine that Jesus had a narrative that included being saved from this painful, humiliating situation. But death was really happening, and here at the end obviously no legion of angels was coming to the rescue. Well, if not rescued, at least Jesus could have expected to have his work and mission confirmed or affirmed in some manner. But God didn't show up in any discernable way. The same God who had sent angels to herald his birth, who had affirmed this Son's belovedness at baptism and been present at the transfiguration, was now silent, seemingly profoundly absent. Being fully human, Jesus must have felt abandoned and betrayed, left totally alone now by the One who sent him. Isn't the coming of untimely death, along with the sense of being abandoned and betrayed, significantly threatening? And in response to these threats, did Jesus not express anger, along with confusion and fear, when he "cried out with a loud voice, . . . 'My God, my God, why have you forsaken me'" (Matt. 27:46; Mark 15:34; quoting Ps. 22:1)?

Other Experiences of Anger

While there is not unanimous agreement about the emotional content of other stories, the context and the language easily suggest the presence of anger. The reader who accepts Jesus as fully human, completely incarnated, and takes time to enter the stories, ponder the scene, hear the dialogue, and empathically imagine personal reactions to such situations will find other instances of

Jesus' anger. What emotions might we experience if we were present to hear Jesus say to Herod's messenger, "Go and tell that fox . . ." (Luke 13:32)? How might we perceive him if we had been present when he called the Pharisees "whitewashed tombs," "snakes," and "vipers" (Matt. 23:27, 33)? Doesn't the term "rebuked," used to describe Jesus' confrontations with the unclean spirits (Mark 1:25), suggest that he was angry at their destructive behavior? Even Peter, though a trusted disciple, caught an angry response in Jesus' rebuke: "Get behind me, Satan!" (Matt. 16:23).

Most Christians believe that Jesus experienced and represented God's love. Captured in the theology of the early church is the idea that Jesus expressed this love through compassionate action in accordance with God's will:

> The Spirit of the Lord is upon me,
>   because he has anointed me
>   to bring good news to the poor.
> He has sent me to proclaim release to the captives
>   and recovery of sight to the blind,
>   to let the oppressed go free,
>   to proclaim the year of the Lord's favor.
>   (Luke 4:18–19)

Loving as Jesus loves calls for a willingness to experience and express anger. Beverly Wildung Harrison points out that orthodox Christology often pictures the basic meaning of Jesus' life to be his passive march toward crucifixion. She believes that this interpretation is a misreading of the gospel, suggesting that his uniqueness (and the reason for his crucifixion) was in the radical way he pursued mutuality, which included his willingness to confront with his anger.[31] Pursuing this radical mutuality, this quest for caring friendships with his brothers and sisters, made Jesus vulnerable to events that threatened this purpose.

Because of his personal narratives about injustice and his compassionate response to victims, Jesus is torn to the depths of his being by people and groups who suffer and are marginalized. His experiences of irritation, frustration, indignation, and anger all arise when his values are threatened and, therefore, his anger is in the service of his love and God's love.

CONTRIBUTIONS TO A
PASTORAL THEOLOGY OF ANGER

What contributions does this brief look at the anger of God and Jesus make to the construction of a pastoral theology of anger?

God's Anger as Model

God's wrath is not a "thing" that stirs around in God's psyche like a raging lion, a loose cannon that God's love must constantly monitor. Rather, God has the capacity to be angry because God is love. Anger is one of the responses that grows out of and expresses God's love. Because of God's investment in us and our well-being, behaviors that demean, dehumanize, oppress, and cause physical and emotional suffering threaten God. In response to this threat, God feels and expresses anger. This capacity for anger is activated only as an expression of God's love.

Because God gets angry and because we are created in God's image (*imago Dei*), it seems logical that we reflect God's capacity for anger. Reflecting the Personhood of God includes in some mysterious way the emotional, affective aspects of Being. Surely we should accept this capacity as a gift. Furthermore, we must take responsibility for disciplining ourselves so that our capacity for anger is triggered by the same type of events that trigger God's anger: injustice, radical suffering, and oppression (see chapter 12). Through the actions motivated by this compassionate anger, we fulfill our prophetic call to the ministry of reconciliation and liberation.

When Jesus says, "Be compassionate as God is compassionate" (Luke 6:36, Borg), he is "urging us to love as completely as God loves—concretely, wholeheartedly, and universally."[32] The great commandment to "Love the Lord your God . . . and . . . love your neighbor as yourself" (Matt. 22:37–39) includes that we should love our neighbor in the ways that God has loved us. If God's love for us can be threatened by injustice, resulting in anger, surely that serves as a model for our love. We remember that being created in God's image includes the capacity for anger and know that if God's love is expressed through compassion toward the disenfranchised, and on behalf of the oppressed and victimized, and over against those who perpetrate injustice, then those of us who claim to know God should be acting out of this same compassion. As Hans Küng reminds us, Christian love is not "merely a decision of the will" but "also a venture of the heart" and should be marked by "vitality, emotion, [and] affectivity."[33]

Jesus' Anger as Model

The concept of incarnation, God becoming flesh, means that Jesus was fully human. Jesus came in the flesh in the same way that you and I are in the flesh, and therefore experienced all human emotions. From a neurological perspective, Jesus had the same neurological warning system (see chapter 5) that we have—including the capacity for anger. Fear and anger are normal emotional responses when we are faced with threats. The man from Galilee was no exception. If Jesus is our model, shouldn't we, too, feel comfortable with our capacity for anger?

We remember Jesus' love shown in so many stories; we see him as advocate for those who were marginalized: the sick, the weak, the blind, the lame, children, and women. In many of these stories we sense his implicit, if not explicit, anger at those who denied these people their wholeness, and their rightful place in knowing God's love. All these stories point out that to model Christian living after the example of Jesus demands that we be advocates willing to courageously confront those who would overlook any person and deny them their rightful place in the human community. To be an advocate is to become indignant, even angry, on their behalf; to fight for their rights; and to be in defense of, and to campaign for, their well-being.

Reflecting God's compassion expressed toward us through the incarnation, the carpenter from Nazareth says to us, "Love one another as I have loved you" (John 15:12). This statement clearly establishes that the way Jesus loved us should serve as our model for loving others. If we are to love as Jesus loved, then we must also be angry as Jesus was angry—when the values of the gospel are violated. John Stott concludes: "We know that God's anger is righteous. So was the anger of Jesus. There must be a good and true anger which God's people can learn from him and from their Lord Jesus."[34] Being created in God's image with the capacity for anger, and with Jesus as a model, we then also have the capacity for anger and, furthermore, should be threatened by, and angry at, injustice, oppression, and victimization. Anger may arise, indeed *should* arise, within us as Christians *because* of our love, not *in contradiction* to our love. The more deeply we become committed to certain values, the more we may experience threat. Certain values matter to us because of our Christian commitments, and when they are violated by persons or institutions, we are threatened and angry. In these instances to be threatened is appropriate, an expression of our faith narratives. As the psalmist expresses, "Hot indignation seizes me because of the wicked, those who forsake your law" (119:53). If we didn't love, we wouldn't be threatened. Here anger is *not opposed* to love, but *in the service* of love. We return to this issue in chapter 12.

10

Toward a Pastoral Theology of Anger

Now to the central task of constructing a pastoral theology of anger. In the introduction, I described how pastoral theology works on the border between the human sciences and the theological disciplines to develop theological concepts that inform ministry. Consequently, I explored current research in the neurosciences, constructionist narrative theory, biblical narratives, and historical theology to discover what knowledge from these diverse disciplines could contribute to the task. To have discovered alternative theological perspectives in Scripture and within the Christian tradition that challenge the traditional anger-is-sin doctrine makes the task easier. In fact, contrary to popular perceptions, these alternative stories from Scripture and historical theology present a theological understanding of anger that does *not* contradict the central conclusions of the biological and social sciences. In fact, these diverse sources, both in the sciences and the theological disciplines, are remarkably consistent in their understanding of anger and, therefore, what they contribute to the construction of a pastoral theology of anger.

In chapter 3, I said that a pastoral theology of anger "is dependent on, rooted in, and congruent with valid theological perspectives on emotion in general" and then offered theological reflections about emotion derived from a brief examination of philosophical, psychological, neurological, biblical, and theological materials in chapters 1 and 2. In light of those conclusions, plus the theological reflections at the end of previous chapters, I have chosen to focus this construction of a pastoral theology of anger on embodiment; rooting anger in creation, not sin; anger as represented in the *imago Dei*; anger as a gift; anger as a moral issue; our freedom to choose what, when, and how to be angry; and our personal ethical responsibility for anger.

EMBODIMENT

The neurosciences and the social sciences make clear that all emotion, including the capacity for anger, is deeply embedded in our physiology. Anger is not a disembodied psychological event, but, like all emotion, is dependent on our senses for information that our brain interprets, and to which our bodies and minds can respond. The neurological arousal pattern that prepares us for survival has been developing for eons, with some of its earlier roots in the "life force" that expresses initiative, drive, and goal-oriented behavior. Early in our existence as a species, anger was specifically related to protecting our physical existence. The development of all emotion is explained by evolutionary biologists to have an important role in our surviving and thriving as a species—with anger, along with fear, playing a significant role in dealing with danger. Our ancestors needed to be physiologically mobilized for strength and stamina in the face of threats from nature, or they would not have survived.

From a scientific standpoint, emotions are not an instinct, in the technical sense, because they don't arise within us on the basis of an innate biological need. We are neurologically "wired" with the *capacity* for emotional response, but this capacity is only activated when one part of our brain (either the amygdala or the neocortex) interprets a life situation as deserving of a physiologically aroused response. Therefore, a theological discussion of any emotion, including anger, must acknowledge that all emotions are part of our embodiment, rather than a nonphysical entity.

The neocortex/prefrontal lobe has also been developing during our evolutionary history toward our present level of consciousness and cognitive function. Our ability for narrative structuring, by which we construct the values, beliefs, and meanings that form our basic sense of identity, has developed within that process. The "narratory principle," as Theodore Sarbin calls it, rooted in language, and connected to our dialogical interactions within community—is at the center of our functioning as thinking beings.[1] These narratives, when threatened, activate the brain's defensive warning system, and we experience anger. This biological capacity for anger, both in the "feeling brain" and the "thinking brain," is part of our embodied existence, one of God's ways of equipping humans for surviving and thriving.

Because our capacity for anger, both the mental processes involved in narrative structuring and the neurological arousal pattern, is so embedded in our physical nature, a credible theology of anger must be based in a theological anthropology that confirms the significance of embodiment. It is basic to the Judeo-Christian tradition that human existence is totally embodied.[2] Existentialist theologian John Macquarrie points out that "all human life is incarnate; it takes place 'in the flesh,' in the sphere of the material and the spatio-temporal."[3] Even as he admires the significance of self-transcendence and the "soul," Macquarrie reminds us that "however far human beings may have proceeded along the path of transcendence, they take their bodies with them as a permanent heritage from their humble origins in the dust."[4] All that we are as finite creatures, including our capacity for self-transcendence, is interconnected within our embodied existence.

Traditional Christian doctrine claims that Jesus was fully human. He came in the same type of body that you and I have, embodied in the same way we are embodied, and therefore experienced all human emotions—as we clearly saw in the biblical narratives. From a neurological perspective, then, Jesus had the same neurological warning system (see chapter 5) that we have and, therefore, the same capacity for anger. Fear and anger are normal emotional responses when we are faced with threats, and Jesus was no exception. Given that Jesus accepted and expressed his anger, shouldn't we feel comfortable with our capacity for anger?

The Christian concept of incarnation, God becoming flesh, confirms an important truth about embodiment: it was in God's original plan. During Advent, the church remembers that God chose to fully participate in the embodied human condition, thereby blessing embodiment through the physicality of Jesus' conception, birth, life, and death. During the Eucharist/communion, we participate in some manner (depending on theological tradition) in Christ's body and blood. Our entire embodied existence, including our capacity for anger, was of God's design and purposeful implementation.

Emotion, as a dimension of our embodiment, is connected with every other aspect of our finite experience. Theological discourse that separates anger from embodiment expresses a body/mind dualism that is no longer tenable. Recent research in philosophy, the neurosciences, psychology, and the social sciences demonstrates the impossibility of dividing the experience of anger from cognitive interpretations of our environment. We know that emotion and reasoning are involved in mutually influencing interaction, so that thinking and feeling are interrelated functions. To think of them as independent, unrelated aspects of the human condition is no longer possible. Thus a pastoral theology of anger informed by the neurosciences and constructionist narrative theory will affirm the body/mind connection underlying an experience of anger.[5]

Integrating anger into our selfhood is imperative for the psychosomatic unity that is basic to wholistic human functioning. The data support the theological view that our potential as God's creatures is fulfilled when we function as a unified psychosomatic whole, integrating every component of our being. The capacity for emotional experience is a neurological given; attempts to suppress or eradicate anger, as the Stoics and some early monastics attempted, can lead to physical, emotional, relational, and spiritual problems. When leading the church to attempt to excise this capacity from our selfhood, theology must accept some of the responsibility for the disastrous consequences.

ANGER IS ROOTED IN CREATION, NOT IN SIN

The basic conclusion that anger is rooted in our physicality, part of our embodiment, establishes that our capacity for anger is part of the human condition. This capacity is not a recent development, but has been in process during our entire biological history, particularly during the development of the neocortex. The neurosciences and constructionist narrative theory both demonstrate that anger is inherent to our embodied existence, part of our physical makeup that has been building on primitive brain systems for millions of years and did not suddenly appear as if by mutation. All emotion, both "positive" and "negative," is central to our development—our "becoming" as human beings.

Both Scripture and the alternative stories of the theologians agree, concluding that the capacity for anger is an aspect of our humanness that was included in God's purposeful plan for creation. I argue that anger's rootedness in our neurological system, which connects it with how we were brought into being, means that a pastoral theology of anger should anchor itself in the doctrine of creation, not the doctrine of sin. The capacity for anger is a reality of the human condition, part of our embodiment, and can be defended, or even proclaimed, as part of God's intentional creation.

These conclusions challenge the traditional anger-is-sin theology, which suggests that the experience of anger came into human experience at a point in human history when the first humans chose disobedience, often called the "fall."[6] This traditional position assumes that anger is rooted in sin rather than in God's original design. Historically, therefore, anger has been discussed under the doctrine of sin rather than under the doctrine of creation, contributing to the continuation of the anger-is-sin tradition.

Our capacity for anger, however, is part of the way we have evolved, not a negative character trait that developed contrary to God's design. Neither the Genesis stories nor other biblical writings assign our capacity for anger to a postcreation sneak attack by the Adversary. The biblical narratives *do not* portray an idealistic time in human history when people were free from the capacity to experience anger. Scripture does not suggest that the capacity for anger is contradictory to God's intentional creation, nor that godly people should strive to rid themselves of anger.

While never questioning that the capacity for anger is part of human nature, Scripture is concerned with how anger is expressed, and critical of destructive behavior motivated by anger. Certainly the Bible is troubled when emotion leads to pain and suffering as described in chapter 8. Scripture is clear, however, that the anger which leads to suffering, and is all too common in day-to-day living, results from an expression of anger that has become destructive, not from anger that by its nature is destructive.

Those people who identify all experiences of anger as sinful must try to remove this source of sin from their lives if they are to attain some level of "perfection." This is impossible to accomplish and usually results in denying or avoiding anger. Both biological and psychological research demonstrate how potentially harmful repression and suppression are to physical and emotional health as well as to our relationships in community. Heeding the advice of Proverbs not to deny and ignore anger, we realize the wisdom of suggesting that we "be slow to anger" (14:29; 16:32; 19:11).

Neurological and narrative understandings of the self suggest that the capability for emotionality, including anger, is a universal experience, raising the question "Is there anything universal about this pastoral theology of anger?" Human biology/neurology, though affected by life experience, is generally the same across cultures. The neurological arousal pattern and the mental process of narrative structuring are probably the same, suggesting that all humans share the capacity for emotion—including anger—as part of the human condition. Our individual and collective narratives, however, are significantly different because of centuries of different experience and diverse interpretations of that experience, so the etiology of a particular emotion in a specific culture can be quite different. The actual experience of anger by an individual, family, group, or institution can be very different because of the unique individual and cultural narratives that would influence the interpretation of any life situation. The neurological capacity for anger would be triggered by quite different events. In summary, though the capacity for anger is probably the same for all humans (unless inhibited by brain anomalies), the diversity of individual and cultural narratives would mean that those life situations interpreted as a threat would be very different across cultures.

CREATED IN GOD'S IMAGE

Another conclusion connected to Christian beliefs about creation has to do with the *imago Dei*, that is, the creation of humans in God's image. When God first imagined bringing humans into being, according to the first creation story, God decided that they (male and female) would be constructed in the Creator's image: "Let us make humankind in our image, according to our likeness" (Gen. 1:26–27). This amazing idea, though interpreted in numerous ways, makes basic contributions to theological anthropology. The *imago Dei* is a central affirmation of the Christian doctrine of creation and a foundational plank in our understanding of what it means to be human. In some mysterious manner, defined differently in various theological traditions, we carry in our personhood a finite reflection of God's infinite self, not as a "thing" we possess, but as a capacity that we express within community and through relationships.[7]

We established in chapters 2 and 3 that God's nature, as understood in the Judeo-Christian tradition, includes the capacity for feeling emotion.[8] Recognizing the limitations of language, chapter 3 demonstrated that both in Scripture and in many strands of historical theology, God's Being is believed to include what we call emotions. More specifically, as shown in chapter 9, God has the capacity for anger. I argued that God's love has expressed itself through anger when God's narratives (that which God values and desires for creation) are threatened. Concluding from biblical and theological perspectives that the capacity for anger is an aspect of God's Being, part of God's nature, it can be argued that experiencing and expressing anger is part of what is included in the *imago Dei*. In some mysterious way the capacity for anger, like all emotion, is part of the Creator's original plan for human selfhood. Because creation in God's image includes the emotional, affective aspects of being, logically we reflect God's capacity for love and, therefore, the capacity for anger. In chapter 2, moreover, I demonstrated that according to the biblical narratives, Jesus was an emotional person, feeling the entire range of human feelings, including anger. One can assert, then, that as a participant in the Trinity (regardless of how this is defined/described by a particular tradition), Jesus' experience of anger reflects that the capacity for anger is part of the nature of the Godhead.

Referring to the use of language in the creation stories (God *said*, and God *called*), some theologians have used Storyteller as a meaningful metaphor for God. Our neurological capacity for narrative structuring is a reflection of this metaphor, also part of what it means to be created in the image of God. God has the capacity for creating through narrative structure, and we join with God's creative process through our capacity for "storying" the events in our lives. As with the physiological capacity for anger, this ability for narrative structuring, which is a vital part of our capacity for anger, is part of our finite existence that God blessed (Gen. 1:28) and called "good" (Gen. 1:31).

Because God gets angry and because we are created in God's image (*imago Dei*), our reflection of God's capacity for anger seems logical, and the biblical narratives certainly support this. The Bible assumes that anger is part of the created order, an important aspect of our finite (located in space and time), embodied existence and therefore our "imageness." In summation, reflecting the Personhood of God includes in some mysterious enigmatic way the emotional, affective aspects of Being.

Pastoral theology does need to address the question of destructive anger. What about the terrible abuse, violence, terror, murder, and war that can result from anger? Doesn't the reality of these demonic expressions argue for the connection of anger with sin? When reading and watching the daily news reports, one can easily imagine that all anger must be contrary to God's purposes. We can certainly understand why many in the Christian tradition who have been wounded, victimized, and frightened by the power of anger have chosen to believe that anger is one of the Seven Deadly Sins. Like every aspect of embodied existence (cognition, sexuality, hunger, and so forth), the capacity for anger can unquestionably be misused in the service of evil. As we have seen, Scripture is clearly aware of how the experience of anger makes us vulnerable to destructive behavior, to sinning against our neighbors and ourselves. Our own experience confirms this truth.

I argue in the next section that the capacity for anger is one of God's gifts. We often misuse and pervert it, of course, but anger is a gift nonetheless. Our misuse does not change the fact that its purpose is positive: to serve as an alarm signal that warns us when our self is endangered and to prepare us for defending our selfhood, which is precious to the Creator. The Creator has granted us the freedom to decide how to respond with our anger. Despite all the destruction that may result, we must not confuse the destructive expression of anger with the capacity itself. In fact, our capacity for anger motivates our response to evil, including that evil caused by anger expressed destructively.

Perhaps we are evolving toward being more like the image of God by learning to identify our angry responses more quickly and handle them more creatively. In our evolutionary history, our ancestors had to depend on the quickness of the amygdala's interpretation of danger and the activation of the fight/flight physiological arousal pattern in order to survive. Given the freedom we have—the response-ability, so to speak—to monitor and adapt our narratives, perhaps we can contribute to the ongoing creation of our biological and psychological self in ways that allow us to monitor more quickly when physiological arousal is necessary and unnecessary. In this manner, we can contribute to God's steadfast invitation toward peace and wholeness within ourselves and society.

ANGER AS GIFT: BLESSED BY GOD

Recognizing that anger is connected to creation means that God blessed our capacity to feel anger. When God looked over creation, including the embodied female and male beings brought into existence in the final act, God saw "everything" and rejoiced that "it was very good" (Gen. 1:31). "Everything" has to include the visceral, affective, emotional aspects of our existence as embodied creatures. This pastoral theology of anger affirms that the capacity for anger is a positive aspect of our selfhood as confirmed by its inclusion in the original blessing.

All emotions, as described in chapter 3, are necessary for the process of becoming more fully human: significant for establishing identity, comprehending existence as meaningful, committing to values, connecting with other persons and the environment, and participating in the dynamics of religious experience and faith. The capacity for anger, therefore, can be thought of as a gift from God,[9] one of the Creator's endowments that has at least three important purposes. One is the preparation of our minds and bodies for actions that contribute to our physical and psychological survival; second, being able to activate our capacity for anger in the right situations is necessary for our physical, mental, and spiritual health; third is related to the motivation that we need not only to fight for ourselves, but to join God in working for peace and justice, as I describe further in chapter 12.

The theological position that anger is always sinful implies, and in many cases explicitly demands, that humans should and could do away with anger. I concur, of course, that ridding ourselves of *destructive, unethical expressions* of anger is possible—in fact, it is our responsibility to do so, as discussed later. However, the idea that we can rid ourselves of the *capacity* for anger argues for what is physically impossible. Furthermore, such a position denigrates a part of our humanness that God has blessed as good, and discounts all of the positive purposes of responsibly and effectively expressed anger, as I discuss in part 4. Given that we are created in God's image, to suppress, or try to eradicate, this gift from our lives is to deny the *imago Dei*. Even if it were possible from a physiological and psychological perspective, ridding ourselves of this capacity would *not* be a good idea. After discussing ways to reduce pathological expressions of anger, Panksepp writes of the positive and useful aspects of anger and says that we should not forget that "anger, at a cognitive level, may be not only a destructive but a useful force in society," then adds:

> With sufficient depth of personality, the psychic energy of human anger can be diverted into outrageously creative or constructive efforts. Where would we be today if our ancestors had not had the passion to say: "Give me liberty or give me death."[10]

Though Panksepp says that "psychobiology presently has little of importance to say about the many cognitive components of human anger, especially the fiery human energies that help change societies,"[11] plenty of evidence from the biblical narratives and Christian theologians through the ages confirms anger's contribution to ethical action. In fact, I argue in chapter 12 that if Christians *don't* feel threatened and angry in certain circumstances, we must hold ourselves accountable.

Anger always leaves us vulnerable, particularly to sin, which explains the admonition in Ephesians 4:26 not to sin with our anger. But this vulnerability also creates opportunities for hope, courage, intimacy, self-awareness, and compassion, as I discuss in chapters 11 and 12. A pastoral theology, therefore, should recognize and celebrate the significant contribution that anger can make to the process of becoming fully human and strive to defend the basic goodness of our capacity for anger. Like other emotions, the basic purpose of anger is the promotion of life, not its destruction.

ANGER IS A MORAL ISSUE

In the twentieth century, psychology reached a consensus that emotions, including anger, are natural occurrences that are neither good or bad—they just *are*. Because these emotions can lead to either constructive or destructive actions, of course, the mature, healthy approach is to focus on recognizing when they occur and effectively managing the expression of these emotions. Most psychotherapists, therefore, concentrate on helping persons to accept their anger as a natural occurrence, to identify and acknowledge when they are experiencing anger, and then to determine what to do with their anger— including appropriate expressions and behaviors.

Theological reflection and pastoral practice, particularly the practice of pastoral care and counseling specialists, in the last half of the twentieth century was significantly influenced by psychology. Many Christian practitioners were trained in the social sciences and incorporated the insights of psychology into their practice of care and counseling. Specialists in pastoral care and counseling became aware from their clinical experience that the anger-is-sin tradition caused many problems for Christians, and have appropriately tried to correct this tradition. They began to emphasize the normative psychological perspective that anger is a natural part of the human condition and challenged the idea that all experiences of anger are sinful.

This "anger is natural" stance, however, does include one problem: it tends to assume that *experiences* of anger are morally neutral,[12] which means that since anger simply happens as a natural response to life, humans shouldn't be concerned about *being* angry, but only about how to *express* it. For example, Martin Davis, writing about anger in twelve-step programs, says:

> While anger is traditionally listed among the Seven Sins, anger itself is not sinful. Anger is an emotion and, like any emotion, is neither good nor bad in and of itself. What we do with the emotion of anger may be good or bad.[13]

Psychologists Gary Oliver and H. Norman Wright interpret anger to a Christian audience by stating this idea clearly:

> Anger . . . is like so many other feelings—neither right nor wrong in itself. The problem lies in its mishandling.[14]

> The sin does not lie in the fact of my experience of anger or the emotion of anger but rather in how I choose to express it.[15]

Even representatives of a more conservative theology, who normally take a literalist view of Scripture and a traditional perspective on the human predicament, have taken this morally neutral stance. Tim LaHaye, a noted conservative evangelical author, says: "The truth of the matter is that anger in itself is neither good nor bad. It is just anger. . . . The problem with anger is the direction in which it leads you."[16] Frank Minirth and Paul Meier, two conservative Christian psychiatrists, say, "Anger is an automatic human response."[17]

The implicit conclusion of this position is that we have no choice about *what* makes us angry, no control over *when* we get angry, or no accountability for *why* we get angry. This position assumes that we have no responsibility for evaluating the *experience* of anger, but only bear responsibility for our *behavior*. These assumptions about the nature of anger, which imply that experiences of anger are morally neutral, are not informed by advances in neuroscience, constructionist narrative psychology, historical moral theology, or by theological analysis.

The psychology reflected in this position is dependent on earlier instinctivist ideas about anger (see chapter 5) that tend to believe anger has a life of its own over which we have little control. Rejecting instinct theories by the second half of the twentieth century, many social scientists recognize that instinctual concepts about anger are no longer adequate. As demonstrated in chapter 5, anger is generated only when our brain interprets environmental stimuli to be dangerous to the self. Anger is not an entity in itself that has an ongoing existence somewhere in our body or personality that looks for ways to be expressed.

Furthermore, chapter 6 discussed how anger unrelated to physical survival is activated: violation of narratives we have adopted or created to explain our world triggers our capacity for anger. In contrast to the "anger is instinct" position, constructionist narrative perspectives make us aware that *we have significant control over the narratives that make us vulnerable to threat*. We are, furthermore, able to revise or reconstruct those narratives as we grow and develop. Because our perspectives on events trigger anger, the values, beliefs, and meanings embedded in our narratives play a large part in explaining when and why we get angry. Since we can normally choose what makes us angry by how we construct the narratives that are threatened, I argue that what we allow to trigger our anger is, in fact, a moral issue.[18]

FREEDOM TO CHOOSE

Because we can normally choose which narratives threaten us and which do not, we have a significant amount of freedom to decide not only what we do with our anger, but also what we allow to trigger our anger in the first place. With that freedom comes the recognition that although the *capacity* for anger is a physiological given, every *experience* of anger is not. This freedom to author and re-author our narratives, explored in chapter 6, makes us accountable for deciding what is going to threaten us and, therefore, activate our capacity for anger: "Nothing makes people angry. . . . [P]eople make themselves angry. . . . [A]t their most fundamental level, they have chosen to be angry."[19]

Consider once again the story of Cain and Abel (Gen. 4:3–7). We have already seen that in this story God distinguishes between the experience of anger and the experience of sin, for though Cain was "very angry" (v. 5), sin was still "lurking at the door" (v. 7) and had not yet taken advantage of Cain's vulnerability. Though God did not discount the capacity for anger that had been triggered in Cain, God was concerned about the narrative that made Cain vulnerable to the threat of rejection and caused him to become angry. God's question, "Why are you angry?" (v. 6), invites Cain to identify the current narrative through which he interpreted the rejection of his offering and consider the possibilities of constructing a different narrative that would not leave him threatened and angry. Cain clearly has the freedom to change his story and, therefore, change his behavior related to the sacrifice—"If you do well, will you not be accepted?" (v. 7)—so that the rejection of his sacrifice did not have to threaten him and generate the anger. Furthermore, as one of the earliest scriptural references to free will, God reminds Cain that he has the freedom to resist the temptation to express his anger destructively: "but you must master it" (v. 7). Any time we are angry, we are vulnerable to expressing it in harmful ways, thereby sinning against ourselves and our neighbors. While the capacity for anger itself is not sinful, we are responsible *both for what we allow to trigger this capacity and for how we handle the anger*.

God also critiques Jonah's narrative about what God should do to the people of Nineveh. Jonah's actions spring from his anger at God for rescuing these people (4:1), and God asks him to consider why he is angry (4:4). God invites him to change his narrative to match God's redemptive narrative, but Jonah resists. Finally God confronts him with the silliness of his narratives and the incongruity of being angry over a tree dying, because it deprives him personally of shade, but not valuing the people in Nineveh (4:6–11). God pushes Jonah to reconstruct his narrative so that it includes more compassion for the people of Nineveh.

Re-authoring of narratives may be considered as the transforming work to which God calls us as we grow toward maturity in Christ.[20] This call to reconstruction was consistently demonstrated in Jesus' own ministry. In his interaction with the religious leaders, Jesus acts congruently with the image of God in the Hebrew Bible. Note the number of times Jesus challenged the religious leaders to reconsider their dominant narrative, which prioritized purity codes above love, kindness, mercy, justice, and humility. He showed them that their lived religion was not in keeping with the foundations of Judaism, that their practices were antithetical to God's expressed desires.

Jesus worked during his ministry to change the dominant narrative of the Jewish religious leaders about the priority of law over love. During an interaction with the crowd recorded in John 7:19–24, for example, the crowd was angry because he healed a man on the Sabbath. Jesus then raised questions about the values that caused them to be threatened and angered by his ministry. In vv. 23–24 Jesus says:

> "If a man receives circumcision on the sabbath in order that the law of Moses may not be broken, are you angry with me because I healed a man's whole body on the sabbath? Do not judge by appearances, but judge with right judgment."

Jesus questions their faith narratives, pointing out that their anger resulted from a lack of "right judgment" and was therefore inappropriate to their professed religious convictions. Notice that these angry religious leaders had not yet behaved unethically, at least in this situation, so Jesus is not challenging their behavior. Rather, he is critiquing the fact that they were holding on to a worldview, a narrative, that was not consistent with their own teachings. Their anger was a problem to Jesus because it was triggered by his action of healing, which he considered to be in keeping with God's desire for human well-being. His loving actions were a threat to their story, which was based on legalisms that he did not consider valid, so he challenged them to adopt a different narrative from which to judge actions.

As the religious people of today, we are responsible for examining our anger and exploring the underlying narratives that make us vulnerable to threat. In this way we determine whether our narratives are congruent with the gospel and evaluate whether our lives are consistent with the life that Jesus modeled. In short, we can assess whether our anger measures up to the example of compassionate anger we see in Jesus, as we explore further in chapter 12.

An example of the freedom to choose is seen in this assessment written by a married male in his late thirties who is intentionally working at changing his angry behavior. After describing the physical changes that he experiences when going through an "angry outburst," which included verbal harangues and pounding walls and doors with his fist, he describes his growing awareness of the choices he has while angry:

> These episodes *very rarely* occur in public! I remember how horrified my friends were when they saw my mother have one of her outbursts, so I make every effort to "hold it in" when my wife and I are around other people. My wife raises a good point in respect to this. She has often wondered that if I can control myself in public, then why can't I control myself at home? I suppose that this is very telling of my condition: I do not do it in public because I would not get away with it in public. I do it at home because I can get away with it.

This self-assessment is true of most people who suggest that they can't control their temper, or that angry explosions are part of their physical makeup. This person had noted that earlier in life he defended his behaviors by arguing that "this is the way God made me." But even then, he admitted, he knew his behaviors were "irrational and foolish."

Though many narratives are developed at unconscious levels, they are still fluid and changeable; many do not have to remain unconscious. By intentionally becoming aware of these stories (see chapters 6 and 13), we can expand our understanding of why our anger is triggered, thereby setting the context for deciding whether or not those particular narratives need to be threatened. Even when we can't recover an unconscious narrative that might be motivating particular actions, we can choose different behaviors.

PERSONAL RESPONSIBILITY

To this point I have constructed a pastoral theology that confirms the capacity for anger as part of our embodied creation (a gift from God), and also affirms—on the basis of neuroscience, constructionist narrative theory, and biblical narratives—our freedom to choose when to get angry. This freedom makes it inappropriate to place responsibility for experiences and expressions of anger on anyone or anything beyond ourselves. Our own narratives, created within the context of the larger narratives in our families and cultures, both trigger the anger and shape our verbal and behavioral expressions of it.

In chapter 3 I mentioned the "myth of passivity," which suggests that we are helplessly co-opted by emotions that often seem to overpower us with their intensity. Language about anger promotes this idea: anger "sweeps over us" or "carried us away," or we were "blinded" by it or "couldn't help" ourselves. While we know that a person can become enslaved to anger, this conclusion is hard to defend from a biological perspective.

Even John Wesley, who was ambivalent about anger, believed in our freedom to choose what we do with anger. Responding specifically to the idea that Christians are helpless in the face of "sin which is natural to us," he argued that Christians are responsible for every "natural" tendency. Even those aspects of self that are grounded in our physicality and mental states (other than brain anomalies) are not beyond our responsibility. Can we control emotions? "Yes, we can," Wesley says, and then provides a personal illustration:

> Anger, for instance, is natural to me; yea, irregular, unreasonable anger. I am naturally inclined to this, as I experience every day. Yet I can help it, by the grace of God; and do so, as long as I watch and pray.[21]

Contending that as Christians we are responsible for the way we experience anger, however, does not suggest that denying or suppressing anger is the answer, as Wesley suggests elsewhere.[22]

The existentialists connect responsibility for both our emotions and behaviors to human freedom. As Sartre said, "the peculiar character of man's reality is that it is without excuse."[23] Because freedom and responsibility are integral parts of our basic existence we cannot complain, says Sartre, that anything outside our selves "has decided what we feel, what we live, or what we are."[24] Though existentialists underestimate the significant role of relationships and cultural narratives in our individual constructions of reality, the emphasis on personal responsibility remains valid, reminding us that we must evaluate cultural stories as well as individual stories when assessing responsibility. The constructionist narrative understanding of the processes by which the self makes sense of life demonstrates that we have significant control over *when* we get angry.

The concept of free will from a nontheistic existentialist perspective is summarized by Jean-Paul Sartre, who holds that the exercise of responsibility will always overrule passion:

... there is no determinism, man is free, man is freedom. ... [O]nce thrown into the world, he is responsible for everything he does. The existentialist does not believe in the power of passion. He will never agree that a sweeping passion is a ravaging torrent which fatally leads a man to certain acts and is therefore an excuse. He thinks that man is responsible for his passion.[25]

Given this freedom, pastoral theology must place responsibility for both why we get angry and for our particular expressions of anger on each individual, while at the same time holding accountable those cultures that tolerate, even support, narratives that promote destructive expressions of anger, particularly abuse and violence. This responsibility includes self-critique on the part of the Christian tradition: the necessity to continually investigate, question, interpret, and reconstruct perceptions of God's character as defined by abusive behaviors assigned to God by some biblical stories.

Theologically speaking, this issue of freedom and responsibility is often known as "free will." This idea of freedom is often considered in the abstract, but Panksepp attempts to understand the concept of free will[26] within the framework of our neurophysiology:

In adult humans, higher cortical controls can be refined to the point that we can, to some extent, choose to be angry or not. But also, because of such higher cognitive functions, we can become angry merely in response to symbolic gestures (reflecting how past learning and current appraisals can come to arouse emotional systems).[27]

Panksepp acknowledges two important aspects of free will. First, he confirms that we are able to control and, therefore, be accountable for our experiences of anger through conscious reflection on our constructed realities. Second, he acknowledges the possible limitation to free will because traumatic narratives, particularly from early in life, establish deep and seemingly indelible neural pathways that bypass the neocortex (thinking brain).

We know about limits to our freedom to control our responses to earlier traumas. We do not have perfect control over our embodied existence. As the discussion on memory in chapter 5 reminds us, at times we respond to "symbolic gestures," particularly those that remind us of problematic narratives shaped in the experience of early traumas. These previous stories leave us more vulnerable to spontaneous angry behavior that is connected to neural pathways created during early traumas and which function faster than our cognitive processes, making it more difficult to activate the rational exercise of free will to manage the event. Nevertheless, we must reckon with our freedom to use and misuse our capacity for anger. Even with these deeply ingrained narratives, increased self-awareness allows us to gain control and to change our responses so that they don't leave us so completely vulnerable to threats.

A pastoral theology must not blame our physiology for destructive expressions of anger. On the basis of recent research in neuropsychology, as discussed earlier, the notion is rejected that destructive expressions of anger are instinctual, rooted in our physiology, and, therefore, an unalterable feature of the human condition. Many people attempt to blame their bodies for angry behavior, claiming, for example, that they are helpless to control their temper. With few exceptions, however, angry behavior reflects a person's personal and cultural narratives about how and when to express anger, either of permission or constraint, rather than physiology. With few exceptions the physiological response is not activated unless important narratives are triggered. Our stories betray us, not our bodies.

SUMMARY

Attaching anger to creation allows us to accept the idea that this capacity for anger was present from the beginning, an integral aspect of our embodied existence. As such we welcome it as gift, a blessed part of God's good creation to be used profitably, creatively, and responsibly in the way we see modeled by Jesus of Nazareth, even viewing it as a spiritual ally, a partner in our spiritual journey. With this view we move toward a vision of psychosomatic wholeness and no longer feel the need to remove anger from our selfhood. Instead of trying to exterminate anger, we seek to learn what it can teach us about ourselves by uncovering the narratives that have made us vulnerable to specific threats. We accept the potential of anger to lead us toward growth and transformation through re-authoring these stories, a process that can move us toward spiritual maturation and abundant life. Thus, as I discuss further in part 4, we learn to understand anger and to use it creatively and effectively, accepting its positive contributions and dealing responsibly with all tendencies toward negative and unhelpful actions.

Continuing to place anger on the list of Seven Deadly Sins is a costly mistake. Given what we have learned from the neurosciences, constructionist narrative theory, Scripture, and historical theology, the anger-is-sin tradition is no longer a viable belief. I hope that moral and systematic theologians attend to these alternative stories and work to remove anger from the list of deadly sins. Perhaps they could substitute hostility, hate, abuse, violence, or any other expression of anger that has become destructive. An effective case could be made for the inclusion of any of these, but to include anger on the list, without separating the capacity for anger from destructive expressions of anger, is unfair to this gift from God, denies its relationship to the *imago Dei*, and ignores the many positive contributions that anger makes to our life—as discussed in the following chapters.

PART 4

Dealing with Anger:
Christian Care and Counseling

11

Anger as Spiritual Ally

The awesome power of anger and its potential to wreak havoc in our lives and communities is well known to all of us. We know of the demonic possibilities that exist when anger is aroused, and understand why the early monastic community, philosophers, and social scientists have been suspicious of it. Each of us could give personal examples of harmful anger expressed through behaviors such as silence, verbal abuse, and violence, and we understand why the Bible gives stern warnings against allowing anger to become bitterness, jealousy, hostility, and vengeance. Both Scripture and our own experience convince us that we are quite vulnerable to sinning against ourselves and others when we are angry.

Anger, however, is not necessarily an enemy; it does not have to be destructive and abusive. It doesn't have to wound and victimize. We established in the last chapter that the capacity for anger is part of the *imago Dei*, a gift that has been called "good" and blessed by God, with many possibilities for contributing to our well-being. Now I want to go further and suggest that anger can actually function as a *spiritual ally*. By using the metaphor of spiritual ally, I refer to anger's significant potential as a positive partner in striving toward personal wholeness and in promoting peace, justice, and reconciliation in relationships at all levels.

The theology in chapter 10 established that we have significant levels of freedom to choose what triggers our capacity for anger and, therefore, responsibility for how we express it. But to exercise this responsibility wisely, and claim the significant gifts anger can bring to our lives, we must deal with anger's ambiguities. Perhaps Kathleen Norris speaks for many of us when she writes, "Anger is my best demon, useful whenever I have to go into a Woman Warrior mode, harmful when I use it to gratify myself, either in self-justification, or to deny my fears."[1]

I want those committed to Christian discipleship to consider their capacity for anger—when it is owned, appreciated, and welcomed[2]—as a guide on their spiritual pilgrimage. Anger, when accepted as an ally, can connect with significant and central aspects of our life—hope, courage, and intimacy. It can also play a significant role in the recovery of self, and can function as an "idol detector." Finally, anger can function as a "diagnostic window," helping us identify the life narratives that make us more vulnerable to anger, guiding us to better self-understanding.

ANGER AND HOPE

Hope is a major component of religious experience. Christian faith narratives include significant "future stories"[3] based on trust in a God who loves us and cares for us. When life events seriously threaten these future stories, our visions and dreams for the future, then we become angry. Unexpected events such as divorce, accident, health crises, unemployment, or financial crises can put our hopes and dreams at risk and, therefore, can produce anger.

Pastoral theologian Carroll Saussy distinguishes between the "anger of despair" and the "anger of hope."[4] The anger of despair has no voice, is silenced, neither heard nor respected by another. It is expressed with no sense of a way out, that God is calling us into the future, or that reconciliation and wholeness are possible. In contrast, the anger of hope cries out in lament, gives voice to the pain and suffering, and is blessed with a belief that God hears and can be trusted to act on our behalf. The anger of hope believes that the future is open to change and that peace and justice are possible.

Anger is a spiritual ally, therefore, in its role as an advocate of hope. It can motivate us to defend ourselves, fight to survive, and resist the unfairness and chaos in the universe. The anger we feel in such circumstances is an expression of protest and resistance, perhaps leading to a confrontation, and therefore a sign that we are still hopeful. Angry words and behaviors can change the present reality, therefore contributing to the existence of hope.

Like most marriage and family counselors, for example, my wife and I would rather work with partners who are angry with each other than with an indifferent couple. When partners are angered by threats to the relationship, that often means they are still invested in the partnership and have hope that it can be rescued or transformed. The lack of anger at threats to the relationship usually signifies apathy, indicating that at least one partner has emotionally "moved out" of the relationship and doesn't care enough to feel threatened. Anger, when accurately identified, understood, and communicated, has served as the transforming dynamic for many couples in therapy, serving as a wake-up call, and providing the motivation for changing the attitudes and actions that have put the partnership in jeopardy.[5]

The loss of hope is one of the most damaging consequences of despair, one that is frequently marked by the inability to be angry. In fact, a common symptom of hopelessness is the inability to be angry at events that would normally be threatening. Suppressed anger has been identified with the prevalence of depression in our culture.[6] Many persons who wrestle with despair and depression describe the part that anger played in their recovery of hope. Writing about his own depression, for example, Robert Morris, an Episcopal priest, identified "my habit of suppressing my emotions—especially those that were painful to me in some way" as a major cause of his depression. Central to his healing and the recovery of hope was his willingness to "own my real feelings . . . especially dislike and anger," and his need "to practice living out my anger."[7]

Mary Catherine Bateson writes about the despair she felt as she struggled with sexism in academia. The president of her college died suddenly, and as dean of the faculty she accepted appointment as the acting president. Within a short period of time, however, she felt betrayed, bullied, and shunned by powerful males in the faculty and by the executive committee who advised the all-male board of trustees against retaining her in this position. Moreover, when the new president was hired, she was fired from her post as dean. In reflecting on her experience, Bateson notes the tendency of women to internalize such losses and too easily move into self-blame and self-accusation as a failure. The anger felt is often the main emotion that is internalized, rather than activated in the service of hope. Bateson says of her own experience with hopelessness, "Anger was an achievement, a step away from the chasm of despair."[8]

Marginalized persons may understand the contribution of anger to the experience of hope more than those of us in privileged social locations. Cornell West, an African American scholar, refers to the connection between hope and anger when discussing the rage felt by African Americans who suffer from the continuous assaults of racism.[9] This anger can become the anger of despair, but the intense expression of anger can be an attempt to establish a sense of personal power, regain a sense of worth, and find meaning in life. The constructive expression of anger in the struggle for social equality, West says, can be an antidote to a sense of impotence and the loss of hope.[10]

Feminist scholars such as Mary Daly, Marjorie Procter-Smith, Susan Brooks Thistlethwaite, and Marjorie Suchocki have also recognized the relationship between anger and hope. Mary Daly has observed that reality-based anger can recognize false hopes and guide women toward a more realistic hope. Using constructionist narrative concepts, when a woman's narratives include an awareness of sexist prejudices and inequities, and she is in touch with the anger that these realities generated, then that angry energy can "express itself as original, creative hope."[11] Marjorie Procter-Smith has argued that when motivating a person to compassionately resist causes of suffering, "anger is an expression of hope, and the opposite of despair.[12]

When people finally allow themselves to fully feel their legitimate anger, they often experience a rebirth of hope. Marjorie Suchocki discusses the envisioning role of anger in the hoping process, describing how "rage becomes the vision, which will become the empowering source of hope."[13] Hope comes about because anger "heightens our confidence in the power of the future, and we dare to undertake its creation."[14] Susan Brooks Thistlethwaite has observed how battered women typically turn their intense anger inward and suffer from depression, self-blame, and hopelessness. When victims are supported in identifying their anger and expressing this anger outward toward the sources of their battering, they can become energized and hopeful.[15]

In chapter 9, I noted that the Greek words translated as anger often have additional meanings that incorporate the experience of grief and sadness. Mark 3:5, for example, says that Jesus experienced both anger and sadness at the religious leaders. Social science research and personal experience both tell us that anger often accompanies grief. I frequently observe that clients and parishioners who are either unaware of anger, or afraid of it, are left with the ongoing burden of sadness; their anger is not available to help them resolve or move past the situation. This result is evident in the words of Dorothy, who in her middle years was exploring the painful life events that, as she noted, had caused "the woundedness and suffering that lies deep within me." Reflecting on her experience with anger in the context of identifying the causes of this suffering, she wrote:

> I was urged, by counselors and friends, to "get in touch with my anger." I could not find it. I was deeply sad, but I could not feel angry, and I resisted. . . . With hindsight I realize I turned my anger inwards; the only emotion I could acknowledge being a profound sadness, and this persisted as the undertone of my living.[16]

As she continued her reflections, she wondered about her "resistance" to those who were concerned that she access her anger and decided:

> Perhaps with the benefit of hindsight, it could be said that this resistance represented one small flicker of anger, a faint residual flicker of

autonomy of action represented some hope for recovery, a faint voice speaking for my own identity.

Notice her reference to the hope that was present even in this small expression of anger.

While we remain sad our energy is drained, but when we identify, accept, and communicate the anger we can recover the energy necessary to address the source of suffering and perhaps take on the larger issues of social inequity in our world. Dorothy describes finding and directing her angry energy at suffering:

> I began to find anger, not as may logically be imagined, directed towards the cause of my own suffering, but . . . as anger for those whose suffering was not heard. . . . I raged against what I saw as the diminishing of the person, as if they had no worth. It seemed that though I hardly understood it, my own suffering had sensitized me deeply to the suffering of others, and allowed me to find solidarity and a place of belonging with them.

"In hearing their articulation of pain and anger," she later wrote, "and in beginning to articulate my own, slowly I began to know hope." Perhaps her experience illustrates the anger of despair being transformed into the anger of hope.

ANGER AND COURAGE

Anger by definition, as with all emotion (see chapter 1), involves a desire to take action. The physiological arousal that comes with anger is programming us to act in response to the threat—anger's primary role in survival. When we are appropriately angered by a threat to our safety and well-being, the anger can generate the courage necessary to act at the level of power needed to make change. New Testament scholar G. Walter Hansen remembers becoming enraged at ten years of age by the way his brother was treated:

> Some teenage boys were tormenting my brother Kenny who had Down syndrome. I went ballistic—screaming, scratching, gouging, biting. When the lifeguard pulled me off them, he told me to say I was sorry. I refused to apologize for defending my powerless brother against the "powerful" bullies.[17]

Anger can give us the energy and the willingness to speak up, speak out, march, vote, protest, refuse to participate, resist evil, and blow the whistle. Anger provides courage, one of the gifts we can receive from anger that grows out of love. "Courage," as Eleanor Haney notes, "is nurtured by both love and anger."[18]

Courage is more often attributed to males than females, as if it were genetically determined, but Haney challenges this perspective and blames socialization for this lack of courage. She points out that women are socialized to suppress their anger because of their assigned role in nurturing relationships, making everybody happy, and avoiding conflict. Women, because of their designated roles, often expend their creative energy maintaining the status quo in order to avoid conflict, rather than challenging social evil and systemic suffering. In her call to action, Haney discusses the role of anger in enabling women to break out of their prescribed roles and function as co-creators with God in bringing about what the apostle Paul calls the "new creation" (2 Cor. 5:17). She writes "We *should* be angry; anger is one of the ways we say that the emperor has no clothes. Anger is absolutely essential if we are to be part of the first fruits of new creation."[19] To participate in making space for this new creation demands that the old creation be courageously challenged. Haney demonstrates that through courage the traditional peace-making gifts of women can be "grounded not in fear or the need to placate but in the glimpses of a profound and fierce love of God and her creation that so deeply honors the world that we *must* speak, we *must* risk—even our lives."[20]

Marjorie Procter-Smith has written about a series of articles in a local newspaper on violence against women. The author of one article, Victoria Loe, expressed how her anger provided the courage that enables her continued participation in the fight against this violence.

> I am angry at every man who is still hurting women. I hold them accountable. I am angry at our society, which tells men it is permissible to hurt women because women are less than men. I hold it accountable. . . . I am angry that anyone would dare to tell us our suffering is our fault. . . . We have a right to keep talking about these crimes, and our anger, until the crimes stop. . . . My job is not to be a victim. My job is to stay angry.[21]

If Loe doesn't stay angry, she will lose the courage that keeps her in the fray and motivates her to resist domestic violence despite the personal risks.

Entering the fray is not an easy decision to make, particularly for white middle-class Christians who have been socialized to be suspicious of and to avoid our anger. We must be willing to feel appropriate anger based on our faith narratives in order to gain the courage to move against injustice and oppression (see chapter 12). People who suppress their capacity for anger are often good at intellectually analyzing the oppressive structures and organizing a response, but the absence of compassionate anger usually leaves them above the fray. Being free to experience appropriate anger and combining that anger with intellectual analysis of social evils has been called *"embodied* learning" because the emotional component provides the courage and commitment that pushes one to physically join the fray.[22]

ANGER AND RECOVERY OF SELF

Persons victimized by unjust relationships and social structures often lose significant aspects of their identity—their sense of being a particular self in relationship to other persons and to the world around them. They have lost their sense of worth; the awareness that they have the right to think, feel, and act in ways that affect the world around them has been taken away. Powerlessness and helplessness often characterize their acceptance of the "way things are." Symptomatic of this loss of self is the inability to be threatened and angry at the powerlessness; appropriate narratives of self-identity are underpowered. Anger, therefore, is not available to serve in one of its most precious roles: defender of the self, protector of self-integrity, and guardian of the self's emotional boundaries. Earlier I quoted Dorothy, a middle-aged woman who was saddened by several life events but unable to feel any anger. She explained her understanding of her lack of anger this way:

> To feel anger, I think one must have a sense of self, a sense of one's own worth and identity. Today I recognize that the sadness was accompanied by disallowed anger, but it could not be expressed as such for I had little sense of self-esteem and no sense of self value or worth that could have allowed me to feel justifiably threatened or legitimately angry. Unable to believe I had worth, there was no "self" to defend. I had no rational basis for feeling either threat or anger. There was only a murky whirlpool of undefined but very painful sadness. The anger mechanism it seems was de-activated, rendered invalid, paralyzed by the destruction of any sense of self-worth.

Since the wholeness of humanity, individually and collectively, is important to God, then defense of that wholeness and integrity of both individuals and communities (in fact, the whole creation!) must be important, a part of faithful living within our world. I contend, therefore, that anger generated by a threat to self boundaries, if expressed and acted upon creatively, can protect a person from violation or restore boundaries that have been invaded, and that such action would constitute part of our faithful response to God.

People who have been wounded, victimized, and oppressed often repress or suppress both the event and the attending anger, which can lead to dissociation. Persons who have been through trauma early in life, such as in incest situations, and are left unable to communicate their fear and anger for fear of retaliation or rejection may have learned not to allow the anger to occur at conscious levels. The most intense way this separation occurs is through repression, the psychological term that describes what happens when a person's conscious process does not allow itself to be aware of something. A different level of response is when a person becomes aware of anger and it is immediately pushed out of awareness, dismissed from conscious concern—a process called suppression. Anger, then, can be lost as an expression of selfhood through either repression or suppression. In either case, a person's voice is lost.

One way of assessing the damage that repressed anger does is to examine the phenomenon of dissociation.[23] Mary Daly reminds us that Aquinas could not find a "contrary" emotion to anger, and she argues that dissociation should be anger's contrary.[24] Daly connects dissociation with the psychiatric condition called "multiple personality disorder." She points out that in situations of helplessness and powerlessness, the anger that would normally be experienced is dissociated and the energy invested in creating other selves.[25] People suffering from multiple personality disorder are frequently the victims of long-term severe sexual and/or physical abuse; in fact this history is the most common dynamic in persons suffering from this mental disturbance, a situation that makes identifing and expressing anger very difficult.

When anger is suppressed or pushed out of awareness, persons experience more difficulty in reaching the center of the self, which theologian Rita Nakashima Brock identifies as the "heart" of our identity. One of "the first steps to reclaiming self and intimacy" is to bring the suffering to consciousness, so the anger arising out of the pain is acknowledged and expressed.[26] Anger that is finally acknowledged often points to painful self narratives that have been kept at semiconscious levels, including dreams and hopes for the self that are suppressed because attaining them seems impossible. Brock reminds us that anger is a crucial path into these suppressed narratives, into the "heart" of the self: "Anger that we integrate . . . leads us to self-assertion and self-acceptance . . . to find our own centered existence."[27]

A specific incident of anger can reveal much about our self-narratives that is important in our journey toward wholeness. Therefore, says Haney, "If our anger remains buried, we are cut off from parts of ourselves . . . [whereas] expressing anger enables us to acknowledge buried dimensions of ourselves,"[28] particularly for women who have been burdened with interpretations of the virtue of humility that lead to exaggerated self-abnegation. Some women have been taught that to become "good" Christians they must give up their self, sacrificing their identity to husband, children, and hospitality.[29] To Rosemary Ruether, recovering a sense of self—as a person who can think and act with perspectives that are not necessarily tied to overdependency on others for identity—demands of women "a willingness to get in touch with their own anger," which can motivate "a turning around in which they literally discover themselves as persons, as centers of being upon which they can stand and build their own identity,"[30] and, we might add, a Christian identity that has the strength exhibited by Jesus and desired by God for all persons. The power of this "liberating anger" becomes the vehicle for reclaiming self by granting "the courage to stand up."[31]

To various extents, Daly, Brock, Haney, and Ruether have all been influenced by psychological concepts of anger that include some instinctivist flavor, rather than by a specific theological perspective. They tend to assume that anger is a "something" that is down inside which must be found, rather than existing only when there are narratives to be threatened. However, they clearly reflect most of the theological tenets for which I argued in chapter 10: conceiving anger as an important part of our existence, with positive potential for accomplishing God's purposes. Their concerns about people "finding" and "recovering" suppressed anger can be interpreted from a constructionist narrative perspective to refer to the narratives about the worth of all persons that they want everyone to have. They desire, as God's representatives, that people have narratives that claim their rights to have an equal voice in giving shape to their lives and to be safe from abuse and violence. Their assumption, that anger is an appropriate response when such narratives are violated, is ethically defendable.

At other times, anger, even when kept at arm's length, functions as a basic connection, perhaps the primary connection, with life. Dorothy identifies this dynamic in her life:

> [Sometimes] anger is all that is left of a person's identity . . . a last handle on an elusive and battered self, a place where anger is perhaps our only possession, the last fragment of identity. It is a place I think where if there was not anger there would be nothing, only the voicelessness of suffering, a dense soul-searing silence or the animal moan that Soelle describes, the apathy of suffering (Soelle) and the faceless clay existence that O'Donohue[32] describes.
>
> My own experience of anger is of an anger that is a deep well, that perhaps is my life force. This anger is seen most especially when it acts on behalf of another. It is anger that is energizing. It seems deeply woven into the fabric of my being, so that its separateness is imperceptible. This anger, known mostly in the guise of sorrow, is my life, though I did not know it till recently. In my ignorance I had denied anger any place, describing it as a "pointless @#$%^%$# emotion!" and too often I had disparaged and despised my sorrow. In this I denied my life and my value, and my ability to use the things which I had suffered in the service of others. It does not surprise me now that my self-esteem and self image then reflected those words I directed at anger—I saw myself as pointless and meaningless.

In a situation like this, the next steps include bringing further into consciousness the narratives that were threatened and the resulting anger, accepting the legitimacy of its role in protesting against unnecessary suffering, and using anger's energy to respond courageously to both personal and systemic injustice.

ANGER AND INTIMACY

Meaningful relationships are a significant contributor to abundant life and basic to our very existence, and recovery of self is necessary in order to participate in healthy relationships. Every intimate relationship, however, includes behaviors, attitudes, conflicting values, and unmet expectations that create threats to each partner and, therefore, generate anger.[33] This anger has the capacity to create intimacy, but too often is allowed to become bitterness, jealous, or hatred—the dividing wall of hostility that destroys intimacy. Brock writes that anger "is extremely powerful because it rests in the most important energy of all: the need for self-affirmation and connection."[34] If we suppress our anger, and are not able or willing to recognize and acknowledge our anger, says Brock, "we cannot love ourselves or connect fully with others."[35] When anger is acknowledged, however, "We are capable of the fullest possible relationships, because we bring a self-aware, centered self to any relationship. We bring heart."[36] Intimacy is difficult without an identified self, because that person will usually be in the "under" position in an over/under relationship.

I have said that anger is not contrary to love but is an expression of love, which is true both of God's anger and human anger. Many scholars, both theologians and social scientists, agree that anger is a necessary path into intimacy.[37] Furthermore, the love between two persons can be lost when anger is not resolved. When anger is denied or avoided, then honesty and trust are compromised and communication is constrained as one or both partners use energy to hide their anger. Dana Crowley Jack writes of the problems that develop between partners when one chooses not to deal with the anger that emerges within the relationship: "The bitter irony is that in the hope of saving relationship and furthering intimacy, the women eliminate any possibility of real mutuality, intimacy's prerequisite, which requires two selves interacting in dialogue."[38] Separation results from the unresolved anger, and intimacy is compromised. I agree with Beverly Wildung Harrison that "we Christians have come very close to killing love precisely because we have understood anger to be a deadly sin."[39] But when the anger is accepted, identified, understood, and expressed creatively, then healing can occur. As Kathleen Norris writes, "in exorcising the demon of anger, that which could kill is converted, transformed into that which can heal."[40]

Rather than being in opposition to love, our anger serves the purposes of love by being a "feeling-signal," or warning sign, that something is wrong in one of our specific relationships, or within our institutions, or within our larger community.[41] Being aware of anger as a gift that can alert us when a relationship is in danger "is a critical first step in understanding the power of anger in the work of love."[42] When anger is acknowledged, we can then move to confrontation that may repair the relationship, leading to reconciliation with those persons to whom we want to be connected.

Christians find this progression to be true in their spiritual journey. Anger can make us aware that our relationship with God is being challenged or threatened by some life event. Being open and honest with this anger can restore intimacy and revitalize our trust and faith in the God who loves us. The experience of Jon, a minister, whose anger at God, when he finally recognized and expressed it, led to a deeper sense of connection and acceptance is illustrative. After graduation from seminary, which he had sacrificed to attend and was already married with children, Jon found no jobs in ministry available. He wrote this summary of his response:

> During those two years my anger at God grew more and more. I began by questioning why God would "call" me to leave my job, family, and home, just to come to [seminary] and fail. That eventually escalated to questioning why God was preventing me from doing the ministry I gave up everything for. As the days turned to weeks and then months, my anger at God was growing at an unhealthy rate. I had never even considered the possibility of voicing my anger to God; that was sure blasphemy, and when your theology said that God's love for you is based on your goodness, getting angry with God was not an option.
>
> I had never read anything that talked about expressing anger to God, [but] I will always remember that afternoon when I told God exactly what I thought. I had spent many hours in prayer asking God for answers, only to find a big black hole where my prayers, and apparently my resumes, had gone. One afternoon I finally slammed my Bible shut and began a five-to-ten minute tirade that was aimed directly at God. I began with every cuss word I had ever heard, and moved to threatening to kick God's ass if he would just be man enough to show himself to me. You can say a lot of cuss words and make a lot of threats in ten minutes, so before long I was repeating everything in every possible way I knew. What happened next was one of those experiences that I will never forget. By the end of the ten minutes, I was pretty exhausted and so I finally sat down and was quiet. At that moment I heard what I would always believe to be the voice of God saying, "now that you've gotten that out of your system, let's talk for a while." I was so shocked, literally stunned, that I had to look around

for a few minutes to ensure that I was truly alone. The next few hours were filled with a tremendous sense of release from all the emotions that had been pent up. For the first time I really began to believe that God's love for me was based on God, rather than on how good I was. What this meant for me was that I could really be free to say and be who I was, and God would love me because of it or in spite of it. This was the experience of a weight being lifted off of me. If God could love me in spite of all the horrible things I had begun to think and believe about God, then that must be a love I could trust to know me completely.

From that experience I learned that I could be exactly who I was, which included sharing my anger, and God would not reject me. That was a tremendous time of personal growth for me. God never has answered why, and my experience since then has almost gotten me to the point of not asking anymore. I now believe that not only is it OK to be real with God, but I believe God truly prefers my honesty and sincerity.

Contrary to what Christians are sometimes taught, being angry at God is not necessarily an act of disobedience, rebelliousness, or lack of faith. In Job and the Psalms of lament we have plenty of examples of people of faith expressing their anger at God. Walter Brueggemann reminds us that within the covenant we have with God "it is a faithful human action to rage and protest" when we are suffering.[43] In fact, being angry at God is an expression of faith, because we wouldn't be angry unless we assumed God existed. Caregiving with people whose anger at God has caused alienation can include helping them express their anger. Some possibilities are to read them the Psalms of lament, include their expressed anger in our prayers for and with them, help them learn how to "pray the Psalms," and teach them to write their own prayers of lament.[44] Having expressed their anger, a sense of calm and connection often occurs.

ANGER AS IDOL DETECTOR

We get the angriest when those things we have put at the center of our lives are threatened. When we extend our self into things, ideas, and people and *they* are threatened, then *we* feel threatened and get angry on their behalf. Because anger is often a response to perceived threats to the narratives in which our beliefs and value systems are encased, that which makes us angry reveals much about our values.

Many of us hide from ourselves those values that are contradictory to our conscious faith narratives, but when a situation arises that threatens one of these "hidden" values, our angry response will clearly identify them. Much like the dyes that physicians inject into our bodies to identify a medical problem, anger will reveal hidden values if we pay attention. In this sense, anger can serve as an "idol detector," pointing out those values that have gained prominence in our lives and detract from our commitment to the living God. Some brief examples:

Madeline, whom we will meet again in chapter 13, became angry in the context of visits from her parents. She and her husband both believed that the anxiety and anger she experienced before, during, and after these visits were the result of her mother's constant put-downs and criticism of how she functioned as wife, cook, and home-maker, and how she presented herself physically. Madeline elaborated on how desperate she was for the mother's approval, which she had never received. The threat to the narrative that contained this desire was intense, as was the resulting anger. During the process of exploring her anger in the context of her faith, Madeline was able to realize that the dynamics of how she "worshiped" her mother and her mother's opinions had indeed become an idol.

Jackson visited his pastor, at his wife's insistence, because he had physically assaulted his two children, nine and eleven years of age, for hiding his cigarettes. They were hoping he would quit smoking and had argued that it was an addiction, an argument he disputed. Because of his high respect for the pastor, and the pastor's ability to invite Jackson's curiosity around violence over something as supposedly unimportant as a cigarette, Jackson was willing to discuss this issue in the context of what he believed as a Christian. The metaphor of "idol" caught his attention and enabled him to admit that "perhaps he did need the cigarettes more than I have admitted." This metaphor enabled him to decide, on the basis of his faith narrative, to apologize to his children and begin a program that he hoped would help him "break the habit."

Another common example is the commitment to sports teams. You can tease many people about their favorite teams, but some people get angry when their team is ridiculed or criticized. They have invested so much of their self-hood in the team that any teasing feels threatening. The team has become the central commitment in life, the highest value, that which they adore.

Theologically speaking, all these examples have in common a human attachment that has been allowed to gain the strength of meaning and importance that we usually reserve for God. The living God does not have to be defended, but idols are weak and do have to be defended—hence our anger on their behalf when they are threatened. Our Christian responsibility in this situation is to evaluate whether our investments are valid (see chapter 12), or whether they represent our "worship" of values that don't measure up to our faith narratives.

ANGER AS A GUIDE
TOWARD SELF-UNDERSTANDING

Anger can also be a source of revelation, revealing those aspects of our life narrative that need to be worked on, corrected, and transformed by the gospel. Anger, for example, can serve as a spiritual ally when we allow it to become a "diagnostic window." By this I mean that if we "enter" an experience of anger to understand why we are threatened, we have the opportunity to learn something about ourselves that can be more clearly revealed by the experience of anger than in any other context.

A fever attracts our attention because it signals that something is wrong.[45] If a fever is high, then attention must be focused on reducing the temperature because the high fever can harm the body. While attending a fever, however, physicians look for the deeper cause. Fevers don't occur without an underlying condition. To treat only the fever without paying attention to the cause would be foolish and irresponsible. Likewise, we must attend to early indications of anger and take responsibility for keeping it from becoming destructively intense. Attending to anger without asking why it happened is not responsible. Just as a fever that continuously reoccurs indicates an underlying cause, anger that is repetitious—that is, anger that always occurs in certain circumstances (such as visiting one's in-laws, relating to one of your children, in response to a particular colleague, at a particular group)—without a clearly understood reason also needs attention. In these situations, anger can serve as a diagnostic window.

> Watson, a fifty-six-year-old dentist, had a mild heart attack on his way back from lunch. He was quickly stabilized in the ER (from where he asked his wife to call me) and then moved to the cardiac care unit. We had known each other since I was involved in a strategic intervention with one of his children some years earlier. Watson wanted to talk about his experience, particularly about the anger he had toward his primary care physician. The heart attack confirmed his original suspicion that heart catheterization triggered heart attacks. But his physician had "talked me into it anyway," and Watson was angrily blaming him for his heart attack. His anger was overpowering any other feelings and concerns that he was having at the time. Even after the threat of a serious attack subsided, the only thing Watson could talk about was his anger at the physician.
>
> Later that night I visited again, and Watson was still verbalizing his anger, which seemed out of proportion to the situation, since he admitted that he made the decision to go through with the test on his own and that "no one twisted my arm." I was beginning to wonder about the real agenda when his wife, who was present during both visits, said that Watson being this angry was very unusual, particularly

because his doctor was an admired friend. He responded to her remark by defending his "right to be angry" and continued this uncharacteristic hostility.

Two days later, I visited Watson at home where he was supposed to be resting before returning to the office. His attitude had made a 180-degree turn. Now he was apologetic for his anger at the primary care physician, blaming himself for being unfair, and saying several times, "I don't know what got into me." After a few minutes I picked up on his innocent question and asked, "How interested are you in finding out 'what got into you'?" He asked me to explain, so I reminded him of his statements that he didn't know what got into him and then casually mentioned that anger, particularly anger we don't understand, usually has something to teach us. He thought that would be an interesting search, so we began what became four conversations that revealed two narratives that were important to him, but largely unidentified.

First was his fear of death. When he realized he was having a heart attack, Watson immediately thought he would die—in fact, that is why he asked his wife to call me. Why? He was overweight and smoked, and had wondered if he was "tempting fate." As we talked it became clear to him that he had much more guilt, even some self-loathing, at these two realities about himself. He had thought often about changing, and his wife had frequently confronted him about the incongruity of being overweight and smoking, given his Christian belief in "being healthy."

Second was that in the first minute of the heart attack, when Watson realized what was happening and thought he might die, he became very angry at God. As a lifelong Christian who assumed that being angry at God was inappropriate, he had suppressed these feelings after being stabilized at the hospital and feeling safe. Only in response to questions that asked him to recall his most immediate feelings about the episode did he remember his anger at God. The next questions focused on what faith narratives he had that would lead to such feelings. Over a week he identified two: that God would protect good people from such "unnecessary" health crises and that if a crisis did occur, God should be immediately present "as the good Shepherd" to fix it.

Identifying these two narratives, which may never have happened if he hadn't been willing to explore this intense experience of anger, gave Watson the freedom to reconstruct both his story about how he wanted to manage his own health and to explore the faith narratives that were connected to his anger at God. He decided that his two faith narratives were not informed by his more conscious images of God, and committed to read some books that would help him expand and nuance his ideas about how God works in the world.

On a day-to-day basis we experience many threats to our psychological well-being: to our sense of integrity, our desires and purposes, to the special relationships that are so important, and to our spiritual identity. Certain life situations feel threatening because we feel attacked at our deepest, most vulnerable points, many of which are no longer part of our conscious story. Being willing to use anger as a "diagnostic window" allows us to uncover some of the significant narratives that have made us vulnerable to specific threats, and thereby increase our level of self-awareness and open another path toward well-being.

Hopefully this chapter has increased your perspective on the many positive roles that anger can play in life. Indeed, anger can serve as a life-enhancing ally on our spiritual pilgrimage. Now I move to discuss an idea that may seem to contradict your perceptions of Christian ethics: at times, we *should* be angry.

12

Compassionate Anger

The pastoral theology of anger developed in chapter 10 establishes that our capacity for anger, as a gift from the Creator, serves the basic function of mobilizing us to fight for physical and psychosocial survival. We also know that anger can serve positive purposes in our lives as an ally in our spiritual pilgrimage toward personal wholeness. Now I want to focus more specifically on anger as a spiritual ally as it informs our responsibility as members of the larger social, cultural, and international community. In this chapter, therefore, I discuss a further purpose for anger: providing the motivation for ethical action in the face of threats from injustice, radical suffering, and oppression.

I argued in chapter 9 that anger and love are *not* equal in the nature of God, but that God's anger is rooted in God's love. I concluded, moreover, that God's anger is activated in the service of love: when God's values and desires for the creation are threatened, the compassionate God we worship gets angry. Being created in God's image with the capacity for both love and anger and, ideally, committed to the same ethical narratives, we have the responsibility for shaping faith narratives that are threatened by the same events that activate God's anger. This compassionate anger should motivate out ministry of liberation and reconciliation.

ANGER AND LOVE

People struggling with their anger often assume that love and anger are opposites. In pastoral counseling sessions I frequently hear concerns such as, "I shouldn't be angry at her, because I love her," or "What kind of mother would be angry at her children?" Most Christians agree that "love your neighbor as yourself" is the primary commandment of Jesus and therefore the central criteria that should guide our relationships with others. Unquestionably loving our neighbor (Lev. 19:18) is the basic criterion for ethics. John goes to the heart of the matter:

> Beloved, let us love one another, because love is from God; everyone who loves is born of God and knows God. Whoever does not love does not know God, for God is love. (1 John 4:7–8)

And in his Gospel, John sums up this ethical imperative: "I am giving you these commands so that you may love one another" (John 15:17).

When Christians believe in the anger-is-sin tradition, they often conclude that anger is an unloving response to others. In his work on the Seven Deadly Sins, for example, religious writer Henry Fairlie defines anger as "perverted love" and suggests that almost any expression of anger is, therefore, the opposite of love.[1]

I believe the opposite is often true: *in many situations, anger is the most loving and, therefore, the most Christian response.* Rather than squelching anger, I suggest the commandment to "love your neighbor as yourself" should often motivate us to be angry. For Christians, a faithful response when our deeply held beliefs—central to our integrity and moral commitments—are contradicted or transgressed is to be threatened and feel angry. Anger can be the logical and ethical requirement of loving others as God has loved us.

Ideally, our capacity for anger should be activated when the values we have adopted as Christians are threatened. In these situations, anger is not the opposite of love, but an expression of love. Anger may arise, indeed *should* arise, within us as Christians *because* of our love, not *in contradiction* to our love. The more deeply we become committed to certain values, the more we may experience threat. Certain values matter to us because of our maturing commitments, and when they are violated by persons or institutions we are threatened and angry. In these instances to be threatened is appropriate, an expression of our faith narratives. If we didn't love, we wouldn't be threatened. Here anger is *not opposed* to love, but is *in the service* of love.

GOOD CHRISTIANS SHOULD BE ANGRY

Some Christians argue that no such thing as "righteous anger" should exist. For example, Paul Hauck, a Christian psychologist, argues against any anger, including righteous anger against perpetrators, because "You and I are not

God and don't run the universe. So let's allow people to be what they will. If they hurt you or me, let's not get righteously angry over their dumb acts."[2] He describes bullies and criminals as examples of people involved in destructive behaviors that cause pain, but insists that they have "the right to be wrong" and that "we have no God-given right to insist they *can't* be that way."[3] Hauck seems to feel no responsibility to resist evil, confront injustice, or protest radical suffering. By his definitions, Hauck would have to label Jesus' angry behavior, which I described in chapter 9, as inappropriate and immature.

I believe, in contrast, that *not being angry* at evil in all of its manifestations is sinful. In these circumstances, anger is a moral response. In a recent lecture,[4] Elie Wiesel discussed God's continuous involvement in justice issues and stressed his belief that God has given us an important eleventh commandment: "Thou shalt not stand idly by!" On the basis of this unwritten, but clearly communicated, commandment, Wiesel proclaimed, "I believe in compassionate anger!" and connected compassionate anger to moral action: "righteous anger is the morally appropriate response to the effects of hatred." Beverly Wildung Harrison reminds us, "We must never lose touch with the fact that all serious human moral activity, especially action for social change, takes its bearings from the rising power of human anger."[5] She goes further, in fact, and attributes moral escapism in the church to Christians who fear their emotions and who, more specifically, are afraid of the power of anger.[6] If anger serves as a spiritual ally and if Christians *should* in fact become angry at injustice, radical suffering, and oppression, then I would argue that trying to attain an anger-free existence cannot be considered a spiritual victory, as some argue, but is actually counterproductive to the Christian life.

The idea that anger can be an appropriate moral response assumes that we have adopted moral values that are, in fact, expressions of God's values. Determining God's values is a task fraught with the possibility of error, for as human beings we have a long history of self-deception and the willingness to confuse our values with God's. Furthermore, because of disagreements about sources of authority and understandings of God's work in the world, Christians disagree among themselves about moral values. Religious people do great harm in their attempt to defend (often by attacking others) their perceptions of what God values. From our finite perspective, we cannot know definitively the mystery of God, nor be absolutely sure we understand God's values.

At the same time, to make no commitments, to refuse to adopt any values, is to neglect John's command to "love one another" (John 15:17). To love means we do not cross to the other side of the road when we see suffering, nor do we wash our hands of moral issues related to this suffering. In my view, we are left with no option but to join together as a Christian community in our attempt to understand Scripture and tradition and, adding reason and experience, pursue the task of "hearing" God's directives.

Given our extensive freedom to choose when to be angry (on the basis of the narratives we adopt and create), we are responsible for assessing our anger to discern whether the narratives that are threatened are ethical or unethical in light of our theological commitments (as I pursue in chapter 13). We must ask, "Do I need to be threatened in this situation?" I argue that for Christians, the answer is often "Yes!" From a faith perspective, to be threatened in certain circumstances is legitimate. Our responsibility is to discern from the Judeo-Christian narratives those values that offer direction to loving others as Jesus loved us.

Among the possibilities, many Christians perceive three frequently intertwined human actions and situations to be unacceptable to God: injustice, radical suffering, and oppression. If God's love is threatened and responds with anger to these situations, shouldn't they also threaten us and make us angry? I strongly disagree with those Christians who interpret these human situations as something God has done in order to punish or teach a lesson and, with Dorothee Soelle, interpret such an attitude as "theological sadism" and "theological masochism."[7]

Anger at Injustice

Many theologians have reflected on God's concern for justice as reflected in Scripture. God's desire for justice, for example, is clearly expressed by the prophets Amos and Micah. Micah chastises his congregation for thinking they could please God through worship even as they lived unrighteously. He reminds them that God's real desire had been clearly revealed, "He has told you, O mortal, what is good; and what does the LORD require of you but to do justice, and to love kindness, and to walk humbly with your God" (6:8). God is not pleased unless our ways of relating to one another are characterized by justice and righteousness and marked by kindness and humility.

The word "justice" in our culture is often used to describe what guilty people deserve in the way of punishment. In Scripture, however, the concept of justice has a different connotation, referring to God's concern for the right of all persons to be treated with respect and to have the community meet their basic needs. This is the heart of God's expectation as addressed through the prophet Amos, who reminds us of what God really requires: "Let justice roll down like waters, and righteousness like an ever-flowing stream" (5:24). Justice intertwined with righteousness demands that we be fair, and see to it that no one is hurt, hungry, or abused by those in authority, particularly by the rich. Being righteous calls for employing attitudes and actions that enable others to find physical, mental, and spiritual wholeness.

The words "anger" and "justice" are "nearly synonymous," John Wesley believed, because "anger stands in the same relation to justice, as love does to mercy." Anger, he believed, is the passion that corresponds to justice, and those who deny that God is capable of anger consistently deny God's concern for justice.[8] We perceive evil, Wesley claimed, not only through reasoning but also through "an emotion of mind, a sensation or passion suitable thereto," which he called anger, and went so far as to say that anger *at* sin is not itself a sin but "rather a duty."[9]

Ideally, we have incorporated into our faith narrative the belief that injustice is wrong. Theologians from a variety of perspectives agree that it is appropriate to feel angry in the face of injustice, as experienced, for example, through violence, exploitation, poverty, or prejudice. John Stott argues as follows: "There is a great need in the contemporary world for more Christian anger. . . . In the face of blatant evil we should be indignant not tolerant, angry not apathetic. . . . If evil arouses [God's] anger, it should arouse ours also."[10] Mary Daly, a post-Christian philosopher, identifies a "deep ontological Fury" that is not "an agitated state of chronic or acute anger that immobilizes, or that misfires at the wrong target" but "a focused gynergetic will to break through . . . and accomplish justice."[11] A more conservative scholar, Carl F. H. Henry, can claim that "The believer is to be . . . angry with the wicked," and "Anger, if consecrated to righteousness, may sometimes be an ethical duty."[12] When certain actions and behaviors by individuals or systems violate our ethical values, then to be threatened on behalf of others and angry at the perpetrators makes sense from a spiritual point of view.

Anger as a faithful response to God's concern for justice is demonstrated in David's experience in 2 Samuel 11–12. David's lust for Bathsheba, jealousy of her husband Uriah the Hittite, and greed leads him to abuse his power, murder Uriah, and take Bathsheba as his own possession. Nathan is the prophet sent to confront David. He chooses to do so by telling David a story about a rich man who, instead of using one of his own lambs to feed a visitor, steals one from a poor man. To David's credit, his spontaneous response to this story is informed by his understanding of God's standards of justice. His beliefs about righteousness are threatened on behalf of the exploited man in Nathan's story and "David's anger was greatly kindled against the [rich] man" (12:5). He also declares that the rich man would be expected to "restore the lamb fourfold" (v. 6) and even "deserves to die" (v. 5). David's anger is "on behalf of" another person who has suffered an injustice. When Nathan reveals to David that he is the man, David is convicted by his own sinful behavior. David's story is an example of how a person committed to God and to God's values can be appropriately threatened and angry in the presence of injustice.

Because David found this injustice in himself, as well as in the rich man in

Nathan's story, each of us is reminded that to be angry at ourselves is also appropriate when we find that we are the perpetrators of an injustice. Our own weaknesses, selfishness, greed, lust for sex, and desire for power can lead us to treat others unjustly. To be confronted with our sin, by others or by our own insight, should threaten our commitments and lead to responsible self-anger. We must note how easy it is to project this anger on others rather than to aim it at the real perpetrators: ourselves.

Anger at Radical Suffering

Many types of suffering plague human existence,[13] but for our purposes, suffering that is unnecessary and unchosen, the fruit of our inhumanity to each other, is the issue. This suffering has human corruption, injustice, and oppression as its root causes. Theologian Wendy Farley uses the term "radical suffering" to describe the undeserved and dehumanizing suffering of individuals and communities at the hands of other human beings.[14] This treatment is not chosen and has no obvious meaning. Such radical suffering, says Nancy Ramsay, "turns people into victims and robs them of a sense of value, dignity, and freedom central to being human."[15] Often radical suffering is the result of anger that becomes "demonic."

Anger becomes demonic when it turns into hate or hostility, when normal desires deteriorate into jealousy, greed, and lust and are unleashed against the well-being of others. Hatred poisons both the mind and spirit, disconnecting the angry person from the humanity of others. This type of anger "gone bad" views others as people who deserve to suffer. The dehumanizing of others leads to brutality and vengeance, making it possible to move beyond even an "eye for an eye" mentality and seek to destroy others.[16] So, yes, one way we can sin with our anger is to become a perpetrator of radical suffering.

But anger also serves love when it motivates resistance to radical suffering. Philosophical ethicist Martha Nussbaum reports a story told by Elie Wiesel about his internment in a Nazi death camp.[17] After seeing the incredible suffering in the camp, an officer who entered the camp with the Allied forces began to shout and curse at the top of his voice, and continued expressing his protest at this outrage for a long time. Although Wiesel was just a child, as he watched and listened to this soldier's intense anger he realized it was a signal that humanity had returned to that place.[18] Such a reaction displays the positive side of anger, anger as a valid response to radical suffering. As Nussbaum observes:

> . . . *not* to get angry when horrible things take place seems itself to be a diminution of one's humanity. In circumstances where evil prevails,

anger is an assertion of concern for human well-being and human dignity; and *the failure to become angry* seems . . . at worst a collaboration with evil. . . . [I]t was just on account of the extremity of [the Allied soldier's] justified rage that the child Wiesel saw him as a messenger of humanity.[19]

Consciously or not, the American soldier expressed the anger that God experiences in response to the perpetration of radical suffering. The root of such compassionate anger is love that seeks to redeem humankind from the ravages of radical suffering. Marjorie Procter-Smith has argued:

Far from being a deadly sin, anger is an indispensable resource in the face of injustice, unnecessary suffering and evil. It is the essential source of energy which can fuel actions intended to put an end to unnecessary suffering, and to resist evil.[20]

As believers we cannot remain unmoved by monstrous evil: outrage is the compassionate, loving response.[21] Steadfast love is consistent in its resistance to evil.

Anger at Oppression

Oppression is a constant reality within social relationships where power imbalances exist, including hierarchical marriages, patriarchal institutions, and political dictatorships. Such oppression is the opposite of the freedom and dignity that is basic to the gospel, for Christians are admonished by Scripture to toss off the yoke of slavery, both our own and that of others (Gal. 5:1). When Jesus describes his call in Luke 4, notice the emphasis on freedom and liberation.

> The Spirit of the Lord is upon me,
> because he has anointed me
> to bring good news to the poor.
> He has sent me to proclaim release to the captives
> and recovery of sight to the blind,
> to let the oppressed go free,
> to proclaim the year of the Lord's favor.
> (Luke 4:18–19)

This ministry of liberation is the prophetic responsibility of the church. The ultimate source of power for prophetic confrontation with evil and the oppressors is the love of God and God's desire for justice. The capacity for anger with which God has created us is the finite source that generates the prophetic behaviors that lead toward liberation.

Many theological voices have expressed commitment to setting prisoners free from whatever enslaves them. Theologian Hans Küng urges commitment to a theology of liberation that would seek "political, economic, cultural, and sexual liberation, as a true sign and anticipation of the definitive eschatological project of complete freedom in the kingdom of God."[22] This would include liberation

> for all who are legally destroyed as human beings and who have no real opportunity . . . whose poverty is not a natural necessity but the side effect of a cruel social system; for the classes of people directly or indirectly exploited, cultures despised, races suffering from discrimination . . . [from] all brutal oppression . . .[23]

African American theologian James Cone speaks of "passionate theology" that is focused not on an abstract understanding of human beings but on concrete human conditions and specific persons, particularly the oppressed. African American theology is connected to Jesus Christ, he argues, when it is "a participation in passion on behalf of the oppressed."[24] Mary Daly points out that when a woman gets past what she calls "plastic passions" about irrelevant issues and "experiences real anger—that is, Rage—at her oppressor/suppressor she is moved to action by her Rage."[25] The motivating force toward living a life committed to liberation from oppression of both ourselves and others is the compassionate anger that our love for God, self, and neighbor triggers in us when faced with oppression.

When Jesus says, "Be compassionate as God is compassionate" (Luke 6:36, Borg), he is urging us to love our neighbor as God has loved us. God's love for us is threatened by injustice, oppression, and radical suffering, resulting in anger, which can serve as a model for our love. If God's love is expressed through compassion toward the disenfranchised, on behalf of the victimized, and over against perpetrators, then we can do no less.

COMPASSION AND ANGER

Compassion and anger are connected because both are based in love and attest to our identity as people created by the God who loves. Love nurtures our empathy for others, which allows us to identify with their pain and suffering. Some authors suggest that anger only occurs when we ourselves are the focus of the threat.[26] This viewpoint is limited by its assumption that people are basically selfish and egotistical. Such an assessment might be true during our narcissistic stages, but many people mature developmentally and spiritually to include others in their world. Without empathy born of love, we would not feel threatened by the hurt and pain of others. For Christians, the concept of "self" is expanded to include others whom we love, which means we become threatened not only for ourselves, but also on behalf of the neighbor we love as ourselves. Our responsibility as Christians is to transform this anger into compassionate action.

Dorothee Soelle tells of watching an act of violence that quickly gave "a feeling of rage in the pit of my stomach." She believes such physical revulsion is part of the way God has formed humans, part of the *imago Dei*, and therefore a universal response.[27] Indeed, the ethical expectation for the expression of anger at perpetrators of pain and suffering is not confined to the Christian tradition. Aristotle considered it an ethical "deficiency" to fail to be angry at those who deserve it and imagined that people without anger are "without perception or pain."[28] That is, a person who does not get angry when "reason" calls for anger suffers from a lack of empathy. Aristotle knew that once we become deeply attached to another person, we open ourselves to be angry when they are threatened.[29]

God created us as relational beings who need each other to experience the fullness of abundant life. When one person suffers, we are all affected, so not being angry and acting against perpetrators and oppressors is uncaring for both the community and ourselves.[30] Given our beliefs about the communal nature of humankind, our deep connections with each other and with the created order, we *should* be threatened by that which destroys wholeness and unity in any realm of the creation. Yes, love does express itself as concern, comfort, grief, kindness, mercy, and forgiveness, but when love's values and commitments are threatened, love also expresses itself as compassionate anger—the power of God that is over against evil, advocating for people who suffer, and resisting those who victimize others.

If we believe that all humans are created in God's image and, therefore, are precious to and valued by God, that we are threatened when any human is violated makes ethical sense. I suggest, therefore, that the commands to "Be compassionate as God is compassionate" (Luke 6:36, Borg), "Love your neighbor as yourself" (Matt. 22:39), and "Love one another as I have loved you" (John 15:12) are imperatives that convince us that we should be threatened and our capacity for anger activated by that which opposes love. Anger in the face of injustice, radical suffering, and oppression is the mark of a person in fellowship with God, one who has chosen to be on God's side against evil, because, says Küng, "love of neighbor is the exact yardstick of love of God. I love God only as much as I love my neighbor."[31]

In their book *Compassion*, pastoral theologians Donald McNeill, Douglas Morrison, and Henri Nouwen conclude that compassion is not simply one of the Christian virtues but "the center of Christian life." Feeling compassion, and knowing when and how to express compassionate anger, is "the radical challenge of our faith."[32] From the perspective of ethics the question is, "What actions for expressing compassionate anger are ethically appropriate?" I suggest three valid actions: speaking the truth in love, compassionate resistance, and nonviolent confrontation.

Speaking the Truth in Love

We examined the words in Ephesians 4:26, "Be angry but do not sin," to support the contention that anger in and of itself is not sin. Now we examine the larger context. Prior to this verse the author exhorts readers to "grow up . . . into Christ," to mature as a body of believers, which is achieved by "speaking the truth in love" (Eph. 4:15). In v. 25, preceding the words "be angry," we find the admonition, "So then, putting away falsehood, let all of us speak the truth to our neighbors." Notice that the author is again concerned with truth. One way the readers can "put away [their] former way of life" (v. 22) and be clothed "with the new self, created according to the likeness of God in true righteousness and holiness" (v. 24) is by speaking the truth. This advice is followed by the "be angry but do not sin" admonition. The meaning seems clear: when an attitude or behavior of your brothers and sisters in Christ should be challenged, do not lie about it. Do not dodge the truth; do not avoid facing the realities. Speaking the truth in love means verbalizing your anger directly, though in a manner that is not sinful.

New Testament scholar Luke Johnson translates Ephesians 4:25 as "do the truth in love" and points out that "Paul makes 'truthing' a verb, so that 'doing truth' and 'love' are mutually interpretive terms." This interpretation means, says Johnson, that "Christian love must be measured by the truth, and truth in relationships must be measured by love,"[33] and both love and truth are expressed in action. Again, if we really want to love our neighbors, we will consider it our responsibility to truthfully identify any injustice expressed toward ourselves, other members of the church, or any "neighbors." Christians occasionally debate the question, "Who are our neighbors?" Johnson points out that the parable of the Good Samaritan raises this question in reverse; the point of this parable is to raise the question "To whom can I be a neighbor?"[34] In this sense our neighbors are any person in need, people who are oppressed and who suffer. When any person or system moves against another person or community unjustly, our responsibility is to be a neighbor by speaking the truth about this injustice—though we will do it in ways that are loving.[35]

Compassionate Resistance

Wendy Farley uses the phrase "compassionate resistance" to describe anger that functions in the service of God's love.[36] Nancy Ramsay elaborates, "Compassion is the exercise of love that . . . fiercely resists the forces of evil that seek to deform or destroy human life."[37] From an ethical perspective, *not* expressing our anger in appropriate "compassionate resistance" is, in effect, to collude with the injustice, to support perpetrators through our silence.[38]

But unanimity does not surround this issue. Some interpret the Gospel to suggest that resistance, not to mention confrontation, is un-Christian. Their stance is often based on the perception that Jesus chose not to resist his trial and crucifixion. Biblical scholar Walter Wink challenges the perception that Jesus' words in Matthew 5:39: "Do not resist an evildoer" counsel passivity in the face of oppression and evil. The Greek word translated "resist" is *antistenai*, which means, says Wink, "to stand against." This word is used in the Greek version of the Old Testament to describe the violent fighting that took place between two armies on the battlefield. Jesus was not saying "don't resist," Wink argues, but "don't resist violently." He thinks a better interpretation is, "Don't react violently against the one who is evil." This translation leaves room for resistance, though it excludes violence. Wink calls this "the third way" of relating to evil, neither passively nor violently.[39]

Wink regrets that Jesus' advice in Matthew 5:39–42 about turning the other cheek, giving your cloak also, and going the second mile have been interpreted as examples of nonresistance rather than nonviolent resistance. In fact, these metaphors have been used to perpetrate abuse, support domination, and enforce acceptance of bondage by all types of authorities—including slave masters, government officials, church leaders, parents, and husbands. Wink carefully examines the meaning of these statements in the context of first-century Palestinian life to argue that Jesus is actually giving a "revolutionary political statement" that, far from teaching nonresistance, counsels resistance without violence.[40] To turn the other cheek, he declares, "has come to imply a passive, doormat quality that has made the Christian way seem cowardly and complicit in the face of injustice."[41] In reality, turning the cheek forces a brutal superior to choose between having to hit with the fist—a sign of equality—or not slapping a second time.[42]

We can see, in this story written by a colleague who remembered a childhood incident, the kind of change that can occur in an oppressor when faced with strong resistance.

> I can still fairly vividly remember the day when I was about ten and I had been hit with the dog leash (my father's usual weapon for punishment)

for doing something I had not done, when something snapped inside me and I became furious. I knew my father's anger was unjust, that I had not done what he said, that he had made a decision without investigating what had happened, and had belted both my brother and I because he assumed one of us had done "it." So I thrust out my other hand, telling him to hit that too. To my surprise he didn't, nor did I get hit for being "cheeky" or answering back (also a punishable offense). Instead, to my surprise, I got a hug. I was not hit much after that, but somehow I discovered in my own mind the sense that I had made my father small.

Her father, she said, was stunned, embarrassed, and perhaps exposed by the assertive action of presenting her other hand to also be hit (a turning of the other cheek). In response he changed his behavior, and the extent of his abuse was reduced. My colleague described a sense of confusion that her father had become small in her eyes, but that may have contributed to her willingness as an adult to resist injustice and oppression.

Wink also decries the interpretation of going the second mile as a platitude that only means to do something helpful beyond what is expected. In Jesus' day, he argues, going the second mile was not doing something extra to be kind to a soldier, but was actually a method for confronting the oppressive law that allowed Roman soldiers to force a Jew to carry his supplies for a mile. The action was calculated to throw the soldier off balance, taking back the power of choice and reasserting human dignity.[43]

Nonviolent Confrontation

Many theologians and ethicists have urged that compassionate anger express itself in action.[44] McNeill, Morrison, and Nouwen agree that anger activated by threats to our values should motivate us to action and specifically point out the relationship between compassion and confrontation. After reminding us of Jesus' willingness to confront, they conclude, "direct confrontation is a true expression of compassion." Within the context of anger generated by injustice, they describe the responsibility of compassionate Christians:

> The illusion of power must be unmasked, idolatry must be undone, oppression and exploitation must be fought, and all who participate in these evils must be confronted. This is compassion. We cannot suffer with the poor when we are unwilling to confront those persons and systems that cause poverty. We cannot set the captives free when we do not want to confront those who carry the keys. We cannot profess our solidarity with those who are oppressed when we are unwilling to confront the oppressor. Compassion without confrontation fades quickly into fruitless sentimental commiseration.[45]

The power of evil is so strong, they write, that "nothing less than strong and unambiguous confrontation is called for. . . . confrontation is an integral part of compassion."[46] Harrison agrees, writing about the connection between our calling "to a radical activity of love" and the responsibility for confrontation.

> We are called to confront, as Jesus did, that which thwarts the power of human personal and communal becoming, that which twists relationship, which denies human well-being, community, and human solidarity to so many in the world.[47]

The importance of anger in the struggle for liberation is strong. Compassionate anger should be in the service of liberating people from oppression and freeing them to be what God has called them to be. Daly observes that "Rage is not 'a stage.' It is not something to be gotten over. It is a transformative, focusing Force."[48] Rosemary Radford Ruether connects the process of liberation with a growing awareness and affirmation of anger. Only this affirmation allows the oppressed to break "the deep internalized chains of repression." Anger becomes righteous anger when it is "the work of liberating grace . . . the presence of God empowering us to say 'no' to injustice." [49]

But what type of confrontive action is appropriate? Christian theologians and ethicists have consistently advocated nonviolence as the appropriate form of confrontation. Martin Luther King Jr. taught nonviolence as the most practical way of achieving racial justice, and spoke often of the immorality of violence. After surveying the destruction caused by violence, James Cone speaks for most liberation theologians when he says, "Returning violence for violence must be completely rejected as an inappropriate strategy for black liberation in the United States."[50] Wink, following Gandhi and King, claims that to be nonviolent is not to avoid conflict:

> The "peace" that the gospel brings is never the absence of conflict, but an ineffable divine reassurance within the heart of conflict: a peace that surpasses understanding. . . . In fact, nonviolence seeks out conflict, elicits conflict, even initiates conflict, in order to bring it out into the open and lance its poisonous sores. Nonviolence is not idealistic or sentimental about evil; it does not coddle or cajole aggressors but moves against perceived injustice proactively, with the same alacrity as the most hawkish militarist.[51]

Nonviolence as active resistance demands courage and a willingness to suffer the consequences.[52] Gandhi often spoke about the difficulty of making cowards into effective nonviolent activists. He learned that people do not make the move from passive submission to active nonviolence unless they are willing to face their own rage. Wink sums up Gandhi's insight:

> [People] need to be energized by their anger. Then they can freely renounce violence for a nonviolent alternative that transforms the energy of their anger into a dynamic and resolute love.[53]

Anger has the energy to turn cowardice into courage, allowing us to confront the power of evil. People who are fearful of anger either because of personal experience or the teaching that anger is a deadly sin are unable to tap the source of courage and are rarely involved in the fight against injustice.

LOVE SHOULD DIRECT ANGER

Though morally appropriate, anger in response to injustice, radical suffering, or oppression must be expressed in ethical ways. Not only is anger in the service of love, but it must always be under love's direction; in every period of church history, theologians have recognized this connection. Early church theologian Evagrius Ponticus wrote that "love . . . is to be reckoned a great thing indeed in that it is able to bridle anger."[54] Many centuries later, John Wesley observed that "zeal is always guided by knowledge, and tempered, in every thought, and word, and work, with the love of man, as well as the love of God."[55] If separated from love's guiding light or foundational principles, anger's destructive powers will lead us into unethical behavior even as we try to confront unethical behavior.

How can we fight injustice without being unjust ourselves? This question focuses our attention on four ethical guidelines that should inform and direct our expressions of compassionate anger: compassion for perpetrators and oppressors, the danger of self-righteousness, identifying the log in our own eye, and not repaying evil for evil.

Compassion for Perpetrators and Oppressors

Jesus calls us to be compassionate beyond our comfort level. In Luke 6:27–28, he challenges us to make a difficult response toward people who perpetrate injustices: "Love your enemies, do good to those who hate you, bless those who curse you, pray for those who abuse you." When we can choose such behavior, we are loving as God loves, because in doing so we "will be children of the Most High; for he is kind to the ungrateful and the wicked" (v. 35).

Anger at unjust, oppressive behavior must not blind us to the humanity of the perpetrator, who is also a person created in God's image, a child of God who is not beyond redemption. Anger that grows out of love's compassion is all-encompassing and seeks redemption for both the oppressed and the oppressor.[56] Eleanor Haney's words, though written to women, should be heard by men also:

> Learning to be courageous does not mean that we should abandon tactfulness, diplomacy, and sensitivity to others. We can speak on our own behalf, speak out against injustice and harm, and speak to hold another accountable and still recognize that we are speaking with people who are also loved by God.[57]

James McGinnis, founder of Parenting for Peace and Justice Network, points out that anger in the service of love not only works toward justice for the victims, but also includes compassion for the victimizer.[58]

We are not always, as individuals or as a society, receptive to this idea. The death penalty, for instance—a controversial cultural expression of anger at people believed to have committed a serious offense—assumes that a person is beyond redemption. In contrast, Jesus' concern that we love our enemies and pray for them is an attempt to keep us from demonizing them so that we don't lose sight of their humanity and the possibility for transformation.

The Danger of Self-Righteousness

Christians face the particular danger of confusing "self-righteous" anger with "righteous" anger. Interpreting threats to the self as if they were threats to God is easy. When we make such mistakes in interpretation, we become angry "on behalf of" God (as if God needed defending!) when in reality we are defending our own immaturity, arrogance, or insecurity. We can easily think our anger is based on valid ethical commitments when in fact our prejudice, self-esteem, or idols are threatened. When this misinterpretation occurs, as theologian C. S. Song has noted, "righteous anger easily gets turned into self-righteous arrogance that tolerates no difference of opinion and opposition."[59] Song says that self-righteous anger attempts to punish and destroy enemies rather than inviting them to become transformed. Righteous anger, on the other hand, is rooted in and directed by love, so its goals are repentance, reconciliation, and transformation: "[R]ighteous anger is more love in agony and action than anger seeking the punishment and destruction of one's enemies."[60]

Self-righteousness often results from what depth psychologists call "projection," perceiving in someone else the very characteristics that we have suppressed in ourselves. This possibility makes it more imperative to assess any experience of anger to determine the various levels of threat so that we can ascertain whether or not being threatened, and angry, is related to our faith narratives rather than egocentric agendas.

Identifying the Log in Our Own Eye

From the Sermon on the Mount comes this verse that has become part of our culture's vernacular: "Why do you see the speck in your neighbor's eye, but do not notice the log in your own eye?" (Matt. 7:3). Jesus speaks to our ability and willingness to quickly assess the shortcomings of a family member, colleague, parishioner, or other neighbor while being quite blind to similar attitudes and behaviors in our own life.

The story of King David's sin against Uriah and Bathsheba as exposed by Nathan's story helps us to understand our tendency to self-deception and projection. David's anger—expressed outwardly when he first heard Nathan's story—also speaks inwardly to himself (with Nathan's prompting). So our anger asks that we tidy up our own act; we are also finite and flawed. We are all tempted to be like David (seducers, betrayers, murderers if only by thought), like Judas (greedy betrayers), and like Peter (cowardly deniers). We must examine our own hearts and minds and be willing to identify our own unjust thoughts and behaviors toward others. By being open with this reality before God, by repenting and accepting God's acceptance and steadfast love expressed in mercy and forgiveness, we can learn how to be merciful to others.

Only as we know ourselves, including our own lying, cheating, deceiving, betraying behavior, can we show compassionate anger based in righteousness. As we are able to see our own sinfulness, we are reminded of our need for mercy and compassion from others and from God. Projecting anger at the oppressor "out there" and away from the "oppressor" in ourselves is easy, as is forgetting that we are also participants in systems that oppress. Recognizing the oppressor in ourselves enables us to refrain from demonizing the other. Being able to identify with their humanness, we are able to have compassion for the oppressor.

Do Not Repay Evil for Evil

Given our imperfections, what begins as righteous anger can easily become hostility, about which the New Testament is constantly concerned. One of the most glaring truths about revolutions against evil political and social regimes is that the revolutionaries often come to practice the same oppressive behaviors as the government they conquered. Freedom fighters become the next generation of oppressors, unable to effectively deal with the rage, unable to move toward peace and mercy. Vengeance and retaliation are the temptation for the victim who gains the upper hand, who attains power over the oppressor.

In the fourth century St. Basil warned against trying "to cure one evil with another" and against "returning evil for evil." He pointed out that doing so would let the enemy "be your teacher and model."[61] Wink calls this "becoming what you hate" and quotes Friedrich Nietzsche: "Whoever fights monsters should see to it that in the process he does not become a monster."[62] Hans Küng reminds us that Christian love stands for the "renunciation of violence, renunciation of the desire for revenge, readiness to spare opponents, readiness for all-round pardon, resolute action for reconciliation and unselfish good will."[63]

Paul speaks to the temptation to copy or mirror what we hate: "Do not be overcome by evil, but overcome evil with good" (Rom. 12:21). He encourages us to take a different path: "Do not repay anyone evil for evil, but take thought for what is noble in the sight of all" (12:17). "Never avenge yourselves," he warns, suggesting that we turn feelings of revenge over to God (12:19), and instead feed enemies when they are hungry and provide something to drink when they are thirsty (12:20), actions that are the very opposite of hate.

CHRISTIAN CARE AND COUNSELING

Christians who are afraid of anger often find it difficult to feel compassion and to take courageous action in the face of evil. Perhaps for this reason, the church has been hesitant to confront injustice, radical suffering, and oppression. Only when beliefs and values are held with passion can they be threatened and generate the compassionate anger that motivates us to resist social evils. As the church, we contribute to the development of compassionate anger through worship, preaching, teaching, and empathic caring.

Worship, Preaching, and Teaching

Through its worship, preaching, and teaching, the church can give permission for parishioners to experience fully and deeply the anger that comes in the daily flow of life, particularly that which comes with pain and loss. Worship is one of the contexts for us to practice putting our anger "on the table" in our relationship with God. In this context we have the opportunity to join the community of faith in learning to accept our capacity for anger as a good gift from the Creator. We can practice naming, claiming, and taming anger.

Second, in litanies, prayers, hymns, the reading of Scripture, and the homiletic event, parishioners can learn, and perhaps adopt, the faith narratives central to the gospel that allow them to be threatened by injustice, radical suffering, and oppression. In this context we can best strive to connect our anger to God's, learning to feel the same anger that God feels because we take God's stories into our faith narratives and become threatened by that which threatens

God. Worship is where we can experience the transformation of anger into compassion and be challenged to find ways of expressing it ethically and effectively. The church, furthermore, can develop curriculum that provides instruction and training for parishioners on *how* to advocate for the oppressed, to identify injustice, to learn strategies for effectively attacking oppressive structures, to learn how to prevent further harm, and to practice relationships that might transform perpetrators.

In worship, preaching, and teaching, parishioners "hear" images and metaphors that can help them know that God is angry on their behalf and ready to empower their resistance.[64] They experience God standing with them in their suffering, identifying with their woundedness, and being on their side. In worship, care, and counseling, we have the opportunity to help victims "construct images of God's power and love that unequivocally present God's righteous anger over their abuse, fierce commitment to their healing, and tender compassion for their violated bodies and wounded spirits."[65] We must challenge images of God which suggest that suffering is handed down to the sufferer by God as punishment, or "given" to victims as a way to build character.

These images and metaphors for God will be enhanced as brothers and sisters in Christ experience God incarnate in us as we stand beside them. Empathic anger toward the sources of pain can produce hope in victims. Expressions of compassionate anger validate their anger.[66] We join them in solidarity against the oppressors when we identify our anger and act as their advocates. When we identify with their rage at being violated and victimized, and even confront on their behalf, they can begin to think of themselves as worthwhile. Compassionate anger expressed in actions of resistance to and confrontation of evil can serve to empower the victims, bringing hope that can fuel their own ability to resist evil. Our compassionate anger can be empowering when wounded people know we are standing beside them and are attempting to walk in their shoes. Teamed with our tender care of them, our anger "encourages in them a new sense of hope and agency."[67] They can recover hope and begin to act passionately on behalf of themselves and others.

Inviting Advocacy

Therapeutic care and counseling with people who have suffered at the hands of others normally includes encouraging them to conceptualize and describe the situation—and to feel and express the anger. This process of naming and expressing anger is part of the healing process, particularly the recovery of self-worth, self-integrity, and a sense of empowerment. For a Christian to be threatened by, for example, sexism, racism, ageism, violence, exploitation, and poverty is appropriate. The caregiver's task is to help the wounded be fully aware of their anger, accept its appropriateness, and choose actions that allow movement against the injustice.

Caregiving to victims, from my perspective, includes another level of concern. I suggest that the ministry of care and counseling in a Christian context is not finished until we have invited people to consider the possibility of finding a way to stand with other victims. The responsibility, indeed the privilege, of the Christian caregiver is to invite wounded persons (after they are far along on the journey toward recovery!) to consider how their experience prepares them for advocacy. "Full service" care and counseling offers guidance to victims who have gained a new sense of self and are grateful for new and whole life, to consider that one response of gratitude is to stand against oppressive individuals and systems.[68] We have the responsibility as members of the Christian faith to guide victims in establishing solidarity with other victims and, in concern for future victims, to consider using anger creatively as part of their spiritual commitment. We must be careful, of course, that they do not make themselves vulnerable to further rejection, blame, penalties, abuse, or violence by taking a stand before they are safe or strong enough to deal with these consequences. They could easily experience backlash from abusive and controlling parents, bosses, spouses, and other people in authority.

Community and Empowerment

Being courageous is difficult in isolation. Anger is more easily transformed into an expression of hope and translated into courage when dealt with in community. Persons dealing with a major threat and intense anger are more likely to feel hopeless and fearful when isolated from other people. When people feel powerless and helpless, they tend to think they are alone and swallow the rage. In community anger can be directed into creative action so that overwhelming feelings of frustration are less likely to push a person into despair.

Christian care and counseling calls for establishing groups that provide support and encouragement to people who are searching for courage. In these groups, anger can be focused, examples provided, fears confronted, defeats debriefed, and successes celebrated as persons develop and nurture the courage to be compassionately angry in the face of injustice. Feminist writers have been particularly concerned that women coming to consciousness about their anger find a network of communication and support so that the backlash which often comes from family, spouse, and church will not abort their anger.[69]

Religious historian Patricia O'Connell Killen describes how power structures in all eras have attempted to deny the existence of suffering in the lives of the people they dominate. If denial doesn't work, these power structures "minimize and delegitimize [suffering] by encouraging individuals to endure pain privately and to take total responsibility for any pain in their lives. Oppressive cultural and institutional forces work insidiously to keep those who suffer both silent and isolated."[70] Dealing with anger in community, therefore, is imperative for finding power and motivation. Killen notes that when people are willing to express their pain in community:

> It generates a communal anger that may develop into risky but real social power. When individuals risk feeling and expressing their pain with others, the cry of pain begins the formation of a new community around an alternative perception of reality. The source of such a counter community is trust in one's pain and in the pain of one's neighbor, which is very much like one's own.[71]

Support groups provide a safe place where intense emotions can be identified, expressed, affirmed, and then focused into effective actions.[72] Marjorie Suchocki notes that "the support group . . . provides the stability which can sustain the rage and begin to direct its force into actions for effective social change."[73] Groups such as Mothers Against Drunk Driving (MADD) allow members to share their experiences and their anger, which often allows them to overcome the sense of helplessness and powerlessness.[74]

Self-Care

Using our energies and abilities to protest radical suffering is part of being a disciple and can be taught as a spiritual discipline.[75] But anger should not rule our lives. Time and energy for joy and celebration are necessities. Other expressions of love such as comfort, mercy, and forgiveness are imperative for abundant life. We do not need to separate anger from our tenderness and gentleness, or from other fruits of the spirit.

Sue Monk Kidd writes about her awakening to the oppressive results of sexism. As she became more conscious of the injustices, she realized that she would have to allow anger to have its place in confronting them. Later, she recognized that the anger would have to be "transfigured," by which she means that

> anger becomes a "fire that cooks things rather than a fire of conflagration." A conflagration may embolden and impassion you for a while, but if you get stuck in it, it can burn you up. A fire that cooks things, however, can feed you and a whole lot of other people.[76]

We must guard against allowing our compassionate anger to turn destructive because of our failures to achieve justice, or because of overcommitment and stress. Jesus did not stay constantly angry, but models for us the many expressions of love and types of caring.

I have established some of the positive potential of anger when expressed in the service of love, explaining the many ways it can be a spiritual ally and motivate us for ethical action. I turn in the last chapter to explore the particular steps that enable us to handle anger creatively, making sure its enormous power is used for good, and not for evil.

13

Handling Anger Creatively

Our capacity for anger is a gift from the Creator that, though it has the potential for harm, serves useful purposes in human life. Our ethical responsibility is to handle anger in ways that are life-enhancing for ourselves and our community, rather than life-destroying. Scripture reminds us that we have the freedom, indeed the responsibility, to handle anger creatively. Remember that after questioning Cain about being angry (Gen. 4:6–7), God reminded him that he could "master" sin that was lurking at the door. The author of Ephesians also believed that we can choose to keep anger from being destructive, advising, "Be angry, but do not sin" (4:26). Then, in 4:31, the author instructs readers that as followers of Christ they should "put away" bitterness, wrath, slander, and malice, those expressions of anger that are destructive rather than creative. Both these narratives assume that we have control over how to express our anger. How can we choose the constructive alternative?

Anger can be expressed creatively and effectively if we exercise our freedom to handle it wisely and redemptively. The wise strategy, say Evelyn and James Whitehead, is to "honor" anger by treating with "awe" and "respect"[1] its power and potential for both harm and good. Since anger is included in our "imageness," recognized as a gift bestowed by and blessed by the Creator (chapter 10), then to honor anger as a potential "spiritual ally" (chapter 11) is an appropriate response. The Whiteheads also suggest that "befriending" anger, by paying attention to its creative possibilities, is an appropriate spiritual stance toward this powerful emotion.[2] Intentionally honoring and befriending anger serves as an antidote to the deep, even unconscious, hold that the anger-is-sin tradition has on many of us who grew up in the church.

This positive, rather than negative, response to anger can free us to deal with it more creatively.

This chapter sets forth a process for handling anger in a manner that serves our ethical responsibility for not doing harm, but also for intentionally activating anger in the service of love. I suggest eight steps that are normally necessary to take when an incident of anger occurs. A preliminary step in preparing to handle anger responsibly, identifying and changing core narratives about anger from our past, is discussed in chapter 6. The eight steps described below may or may not need to be considered in this order, but to handle anger wisely, using its power for good rather than evil, attending to each of these steps is necessary: recognizing anger, acknowledging anger, demobilizing our bodies, identifying the narratives that are threatened, evaluating the validity of the threat, transforming those stories that make us unnecessarily vulnerable to threats, changing previous patterns of dealing with anger, and expressing anger creatively. Following these steps guides our thinking about how to handle a given experience of anger, but also provides a guideline for providing care and counseling with persons, families, and institutions struggling with anger and conflict.

RECOGNIZING ANGER

The first step is to develop our ability to recognize anger when it occurs. We cannot act responsibly with anger we don't recognize, and anger that is unidentified and thereby ignored becomes even more dangerous. Denial and avoidance are constant temptations because of our fear of anger or our belief in the anger-is-sin tradition. A "quick-tempered" person, of course, who regularly expresses spontaneous anger that is disturbing and problematic might think that increasing the ability to recognize anger is the last suggestion needed. The reality, however, is that the sooner in the process of being threatened we recognize our anger, the more quickly we can bring resources to bear on handling it before it becomes so "hot."

Yet, most of us, whether we tend to suppress or to explode, know the difficulty of recognizing our own anger—not because the signs are hard to read, but because we don't want to admit to ourselves, much less others, that we are angry. Fortunately for our discernment process, anger can't easily hide itself; it leaves clues to its presence. Our responsibility is to do the detective work necessary to identify our unique physical, mental, and behavioral signs of anger.

Anger, as with all genuine emotions, is embedded in our physiology and includes the neurological arousal patterns described in chapter 5. By paying attention, we can easily recognize the physical signs and symptoms that accompany true experiences of anger. Blood pressure rises, heartbeat increases, muscles tense, and blood chemistry changes as the body becomes primed to defend or attack. Studying and understanding our body's reaction to anger lets us learn to read the unique evidence (grinding teeth, clenched fists, tight neck, cramping abdomen, headaches, indigestion, gas, constipation, diarrhea, and so forth) of how anger affects us physiologically. Any number of other things may cause these physical symptoms, and may even require medical attention, but they *can* be a sign that we are, or have been, angry.

Our moods also reveal the presence of anger. Being grouchy, cranky, cross, or touchy may indicate that we are angry. People around us may ask, "Why are you frowning?" or "What got you so on edge?" or they may state, "You got up on the wrong side of the bed this morning." Language also provides clues: the words "irritated," "frustrated," "annoyed," "disappointed," "hurt," or "jealous" usually indicate that some life circumstance has threatened us.

Most of us can identify several behaviors that are more likely to occur when we have not admitted our anger to consciousness. Anger can be expressed through nagging, hostile humor, abusive language, or passive-aggressive behavior even before we are aware of, or willing to admit, the anger. Behaviors as diverse as alcohol abuse, overeating, being obsessed by an event, and depression may also indicate unrecognized anger.

Any of these events might be brushed off as irrelevant, but unless we identify and deal with the anger these behaviors will continue. Sensitizing ourselves to these behaviors, physical symptoms, and moods may help us recognize anger and allow us to be more creative in dealing with it. Why focus attention on a step that may seem so obvious that it hardly needs mentioning? Because, when committed either consciously or unconsciously to theological or psychological beliefs that pathologize anger, we often respond by denying the anger, not willing to admit that the feeling even occurred. Our strong need to belong, our concern that conflict will cause people we need to abandon us, our need to be in control, or our fear of retaliation can keep us from allowing anger to stay conscious. This suppressive response can produce any number of significant narratives that prohibit a person from entertaining anger.

This way of ignoring or pretending that anger doesn't exist only heightens the probability that it will do harm, because by ignoring anger we cannot bring our reasoning powers, our volitional ability, and our spiritual resources to understanding it or directing its behavior. For this reason, psychotherapists invite patients "to get in touch with their feelings" and "to take responsibility for these feelings." In light of all this, we can easily say that a basic ethical principle for dealing with anger is our responsibility to be aware of it and keep it conscious.

Destructive experiences with anger can make us yearn for a magic wand to eliminate anger from us and the world. Denial and suppression, however, are not the answer. Anger cannot be banished from our lives, but needs to be accepted as a potential spiritual ally, learned from, and used in the service of love. Bringing the anger to conscious awareness is essential, for anger that remains below the conscious level is more likely to be expressed destructively rather than constructively. As the pastoral theology in chapter 10 established, people who suppress anger have denied an important aspect of the image of God reflected in us, and have refused to accept one of God's gifts. People who attempt to eradicate the experience of anger by repression or suppression become mentally or spiritually truncated.

ACKNOWLEDGING ANGER

After recognizing anger, the second step is to acknowledge it, by which I mean accepting what we feel: to name it and claim it as ours. Naming something gives it an identity and makes it more difficult to brush aside or discount its significance. A nameless experience does not call for our attention, or allow a creative response. By acknowledging anger we capture the reality of it, not allowing it to escape conscious awareness, and confirm that dealing with it is our responsibility. To actually acknowledge our anger we must overcome our fear of anger, or our embarrassment over being angry, that is based on our belief in rationality as the primary mode of existence or our guilt and/or shame over being angry. These last two concerns are particularly problematic in keeping people from acknowledging anger.

We may be unwilling to acknowledge anger because, like modern-day Stoics, our narrative about the reason/emotion issue is to believe that rationality is superior to emotionality and that emotion is irrational or unreasonable in most circumstances. To feel angry, therefore, in a situation we *think* should not create anger may keep us from acknowledging the anger in order to maintain our self-perception as a "rational" person. Avoiding anger is a way of protecting self-esteem that is attached to being both logical and in control of emotion.

Feeling guilty or ashamed over being angry can also hinder us from acknowledging our anger. When we adopt the anger-is-sin concept and believe that Christians should have no cause to be angry, then the fact that we *are* angry becomes an indicator that we have fallen short of the Christian ideal and have sin in our lives, causing guilt for sinning or shame for falling short of our ideals—or both. Shame and guilt are uncomfortable and make it easy to suppress the anger, or fail to acknowledge it, in order to avoid dealing with the guilt and shame. We can feel so guilty or ashamed by the experience of being angry or expressing anger that learning from the experience is difficult. We simply want to forget the incident as quickly as possible. This guilt/shame experience may push us to find a scapegoat[3] in order to feel less guilt or shame about our anger.

One other temptation, which prohibits us from acknowledging anger in the sense of claiming it as our responsibility, is to blame our anger on someone else's behavior. We can quickly accuse a person or institution of doing or saying something that "made" us angry, as if there were universal, objective behaviors that "made" all people angry. Blaming, in effect, attempts to make other persons or institutions responsible for our anger instead of our constructed realities. So we excuse our anger by blaming it on the baby who threw food on the floor, the girlfriend who was flirting, the congregation who voted against our wishes, the driver who cut in front of us, the adolescent who was talking back, or the employer who fired us. The resulting anger creates conflict and we think the "other" should take the blame, avoiding the reality that our anger comes as a result of our narratives and is our responsibility.

We need to recognize that it is not someone else's fault that we are angry, but rather that we are angry because of the way we have interpreted their words or behaviors in the context of our constructed narratives. We are angry because the narratives that create our identity, our sense of self, are threatened by the words or behaviors of an individual or system. As Panksepp summarizes:

> Other people do not cause our anger; they merely trigger certain emotional circuits into action. Ultimately, our feelings come from within, and perhaps only humans have a substantive opportunity, through emotional education or willpower, to choose which stimuli they allow to trigger their emotional circuits into full-blown arousal.[4]

Placing the blame somewhere else in order to protect self-esteem is easy. We may be attached to self-narratives that would make it problematic to admit that we are at fault. If we can believe we were angry because someone else *made* us angry, then we can rationalize and excuse ourselves.

To acknowledge our anger before God is particularly important. If our core narrative about anger is that God is upset with us when we are angry, then we will be tempted to hide the anger from God, but the theology of anger established herein suggests that anger, like every other aspect of our life, is speakable to God. Placing our anger in the context of who we are as believers makes it less likely that we will deny or suppress it. The anger becomes an agenda between God and us, and we are then able to access our spiritual resources while dealing with the anger event, increasing the possibility of handling it ethically. An appropriate prayer is to ask God for help in learning from this event and for guidance in dealing with the anger effectively and not destructively.

When we acknowledge that anger occurred, we often realize that our expressions of anger, verbal and/or behavioral, were unethical. Our response was not a loving response but a response contrary to our commitments; we have sinned with our anger. Moving toward reconciliation calls for us to ask forgiveness from those we have injured with our expressions of anger. New Testament scholar Luke Johnson says that if the intensity of anger is not acknowledged, "then there is no awareness of and acknowledgment of hurt or injury, and there can be no forgiveness. Anger is virtually a prerequisite of reconciliation, for it reveals the reality of estrangement."[5] We must consider restitution where necessary. The purposes of this book do not include an examination of the dynamics of forgiveness, but many good books are available. Professional pastoral counselors, marriage and family therapists, and others are trained to provide such guidance.

DEMOBILIZING THE BODY

Taking responsibility for our anger requires a third step, maintaining as much control over our bodies as possible. Many of us have been in, or read about, situations in which the physical arousal that follows the perception of threat has been invaluable to survival—such as escaping a fire or tornado, resisting a rape attempt, rescuing someone from a wild river, protecting a mother from physical abuse at the hands of a drunken father, or mobilizing the body to fight disease. However, even without physical danger, when the threat is to our values, beliefs, and meanings, our bodies mobilize as if we needed to make a physically demanding response. The resulting chemical and biological changes (see chapter 5) can be destructive to our health unless we learn how to calm our bodies and regain chemical balance in order to take care of ourselves.

When in a state of arousal, we are also more likely to act harmfully with words and actions, to overreact to other provocations. When we are angered by a threat that quickly passes (someone apologizes, for example), the body often returns to neutral naturally, but when the threat is prolonged, as is common when the threat is to our values, the body can stay mobilized for a long time (see chapter 5). In fact, one way to avoid some experiences of anger is by keeping stress to a minimum. When stressed, our bodies are in a semiaroused state, which makes us more vulnerable to become aroused and angry in situations that would not normally threaten us.

So learning how to turn off the body's alarm system, minimize stress, and reduce the need for physical mobilization are important in dealing effectively with anger. You may already use some effective demobilizing processes either intentionally or without realizing it. We can learn, for example, to use music (listening to calming selections),[6] exercise (jogging, working out, gardening), meditation (controlled breathing exercises, relaxation exercises, focused imagery on safe scenes, repetition of a mantra), and massage (working to relax tight muscles). Many Christians also turn to prayer in which they may practice "surrendering" the anger or inviting insight. Meditation may include images of biblical scenes that can bring a sense of security and peace. One of my clients regularly used imagery from Psalm 23 of being led into green pastures and beside still waters as a way of calming down his body.

Using these practices to relieve tension *is not the same as suppressing anger*. Demobilizing the body should not be an attempt to pretend we aren't angry, or to forget or avoid the anger. We are simply recognizing and accepting that our bodies have made an understandable neurological response to a threatening situation, but that this physical arousal is not necessary for a survival response. In fact, a more creative response is usually possible if we calm the physical arousal. Our alarm system has mobilized us for fight or flight, but to preserve our health and to reduce the temptation to act irresponsibly, we need to relax—by moving our body chemistry away from this battle-ready condition to a state of homeostasis. In some circumstances, medication may be needed to turn off the alarm system echoing through the central nervous system in order to accomplish this demobilization. Medication can be helpful in the short term by convincing the limbic system that the danger is not as great as it fears, or as one psychiatrist friend describes it, "This will help until the tiger is out of the room."

IDENTIFYING THE NARRATIVES
THAT ARE THREATENED

The fourth step in handling anger responsibly is to figure out *why* we are angry. Anger is an alarm system activated when one of our important narratives is threatened by a particular life situation. Speaking about the experience of Jonah, Eugene Peterson commented:

> Anger is most useful as a diagnostic tool. When anger erupts in us, it is a signal that something is wrong. Something isn't working right. There is evil, or incompetence, or stupidity lurking about. Anger is our sixth sense for sniffing out wrong in the neighborhood. Diagnostically it is virtually infallible, and we learn to trust it. Anger is infused by a moral/spiritual intensity that carries conviction—when we are angry we know we are on to something that matters, that really counts.[7]

Any incident of anger contains a message that something in our life is not as we expect or desire. Remember that when Cain got angry after his offering had been unacceptable, the first thing God said to him was "Why are you angry?" (Gen. 4:6). God gave Cain a chance to understand why he was angry so that he might deal with it appropriately and gain insight, which, sadly, Cain refused to do. Taking responsibility to discern this message and assess the threat is a basic ethical step.

We begin by attempting to identify the narrative that was threatened. At the end of any mystery story, the clues are put together so that the plot becomes self-evident. The reader or viewer thinks, "Oh, now I see," which means the whole story is now understandable. Things make sense, which is how narrative structuring serves us (see chapter 6). So our task is to explore the whole experience of anger. Questions that can guide the search include: What was the anger all about? With whom am I angry? Why am I angry? What words, actions, or insinuations made me react? What part of my narratives (values, beliefs, meanings) feels attacked or in danger? In answering these questions we are facilitating self-assessment, working to gain insight so we can say, "Oh, now I see why I am threatened." Let me illustrate with Brenda's experience.

> Brenda, thirty-four, was referred by her pastor because of Brenda's concern about the intense emotional response she was having to both her daughter and her best friend. First she explained about her daughter, Lisa, who was choosing to work at a national park in a different part of the country rather than coming home from college for the summer. Brenda had become angry on the phone when Lisa announced her decision and then became "short and curt" with her husband for encouraging Lisa. A few days before we met she was surprised to make what she called an "ugly, angry jab" at her other daughter, a junior in high school: "I suppose you'll run off to another state when you get out of high school too!" Having raised her children to be independent and make their own decisions, she imagined being supportive of Lisa's decision, so although she understood being sad, her anger made no sense to her.
>
> During the same week, her best friend, Cheryl, announced she was moving to another state because her husband was changing jobs. Brenda had become immediately angry with Cheryl and even more angry at Cheryl's husband, making Cheryl come to his defense. Brenda had accused him of being insensitive to Cheryl and was angry at Cheryl for not resisting this "unilateral and insensitive command," all of which caused tension between her and Cheryl. Later Brenda realized how inappropriate she had been with her anger, unable to hear that Cheryl was in favor of, and anticipating, a move that would take them near her family.
>
> In our first two sessions, we raised two questions: how was she threatened and what stories (values, beliefs, and meanings) were under

attack? Brenda was able to see that in both instances she felt that her daughter and her friend were purposefully leaving her; she called it being "deserted." She remembered angrily telling her husband that Cheryl must not be concerned about their friendship or she wouldn't be so happy about the move, and also the "sinking feeling that Lisa didn't want to come home because of me." She went on to say, "I know they care about me, but my heart wonders why they would leave." Exploring her own history for experiences of being "left," Brenda was able to talk about being adopted as a two-month-old, and about being angry at her biological mother for "giving up on me." Brenda said with strong emotion, "She didn't even know me, but decided I wasn't worth keeping!" This intense mix of sadness and anger is not an unusual response to "relinquishment,"[8] but Brenda had never been willing to verbalize this to another person. She rationalized that it was unfair to feel this way toward her birth mother when she didn't know all the circumstances.

Identifying the narratives that were threatened by the choices of her daughter and best friend was relatively easy for Brenda because she recognized fairly quickly that her anger contradicted her conscious values and created unnecessary tension in two important relationships. Her willingness to seek assistance in understanding where this anger came from enabled her to explore this event and identify a core narrative that had formed around her early knowledge that she was adopted. She named the narrative "If you love me, you won't leave me" and summarized it with these words: "Something is wrong with me that makes people give up on me and leave." Giving language to this narrative and sharing it with another person—and later with both her daughter and her friend—provided the context for moving ahead in handling her anger creatively.

Yena, a minister in her late thirties whom you met in chapters 3 and 6, offers another example of identifying main stories that make a person vulnerable to threat. She is not addressing one particular incident of anger, but basic narratives that make it difficult for her to respond to any occurrence of anger. She wrote:

> When I began this [journey], I was not aware of my guilt over feeling anger. I was not aware that I believed the statements offered by so many Christian families to their children: (1) It is not "nice" to get angry, (2) Only bad kids get angry, and (3) I won't be loved, or even liked, if I get angry. However, through journaling about my experiences of anger, I have realized that I indeed do believe these myths. I was taught them as a child and, although intellectually I would not argue for their validity . . . I do operate by them. This philosophy of life I learned as a child runs very deep within me. Throughout my adult years these myths have been reinforced by significant others . . .

who have reacted negatively to my anger and concluded I feel too much anger. These experiences have reinforced these myths, leading me to continue to try to feel less anger, unsuccessfully. I don't believe these myths or their opinions anymore. It seems to me now that feeling anger is better than not feeling anger.

I have been aware for some time of the things that anger me. They are the same things that angered my mother: someone living with me picking up after themselves, helping to keep the house running smoothly by ensuring we don't run out of items, paying the bills on time, and taking care of appliances and tools and machines so they continue to work. When these things are not done perfectly by another, I interpret the inattention as lack of love. When they are not done perfectly by me, I think I have failed. This way of viewing the world has been a dominant narrative for me that I inherited from my mother. I wonder if I feel somehow that I will betray my mother by giving up this narrative? Several narratives are actually operating here: respect and obey your parents at all times; thoughtful acts are signs of love; I can be and am expected to be perfect, as are others; I earn others' love through my perfect actions; machines and tools and appliances don't break if taken care of; we can control our life completely if we try hard enough, among others. Again, while intellectually I am able to argue against the validity of most of these narratives, emotionally I see now that I indeed subscribe to them.

When trying to understand what narratives are threatened by a particular life situation, looking for more than one is important. Behind many experiences of anger are multiple stories being threatened, and frequently one or more are unconscious. Whether trying to understand our own anger, or functioning as a caregiver, a fruitful question to ask is, "What other stories might be threatened?"

Jonathan and Susan, a newly married couple, called me for an appointment because I had worked with them as their premarital counselor. They came because their anger was unexpected and disturbing to them. Jonathan described a recent Sunday morning when he was angry at his wife because they were late to church again. They had already worked with and understood the threat model of understanding anger, so we moved to the question, what narratives are threatened? After exploring many possibilities, and with Susan's assistance, Jonathan identified that one of his important narratives contained the value of being responsible. He confirmed that part of the story is his belief that responsible people are on time. This story was important in his family of origin and he had adopted it as his own. Furthermore, "being on time" for Jonathan means "being in your seat" a few minutes before the event starts.

Susan, on the other hand, also likes to be responsible, but does not connect being responsible with being on time. In fact, for her "being on time" means getting there "before the main event is under way," because, as she says, "nothing starts on time anyway and the warmup stuff isn't worth sitting through." Their clash of stories about the definition of "being on time" often caused conflict about departure times and, when they are late, Jonathan is threatened by his feeling of being irresponsible. He angrily blames Susan for being irresponsible and she gets angry in return because he has "assassinated my character!"

Now why was there so much intensity around an important, but not unsolvable, problem? To the question, "What other stories could there be underneath all this?" Jonathan was able to identify a deeper threat. The clue came when he said that when she made them late he felt "that she doesn't care for me." When he elaborated, Jonathan was able to discuss that since they had been married for almost a year, he believed that "she should know by now how important it is to me to be on time." The fact that, despite constant promises to the contrary, she doesn't make the effort to be on time feels threatening to a more unconscious narrative, which he described as "people who love each other behave in ways that help their partner accomplish goals and feel good about themselves." The fact that she does not choose to be on time, nor function in a way that helps him meet this important criteria, is perceived by him as "not very loving." Susan was surprised by this deeper feeling and had underestimated the extent of Jonathan's feelings.

Jonathan has several obvious narratives: one values being responsible, another connects being responsible with being on time, and a third defines being on time with being what others might consider early. But a deeper narrative is about how people who love each other relate, namely that they work hard to function in ways that assist each other in activities and behaviors that represent their self-identity and maintain integrity. Though he didn't like to be late, it was the more basic interpretation of Susan's behavior as being "unloving" that was the most threatening. Knowing this deeper threat moved both Jonathan and Susan to a more concerned and thorough assessment of their conflict, as discussed later.

In summary, the goal of this step is to identify the situations that create threat and to use the anger event as a "diagnostic window," as described in chapter 11. In each of the illustrations above, clearly identifying the threat was a necessary step in self-discovery that allowed a responsible process of handling conflict.

EVALUATING THE VALIDITY OF THE THREAT

After gaining insight into why we feel threatened, the fifth step is to discern whether feeling threatened is necessary and appropriate. The next question is, "Did I need to be threatened?" Ideally the answer is based on an evaluation of the circumstances, based on those values and meanings that reflect our understanding of the Christian faith and its claims on our life. Such an evaluation focuses the light of the gospel on the narratives that are threatened in order to examine them in the context of our theology, our ethics, and our spiritual experience. On the basis of our faith narratives, we can assess whether or not a maturing Christian needs to be threatened by this particular life circumstance. The faith narratives used might include our understanding of God's character and how God works in the world. The "fruit of the Spirit" found in Galatians 5:22 can help persons assess their behaviors when angry, and the way in which Jesus related to others is a model for evaluating relationships.

By identifying, from the perspective of our theological commitments and our spiritual journey, which persons and events do not *have* to threaten us, we will be able to reduce unnecessary threats and, therefore, our anger. Our continued maturation as people who love God and neighbor as self leads us to identify which life events do not have to be *perceived* as a threat. We find that many of the things we are threatened by do not really need to threaten us, which Brenda's situation can illustrate.

> Brenda's narrative about being abandoned because something is wrong with her leaves her particularly vulnerable to life events that feel like she is being abandoned—relinquished yet again! Long-standing questions about her worth are raised automatically when people "leave" her. Making the story conscious, and intentionally making the connections, allowed her to realize that the narrative under threat was not a valid story. The geographical changes were in no way an indication that they loved her any less.
>
> She was able to begin realizing that the story she developed as a child that her mother "must have known something about me" that made her "not want to keep me" was, as she called it, "irrational." She realized that many other circumstances could have gone into that decision and decided to begin the process of finding out more about her birth family.
>
> Perhaps most important was the question of Brenda, who was a Christian, "What does your faith have to teach you about this narrative you have described?" Over several sessions she pursued describing her understanding of God and particularly her perceptions about how God felt about her. Brenda did believe that God was a loving God, and that God loved everyone. But she was able to admit that on many occasions, particularly when she was feeling that people left her because something was wrong with her, that she didn't include herself among the "everybody."

Brenda used her faith narratives about the character of God and how God feels about her as a particular person as a way to assess the narrative that was threatened.

Some threats, of course, are legitimate, and anger is an appropriate response. From a faith perspective, to be threatened by real physical, social, or relational dangers is legitimate—that is why we were created with the capacity for anger. Furthermore, in chapter 12 I established that certain life circumstances such as injustice, radical suffering, and oppression *should* threaten the theological values encased in our faith narratives.

TRANSFORMING NARRATIVES

The sixth step has to do with answering the question: what do we do when we evaluate a particular experience of anger and discern that, from the perspective of our faith narratives, being threatened by this particular life situation is not necesssary? The answer is to revise, or reconstruct, those particular narratives so that they are more in keeping with our faith narratives and, therefore, not vulnerable to threat. How do we change narratives?

For Brenda, changing the story involved becoming more intentional in recognizing when her unconscious narrative, "If you loved me, you wouldn't leave me," became dominant.

> Brenda began to make a new conscious story about the realities of her daughter's choice and her friend's necessary move. She incorporated the real story as they presented it by writing it down on a small piece of cardboard that she kept by her bathroom sink: "Lisa loves me and chose to work out of state because our love is strong enough so that she has the freedom to make such choices. Cheryl DOES consider me a best friend, and is moving because of her commitment to her husband and to be closer to her family."
>
> Furthermore, she decided that she could trust as a reality what her family and friends communicated by word and deed about their feelings for her. She accepted the idea that it made more sense to believe that her adoptive family, her husband, children, and good friends had a much better knowledge of her than her birth mother, and found her both likeable and loveable. Her anger at Lisa and Cheryl began to dissipate.

We may realize the need to change some faith narratives to reflect a deeper, more accurate understanding of the gospel, thereby reducing our vulnerability to unnecessary threats.

> Brenda quickly realized that it was not rational to leave herself out of the "everyone" that she believed God loved. We discussed some characters in the Bible, including David and Peter, who had failed to measure up to our standards of behavior and faithfulness and her strong

belief that God loved them anyway. She knew that it made no sense, and accepted that this belief had not been "taken into my heart." She began to consciously consider that God's love and acceptance of her could counter the narrative about being "unwanted," "given up," "deserted," and "not good enough to keep." So she wrote a prayer that expressed gratitude to God for loving her, particularly as a child who had been "given up."

After Yena recognized the extent and pervasiveness of her core narrative about anger, this larger picture provided the impetus for beginning to change her patterns of dealing with anger. As she wrote:

> My feelings of anger have been based not on a temperament but on my values and basic "way of life," my immediate perceptions of an event, and my basic philosophy of life. My feelings of anger have been based on my narrative, the way I think life occurs. This narrative has been influenced significantly by my mother's narrative, and in many ways I have simply adopted her narrative. When my narrative, or the way I think life works, is threatened, I feel anger. This understanding of anger eliminates the [need to judge] anger as bad or sinful. It accepts the reality that anger occurs, and eliminates the [need to judge myself] as a bad or un-Christian person because I experience anger. It sets the stage for adopting an approach to dealing with anger that, at the onset, appears to have more credibility and possibility of success than previous approaches I have attempted.
>
> Although I know it will not be easy to change this dominant narrative that anger is bad, I believe this is the first step for me. I must change my view of anger from a negative emotion to be avoided to a neutral emotion, or even a positive emotion to be accepted and used for personal growth and development.
>
> I do think letting go of them has been tied to a belief that doing so would be a betrayal of my mother. While again I know that changing these narratives will not be easy, I believe I must do so not only to deal effectively with anger but to be a responsible, mature Christian in the world.

The results of transforming the narratives that make us vulnerable to unnecessary threat is the freedom from so much anger.

Narratives that are deeply ingrained, so basic to our identity that they are easily threatened, are not easy to change. After several months of intentionally working with her narratives about anger, both those with which she grew up and the ones she has adopted, Yena is aware that changing narratives is difficult.

> Another narrative I have to change is the belief that if I don't fix it now, remedy the situation that has angered me, the future of our relationship is questionable. This, I believe, is a matter of security. I have been

insecure in my primary relationships, not quite believing the other really loves me. This insecurity fosters a fear of loss of love, of abandonment, that I think underlies my interpretation of the other's behavior as a sign of lack of love. I must become less fearful, more secure, and therefore less threatened. The narrative at the core of this insecurity is that I am not lovable. This comes from feeling my mother was never pleased, didn't really want me, and therefore didn't ever love me. This has left me feeling unlovable. After all, if your mother doesn't love you, who can? I know this narrative operates inside me. I can feel when it becomes the dominant narrative out of which I operate. I also know at other times I operate out of a different narrative, one that says that she loved me as best she could, that her expression of love for me is about her, not me. It is as if these two narratives co-exist inside me, fighting for the dominant position. The former has a better chance of winning out when I am in a heightened state of arousal. Therefore, one way I can help to foster the latter being my dominant narrative is to live life in such a way that my arousal is decreased: exercising, eating healthily, praying, taking time for relaxation, and not taking on too many responsibilities or demands that keep me too busy. Another way is of course to be consciously aware of the narratives and actively work on dispelling the one and integrating the other.

Yena's final reflections focused on the larger picture of how she thinks and feels about anger and the need for a reconstructed narrative about anger. She connects this need with her spiritual pilgrimage and makes a commitment to construct a new understanding of anger and a new way of behaving with anger.

I think the thing I have learned that will have the most profound affect on the way I deal with anger and help others to deal with anger is the way I view anger itself. I had never thought of anger as a "spiritual ally" or a "call to action." Deconstructing my narrative of anger and reconstructing it is necessary. Seeing anger as an indication that something is amiss is I think warranted. Anger dictates taking the time to hear the call, discerning God's lure and strategizing a response. In this way, anger, instead of being something to dread, avoid, or pray away, is transformed into "a positive partner in our growth and development, in our maturity as people who are committed to being Christian disciples." This reconstruction requires discipline, not unlike other spiritual disciplines. Having a history of practicing spiritual disciplines, this notion of disciplined reconstruction resonates with me and helps me to put anger into a completely different category—usefulness instead of vice. I believe this reconstruction will be the key to my finally learning to deal with anger in a healthy and constructive way in my life and thereby be able to assist others in doing the same.

Yena illustrates the importance of caregivers' attending to our own narratives about anger if we are to be effective in helping people with theirs. Our sensitivity to injustice is often based in our own past hurt. Therefore we can respond from a sense of our own outrage and pain, but mask it as being concern for another. This does not mean we are in error or that our anger is unjustified, but that we must be on guard lest we overreact or project our pain onto the other and exaggerate their situation because of our own history. Only by clearly knowing our own narratives can we minimize this risk.

This step reminds us of our responsibility to work toward transforming those narratives that wouldn't be threatened by a particular event if we were living our lives more clearly attuned to the most central values of our faith. In this way we reduce the number of situations in which we feel threatened and angry.

CHANGING PREVIOUS PATTERNS OF DEALING WITH ANGER

Taking ethical responsibility for our anger includes this seventh step: changing previous patterns of dealing with it. Our theology is clear; we have the ability to change. As a person becomes aware that previous patterns were ineffective at best, and destructive at worse, then beginning to change those patterns becomes an important step in dealing creatively with anger. Everyone has unique ways of expressing anger, but some patterns are discernable. In the introduction, I mentioned such common behaviors as silence, withdrawal, nagging, fussing, hostile humor, verbal abuse, and violence. Some people have learned to express anger in a dominating, intimidating way in order to maintain control. Others adopt patterns of acting impulsively, either verbally or physically, in ways that are hurtful to others. Still others pretend that they have a temper that they can't control.

Yena describes how her experiences growing up and the dominant stories about anger she brought into adulthood influence the way she handles anger in the present.

> When I do handle anger in the moment I feel it, I handle it in a way very similar to the way my mother handled anger: indirectly. I give clues I am angry, expecting you to pick up on my displeasure, recognize the injustice that is causing my anger, and rectify the injustice, thus eliminating my anger.

Next Yena describes how she handles anger in close relationships, particularly within romantic relationships, and that reflects her dominant narratives and the modeling she did after her mother.

I find myself most often angry at those I am living with or in a romantic relationship with, someone I would consider "family." In these situations, I express anger in a way indicative of my family of origin. I use
verbal and nonverbal expressions that make clear my displeasure. My
tone of voice is unloving, I slam doors, and I ask questions that are
interpreted as attacking. I rationalize that I am being honest by bringing up the situation that is bothering me.

In dealing with anger with a significant other, my pattern is to
immediately address the situation, albeit in an indirect and unhealthy
way, forcing conversation about it. I have to admit that this has not
proven to be very effective. The statement "Most people don't know
how to express anger without attacking or belittling" certainly applies
to me at times, particularly when I am expressing anger to my significant other. I have had experience after experience support the claim
that "verbal aggression usually fails because it riles up the other person and makes him or her inclined to strike back."

Changing how she expresses anger is the next agenda that Yena addresses.

I believe taking time, counting to ten, or one hundred, or even not
raising some issues at all may be beneficial. At the very least, taking
time will allow me to process my anger before acting on it. This time
will allow me, when I am "feeling bothered," to figure out what is
occurring within me (am I angry?), acknowledge anger if it is present,
identify the threat causing my anger, and discern if the threat is justi-
fiable. If I am unable to change anything else except to simply take
more time to process internally before expressing externally, my way
of dealing with anger will be dramatically altered.

For me to deal healthily with the anger requires thought, deliber-
ate action, and energy because it is not a pattern I have established; it
is not something that is automatic or comes easy for me. It is uncomfortable. It is a challenge.

Passive-aggressive people don't get mad, they get even. Their anger is often
expressed through indirect retaliation as they satisfy their need for revenge, or
to "pay back." Continuing with Jonathan and Susan's story will illustrate:

After realizing that her choice to be late made Jonathan question her
love, Susan made a decision to change her behavior and be on time.
She assumed that this would be an easy commitment to make, but over
the next month she was still late on a number of occasions. In the sessions we focused on why Susan thought she could not mobilize her
"willing powers" to change this behavior. Over several weeks of trying to identify what made the difference between those times she was
on time and those when she wasn't, she discerned that it was related
to "how close" she felt to Jonathan. When asked what made the difference in level of closeness, she was able to identify anger that she felt
about something in their relationship. She read a layperson's descrip-

tion of passive-aggression and concluded that her resistance to his desire to be on time represented a passive-aggressive response.

   This awareness, and her disgust with herself for being indirect with her anger, led to a different pattern of communication for both of them. They committed to what they labeled "straight talk" when either was dissatisfied or annoyed with the other. Because they worked overlapping shifts, and because she wasn't sure how easy it would be to break her long history of hiding many of her negative feelings, they decided to keep a small notebook on a counter in the kitchen in which they would note "affirmations and concerns" about their day-to-day life. Then at two appointed times during the week, they pledged to take time to discuss thoroughly what they had written.

Passive-aggressive behaviors can be identified and changed so that a person handles anger more directly, as described in the following section. Again, note that in this step we take responsibility for changing our patterns of handling anger so that they fit our ethical commitments about behavior that is appropriate.

CREATIVE EXPRESSIONS OF ANGER

The eighth step in handling anger responsibly is to attend to the way in which anger is expressed. Handling our anger responsibly certainly includes the expectation that we not wound people with our expressions of anger. This step is important *whether or not we discern that the anger is valid*. Often we are aware that anger in a certain situation is our problem, not someone else's problem. That is, we are experiencing anger but we know that the threatened narrative needs to be changed, that no reason exists from a faith perspective to be threatened, yet we are angry. So we have to express that anger in a way that is creative and does no harm.

Communicating Directly with the Source of Threat

When we have assessed that the narrative which is threatened is a valid narrative and decided that our anger is an ethically appropriate response, then directly communicating this to the other person(s) involved may be the appropriate option. Whether to take this option depends on the circumstances; direct communication is not always the most effective option. Those people closest to us, however, usually sense when we are angry because they recognize the clues (facial expressions, tone of voice, and other behaviors), so we might as well acknowledge the feeling. In a close relationship important actions are usually acknowledging the anger, admitting our inability to deal

with it at the moment, and then committing to deal with it creatively later, saying something like, "I don't want this to create distance between us and will
come back to it with you as soon as possible." If we spoke or acted in some way
that hurt the other person or damaged the relationship, then an apology may
be in order.

Sometimes communicating directly means a confrontation with an individual with whom we are angry. Matthew 18 provides a scriptural model for
dealing with our anger directly:

> If another member of the church sins against you, go and point out
> the fault when the two of you are alone. If the member listens to you,
> you have regained that one. But if you are not listened to, take one or
> two others along with you, so that every word may be confirmed by
> the evidence of two or three witnesses. If the member refuses to listen
> to them, tell it to the church. . . . (Matt. 18:15–17)

Jesus knew what harm could be done by unresolved anger. Therefore, he
instructs the disciples to take initiative in seeking reconciliation with those
with whom we are angry. If this individual initiative does not work, we should
next take one or two other people with us to facilitate communication. As
counselors well know, often another person or two present allows narratives
to be expressed, more fully expanded, and heard. With one or two witnesses,
accountability seems to increase. If this approach does not work, then a small
group consultation or confrontation may be the next step. Here representatives of the community of faith try to mediate the dispute. This process of
mediation can often facilitate more thorough and effective communication,
provide more complete insight and understanding, explore new possibilities
for change, and lead to problem solving and reconciliation.

Confrontation in the larger social arena is more difficult, but perhaps the
same strategies apply. Ideally, for example, when confrontation of a larger system, such as a corporation or an organization, is called for, the whole community of faith can join together for thoughtful and creative action, as
discussed in chapter 12.

Expressing Anger to a Trusted Other

At times, of course, directly approaching a source of threat is impossible or
imprudent. Acknowledging anger to the other person may not be wise; perhaps the time, place, or situation is not appropriate. Perhaps people not
involved are present and would not understand, or we are wound tight from
stress and know we would not express our anger creatively.

Confrontation, even of the mildest type, might feel dangerous to a person who is very dependent on a particular relationship. A person in a dependent relationship may fear that expressing anger toward an employer, professor, supervisor, doctor, spouse, or parent, for example, could be perceived as an attack, or at least disrespectful, and either break the relationship or be countered with retribution or punishment. These relationships usually involve power differential, and anger is difficult to express toward someone who has the power to hurt us emotionally, socially, financially, or physically—by divorcing or firing, or with physical violence. Acknowledging anger might even be dangerous when it has the potential to elicit a destructive response from a defensive coworker, abusive spouse, arrogant boss, or armed intruder. We know that taking time to think through our feelings—to decide how to express the anger and toward whom—would be the wiser choice.

The other side of this situation occurs when a person is angry at someone over whom he or she has control. A parent may be aware of intense anger toward a child, for example, yet also aware that the child's behavior is mostly related to the age and stage that the child is passing through, so that to express the anger at the child could be destructive.

We may also share our anger with another person when the source of the threat is not available—because of death, age, mental health, or geography. Fredrick's experience provides an example when the age of the antagonist made direct communication of anger inappropriate:

> After several sessions of counseling, Fredrick, at age forty-seven, was able to admit his intense anger toward his father for the father's behavior toward Fredrick when he was an adolescent, particularly related to his unrelenting criticism of Fredrick 's intellectual and physical attributes. After several weeks of processing the effects of this anger in his present relationships, Fredrick considered the possibility of overcoming the alienation that characterized his relationship with his father for the last thirty-three years. He imagined expressing this anger directly to his father. However, his father was now in a nursing home in frail health, so Fredrick decided that it would not be a caring action to, as he said, "dump all this old crap in my father's lap now." So he decided to express his anger through writing a long letter to his father and reading his words to me as his pastoral counselor. The letter did become part of his healing process and freed him to choose behaviors that he hoped would communicate to his father a desire for reconciliation.

In therapy a person might uncover anger toward someone who is now dead—a mother who deserted the family to marry another man, a father who was abusive, a drunk driver, a person who committed suicide, and so forth—for actions that were emotionally or physically painful. Caregiving at the time of a tragedy may include listening to, and then facilitating, anger toward another who cannot now respond.

Tonya's husband was killed in an automobile accident in which he had been at fault. This thirty-three-year-old widow was very angry with him for driving carelessly, which she had warned him about repeatedly. She was angry that he had lost his life and left her in financial difficulty with two young children. She was frustrated that he was not available, as she said, "to feel my heat," but she chose to share all this with me as a trusted other. Later, in a manner that was as close as she could get to a direct confrontation, she wrote a long letter to her deceased husband, expressing in detail her anger at his irresponsibility and abandonment. After writing this letter she began to look for alternative stories that would help her lay the anger aside. After a few weeks she decided to claim the positive aspects of the relationship, so she re-storied her narrative to focus on the "good times." Then she began a process of accepting his choices and hoped that "I can forgive him some day." She also developed a future narrative about herself that provided hope: surviving and thriving as a mother and an individual who might remarry. Two months later she wrote him a good-bye note and was ready to "get on with my life."

You can see that in these situations, finding another person with whom to share the feelings can be helpful. If you are aware of anger concerning either a past or present event or relationship, it is possible to explore more thoroughly the causes and effects by sharing the anger with a trustworthy person. Find a pastor, priest, or therapist who is knowledgeable and competent in guiding an angry person through the processes described in these chapters. After listening to you, if this person doesn't feel competent or have the time to participate with you in this process, he or she will know persons in your community who are fully trained to do so.

Journaling

Closely related to verbalization is writing the words that we would like to speak. Keeping a journal can help us capture the feelings, identify and understand the threat, and decide on the best manner of being responsible with the anger. If I wake up thinking about some situation that angers me but stay in bed ruminating about the situation, then I become more physically aroused and mentally upset—which keeps me from going back to sleep. However, if I go to the computer and express the feelings in my journal, the process of writing often dissipates much of the physical arousal; my body is demobilized and I can return to sleep. How does this work?

For me, journaling is an action that helps me move toward decisions, which I don't do while lying in bed. Capturing anger in my journal gives language to my feelings, allowing me to express myself specifically and thoroughly. Writing it down serves the purpose of acknowledging the anger both to myself and to God. Once the anger is expressed, I pursue the process of identifying the narrative that is threatened and assessing whether being threatened in this circumstance is justified. Then I think through possible responses and decide on a particular next step. Often I move directly from journaling to writing a letter, to either myself or another person, that deals with the event—hopefully in a creative, ethical manner. In addition, having a long-term written record of situations in which I get angry has allowed me to investigate the types of threat to which I am most vulnerable.

CHRISTIAN CARE AND COUNSELING

A purpose of this book is to provide assistance for ministers in offering care and counseling, which does not necessitate the development of new or different methods and techniques. My assumption is that the skills you already possess are adequate for the task of caring for angry people. I have focused on what needs to happen in the caregiving relationship.

Christian caregiving and counseling includes inviting, sometimes challenging, people to take responsibility to change those narratives that make them unnecessarily vulnerable to threats—stories that are negative, painful, or problematic. From a narrative perspective, stories are constructed, and therefore changed, through the interactive process of dialogue, what one author calls "the world of conversational narrative." Therefore, change in a person's story is most likely to occur in the context of conversation—what narrative therapists Harry Goolishian and Harlene Anderson call "collaborative language."[9] Through language we describe other possible stories, or interpretations, that have been overlooked.[10]

Reconstructing/Deconstructing Threatened Narratives

Reconstructing a narrative usually proceeds in tandem with the process of deconstructing a present story. The concept of "deconstruction" has a long history in philosophy, but I borrow the term from two disciplines: literary criticism and psychotherapy. In literary criticism, the term "deconstruction" describes the process of dissecting a text for analysis. Since constructionist narrative theory sees human life as storied, deconstruction describes a process of studying a person's story to see what parts are causing problems and challenging those aspects that need to be changed.

In psychotherapy, the term "deconstruction" describes a therapist's attempt to change a clients' perception of the validity of some part of their story. The term refers specifically to the process by which a therapist guides clients in identifying the inconsistencies in particular narratives. To deconstruct in therapy is to challenge a client's view of reality, or as Steve de Shazer describes the process, the therapist "seeks to find the . . . thread . . . which will unravel it all, or the loose stone which will pull down the whole building."[11] In counseling angry souls, we may need to do the same.

Madeline and her husband, Kenneth, were both twenty-six years old and had been married almost two years when they invited me to join their story. They were bothered by critical anger that she would express at him for reasons both agreed were minor. Furthermore, both of them were insightful people and had identified that this anger almost always occurred around weekend visits from her parents. Her parents made this hour-and-forty-five-minute trip about every other weekend. Kenneth described Madeline's agitation before such visits, the conflict that occurred during the visit, and the depressiveness and anger that she experienced for several days afterwards. What was the conflict about? Madeline's mother, a woman who was strong and opinionated, constantly criticized her for the way she kept house, cooked, wore her clothes and makeup, and functioned as a wife. They both believed that her bouts of self-doubt and questioning her worth as a person were rooted in threats she felt from her mother's critical and judgmental attitudes.

I pointed out that while most women desired approval from their mothers, others realized that their mother's expectations or projections made it difficult to take their critique to heart; what made the difference for her? Madeline described her long story of trying to function in ways that gained her mother's unconditional support and approval. She was able to describe her narrative as believing that unless she somehow earned this approval, she was "not a very good person." Furthermore, the mother's expectations, as perfectionistic as they were, found support in some of the cultural expectations that Madeline carried within her stories.

The pastoral conversation moved in several directions to deconstruct the story. The most helpful was in seeking what narrative therapists call an alternative story. I asked her to help me understand the story about her that was held by three other people that knew her well. We agreed on her husband, her sister, and her best friend. Then she carried out the assignment to ask them specifically how they evaluated her as wife, cook, and homemaker, and how she presented herself physically. As she listened to them tell their stories about her, and then as she listened to herself tell me these stories, she began to realize that an alternative story existed that she had not heard. That is, she had not taken into her story other pieces of relevant data.

The next piece had to do with looking for the "loose stone which will pull down the whole building." By then it was clear that unconsciously she had given her mother's opinion of her (as she perceived it) power over her self-identity. Many possibilities existed as to why she

might have done this, but I approached the issue by making this statement, "Wow, as much weight as you give to your mother's opinions,
you must greatly admire her as a judge of character! She must have
wonderful insight into people." Her immediate response was, "Oh no,
Mother is critical of everyone!" I said, "But don't you think she is a
better judge of people than your sister?" "No." "Your best friend?"
"No." "Your husband?" "No." "Well, how does she gain veto power
over the votes of these other people when it comes to evaluating you?"
The incongruity of this conversation began to challenge her core narrative about her mother. She began to realize that she had given her
mother's observations power that didn't make sense according to her
own assessment of her mother, particularly when compared with the
trusted observations of the other three persons.

Challenging a Dominant Narrative

Mary and Kenneth Gergen, social psychologists and constructionist narrative
theorists, use the term "dialectic narrative" to indicate the presence of two or
more stories that are in conflict with each other.[12] I adopt the term to describe
a narrative that is different than, thereby causing conflict with, an existing narrative. From the clash of contradictory stories comes the possibility that a
transformation will occur. A therapist may purposefully introduce an alternative story in hopes of creating dialectical tension with the possibility that the
client will choose the new story. A counselor can facilitate change, therefore,
by enabling a person to develop an "alternative story" that can serve a dialectic purpose, a story with the power to confront a person's current story. Consider this example:

> I was the visiting preacher at a small church (they were without a pas-
> tor) and was now standing to the side of the altar after the worship ser-
> vice talking with five parishioners. Two of them, Len and Marsha,
> were a married couple with whom I had been working as a pastoral
> counselor/marriage and family therapist for over a month. They had
> not attended any church for years, and had been members of this con-
> gregation for only ten months. As we talked together, I noticed Len
> frown, clench his teeth, and then step out of the group to say in a low,
> but intense voice, "How many times have I told you not to run in the
> church!" I realized that his two sons, five and three years of age, were
> chasing each other from the educational wing through the double
> doors into the sanctuary. Len grabbed their upper arms too tightly and
> herded them back out the side door. The conversation ended, and the
> next time I saw them was at their weekly session three days later.
>
> One of the problems that had brought them into the counseling
> process was Len's harsh expressions of anger within the family, partic-
> ularly toward the two children. He had embarrassed himself several
> times in public by his overly physical discipline of the two boys and

requested that his wife help him find a counselor. Their former pastor referred them to me. Prior to the incident mentioned above, we had already discussed the threat model for understanding anger, and both of them were able to understand it quickly. So, at our next session, after listening to his guilt about Sunday's incident, I invited him to apply those concepts and see what he could learn.

During that session Len searched his narratives to see if he could understand why he was threatened by the children's behavior. The first threat was quickly identified and had to do with the children's seeming disobedience. His narrative about children is that they should automatically do anything a parent tells them to do. He had told them before they got out of the car, as he did every Sunday, to behave themselves, which included "don't run in the church." Adding to the intensity of this threat was the fact that many fellow parishioners were still around and Len was able to acknowledge his fear that if they saw his children running in the church they would think of him as a poor father. The second narrative, therefore, had to do with his strong need to have other people think of him as a good parent, which he assumed would only occur if his children were obedient. But what about the harsh discipline? He realized that he had accepted as a model his grandfather's explosive, physical response when something didn't go according to his expectations. Marsha helped him verbalize his negative response to his grandfather's approach and he confirmed that he had wanted to be different, but in his frustration, and his desire that his children would "be good kids," he often resorted to this model.

Len invited Marsha to help him tackle the first narrative, and they decided to start with an educational approach to learning more about parenting. Len would take responsibility for educating himself on "what a good father would do." In the next month they read two assigned books on parenting. Then, with the aid of the new pastor, they organized a group of parents of younger children and invited (and paid for) a minister to children from a large suburban church in a nearby city to lead a three-hour workshop on "Christian Parenting." He learned during the discussion in the seminar that other men in the church also struggled with how to be good fathers. From both the books and the seminar discussion, he began to develop new ideas about discipline and began experimenting with more gentle interactions with his boys. As his confidence grew, he was less threatened by his children's behaviors. He was changing the narrative about his incompetence.

The Christian story provides alternative stories by which we can confront dysfunctional narratives about anger. As representatives of God, our privilege and responsibility are to facilitate the confrontation between Christians and the gospel in order to develop more valid faith narratives, which is part of both the priestly and the prophetic function. A Christian caregiver can facilitate change, therefore, by introducing a dialectic story from the gospel that has the power to challenge and transform a current story.

Later, I asked Len how he came to believe that children shouldn't run in church. He was surprised by my question and said, "Well, the church is a place to be reverent." I asked, "So, as far as you know, when God sees kids running in church, God gets upset with them?" "Well, yes," he said tentatively, "or maybe he blames their parents for not teaching them how to behave at church." As we pursued this conversation, it became clear to him that another narrative, largely unconscious, which influenced his reaction to the boys at the church, was that God was irritated when children ran in church and, furthermore, held parents accountable. He realized this narrative was emotionally strong, but when it was spoken he wasn't sure he really believed it.

Pursuing the history of that image of God, he discussed his father's death when he was four and his mother's choice to attend college about twenty miles from their home. Because she often worked at night and on weekends to support the two of them, Len spent much time with his grandparents, who lived close by. His mother had never gone to church, but he had to go with his grandparents. They were very stern in their expectations about his behavior and he had to "toe the line," which meant no noise, little movement ("I could hardly wiggle my fingers"), and "certainly no running!" We discussed the images of God that grew out of his experiences with his grandparents. Len realized that he not only modeled his parenting after his grandfather, but also had adopted some of his image of God from both grandparents.

He was willing to explore more thoroughly the content of his God images. We listed various characteristics about God that he learned from his grandparents and another list of characteristics that he had heard from other sources, including in recent months at their current church. He was clear that the current list was the one he thought to be most valid based on his new knowledge of Scripture and the tradition of this church. In short, he was deconstructing the narrative about God learned as a child at the same time he was constructing a new narrative based on his current study and experience in both worship and the teaching ministry of his current church. He decided, in his words, "that God was probably smiling, rather than frowning, when children were having any kind of fun in the church."

The Gospel as Dialectic Narrative

This process of deconstruction is not unlike the use of parables in the teachings of Jesus. Parables are an example of deconstruction as they present a dialectic narrative that confronts the existing worldview of the listeners. The parabolic teachings of Jesus represent a different reality, an alternative story that, if understood, calls the dominant narrative into question. The parable becomes a dialectic narrative that has the potential of deconstructing the current worldview, challenging the hearer to construct a new understanding of reality or, in narrative language, a new story. Parables challenge the dominant story of individuals, the larger community (like a local church), and the whole society.

The church has the privilege and responsibility of bringing the perspective of the Christian story into confrontation with a person's personal story. In worship, preaching, and teaching, the gospel can function as a dialectic narrative, challenging our embedded dogmas, revealing our incongruent narratives, and confronting stories in our life that have not been transformed. Through the interactive processes of litanies, prayers, hymns, lessons, sermons, and the reading of Scripture, the church enters the parishioners' stories, hoping to facilitate a transformation in accordance with the sacred story.

Notes

Introduction: The Problem with Anger

1. See chapter 4 in Andrew D. Lester and Judith L. Lester, *It Takes Two: The Joy of Intimate Marriage* (Louisville, Ky: Westminster John Knox Press, 1998).
2. Judy is also a licensed marriage and family therapist and a member of the American Association of Pastoral Counselors. We have often worked as a therapy team when counseling couples.
3. See "Anger" in the *Dictionary of Pastoral Care and Counseling*, gen. ed. Rodney Hunter (Nashville: Abingdon Press, 1990), 39. This article concurs, describing "the erroneous belief that all anger is sinful (and that this is the Bible's teaching)" as the dominant contemporary misconception about anger that keeps Christians from handling it well.
4. Redford and Virginia Williams, *Anger Kills: Seventeen Strategies for Controlling the Hostility That Can Harm Your Health* (New York: Harper Perennial, 1993).
5. Notice the frequent connection between humor and violence in certain cartoons (Beetle Bailey and Popeye) and movies (*The Three Stooges*).
6. Personal correspondence, summer 2001. Name withheld.
7. For one example, see *The Treasure of Earthen Vessels: Essays in Theological Anthropology*, ed. Brian H. Childs and David W. Waanders (Louisville, Ky.: Westminster John Knox Press, 1994).
8. For other descriptions of pastoral theology, see the *Dictionary of Pastoral Care and Counseling*; the *Journal of Pastoral Theology*, 1991–current (Dayton, Ohio: Society for Pastoral Theology); and *The New Dictionary of Pastoral Studies*, ed. Wesley Carr (Grand Rapids: William B. Eerdmans Publishing Company, 2002), 258–59.
9. For further study, see Tobin Hart, Peter Nelson, and Kaisa Puhakka, eds., *Transpersonal Knowing: Exploring the Horizon of Consciousness* (New York: State University of New York Press, 2000).
10. Pauline Marie Rosenau, *Post-Modernism and the Social Sciences: Insights, Inroads, and Intrusions* (Princeton, N.J.: Princeton University Press, 1992), 117. See also

Axel O. Hirschman, "The Search for Paradigms as a Hindrance to Understanding," in *Interpretive Social Science: A Second Look*, ed. Paul Rabinow and
William M. Sullivan (Berkeley, Calif.: University of California Press, 1987).

11. Pastoral theology and practical theology have much in common, though I do
not see them as the same.

12. John Macquarrie, "Pilgrimage in Theology," *Epworth Review* 7, no. 1 (January
1980): 47–52.

13. Wolfhart Pannenberg, *Anthropology in Theological Perspective*, trans. Matthew J.
O'Connell (Philadelphia: The Westminster Press, 1985), 11. Pannenberg
argues that "Christian theology in the modern age must provide itself with a
foundation in general anthropological studies," 15.

14. Ibid., 15.

15. Ibid., 21.

16. Carroll Saussy, *The Gift of Anger: A Call to Faithful Action* (Louisville, Ky.:
Westminster John Knox Press, 1995), 66.

Chapter 1: The Significance of Emotion

1. John M. Cooper, *Reason and Emotion: Essays on Ancient Moral Psychology and Ethical Theory* (Princeton, N.J.: Princeton University Press, 1999), 411. For a summary of Aristotle's ideas about emotion, see 406–23.

2. See *Webster's Third New International Dictionary, Unabridged* (Springfield,
Mass.: Merriam-Webster, Inc., 1986), 742.

3. Jaak Panksepp, *Affective Neuroscience: The Foundations of Human and Animal
Emotions* (New York: Oxford University Press, 1998), 47. For a psychoneural
definition, see 48.

4. Robert Solomon, *The Passions: The Myth and Nature of Human Emotions* (Notre
Dame, Ind.: University of Notre Dame Press, 1983), x.

5. For a more detailed discussion, see David M. Rosenthal, "Emotions and the
Self," in *Emotion: Philosophical Studies*, ed. Gerald E. Myers and K. D. Irani
(New York: Haven Publications, 1983), 164–91.

6. James E. Gilman, "Reenfranchising the Heart: Narrative Emotions and Contemporary Theology," *Journal of Religion* 74 (April 1994): 219.

7. See Rosenthal.

8. Gilman, 219.

9. Quoted in James D. Whitehead and Evelyn Eaton Whitehead, *Shadows of the
Heart: A Spirituality of the Negative Emotions* (New York: Crossroad Publishing
Company, 1994), 6.

10. Martha Nussbaum, *Love's Knowledge: Essays on Philosophy and Literature* (New
York: Oxford University Press, 1990), 40–41.

11. Quoted in Whitehead and Whitehead, 6.

12. Roberto Unger, *Passions: An Essay on Personality* (New York: Free Press, 1984),
101ff.

13. See Nussbaum, 40–41.

14. Solomon, viii. He says that in the modern era "passion got no respect in philosophy."

15. Ibid., xvi.

16. For a detailed summary of psychological research prior to 1960, see James Hillman, *Emotions: A Comprehensive Phenomenology of Theories and Their Meanings
for Therapy* (Evanston, Ill.: Northwestern University Press, 1992).

17. John Macquarrie, *Principles of Christian Theology* (New York: Charles Scribner's
Sons, 1966), 119.

18. Solomon, 193.
19. Daniel Goleman, *Emotional Intelligence* (New York: Bantam Books, 1995), 56.
20. Gilman, 224.
21. Solomon, ix.
22. Stanley J. Grenz, *A Primer on Postmodernism* (Grand Rapids: William B. Eerdmans Publishing Company, 1996), 5–9. See his work for discussion of a Christian response to postmodernism.
23. Goleman, 4.
24. Andrew Ortony, Gerald Close, and Allen Collins, *The Cognitive Structure of Emotions* (New York: Cambridge University Press, 1988), 5.
25. Solomon, 251.
26. Jean-Paul Sartre, *The Emotions: Outline of a Theory*, trans. Bernard Frechtman (New York: Philosophical Library, 1948), 52.
27. Solomon, ix.
28. Pauline Marie Rosenau, *Post-Modernism and the Social Sciences: Insights, Inroads, and Intrusions* (Princeton, N.J.: Princeton University Press, 1992), 129.
29. Grenz, 14.
30. Warren S. Brown, Nancey Murphy, and H. Newton Malony, eds., *Whatever Happened to the Soul? Scientific and Theological Portraits of Human Nature* (Minneapolis: Fortress Press, 1998), 121.
31. See Solomon, chap. 7. Also see Unger's description as an example.
32. Hillman, 188.
33. Ibid., xii.
34. Ibid., ix. See Solomon as well.
35. John Macquarrie, *Existentialism* (Philadelphia: Westminster Press, 1972), 119.
36. Rosenthal, 179.
37. Ibid., 180.
38. Panksepp, 42.
39. Macquarrie, 121.
40. See Graeme J. Taylor, R. Michael Bagby, and James D. A. Parker, *Disorders of Affect Regulation: Alexithymia in Medical and Psychiatric Illness* (New York: Cambridge University Press, 1997), xi–45.
41. Panksepp, 42.
42. Solomon, ix.
43. Unger, 95–271.
44. Sartre, 93.
45. Unger, 107ff.
46. Joseph LeDoux, *The Emotional Brain: The Mysterious Underpinnings of Emotional Life* (New York: Simon & Schuster, Inc., 1996), 12–13.
47. Panksepp, 41.
48. Goleman, 289–90.
49. The connections between fear and anger are explored further in chapter 5.
50. For an overview of this debate, see Paul Ekman and Richard Davidson, eds., *Fundamental Questions about Emotions* (New York: Oxford University Press, 1990).
51. See LeDoux specific work on fear, *The Emotional Brain*, for an example of research that pursues the unique neurological processes in differing emotions.
52. See LeDoux, chap. 7.
53. Ibid., 179–224.
54. Panksepp, 43.
55. Richard J. Davidson, "Neuropsychological Perspectives on Affective Styles

and Their Cognitive Consequences," in *Handbook of Cognition and Emotion*, ed. Tim Dalgleish and Mick J. Power (Chichester, U.K.: John Wiley & Sons, 1999), 115. See his references for further information.

56. Panksepp, 43.
57. Ibid., 42. He says, "The function of ancient emotional systems is to energize and guide organisms in their interactions with the world." Panksepp adds that emotions "actually arise from the activities of ancient brain processes that we have inherited from ancestral species."
58. Ibid., 48. He says, "Their essential and archaic nature was cobbled together during the long course of brain evolution so as to provide organisms ready solutions to the major survival problems confronting them."
59. Robert H. Frank, *Passions within Reason: The Strategic Role of the Emotions* (New York: W. W. Norton & Company, 1988).
60. Panksepp, 42, 49. He says that it is external stimuli that "trigger prepared states of the nervous system." Like other neuroscientists, Panksepp believes that "the emotional tendencies of the brain were designed to respond to various types of real-world events."
61. Goleman, 290.
62. For an excellent description of the effect of trauma on neurology, see Babette Rothchild, *The Body Remembers: The Psychophysiology of Trauma and Trauma Treatment* (New York: W. W. Norton & Company, 2000).
63. Panksepp, 49.
64. Ibid., 42.
65. Davidson, 106.

Chapter 2: The Christian Tradition and Emotion

1. James D. Whitehead and Evelyn Eaton Whitehead, *Shadows of the Heart: A Spirituality of the Negative Emotions* (New York: Crossroad Publishing Company, 1994), 13.
2. Ibid., 14.
3. Ibid.
4. Ibid., 15.
5. Bruce Metzger, *A Textual Commentary on the Greek New Testament* (New York: United Bible Societies, 1971).
6. See J. Bardarah McCandless, "Christian Commitment and a 'Docetic' View of Human Emotions," *Journal of Religion and Health* 23, no. 2 (1984): 125–37.
7. Marcus J. Borg, *Meeting Jesus Again for the First Time: The Historical Jesus & the Heart of Contemporary Faith* (San Francisco: HarperSanFrancisco, 1994).
8. Donald P. McNeill, Douglas A. Morrison, and Henri J. M. Nouwen, *Compassion: A Reflection on the Christian Life* (Garden City, N.Y.: Doubleday & Company, Inc., 1982), 16.
9. Ibid.
10. Speaking of emotion as part of God's nature necessitates using anthropomorphic language, which like all human language is limited, making it difficult to find meaningful language about God. A stream of thought within the mystical/monastic tradition, often called the apophatic way, recognizes that the Creator is beyond knowing, beyond understanding, even beyond naming, and therefore any words to describe God or God's activity are useless and inadequate. Many of us have experienced the apophatic option, either being driven on to this path by life's traumas or intentionally choosing it as a spiritual

assumption to set a context for a period of meditation. But a second stream of thought, often called the kataphatic way, recognizes the need of humans to make attempts to understand and describe God's nature. Most Christians have felt free (and sometimes compelled) to use various forms of language to seek to understand, describe, and know God—including adjectives, analogies, metaphors, poetry, and stories. To take this path, we are entirely dependent on our ability to "language" the unknown. For a discussion of apophatic and kataphatic spirituality, see Belden C. Lane, *The Solace of Fierce Landscapes: Exploring Desert and Mountain Spirituality* (New York: Oxford University Press, 1998), 62–78.

11. This is only a small sample of the references to God's capacity to feel emotion.

12. I am using Marcus Borg's translation here. He believes the word "compassion" is a more accurate translation than "merciful," as does the NEB and the Jerusalem Bible, but changes "Father" to God to be more inclusive. See Borg, 47–48, and note 1, 62. McNeill, Morrison, and Nouwen also agree with this interpretation/translation, 7.

13. Borg, 46.

14. Phyllis Trible, *God and the Rhetoric of Sexuality* (Philadelphia: Fortress, 1978), chaps. 2 and 3.

15. See Borg, 48, for elaboration.

16. I concur with the spontaneous response to this paragraph by one of my colleagues in the field of pastoral care, Dorothy Panelli, of Melbourne, Australia, which in June 2002 she expressed as follows:

> It is still hard for me to imagine how one can love, worship and adore, indeed feel at all for an "unfeeling" God. Perhaps it is only my feminine need, but I need a God who is passionate and intense, else I feel about him much as I felt about Michelangelo's David when I first saw it—awestruck by its power, its beauty and its presence. Though I was breath-taken by Michelangelo's sculptor-skill, finding his work very beautiful and impacting, I could not worship or even love this sculpture intensely and passionately. Nor can I love with an all-commanding, all-desiring passion a God of only reasoned response, a God inert and unmoved to depth of feeling. Surely this immutable, dispassionate, thoroughly intellectual God could only be an academic male creation. Yet I read that many of these Theologians had deep experiences with God. It is hard for me to imagine this, given what I perceive as the lack of emotion and feeling in their writing. Perhaps in saying all of this I have yet again simply confirmed that our metaphors for God are only that—metaphors—constructed to answer our own need, constructed to speak into our own social context, thus "evangelizing" our world at the particular time and in the particular, internal as well as external, spaces in which "we live and move and have our being."

17. Seneca, "De Ira," in *Seneca: Moral Essays*, vol. 1, trans. John W. Basore (Cambridge, Mass.: Harvard University Press, 1963), 125–27.

18. For a discussion of several Greek perspectives on emotion, see John M. Cooper, *Reason and Emotion: Essays on Ancient Moral Psychology and Ethical Theory* (Princeton, N.J.: Princeton University Press, 1999), 449–77.

19. Vernon McCasland, *The Interpreter's Bible*, vol. 7 (New York: Abingdon Press, 1951), 86.

20. See Gregory the Great's work as an example.
21. Saint Augustine, *The City of God*, trans. Marcus Dods (New York: The Modern Library, 1993), 285.
22. John Cassian, *The Monastic Institutes, Consisting of On the Training of a Monk and The Eight Deadly Sins*, Eighth Book, trans. Father Jerome Bertram (London: The Saint Austin Press, 1999), 127.
23. Ibid.
24. Thomas Aquinas, *Summa Theologiae*, vol. 19, *The Emotions*, trans. Eric D'Arcy (London: Blackfriars, 1967), 15.
25. Quoted in William J. Bouwsma, *John Calvin: A Sixteenth-Century Portrait* (New York: Oxford University Press, 1988), 105.
26. See *The Cloud of Unknowing*; John of the Cross's *Dark Night of the Soul*; and Teresa of Avila's *The Interior Castle*.
27. John Patrick Reid, Introduction to *Summa Theologiae*, vol. 21, *Fear and Anger*, by Thomas Aquinas (London: Blackfriars, 1965), xxi.
28. Ellen T. Charry, *By the Renewing of Your Minds: The Pastoral Function of Christian Doctrine* (New York: Oxford University Press, 1997), 137.
29. Augustine, 284–85.
30. Saint Gregory of Nyssa, "On the Soul and the Resurrection," in *The Fathers of the Church*, vol. 58, *Ascetical Works*, trans. Virginia Woods Callaban (Washington, D.C.: The Catholic University of America Press, 1967), 218.
31. Ibid., 222.
32. Ibid.
33. Ibid., 223.
34. For a discussion of the use of "emotion" to translate the word *passions* in Aquinas, see Eric D'Arcy, notes in Thomas Aquinas, *Summa Theologiae*, vol. 19, *The Emotions* (London: Blackfriars, 1965), xxi–xxiii.
35. Edward J. Gratsch, *Aquinas' Summa: An Introduction and Interpretation* (New York: Society of St. Paul, Alba House, 1985), 89.
36. *What Luther Says: An Anthology*, vol. 1, comp. Ewald M. Plass (St. Louis: Concordia Publishing House, 1959), 510.
37. Ibid.
38. Ibid.
39. Ibid.
40. Ibid., 511.
41. Jan Lindhardt, *Martin Luther: Knowledge and Mediation in the Renaissance* (Lewiston, N.Y.: The Edwin Mellen Press, 1986), 102–12.
42. Martin Luther, *Luther's Works*, vol. 11, ed. Hilton C. Oswald (St. Louis: Concordia Publishing House, 1955), 485.
43. See Steven E. Ozment, *Homo Spiritualis: A Comparative Study of the Anthropology of Johannes Tauler, Jean Gerson and Martin Luther (1509–16) in the Context of Their Theological Thought* (Leiden: E. J. Brill, 1969), 114–17.
44. See Peter J. Leithart, "Stoic Elements in Calvin's Doctrine of the Christian Life," *Westminster Theological Journal* 55 (spring 1993): 47–49. Also see Bouwsma, 79–80.
45. See Bouwsma, 80.
46. Ibid.
47. Ibid., 79.
48. Ibid., 134.
49. Ibid.
50. Ibid.

51. John Calvin, *Institutes of the Christian Religion*, vol. 1, book 1, trans. Henry Beveridge (Grand Rapids: Wm. B. Eerdmans Publishing Company, 1953), 57.

52. Richard A. Muller, "*Fides* and *Cognitio* in Relation to the Problem of Intellect and Will in the Theology of John Calvin," *Calvin Theological Journal* 25, no. 2 (November 1990): 217.

53. Calvin, *Institutes of the Christian Religion*, vol. 1, book 3, trans. Henry Beveridge (Grand Rapids: Wm. B. Eerdmans Publishing Company, 1953), 499.

54. Quoted in Muller, 217.

55. John Wesley, "What Is Man?" Sermon CIX, *The Works of John Wesley*, vol. 7 (Grand Rapids: Zondervan Publishing House, 1958), 226–27.

56. Ibid., 228.

57. Ibid.

58. John E. Smith, introduction to *Works of Jonathan Edwards*, vol. 2: *Religious Affections* (New Haven: Yale University Press, 1959), 2–24.

59. See Ibid., 93–124, for Edwards's ideas on the interrelatedness of these aspects of our self.

60. Ibid., 95.

61. Edwards is one of the thinkers examined in William J. Wainwright's *Reason and the Heart: A Prolegomenon to a Critique of Passional Reason* (Ithaca, N.Y.: Cornell University Press, 1995).

62. See Joseph Layton Mangina, "The Practical Voice of Dogmatic Theology: Karl Barth on the Christian Life" (Ph.D. diss., Yale University, 1994), 226–36.

63. Karl Barth, *Ethics*, trans. Geoffrey W. Bromiley (New York: The Seabury Press, 1981), 418.

64. Karl Barth, *The Doctrine of the Word of God, Church Dogmatics* I/I (Edinburgh: T. & T. Clark, 1936), 148.

65. Emil Brunner, *Revelation and Reason: The Christian Doctrine of Faith and Knowledge*, trans. Olive Wyon (Philadelphia: The Westminster Press, 1946).

66. Emil Brunner, *The Christian Doctrine of Creation and Redemption, Dogmatics*, vol. 2, trans. Olive Wyon (Philadelphia: The Westminster Press, 1952), 61.

67. Brunner, *The Christian Doctrine*, 61–63.

68. Reinhold Niebuhr, *The Nature and Destiny of Man: A Christian Interpretation*, vols. 1 and 2 (New York: Charles Scribner's Sons, 1941 and 1943).

69. Reinhold Niebuhr, *The Self and the Dramas of History* (New York: Charles Scribner's Sons, 1955).

70. Richard Niebuhr, *Experiential Religion* (New York: Harper & Row Publishers, 1972), 45.

71. Paul Tillich, *Systematic Theology*, vol. 1 (Chicago: The University of Chicago Press, 1951), 77.

72. Ibid., 98.

73. Ibid., 153–54.

74. Paul Tillich, *Systematic Theology*, vol. 2, *Existence and the Christ* (Chicago: The University of Chicago Press, 1957), 19–78.

75. Paul Tillich, *Systematic Theology*, vol. 3, *Life and the Spirit, History and the Kingdom of God* (Chicago: The University of Chicago Press, 1963), 11–137.

76. Paul Tillich, *The Courage to Be* (New Haven: Yale University Press, 1952).

77. Ibid., 35.

78. Ibid., 45–54.

79. Hans Küng, *On Being a Christian* (Garden City, N.Y.: Doubleday & Company, Inc., 1976), 262.

80. Küng, 530.

81. Wolfhart Pannenberg, *Anthropology in Theological Perspective*, trans. Matthew J. O'Connell (Philadelphia: The Westminster Press, 1985).
82. Ibid., 243.
83. Ibid., 250.
84. Ibid., 251.
85. Ibid., 308.
86. Ibid.
87. Ibid., 312.
88. See D'Arcy's introduction to Aquinas, xxxi.
89. Richard Niebuhr, "Dread and Joyfulness: The View of Man as Affectional Being," in *Religion in Life: A Christian Quarterly of Opinion and Discussion* 31, no. 3 (summer 1962): 443–64.
90. Which would reflect a traditionally masculine perspective on reality.
91. Patricia Beattie Jung, "Emotion," *Dictionary of Feminist Theologies*, ed. Letty M. Russell and J. Shannon Clarkson (Louisville, Ky.: Westminster John Knox Press, 1996), 83.
92. For a brief description of the debate, see Charry, 19–28. For a more thorough description see Carol Zander Malatesta and Caroll E. Izard, eds., *Emotion in Adult Development* (Beverly Hills, Calif.: Sage Publishers, 1984).
93. Charry, 21, 27.
94. Beverly Wildung Harrison, "The Place of Anger in the Works of Love," in *Making the Connections: Essays in Feminist Social Ethics*, ed. Carol S. Robb (Boston: Beacon Press, 1985), 13.
95. Sidney Callahan, *In Good Conscience: Reason and Emotion in Moral Decision Making* (San Francisco: Harper/Collins, 1991). Ideas about the connection of emotions to morality in two influential theologians, Thomas Aquinas and Jonathan Edwards, are compared with some modern perspectives in Paul Allen Lewis, "Rethinking Emotions and the Moral Life in Light of Thomas Aquinas and Jonathan Edwards" (Ph.D. diss., Duke University, 1991).
96. For one critique of Callahan's conclusions, see Stanley Hauerwas, "Whose Conscience? Whose Emotion?" *Hastings Center Report* (January–February 1992): 48–49.
97. C. Robert Mesle, *Process Theology: A Basic Introduction* (St. Louis: Chalice Press, 1993), 30.
98. L. Bryant Keeling, "Feeling as a Metaphysical Category: Hartshorne from an Analytical View," *Process Studies* 6, no. 1 (spring 1976): 65.
99. George Wolf, "The Place of the Brain in an Ocean of Feelings," in *Existence and Actuality: Conversations with Charles Hartshorne*, ed. John B. Cobb Jr. and Franklin I. Gamwell (Chicago: The University of Chicago Press, 1984), 167.
100. Alfred North Whitehead, *Process and Reality: An Essay in Cosmology*, corrected edition, ed. David Ray Griffin and Donald W. Sherburne (New York: The Free Press, 1978), 344.
101. Ibid., 18.
102. Keeling, 55.

Chapter 3: Theological Reflections on Emotion

1. Archibald Hart, *Christian Counseling Connection*, 1 (2000): 1.
2. John Macquarrie, *Existentialism* (Philadelphia: Westminster Press, 1972), 118.
3. Patricia Beattie Jung, "Emotion," *Dictionary of Feminist Theologies*, ed. Letty M. Russell and J. Shannon Clarkson (Louisville, Ky.: Westminster John Knox Press, 1996), 83.

4. Jaak Panksepp, *Affective Neuroscience: The Foundations of Human and Animal Emotions* (New York: Oxford University Press, 1998), 51.

5. Beverly Wildung Harrison, "The Place of Anger in the Works of Love," in *Making the Connections: Essays in Feminist Social Ethics*, ed. Carol S. Robb (Boston: Beacon Press, 1985), 13.

6. Jean-Paul Sartre, *The Emotions: Outline of a Theory*, trans. Bernard Frechtman (New York: Philosophical Library, 1948), 93.

7. Harrison, 13.

8. Robert Solomon, *The Passions: The Myth and Nature of Human Emotions* (Notre Dame, Ind.: University of Notre Dame Press, 1983), xiv.

9. Roberto Unger, *Passions: An Essay on Personality* (New York: Free Press, 1984), 107.

10. Ibid., 95–271.

11. Ibid., 107 ff.

12. Even in the Whiteheads' excellent treatment of emotions and spirituality in their *Shadows of the Heart*, their subtitle focuses on *Negative Emotions*. James D. Whitehead and Evelyn Eaton Whitehead, *Shadows of the Heart: A Spirituality of the Negative Emotions* (New York: Crossroad Publishing Company, 1994).

13. Ibid., 6.

14. Jung, 83.

15. For an excellent overview, see James D. G. Dunn, *The Theology of Paul the Apostle* (Grand Rapids: William B. Eerdmans Publishing Company, 1998), 51–78.

16. Warren S. Brown, Nancey Murphy, and H. Newton Malony, eds., *Whatever Happened to the Soul? Scientific and Theological Portraits of Human Nature* (Minneapolis: Fortress Press, 1998), 24–25.

17. Ibid., 224–25.

18. Ibid., 147.

19. Harrison, 13.

20. Søren Kierkegaard, *Purity of Heart Is to Will One Thing: Spiritual Preparation for the Office of Confession*, trans. Douglas V. Steere (New York: Harper, 1948).

21. Parker J. Palmer, *To Know as We Are Known: A Spirituality of Education* (San Francisco: Harper & Row, Publishers, 1983), xi.

22. Ibid., xii.

23. For a study of emotions that emphasizes our responsibility for them, see James Hillman, *Emotions* (Evanston, Ill.: Northwestern University Press, 1992).

24. See Paul Ekman and Richard J. Davidson, eds., *The Nature of Emotion: Fundamental Questions* (New York: Oxford University Press, 1995), 265–81.

Chapter 4: Anger or Aggression?

1. David W. Augsburger, "Anger and Aggression," in Robert J. Wicks, Richard D. Parsons, and Donald E. Capps., eds., *Clinical Handbook of Pastoral Counseling* (New York: Paulist Press, 1985), 482. A pastoral theologian and counselor, Augsburger views "anger as emotional energy, aggression as its physical expression." One problem with this definition, however, is the implication that all aggression is related to the emotion of anger.

2. See Dolf Zillman, *Hostility and Aggression* (Hillsdale, N.J.: Lawrence Erlbaum Associates, Publishers, 1979), for a thorough overview of this period.

3. For a readable discussion of this issue see Stephen Budiansky, *If a Lion Could Talk: Animal Intelligence and the Evolution of Consciousness* (New York: The Free Press, 1998), and Lesley J. Rogers, *Minds of Their Own: Thinking and Awareness in Animals* (Boulder, Col.: Westview Press, 1997).

4. Erich Fromm, *The Anatomy of Human Destructiveness* (New York: Holt, Rinehart and Winston, 1973), xvi.
5. Jaak Panksepp, *Affective Neuroscience: The Foundations of Human and Animal Emotions* (New York: Oxford University Press, 1998), 188.
6. Theodore Lidz, *The Person* (New York: Basic Books, Inc., 1968), 31.
7. Panksepp, 197–198. Panksepp details at least six parts of the brain involved in this system with the periaqueductal gray area serving as the integrative source.
8. Ibid., 190.
9. For information on the biology of aggression see "The Neurobehavioral Genetics of Aggression," a special issue of *Behavior Genetics* 26, no. 5 (September 1996): 459–532.
10. Zillman, vi.
11. Ibid.
12. Konrad Lorenz, *On Aggression*, trans. Marjorie Kerr Wilson (New York: Harcourt, Brace & World, Inc., 1966). See particularly chaps. 13 and 14.
13. For further discussion of the problems with Lorenz's application to humans, see Fromm, 13–32.
14. Robert Ardrey, *African Genesis: A Personal Investigation into the Animal Origins and Nature of Man* (New York: Atheneum, 1961), 317.
15. Robert Ardrey, *The Territorial Imperative: A Personal Inquiry into the Animal Origins of Property and Nations* (New York: Atheneum, 1966).
16. Desmond Morris, *The Naked Ape: A Zoologist's Study of the Human Animal* (New York: McGraw-Hill, 1967), and *The Human Zoo* (New York: McGraw-Hill, 1969).
17. Dolf Zillman, "Mental Control of Angry Aggression," in *Handbook of Mental Control*, ed. Daniel N. Wegner and James W. Pennebaker (Englewood Cliffs, N.J.: Prentice Hall, 1993), 370.
18. Ibid.
19. The frustration-aggression hypothesis was put forth in J. Dollard, N. E. Miller, O. Hobart Mowrer, G. H. Sears, and R. R. Sears, *Frustration and Aggression* (New Haven, Conn.: Yale University Press, 1939). This theoretical concept has been carefully critiqued and modified in the intervening years by Leonard Berkowitz, ed., in *The Roots of Aggression: A Re-examination of the Frustration-Aggression Hypothesis* (New York: Atherton, 1969).
20. Kathleen J. Greider, "'Too Militant'? Aggression, Gender, and the Construction of Justice," in Jeanne Stevenson Moessner, ed., *Through the Eyes of Women: Insights for Pastoral Care* (Minneapolis: Augsburg Fortress, 1996), 125. Greider's book *Reckoning with Aggression: Theology, Violence, and Vitality* (Louisville, Ky.: Westminster John Knox Press, 1997) is an excellent pastoral theological discussion of aggression.
21. James D. Whitehead and Evelyn Eaton Whitehead, *Shadows of the Heart: A Spirituality of the Negative Emotions* (New York: Crossroad, 1994), 45.
22. Jean M. Blomquist, "Discovering Our Deep Gladness: The Healing Power of Work," *Weavings* 8, no. 1 (January/February 1993): 24.
23. Greider, "'Too Militant'? Aggression, Gender, and the Construction of Justice," 126.
24. Ibid., 126–27.
25. Ibid.
26. Ibid., 125.
27. Marjorie Suchocki, "Anxiety and Trust in Feminist Experience," *The Journal of Religion* 60, no. 4 (October 1980): 464.

28. Though the very concept of aggression, when mixed with the perspective that aggression is a male characteristic, or at least a male prerogative, risks providing support for the idea that God is male.
29. Suchocki, 464.
30. Ibid., 465.
31. One of my friends, Mahan Siler, expressed it well in a personal communication: "I, too, think of God more as love than aggression, but have come to appreciate more the passionate, persuading, pursuing, wooing of God's love, which has an aggressive edge, though never coercive, violating our freedom."
32. It is difficult for me to think of the Christian tradition making the statement "God is aggression," making this characteristic equal to love in God's character. This parallels the concerns I discuss in chapter 9 about theologies that claim love and wrath are equal characteristics of God that are often at odds.

Chapter 5: Where Does Anger Come From?

1. I presented an early version of this model in *Coping with Your Anger: A Christian Guide* (Philadelphia: Westminster Press, 1983).
2. The following description comes from many sources. For more information that is quite readable, see Babette Rothchild, *The Body Remembers: The Psychophysiology of Trauma and Trauma Treatment* (New York: W. W. Norton & Company, 2000), and Joseph LeDoux, *The Emotional Brain: The Mysterious Underpinnings of Emotional Life* (New York: Simon & Schuster Inc, 1996).
3. See LeDoux, chap. 7.
4. Ibid., 179–224.
5. Rothchild, 12–13; LeDoux, chap. 7.
6. Richard J. Davidson, "Neuropsychological Perspectives on Affective Styles and Their Cognitive Consequences," in *Handbook of Cognition and Emotion*, ed. Tim Dalgleish and Mick J. Power (Chichester, U.K.: John Wiley & Sons, 1999), 115. See his references for further information.
7. Jaak Panksepp, *Affective Neuroscience: The Foundations of Human and Animal Emotions* (New York: Oxford University Press, 1998), 190.
8. Ibid., 42.
9. Other messages pass to, and through, the sympathetic branch of the autonomic nervous system preparing our body internally for response to this crisis situation. The main chemical transmitter of this system is epinephrine (also known as adrenaline), which functions as both a neurotransmitter and as a circulating hormone in order to
   1. ensure maximum blood supply to organs that need to be active—the muscles, heart, and brain
   2. increase cardiac output by increasing blood pressure, pulse rate, and stroke volume (the amount of blood pumped with each heartbeat)
   3. dilate blood vessels in muscles while constricting those in less important areas of the body, thus ensuring an increased blood supply (which increases oxygen and removes waste product such as carbon dioxide and lactic acid) to both skeletal and heart muscle

The hypothalamus, pituitary gland, and other endocrine glands release additional hormones (chemical messengers) into the blood to ensure that blood sugar levels rise, and insulin and growth hormone levels are reduced, all with the effect of making increased quantities of glucose, and thus energy, available to muscles.

10. Rothchild, 12–13; LeDoux, chap. 7.
11. Panksepp, 187.
12. See LeDoux's explanation.
13. Panksepp, 53.
14. Ibid., 54 (his capitalization).
15. Ibid., 203.
16. Davidson, 108.
17. Panksepp, 188.
18. Dolf Zillman, *Hostility and Aggression* (Hillsdale, N.J.: Lawrence Erlbaum Associates, Publishers, 1979), 308. Also see Willard Gaylin's *The Rage Within: Anger in Modern Life* (New York: Simon and Schuster, 1989), 25–48.
19. Andrew D. Lester, *Hope in Pastoral Care and Counseling* (Louisville, Ky.: Westminster John Knox Press, 1995).
20. John M. Cooper, *Reason and Emotion: Essays on Ancient Moral Psychology and Ethical Theory* (Princeton, N.J.: Princeton University Press, 1999), 421.
21. Panksepp, 56. He describes, for example, how receptor fields undergo permanent change in response to external events and neurons expand or shrink on the basis of environmental pressures.
22. Ibid., 56.
23. Ibid., 48.
24. Ibid., 55.
25. Ibid., 204.
26. Ibid., 187.
27. Quoted in Daniel Goleman, *Emotional Intelligence* (New York: Bantam Books, 1995), 311.

Chapter 6: Why Do People Get Angry?

1. Jaak Panksepp, *Affective Neuroscience: The Foundation of Human and Animal Emotions* (New York: Oxford University Press, 1998), 205.
2. This inclusive phrase pulls together constructionist thought with narrative theory and is based on a slightly different phrase used by Donald Meichenbaum and D. Fitzpatrick, "A Constructivist Narrative Perspective of Stress and Coping," in *Handbook of Stress*, ed. L. Goldberger and S. Breznitz (New York: Free Press, 1992). Though I will discuss constructivist thought, my overall approach stresses the social and relational aspects of existence emphasized in constructionist theory rather than the individualistic emphasis in constructivist thought.
3. For a brief history of constructivism, see Ernst von Glasersfeld, "An Introduction to Radical Constructivism," in *The Invented Reality*, ed. Paul Watzlawick (New York: W. W. Norton, 1984), 17–40.
4. See Gregory Bateson, *Steps to an Ecology of Mind* (New York: Ballantine, 1972).
5. For a well-known introduction to the neurological limitations on our perception, and therefore our construction of reality, see Heinz von Foerster, "On Constructing a Reality," in Watzlawick, 41–61.
6. Bebe Speed, "How Really Real Is Real?" *Family Process* 23, no. 4 (December 1984): 511–20. Also see Speed's "Reality Exists, OK? An Argument Against Constructivism and Social Constructionism," *Journal of Family Therapy* 13, no. 4 (November 1991): 395–410.
7. Speed, "Reality Exists, OK?" 401–8.
8. Kenneth Gergen, "The Social Constructionist Movement in Modern Psychology," *American Psychologist* 40, no. 3 (March 1985): 266–75.

9. John L. Walter and Jane E. Peller, "Rethinking Our Assumptions: Assuming Anew in a Postmodern World," in *Handbook of Solution-Focused Brief Therapy*, ed. Scott D. Miller, Mark A. Hubble, and Barry L. Duncan (San Francisco: Jossey-Bass Publishers, 1996), 14.

10. Jerome Bruner, "Life as Narrative," *Social Research* 54, no. 1 (spring 1987): 32.

11. Don P. McAdams, *The Stories We Live By: Personal Myths and the Making of the Self* (New York: William Morrow and Company, Inc., 1993), 39–65.

12. Stephen Crites, "The Narrative Quality of Experience," *Journal of the American Academy of Religion* 39, no. 3 (September 1971): 291.

13. Walter and Peller, "Rethinking Our Assumptions," 12–13.

14. Theodore R. Sarbin, "The Narrative as a Root Metaphor for Psychology," in *Narrative Psychology: The Storied Nature of Human Conduct*, ed. Theodore R. Sarbin (New York: Prager, 1986), 4. Sarbin borrows the concept of metaphor from Stephen Pepper, *World Hypotheses* (Berkeley: University of California Press, 1942).

15. Crites, "The Narrative Quality of Experience," 291.

16. See essays in Sarbin's *Narrative Psychology*. Also see McAdams, *The Stories We Live By*; Michael M. White and David Epston, *Narrative Means to Therapeutic Ends* (New York: Norton, 1990); and Donald P. Spence, *Narrative Truth and Historical Truth: Meaning and Interpretation in Psychoanalysis* (New York: W. W. Norton, 1982).

17. Sarbin, *Narrative Psychology*, 8. Narrative theorists from philosophy, literature, and the social sciences point out how much of human life is not only creating stories, but the unrelenting quest for stories. Children love to hear stories, read stories, and make up stories. Adults spend hours attending to stories in the media that follow our culture's ongoing sagas.

18. John Navone, *Toward a Theology of Story* (Slough, England: St. Paul Publications, 1977), 78.

19. Sarbin, *Narrative Psychology*, 9, says "narrative structure" is a meaningful organizing principle for explaining how "human beings impose structure on the flow of experience."

20. Crites, "The Narrative Quality of Experience," 29. See also George Stroup, *The Promise of Narrative Theology: Recovering the Gospel in the Church* (Atlanta: John Knox Press, 1981), 101–18.

21. Bruner, "Life as Narrative," 13.

22. M. Mair, *Between Psychology and Psychotherapy* (London: Routledge & Kegan Paul, 1988), 127.

23. Mary M. Gergen and Kenneth J. Gergen, "The Social Construction of Narrative Accounts," in *Historical Social Psychology*, ed. Kenneth J. Gergen and Mary M. Gergen (Hillsdale, N.J.: Lawrence Eribaum Associates, 1984), 174–75.

24. See Andrew D. Lester, *Hope in Pastoral Care and Counseling* (Louisville, Ky.: Westminster John Knox Press, 1995).

25. Some social constructionist approaches ignore or deny the seemingly obvious function of neurobiological processes in the emotional life of humans and do not take embodiment seriously. Panksepp describes the "componential" approach that combines constructivist perspectives (the importance of appraisal processes within the neocortex that seem to initiate emotional response) with an understanding of the neurobiological functions of the brain. See Panksepp, *Affective Neuroscience*, 44–45.

26. As interpreted by Martha Nussbaum, *Love's Knowledge: Essays on Philosophy and Literature* (New York: Oxford University Press, 1990), 89.

27. Nussbaum, *Love's Knowledge*, 90.
28. Alasdair MacIntyre, *After Virtue: A Study in Moral Theory*, 2d ed. (Notre Dame, Ind.: University of Notre Dame Press, 1984), 205–14.
29. Stanley Hauerwas, "Story and Theology," *Religion in Life* 45, no. 3 (Autumn 1976): 343.
30. MacIntyre, *After Virtue*, 208.
31. Ibid., 209.
32. Hauerwas, "Story and Theology," 344.
33. Richard J. Davidson, "Neuropsychological Perspectives on Affective Styles and Their Cognitive Consequences," in *Handbook of Cognition and Emotion*, ed. Tim Dalgleish and Mick J. Power (Chichester, U.K.: John Wiley & Sons, 1999), 103.
34. Crites, "The Narrative Quality of Experience," 83.
35. See Hans-Georg Gadamer, *Truth and Method*, trans. Garrett Barden and John Cumming (New York: Seabury Press, 1975), 397–447.
36. Davidson, "Neuropsychological Perspectives," 104.
37. See my discussion of Kierkegaard's emphasis on future in *Hope in Pastoral Care and Counseling*, 13–14 and my discussion of future stores, 35–37.
38. To explore the various cognitive structures that influence the difficulty of changing stories, see Donald Meichenbaum and Geoffrey T. Fong, "How Individuals Control Their Own Minds: A Constructive Narrative Perspective," in *Handbook of Mental Control*, ed. Daniel N. Wegner and James W. Pennebaker (Englewood Cliffs, N.J.: Prentice Hall, 1993).
39. Ibid. We see the "basic stuff" of our friends and family over decades and realize how much of what they have constructed in their past has become quite essential to their self in the present. As we create self from infancy forward, some of this created self becomes the core of personhood and includes the essential elements of the self by which people come to know us.
40. See Søren Kierkegaard, *The Concept of Anxiety*, ed. and trans. with introduction and notes by Reidar Thomte in collaboration with Albert B. Anderson (Princeton, N.J.: Princeton University Press, 1980), particularly chaps. 1 and 2.
41. John Macquarrie, *In Search of Humanity: A Theological and Philosophical Approach* (New York: Crossroads, 1989), 48–51.
42. Jean-Paul Sartre, *Existentialism and Human Emotions* (New York: The Wisdom Library, 1957), 52.
43. See my *Hope in Pastoral Care and Counseling* for a discussion of the connection between hope and future stories.

Chapter 7: Why Is Anger One of the Seven "Deadly Sins"?

1. Herbert E. Hohenstein, "Oh Blessed Rage," *Currents in Theology and Mission* 10, no. 3 (June 1983): 162.
2. Rosemary Radford Ruether, *Sexism and God-Talk: Toward a Feminist Theology* (Boston: Beacon Press, 1983), 185–86.
3. Rita Nakashima Brock, *Journeys by Heart: A Christology of Erotic Power* (New York: Crossroad, 1996), 19.
4. For a brief description, see John T. Fitzgerald, "Virtue/Vice Lists," *The Anchor Bible Dictionary*, vol. 6, ed. David N. Freedman (New York: Doubleday, 1992), 857–859. Galatians 5:19–23 is one of the best known.
5. See Fitzgerald, "Virtue/Vice Lists," for a list of these references.
6. For a brief but thorough history of this concept, see Morton W. Bloomfield, *The Seven Deadly Sins: An Introduction to the History of a Religious Concept with*

Special Reference to Medieval English Literature (East Lansing: Michigan State University Press, 1952).

7. Quoted in Daniel Goleman, *Emotional Intelligence* (New York: Bantam Books, 1995), ix.

8. Aristotle, "Nicomachean Ethics," book 2, chap. 5, trans. W. D. Ross, in *The Works of Aristotle: II*, vol. 9 of *The Great Books of the Western World* series, editor-in-chief Robert Maynard Hutchins (Chicago: Encyclopedia Britannica, Inc., 1952), 351.

9. Probably the best survey of the concern about dealing with anger in this tradition is William V. Harris, *Restraining Rage: The Idea of Anger Control in Classical Antiquity* (Cambridge, Mass.: Harvard University Press, 2001).

10. Martha Nussbaum, *Love's Knowledge: Essays on Philosophy and Literature* (New York: Oxford University Press, 1990), 90, 243.

11. Seneca, "Epistle CXVI on Self-Control," in *Seneca: Moral Essays*, trans. John W. Basore (London: William Heinemann LTD, 1935), 333.

12. Seneca, "De Ira" in *Seneca: Moral Essays*, vol. 1, book 3, trans. John W. Basore (Cambridge, Mass.: Harvard University Press, 1963), 173.

13. Ibid., 157.

14. Ibid., 129.

15. Ibid.

16. Nussbaum, 407–28.

17. Seneca, *De Ira*, 351.

18. Saint Augustine, *The City of God*, book nine, chap. 5, trans. Marcus Dods (New York: The Modern Library, 1993), 285.

19. John Cassian, *The Institutes*, eighth book, chap. 4, sec. 3, trans. Boniface Ramsay, O.P. (New York: The Newman Press, 2000), 195.

20. Ibid., chap. 2, 193.

21. Ibid. For a discussion of "taint" as sin, see Paul Ricoeur's *The Symbolism of Evil*, trans. Emerson Buchanan (Boston: Beacon Press, 1969).

22. Cassian, *The Institutes*, chap. 2, 194.

23. Ibid., chap. 4, 194.

24. Though some scholars note that Paul suggests in his Athens speech (Acts 17:25) that God doesn't need anything, which is close to saying that God is immutable.

25. The biographical material summarized here can be found in David Hugh Farmer, *The Oxford Dictionary of Saints*, 4th ed. (Oxford: Oxford University Press, 1997), 42–43.

26. Saint Basil, "Against Those Who Are Prone to Anger," Homily 10 in *Ascetical Works*, trans. M. Monica Wagner (Washington, D.C.: The Catholic University of America Press, 1962), 447–48.

27. Ibid., 448.

28. Ibid., 449.

29. Ibid., 448.

30. Ibid., 456.

31. Ibid., 457.

32. Ibid., 456.

33. Ibid., 456–57.

34. Ibid., 457.

35. Ibid., 458.

36. See the introduction to Evagrius in *The Philokalia*, vol. 1, trans. G. E. H. Palmer, Philip Sherrard, and Kallistos Ware (London: Faber and Faber, 1979), 29 ff.

37. Evagrius Ponticus, *The Praktikos: Chapters on Prayer*, trans. John Eudes Bamberger (Spencer, Mass.: Cisterian Publications, 1970), 18, 22.
38. Ibid., 36.
39. Ibid., 62.
40. Ibid., 59.
41. Ibid., 58–59.
42. Ibid., 17.
43. Ibid., 23.
44. Ibid., 27.
45. Ibid.
46. *The Westminster Dictionary of Church History*, ed. Jerald C. Brauer (Philadelphia: The Westminster Press, 1971), 72.
47. Ibid., and Farmer, *The Oxford Dictionary of Saints*, 25–26.
48. Saint Augustine, *The City of God*, book fourteen, chap. 15, trans. Marcus Dods (New York: The Modern Library, 1993), 464.
49. Augustine, *The City of God*, book nine, chap. 5, 285.
50. Ibid.
51. For brief biographical data, see Cassian, *The Institutes*, 3–8.
52. Cassian, *The Institutes*, eighth book, chap. 2, 194.
53. Ibid., chap. 1, 193.
54. Ibid., chap. 5, 196.
55. Ibid., chap. 5, 195.
56. Ibid., chap. 1, 193.
57. Ibid., chap. 7, 196.
58. Ibid., chap. 9, 197.
59. This information is summarized from Jeffrey Richards, *Consul of God: The Life and Times of Gregory the Great* (Boston: Routledge & Kegan Paul, 1980).
60. Summarized from F. H. Dudden in Matthew Baasten, *Pride According to Gregory the Great* (Queenston, Ontario: The Edwin Mellen Press, 1986), 6–7.
61. Ibid., 5.
62. These quotes are found in Joseph Gildea, *Source Book of Self-Discipline: A Synthesis of "Moralia in Job" by Gregory the Great: A Translation of Peter of Waltham's "Remediarium Conversorum"* (New York: Peter Lang Publishers, 1991), 98.
63. Ibid.
64. Ibid., 100.
65. Ibid., 101.
66. Ibid.
67. Ibid.
68. Ibid., 102.
69. The exact years of John's life are debated. See *John Climacus: The Ladder of Divine Ascent*, in *The Classics of Western Spirituality* series, 2–3, trans. Colm Luibheid and Norman Victor Russell (New York: Paulist Press, 1982).
70. Ibid., 1.
71. Ibid., 147.
72. Ibid., 150.
73. Ibid., 151.
74. Ibid., 150.
75. Ibid.
76. Ibid.
77. Ibid.

78. For more information about the life of Aquinas, see Robert Barron, *Thomas Aquinas: Spiritual Master* (New York: The Crossroad Publishing Company, 1996).

79. Edward J. Gratsch, *Aquinas' Summa: An Introduction and Interpretation* (New York: Society of St. Paul, Alba House, 1985), ix.

80. Baasten, 130–35.

81. Diana Fritz Cates, "Taking Women's Experience Seriously: Thomas Aquinas and Audre Lorde on Anger," in *Aquinas and Empowerment: Classical Ethics for Ordinary Lives*, ed. G. Simon Harak, S.J. (Washington, D.C., Georgetown University Press, 1996), 55.

82. Cates, 55.

83. St. Thomas Aquinas, *Summa Theologiae*, vol. 21, *Fear and Anger* (New York: McGraw-Hill Book Company, 1965), 91.

84. Aquinas, *Summa Theologiae, Fear and Anger,* 97.

85. Ibid., 103.

86. Ibid., 117.

87. *The Westminster Dictionary of Church History*, ed. Jerald C. Brauer (Philadelphia: The Westminster Press, 1971), 512.

88. Martin Luther, *What Luther Says: An Anthology*, vol. 1, comp. Ewald M. Plass (St. Louis: Concordia Publishing House, 1959), entry no. 74, 27.

89. Ibid., entry no. 77, 28.

90. Ibid.

91. Ibid.

92. Ibid., entry no. 79, 29.

93. Ibid., entries no. 1530 and 1531, 511.

94. Ibid., entry no. 1530.

95. Quoted in Charles Scot Giles, "The Practical Theology of Martin Luther," *Religious Humanism* 18, no. 1 (1984): 18.

96. Luther, *What Luther Says*, entry no. 80, 29.

97. *The Westminster Dictionary of Church History*, 149.

98. Ibid.

99. Quoted in William J. Bouwsma, *John Calvin: A Sixteenth-Century Portrait* (New York: Oxford University Press, 1988), 105.

100. Ibid.

101. Ibid., 88–89.

102. Ibid., 32.

103. Ibid., 89.

104. John Calvin, *Commentaries on the Last Four Books of Moses Arranged in the Form of a Harmony* (Grand Rapids: Wm. B. Eerdmans Publishing Company, 1950), 347.

105. Ibid., 346.

106. For more information on the life of John Wesley, see Kenneth J. Collins, *A Real Christian: The Life of John Wesley* (Nashville: Abingdon Press, 1999).

107. John Wesley, "The Way to the Kingdom," sermon VII, *The Works of John Wesley*, vol. 5 (Grand Rapids: Zondervan Publishing House, 1958), 82.

108. Albert C. Outler, ed., *The Works of John Wesley*, vol. 2 (Nashville: Abingdon Press, 1985), 516.

109. John Wesley, "On Sin in Believers," sermon XIII, *The Works of John Wesley*, vol. 5 (Grand Rapids: Zondervan Publishing House, 1958), 153.

110. Ibid., 154.

111. Ibid., 153.

112. John Wesley, "Upon Our Lord's Sermon on the Mount," sermon XXXIII, *The Works of John Wesley*, vol. 5 (Grand Rapids: Zondervan Publishing House, 1958), 432.

113. Ibid., 263.

114. Ibid.

115. John Wesley, "Christian Perfection," sermon XL, *The Works of John Wesley*, vol. 6 (Grand Rapids: Zondervan Publishing House, 1958), 17.

116. John Wesley, "Upon Our Lord's Sermon on the Mount," sermon XXII, 264.

117. See Karl Barth, *Ethics*, trans. Geoffrey W. Bromiley (New York: Seabury Press, 1981), and Dietrich Bonhoeffer, *Ethics* (New York: Simon & Schuster, 1995).

118. In a paper being reviewed for publication, Xolani Kacela describes his search without success of African American theologians for such a theological discussion. He reports on his discussions about his findings with other African American scholars who have been unable to offer any further resources.

119. Marjorie Suchocki, "Anxiety and Trust in Feminist Experience," *The Journal of Religion* 60, no. 4 (October 1980): 467.

120. Beverly Wildung Harrison, "Anger/Wrath," *Dictionary of Feminist Theologies*, (Louisville, Ky.: Westminster John Knox Press, 1996), 8.

121. "The Place of Anger in the Works of Love," in *Making the Connections: Essays in Feminist Social Ethics*, ed. Carol S. Robb (Boston: Beacon Press, 1985), 4.

122. Ibid., 14.

Chapter 8: Biblical Perspectives

1. *The Interpreter's Dictionary of the Bible: An Illustrated Encyclopedia* (Nashville: Abingdon Press, 1962), 135.

2. Ibid. See also W. E. Vine, *Vine's Expository Dictionary of Old and New Testament Words* (Old Tappan, N.J.: Fleming H. Revell Company, 1981), 55–56.

3. For one estimate, see Alistair V. Campbell, *The Gospel of Anger* (Great Britain: SPCK, 1986), 33. Another source is Bruce Edward Baloian, *Anger in the Old Testament* (New York: P. Lang, 1992), 73.

4. Leland Ryken, James C. Wilhoit, Tremper Longman III, gen. eds., *Dictionary of Biblical Imagery* (Downers Grove, Ill.: InterVarsity Press, 1998), 25. Other examples of a careful response are Judg. 9:30; 2 Sam. 12:5; Neh. 5:6.

5. Besides the Brueggemann reference that follows, see also Ellen van Wolde, *Words Become Worlds: Semantic Studies of Genesis 1–11* (Leiden: E. J. Brill, 1994), for another scholarly account of Cain and Abel. Ricardo J. Quinones has written an interesting nontheological account of the story as well. See his *The Changes of Cain: Violence and the Lost Brothers in Cain and Abel Literature* (Princeton, N.J.: Princeton University Press, 1991).

6. Walter Brueggemann, *Genesis*, in the series *Interpretation: A Bible Commentary for Teaching and Preaching* (Atlanta: John Knox Press, 1982), 57.

7. Ibid.

8. For interesting scholarly works on wisdom literature, see Dianne Bergant, *Israel's Wisdom Literature: A Liberation-Critical Reading* (Minneapolis: Fortress Press, 1997); Roland E. Murphy, *The Tree of Life: An Exploration of Biblical Wisdom Literature*, 3d ed. (Grand Rapids: William B. Eerdmans Publishing Company, 2002); and Leo Perdue, *Wisdom and Creation: The Theology of Wisdom Literature* (Nashville: Abingdon Press, 1994).

9. See James L. Crenshaw, *A Whirlpool of Torment: Israelite Traditions of God as an Oppressive Presence* (Philadelphia: Fortress Press, 1984). The five biblical passages, with Crenshaw's titles, are Gen. 22, "A Monstrous Test"; Jer. 20:7,

"Seduction and Rape" of Jeremiah; Job, "Murder without Cause"; Ecclesiastes, "The Silence of Eternity"; and Psalm 73, "Standing near the Flame."

10. Walter Brueggemann, "Foreword," in Ann Weems, *Psalms of Lament* (Louisville, Ky.: Westminster John Knox Press, 1995), xii.
11. Ibid., xii–xiii.
12. Dwight Matthew Sullivan, "An Anthropology of Anger: A Possible Dialogue between Sigmund Freud and the Bible" (Rel.D. diss., School of Theology at Claremont, 1974), 132.
13. *Matthew: A Commentary on His Literary and Theological Art* (Grand Rapids: Eerdmans, 1982), 138–39. Quoted in Sarah Chambers, "A Biblical Theology of Godly Human Anger" (Ph.D. diss., Trinity Evangelical Divinity School, 1996), 141.
14. M. Eugene Boring, "Matthew: Introduction, Commentary, and Reflections," in *The New Interpreter's Bible: A Commentary in Twelve Volumes* (Nashville: Abingdon Press, 1995), 190.
15. See Carl G. Vaught, *The Sermon on the Mount: A Theological Investigation*, rev. ed. (Waco, Tex.: Baylor University Press, 2001), 64. Vaught says ὀργίζω implies the kind of anger that is a "smoldering, festering cauldron."
16. Charles B. Williams, *The New Testament in the Language of the People* (Nashville: Holman Bible Publishers, 1937), 19.
17. *The New English Bible*, 2d ed. (n.p.: Oxford University Press, 1970), 9.
18. Boring, 188.
19. Though one scholar has argued for its inclusion. See David Alan Black, "Jesus on Anger: The Text of Matthew 5:22a Revisited," in *Novum Testamentum: An International Quarterly for New Testament and Related Studies* 30, no. 1 (1988): 1–8.
20. See Roland H. Worth Jr., *The Sermon on the Mount: Its Old Testament Roots* (New York: Paulist Press, 1997), 133–54. Worth writes on pages 134–35:

> [N]owhere in the verse does [Jesus] actually call anger an inherent sin. What he does assert is that anger is always *dangerous*. He does not say that one will be the subject of "judgment," "the council," or "hell fire" for anger *alone*, but that one would be "in *danger of*." Even when one is righteously angry, there still remains a potential risk, and Jesus was too worldly-wise to deny it. Hence, he sets out to demand that control of anger rather than the *elimination* of it.

21. For a thorough description of the Greek usage, and the history of scholarship on this verse, see Daniel B. Wallace, "ΟΡΓΙΖΕΣΘΕ in Ephesians 4:26: Command or Condition?" in *Criswell Theological Review* 3, no. 2 (spring 1989): 353–72.
22. *The New English Bible*, 332.
23. For further research on this verse, see Martin Kitchen, *Ephesians* (London: Routledge, 1994), 87; Watson E. Mills and Richard F. Wilson, eds., *Mercer Commentary on the Bible* (Macon, Ga.: Mercer University Press, 1995), 1223; John Muddiman, *A Commentary on the Epistle to the Ephesians* (London: Continuum, 2001), 225; and Peter T. O'Brien, *The Letter to the Ephesians* (Grand Rapids: William B. Eerdmans Publishing Company, 1999), 339.
24. Wallace, 363.
25. See John T. Fitzgerald, "Virtue/Vice Lists," in *The Anchor Bible Dictionary*, vol. 6, ed. David N. Freedman (New York: Doubleday, 1992), 857–59.

26. Victor Paul Furnish, *Theology and Ethics in Paul* (Nashville: Abingdon Press, 1968), 84–86.

27. For a classic article on these lists, see Burton Scott Easton, "New Testament Ethical Lists," in *Journal of Biblical Literature* 51 (1932): 1–12.

28. See Lewis R. Donelson, "The Vice Lists of the Pastoral Epistles" in *The Catholic Biblical Quarterly* 36, no. 2 (April 1974): 203–19.

29. M. Jack Suggs, "The Christian Two Ways Tradition: Its Antiquity, Form and Function," in *Studies in New Testament and Early Christian Literature* (Leiden: E. J. Brill, 1972), 74.

30. Furnish, 84.

31. This is also the view of Mills and Wilson, eds., *Mercer Commentary*, 1286 and Douglas J. Moo, *The Letter of James* (Grand Rapids: Williams B. Eerdmans Publishing Company, 2000), 83.

32. Luke Johnson, *Faith's Freedom: A Classic Spirituality for Contemporary Christians* (Minneapolis: Fortress Press, 1990), 138.

Chapter 9: The Anger of God and Jesus

1. For an overview of the meanings of this Greek word, see Sarah Chambers, "A Biblical Theology of Godly Human Anger" (Ph.D. diss., Trinity Evangelical Divinity School, 1996), 78–113.

2. Anthony Hanson provides an overview of the wrath of God in *The Wrath of the Lamb* (London: SPCK, 1957).

3. For an overview of this problem, see Alastair V. Campbell, *The Gospel of Anger* (London: SPCK, 1986).

4. Chambers, 76.

5. James D. Whitehead and Evelyn Eaton Whitehead, *Shadows of the Heart: A Spirituality of the Negative Emotions* (New York: Crossroad Publishing Company, 1994), 133.

6. See Tillich's brief description of this position in Paul Tillich, *Systematic Theology*, vol. 2 (Chicago: University of Chicago Press, 1959), 77.

7. Paul Tillich, *Systematic Theology*, vol. 1 (Chicago: The University of Chicago Press, 1951), 284.

8. David R. Blumenthal, *Facing the Abusing God: A Theology of Protest* (Louisville, Ky.: Westminster/John Knox Press, 1993).

9. See Renita Weems, *Battered Love: Marriage, Sex, and Violence in the Hebrew Prophets* (Minneapolis: Fortress Press, 1995); Gracia Fay Ellwood, *Batter My Heart* (Wallingford, Pa.: Pendle Hill Pamphlets, 1988); and Blumenthal, 240–43.

10. For a summary of several perspectives, see Carroll Saussy, *The Gift of Anger: A Call to Faithful Action* (Louisville, Ky.: Westminster John Knox Press, 1995), 65–80.

11. J. K. Mozley, *The Impassibility of God: A Survey of Christian Thought* (Cambridge, England: The University Press, 1926), 19. Please refer to this work for references to original documents.

12. Ibid., 23.

13. Ibid., 55.

14. Ibid., 60.

15. Ibid., 59, 62.

16. See C. H. Dodd's *The Epistle of Paul to the Romans* (New York: Harper and Brothers Publishers, 1932), 18–24. Also see Campbell, 33–49.

17. For scholarly discussion of this issue, see Stephen T. Davis, ed. *Encountering Evil: Live Options in Theodicy* (Atlanta: John Knox, 1981). An excellent popular

account of these perspectives is found in Harold Kushner's *Why Bad Things Happen to Good People* (New York: Schocken Books, 1981).

18. Blumenthal, 245.
19. Ibid., 17–18, 246.
20. Ibid., 14–20. While this is accurate as far as it goes, I would assert as well that as *we* have freedom to restrain from violence, so does God.
21. Ibid., 261–62.
22. Ibid., 266.
23. This connection occurred to me when reading Nancy Ramsay's "Compassionate Resistance: An Ethic for Pastoral Care and Counseling," *The Journal of Pastoral Care* 52, no. 3 (fall 1998): 220–21.
24. C. S. Lewis, *Letters to Malcolm* (New York: Harcourt Brace Jovanich, 1963), 97.
25. See, for example, Paul Tillich, *Love, Power, and Justice: Ontological Analyses and Ethical Application* (London: Oxford University Press, 1954).
26. For a thoughtful, personal summary by a New Testament scholar, see Marcus J. Borg, *Meeting Jesus Again for the First Time* (San Francisco: HarperCollins Publishers, 1994). For more scholarly research, see the publications of the "Jesus Seminar."
27. One other example may be a textual variant of Mark 1:41 in which the dominant text has Jesus "moved with pity"—σπλαγχνυσθείς, meaning to have compassion. The Western text, manuscript D, uses the word ὀργίζεσθε and translates this verse to show that Jesus was moved with "anger."
28. Personal correspondence from John T. Fitzgerald, professor at the University of Miami in Coral Gables, Florida, August 2002.
29. Is it possible that retention of the emotive context gives credence to the possibility that this Gospel reflects the views of a woman ("the textual alter ego of the evangelist")? See Sandra M. Schneiders, 'Because of Women's Testimony . . .:' Reexamining the Issue of Authorship in the Fourth Gospel," *New Testament Studies* 44, no. 4 (October 1998): 513–35.
30. Arthur Gossip, *The Interpreter's Bible*, vol. 8, George Arthur Buttrick, gen. ed. (New York: Abingdon-Cokesbury Press, 1952), 497–98.
31. Beverly Wildung Harrison, "The Place of Anger in the Works of Love," in *Making the Connections: Essays in Feminist Social Ethics*, ed. Carol S. Robb (Boston: Beacon Press, 1985), 18.
32. James McGinnis, "Mercy in Hard Times and Places," *Weavings* 15, no. 5 (September/October 2000): 24.
33. Hans Küng, *On Being a Christian*, trans. Edward Quinn (Garden City, N.Y.: Doubleday & Company, Inc., 1968), 262.
34. John R. W. Stott, *God's New Society: The Message of Ephesians* (Downers Grove, Ill.: InterVarsity Press, 1979), 185–86.

Chapter 10: Toward a Pastoral Theology of Anger

1. Theodore R. Sarbin, "The Narrative as a Root Metaphor for Psychology," in *Narrative Psychology: The Storied Nature of Human Conduct*, ed. Theodore R. Sarbin (New York: Prager, 1986), 8.
2. John Macquarrie, *In Search of Humanity: A Theological and Philosophical Approach* (New York: Crossroads, 1989), 47, says "all human life, as we know it, is embodied."
3. Ibid.
4. Ibid. He writes that "in a sense the miracle of 'the word made flesh' is to be seen in every human being."

5. As Macquarrie says; "Feeling is always a constituent factor in existing. At any given time, feeling, understanding, and willing . . . are all three together in existing. They are distinguishable . . . , but they cannot be separated. . . ." John Macquarrie, *Principles of Christian Theology* (New York: Charles Scribner's Sons, 1966), 87. For a later discussion of theological anthropology, see Wolfhart Pannenberg, *Anthropology in Theological Perspective*, trans. Matthew J. O'Connell (Philadelphia: The Westminster Press, 1985).

6. The "fall" metaphor may continue to serve some traditions in describing how we developed the willingness to be destructive with this originally good capacity. See Peter C. Hodgson, *Winds of the Spirit: A Constructive Christian Theology* (Louisville, Ky.: Westminster/John Knox, 1994), 209 ff.

7. Moving beyond the postmodern critique of the individualistic, self-contained "self," theologian Stanley Grenz discusses a "trinitarian anthropology of the self" that uses social, relational understandings of God's nature to painstakingly develop a communal understanding of *imago Dei*, which he claims is the center of Christian anthropology. See Stanley J. Grenz, *The Social God and the Relational Self: A Trinitarian Theology of the* Imago Dei (Louisville, Ky.: Westminster John Knox Press, 2001).

8. See note 10 in chap. 2.

9. Carroll Saussy expands this concept in her helpful book *The Gift of Anger: A Call to Faithful Action* (Louisville, Ky.: Westminster John Knox Press, 1995).

10. Jaak Panksepp, *Affective Neuroscience: The Foundations of Human and Animal Emotions* (New York: Oxford University Press, 1998), 205.

11. Ibid.

12. Sarah Chambers argues against the idea that anger is neutral and also points out how much modern Christian writers depend on Greek philosophy and psychology for their ideas on anger. See Sarah Chambers, "A Biblical Theology of Godly Human Anger" (Ph.D. diss., Trinity Evangelical Divinity School, 1996), 5–28.

13. Quoted in Chambers, 20.

14. Gary Oliver and H. Norman Wright, *When Anger Hits Home* (Chicago: Moody Press, 1994), 10.

15. Ibid., 48.

16. Tim LaHaye, *Anger Is a Choice* (Grand Rapids: Zondervan, 1982), quoted in Chambers, 42.

17. Frank Minirth and Paul Meier, *Happiness Is a Choice*, 2d ed. (Grand Rapids: Baker Book House, 1994), 39.

18. For an overview of this issue, see Chambers, 41–53. She argues that biblical stories consistently present the experience of anger as "morally charged even before it is expressed in human behavior" (45), and since anger "is a reaction of judgment; it implies an appraisal of the morality of things" (52).

19. Mark Cosgrove, *Counseling for Anger* (Dallas: Word, 1988), 44–45.

20. Illustrated by the work of Herbert Anderson and Edward Foley, *Mighty Stories, Dangerous Rituals: Weaving Together the Human and the Divine* (San Francisco: Jossey-Bass, 1998).

21. John Wesley, "The Doctrine of Original Sin According to Scripture, Reason, and Experience," *The Works of John Wesley*, vol. 9 (Grand Rapids: Zondervan Publishing House, 1958), 311.

22. See the material on Wesley in chap. 7.

23. Jean-Paul Sartre, *Existentialism and Human Emotions* (New York: The Wisdom Library, 1957), 55.

24. Ibid., 53.
25. Ibid., 23.
26. Panksepp, 387.
27. Ibid., 190.

Chapter 11: Anger as a Spiritual Ally

1. Kathleen Norris, *Amazing Grace: A Vocabulary of Faith* (New York: Riverhead Books, 1998), 49.
2. David W. Augsburger, "Anger and Aggression," in *Clinical Handbook of Pastoral Counseling*, vol. 1, ed. Robert J. Wicks, Richard D. Parsons, and Donald E. Capps (New York: Paulist Press, 1993), 482.
3. For a discussion of "future stories," see my *Hope in Pastoral Care and Counseling* (Louisville, Ky.: Westminster John Knox Press, 1995), chap. 2.
4. Carroll Saussy, *The Gift of Anger: A Call to Faithful Action* (Louisville, Ky.: Westminster John Knox Press, 1995), 102–12.
5. See Andrew and Judith Lester, *It Takes Two: The Joy of Intimate Marriage* (Louisville, Ky.: Westminster John Knox Press, 1998), chap. 4.
6. Susan J. Dunlap, *Counseling Depressed Women* (Louisville, Ky.: Westminster John Knox Press, 1997), 102–15.
7. Robert C. Morris, "Enlightening Annoyances: Jesus' Teachings as a Spur to Spiritual Growth," *Weavings* 16, no. 5 (September/October, 2001): 39.
8. Mary Catherine Bateson, *Composing a Life* (New York: Plume, 1990), 205.
9. Cornel West says, "The accumulated effect of the black wounds and scars suffered in a white-dominated society is a deep-seated anger, a boiling sense of rage, and a passionate pessimism regarding America's will to justice," in *Race Matters* (Boston: Beacon Press, 1993), 18.
10. See West's chapter on "Nihilism in Black America." He points out that rage that spills out in violence is a response to powerlessness and is a sign of nihilism, the loss of hope, and the loss of meaning.
11. Mary Daly, *Pure Lust: Elemental Feminist Philosophy* (Boston: Beacon Press, 1984), 258. Daly also connects anger with hope when she says, "Hope and despair are sharpened also by Righteous Rage," 258. Also see her idea of "ontological Fury," 5.
12. Marjorie Procter-Smith, "Our Job Is to Stay Angry," *The Living Pulpit* 2, no. 4 (October–December 1993): 16.
13. Marjorie Suchocki, "Anxiety and Trust in Feminist Experience," *Journal of Religion* 60, no. 4 (October 1980): 469.
14. Ibid., 471.
15. Susan Brooks Thistlethwaite, *Sex, Race, and God: Christian Feminism in Black and White* (New York: Crossroad, 1991), 24.
16. Quotes from Dorothy are from personal correspondence, summer 2002, and are used by permission.
17. G. Walter Hansen, "The Emotions of Jesus," *Christianity Today* (3 February 1997): 44.
18. Eleanor H. Haney, *The Great Commandment: A Theology of Resistance and Transformation* (Cleveland: The Pilgrim Press, 1998), 110.
19. Ibid.
20. Ibid., 112.
21. Victoria Loe, *Dallas Morning News*, 13 June 1993, quoted in Marjorie Procter-Smith, "Our Job Is to Stay Angry," 16.
22. Donna Bivens, Elizabeth Bettenhausen, and Nancy Richardson, "Struggling

Through Injury in the Work of Love," *Journal of Feminist Studies in Religion* 9 nos. 1–2 (spring/fall 1993): 225.

23. See Saussy, 59–60.

24. Daly, 368–70.

25. Ibid., 370. This dissociation process, she argues, may be why some women are "incapable of moral outrage on behalf of their own Selves and other women."

26. Rita Nakashima Brock, *Journeys by Heart: A Christology of Erotic Power* (New York: Crossword, 1996), 19.

27. Ibid.

28. Haney, 110.

29. See Jeanne Stevenson Moessner's chapter on the Good Samaritan, "A New Pastoral Paradigm and Practice," in *Women in Travail and Transition* (Minneapolis: Fortress Press, 1991), 198–225.

30. Rosemary Radford Ruether, *Sexism and God-Talk: Toward a Feminist Theology* (Boston: Beacon Press, 1983), 186.

31. Ibid.

32. Referring to Dorothee Soelle's *Suffering* (Philadelphia: Fortress, 1975), 68–73, and to John O'Donohue's *Eternal Echoes: Exploring Our Hunger to Belong* (London: Bantam Press, 1998), 160–61.

33. See Andrew and Judith Lester, *It Takes Two*, chap. 4.

34. Brock, 19.

35. Ibid.

36. Ibid.

37. Ibid.

38. Dana Crowley Jack, *Silencing the Self: Women and Depression* (Cambridge, Mass.: Harvard University Press, 1991), 137.

39. Beverly Wildung Harrison, "The Place of Anger in the Works of Love," in *Making the Connections: Essays in Feminist Social Ethics*, ed. Carol S. Robb (Boston: Beacon Press, 1985), 14.

40. Norris, 49.

41. Harrison, 14.

42. Ibid.

43. Walter Brueggemann, "Covenanting as Human Vocation: A Discussion of the Relation of Bible and Pastoral Care," *Interpretation* 30, no. 2 (April 1979): 122.

44. Saussy, 118 ff.

45. Willard Gaylin uses this analogy in *The Rage Within: Anger in Modern Life* (New York: Simon and Schuster, 1984), 93. Also see James D. Whitehead and Evelyn Eaton Whitehead, *Shadows of the Heart: A Spirituality of the Negative Emotions* (New York: Crossroad Publishing Company, 1994), 21–22.

Chapter 12: Compassionate Anger

1. Henry Fairlie, *The Seven Deadly Sins Today* (Washington, D.C.: New Republic Books, 1978), 108.

2. Paul A. Hauck, *Overcoming Frustration and Anger* (Philadelphia: The Westminster Press, 1974), 56.

3. Ibid., 55.

4. The Gates of Chai Lectureship, Texas Christian University, 21 September 2000. Elie Wiesel is a Holocaust survivor who is committed to keeping the memory of these atrocities alive for the instruction of coming generations.

5. Beverly Wildung Harrison, "The Place of Anger in the Works of Love," in

Making the Connections: Essays in Feminist Social Ethics, ed. Carol S. Robb (Boston: Beacon Press, 1985), 14.

6. Ibid., 15.
7. See Dorothee Soelle, *Suffering*, trans. E. R. Kalin (Philadelphia: Fortress Press, 1975), 17–32, 41–45.
8. John Wesley, "An Extract of a Letter to the Reverend Mr. Law," in *The Works of John Wesley*, vol. 9 (Grand Rapids: Zondervan Publishing House, 1958), 481.
9. John Wesley, "Thirty-Seven Letters to a Member of the Society," letter CCLIX, in *The Works of John Wesley*, vol. 12 (Grand Rapids: Zondervan Publishing House, 1958), 291.
10. John R. W. Stott, *God's New Society: The Message of Ephesians* (Downers Grove, Ill.: InterVarsity Press, 1979), 186.
11. Mary Daly, *Pure Lust: Elemental Feminist Philosophy* (Boston: Beacon Press, 1984), 5.
12. Carl F. H. Henry, *Christian Personal Ethics* (Grand Rapids: Wm. B. Eerdmans Publishing Co., 1957), 345, 499.
13. Suffering that comes as the result of our own sin (gluttony, adultery, and the like) and from natural occurrences (such as lightning, floods, earthquakes, and the like) are two categories that deserve their own theological review.
14. Wendy Farley, *Tragic Vision and Divine Compassion: A Contemporary Theodicy* (Louisville, Ky.: Westminster/John Knox Press, 1990), 53 ff.
15. Nancy J. Ramsay, "Compassionate Resistance: An Ethic for Pastoral Care and Counseling," *The Journal of Pastoral Care* 52, no. 3 (fall 1998): 218.
16. Martha Nussbaum, *Love's Knowledge: Essays on Philosophy and Literature* (New York: Oxford University Press, 1990), 403.
17. This story was told at West Point and is repeated in Nussbaum, 403.
18. Ibid.
19. Ibid.
20. Marjorie Procter-Smith, "Our Job Is to Stay Angry," *The Living Pulpit* 2, no. 4 (October/December 1993): 16.
21. J. Clinton McCann, *A Theological Introduction to the Book of Psalms* (Nashville: Abingdon Press, 1993), 119. He says, "In the face of monstrous evil, the worst possible response is to feel *nothing*. What *must* be felt is grief, rage, outrage."
22. Hans Küng, *On Being A Christian*, trans. Edward Quinn (Garden City, N.Y.: Doubleday & Company, Inc., 1968), 564.
23. Ibid., 563–64.
24. James H. Cone, *A Black Theology of Liberation* (New York: J. B. Lippincott Company, 1970), 46–47.
25. Daly, 203. See also her comments on feeling "Rage at the oppression of her sisters of all races, of all ethnic groups, of all classes, of all nations," 397.
26. Paul Lauritzen, "Emotions and Religious Ethics," *Journal of Religious Ethics* 16, no. 2 (fall 1988): 312. He says that anger is "a composite of painful feeling with the belief that I have been wronged."
27. Dorothee Soelle and Fulbert Steffensky, *Not Just Yes and Amen: Christians with a Cause* (Philadelphia: Fortress Press, 1985), 8.
28. Quoted in Nussbaum, 95.
29. Ibid., 92.
30. Donna Bivens, Elizabeth Bettenhausen, and Nancy Richardson, "Struggling Through Injury in the Work of Love," *Journal of Feminist Studies in Religion* 9, nos. 1–2 (spring/fall 1993): 217. The assumptions expressed by the Women's

Theological Center include this clear statement: "Anger is an appropriate moral response to such violation and injury."

31. Küng, 263.
32. Donald P. McNeill, Douglas A. Morrison, and Henri J. M. Nouwen, *Compassion: A Reflection on the Christian Life* (Garden City, N.Y.: Doubleday & Company, Inc., 1982), 8.
33. Luke T. Johnson, *Faith's Freedom: A Classic Spirituality for Contemporary Christians* (Minneapolis: Fortress Press, 1990), 133.
34. Ibid., 132.
35. For a thoughtful description by a professor of business of confronting injustice in the workplace, see Debra E. Meyerson, *Tempered Radicals* (Boston: Harvard Business School Press, 2001). Also see Barbara Waugh's *The Soul in the Computer: The Story of a Corporate Revolutionary* (Makawao, Maui, Hawaii: Inner Ocean, 2001) concerning tools used to fight injustice.
36. For a thorough discussion of compassion, see Farley, 69–133.
37. Ramsay, "Compassionate Resistance," 218.
38. Ibid., 220.
39. Walter Wink, *Engaging the Powers: Discernment and Resistance in a World of Domination* (Minneapolis: Fortress Press, 1992). This paragraph is based on chap. 9.
40. Walter Wink, *The Powers That Be: Theology for a New Millennium* (New York: Doubleday, 1998), 98–99.
41. Ibid., 98.
42. Ibid., 101–3.
43. Ibid., 106–8. For a more thorough account of these three examples, see Wink's *Engaging the Powers*, chap. 9.
44. James D. Whitehead and Evelyn Eaton Whitehead, *Shadows of the Heart: A Spirituality of the Negative Emotions* (New York: Crossroad Publishing Company, 1994), 142. Because anger is the "power of resistance in the soul" (142), the Whiteheads believe that the call to prophetic confrontation is an important way of serving God (136–37).
45. McNeill, Morrison, and Nouwen, 124.
46. Ibid.
47. Harrison, 18.
48. Daly, 375.
49. Rosemary Radford Ruether, "Anger and Liberating Grace," *The Living Pulpit* 2, no. 4 (October/December 1993): 7.
50. James H. Cone, *Speaking the Truth: Ecumenism, Liberation, and Black Theology* (Grand Rapids: William B. Eerdmans Publishing Company, 1986), 65.
51. Wink, *The Powers That Be*, 121. For more on nonviolence, see Wink's *Engaging the Powers*, chaps. 11–13.
52. The Baptist Peace Fellowship says, "peace, like war, must be waged" (www.bpfna.org).
53. Wink, *The Powers That Be*, 119.
54. Evagrius Ponticus, *The Praktikos: Chapters on Prayer*, trans. John Eudes Bamberger (Spencer, Mass.: Cisterian Publications, 1970), 26.
55. John Wesley, "Upon Our Lord's Sermon on the Mount," sermon XXII, in *The Works of John Wesley*, vol. 5 (Grand Rapids: Zondervan Publishing House, 1958), 263.
56. James McGinnis, "Mercy in Hard Times and Places," in *Weavings* 15, no. 5 (September/October 2000): 28–29.

57. Eleanor H. Haney, *The Great Commandment: A Theology of Resistance and Trans-formation* (Cleveland: The Pilgrim Press, 1998), 112.
58. McGinnis, 28–29.
59. Quoted from C. S. Song by *The Living Pulpit* 2, no. 4 (October/December, 1993): 5.
60. Ibid.
61. Saint Basil, "Against Those Who Are Prone to Anger," Homily 10 in *Ascetical Works*, trans. M. Monica Wagner (Washington, D.C.: The Catholic University of America Press, 1962), 450.
62. Wink, *The Powers That Be*, 122–27.
63. Küng, 570.
64. Ramsay, "Compassionate Resistance," 223–25, reminded me that the Good Shepherd can be one such metaphor.
65. Nancy Ramsay, an unpublished draft of a book tentatively titled *Counseling with Adult Survivors of Sexual Abuse*. Used by permission from the author.
66. Ramsay, "Compassionate Resistance," 223–25.
67. Ramsay, *Counseling with Adult Survivors of Sexual Abuse*. Used by permission from the author.
68. See Arthur W. Frank, *The Wounded Storyteller* (Chicago: University of Chicago Press, 1997).
69. Rosemary Radford Ruether, *Sexism and God-Talk: Toward a Feminist Theology* (Boston: Beacon Press, 1983), 184.
70. Patricia O'Connell Killen, *Finding Our Voices: Women, Wisdom, and Faith* (New York: Crossroad, 1997), 91.
71. Ibid., 92.
72. Whitehead and Whitehead, 51.
73. Marjorie Suchocki, "Anxiety and Trust in Feminist Experience," *Journal of Religion* 60, no. 4 (October 1980): 470.
74. Though allowing a member's anger to be deeply identified and expressed, the effective support group will *not* allow anger to be continually rehearsed in ways that place it at the center of a person's life so that the anger itself becomes an idol.
75. Marjorie Procter-Smith, "Our Job Is to Stay Angry," 16.
76. Sue Monk Kidd, *Dance of the Dissident Daughter: A Woman's Journey from Christian Tradition to the Sacred Feminine* (San Francisco: Harper Collins, 1996), 186.

Chapter 13: Handling Anger Creatively

1. James D. Whitehead and Evelyn Eaton Whitehead, *Shadows of the Heart: A Spirituality of the Negative Emotions* (New York: Crossroads, 1994), 76.
2. Ibid.
3. For a good analysis of scapegoating, see Walter Wink, *The Powers That Be: Theology for a New Millennium* (New York: Doubleday, 1998), 84–93.
4. Jaak Panksepp, *Affective Neuroscience: The Foundations of Human and Animal Emotions* (New York: Oxford University Press, 1998), 190.
5. Luke T. Johnson, *Faith's Freedom: A Classic Spirituality for Contemporary Christians* (Minneapolis: Fortress Press, 1990), 138.
6. Evagrius suggested that "'psalms and hymns and spiritual canticles'" return us to virtue by "cooling our boiling anger." See Evagrius Ponticus, *The Praktikos: Chapters on Prayer*, trans. John Eudes Bamberger (Spencer, Mass.: Cisterian Publications, 1970), 35.

7. Eugene H. Peterson, "A Pastor's Quarrel with God," *The Princeton Seminary Bulletin* 11, no. 3 (1990): 271.
8. See Ronald J. Nydam, *Adoptees Come of Age* (Louisville, Ky.: Westminster John Knox Press, 1999), 30–47.
9. See Harold A. Anderson and Harlene Goolishian, "Human Systems as Linguistic Systems: Preliminary and Evolving Ideas about the Implications of Clinical Theory," *Family Process* 27 (1988): 371–98.
10. For an excellent overview of narrative therapy, see Jill Freedman and Gene Combs, *Narrative Therapy: The Social Construction of Preferred Realities* (New York: W. W. Norton & Company, 1996), and Gerald Monk, John Winslade, Kathie Crocket, David Epston, eds., *Narrative Therapy in Practice: The Archaeology of Hope* (San Francisco: Jossey-Bass Publishers, 1997).
11. Steve de Shazer, *Putting Differences to Work* (New York: Norton, 1991), 68.
12. Mary M. Gergen and Kenneth J. Gergen, "The Social Construction of Narrative Accounts," in Kenneth J. Gergen and Mary M. Gergen, eds., *Historical Social Psychology* (Hillsdale, N.J.: Lawrence Eribaum Associates, 1984), 178.

Bibliography

Aggleton, J. P., ed. *The Amygdala: Neurobiological Aspects of Emotion, Memory and Mental Dysfunction.* New York: Wiley-Liss, 1992.

Anderson, H., and H. Goolishian. "Human Systems as Linguistic Systems: Preliminary and Evolving Ideas about the Implications of Clinical Theory." *Family Process* 27, no. 4 (1988): 371–98.

Anderson, Herbert, and Edward Foley. *Mighty Stories, Dangerous Rituals: Weaving Together the Human and the Divine.* San Francisco: Jossey-Bass, 1998.

Aquinas, Thomas. *Summa Theologiae.* Vol. 19, *The Emotions.* Translated and introduction by Eric D'Arcy. London: Blackfriars, 1967.

———. *Summa Theologiae.* Vol. 21, *Fear and Anger.* Translated and introduction by John Patrick Reid. London: Blackfriars, 1965.

Ardrey, Robert. *African Genesis: A Personal Investigation into the Animal Origins and Nature of Man.* New York: Atheneum, 1961.

———. *The Territorial Imperative: A Personal Inquiry into the Animal Origins of Property and Nations.* New York: Atheneum, 1966.

Aristotle. "Nicomachean Ethics." Book II, Chap. 5. Translated by W. D. Ross. In *The Works of Aristotle: II.* Vol. 9 of *The Great Books of the Western World* series. Robert Maynard Hutchins, editor-in-chief. Chicago: Encyclopedia Britannica, Inc., 1952.

Ashbrook, James B., and Carol Rausch Albright. *The Humanizing Brain: Where Religion and Neuroscience Meet.* Cleveland: The Pilgrim Press, 1997.

Augsburger, David W. "Anger and Aggression." In *Clinical Handbook of Pastoral Counseling.* Edited by Robert J. Wicks, Richard D. Parsons, and Donald E. Capps. New York: Paulist Press, 1985.

Augustine, Saint. *The City of God.* Translated by Marcus Dods. New York: The Modern Library, 1993.

Austin, James H. *Zen and the Brain: Toward an Understanding of Meditation and Consciousness.* Cambridge, Mass.: MIT Press, 1998.

Averill, J. R. *Anger and Aggression: An Essay on Emotion.* New York: Springer-Verlag, 1982.

Baasten, Matthew. *Pride According to Gregory the Great: A Study of the Moralia.* Queenston, Ontario, Canada: The Edwin Mellen Press, 1986.

Bach, George R., and Herb Goldberg. *Creative Aggression.* Garden City, N.Y.: Doubleday, 1974.

Baloian, Bruce Edward. *Anger in the Old Testament.* New York: P. Lang, 1992.

Barron, Robert. *Thomas Aquinas: Spiritual Master.* New York: The Crossroad Publishing Company, 1996.

Barth, Karl. *The Doctrine of the Word of God, Church Dogmatics* I/I. Edinburgh: T. & T. Clark, 1936.

———. *Ethics.* Translated by Geoffrey W. Bromiley. New York: Seabury Press, 1981.

Basil, Saint. "Against Those Who Are Prone to Anger," Homily 10 in *Ascetical Works.* Translated by M. Monica Wagner. Washington, D.C.: The Catholic University of America Press, 1962.

Bateson, Gregory. *Steps to an Ecology of Mind.* New York: Ballantine, 1972.

Bateson, Mary Catherine. *Composing a Life.* New York: Plume, 1990.

Behavior Genetics. Special issue on "The Neurobehavioral Genetics of Aggression." 26, no. 5 (September 1996): 459–532.

Bergant, Dianne. *Israel's Wisdom Literature: A Liberation-Critical Reading.* Minneapolis: Fortress Press, 1997.

Berkowitz, Leonard, ed. *The Roots of Aggression: A Re-Examination of the Frustration-Aggression Hypothesis.* New York: Atherton, 1969.

Bivens, Donna, Elizabeth Bettenhausen, and Nancy Richardson. "Struggling Through Injury in the Work of Love." *Journal of Feminist Studies in Religion* 9, nos. 1–2 (spring/fall 1993): 215–26.

Black, David Alan. "Jesus on Anger: The Text of Matthew 5:22a Revisited." In *Novum Testamentum: An International Quarterly for New Testament and Related Studies* XXX, no. 1 (January 1988): 1–8.

Blomquist, Jean M. "Discovering Our Deep Gladness: The Healing Power of Work." *Weavings* VIII, no. 1 (January/February 1993): 20–26.

Bloomfield, Morton W. *The Seven Deadly Sins: An Introduction to the History of a Religious Concept with Special Reference to Medieval English Literature.* East Lansing: Michigan State University Press, 1952.

Blumenthal, David R. *Facing the Abusing God: A Theology of Protest.* Louisville, Ky.: John Knox Press, 1993.

Bondi, Roberta C. "Anger: Help from the Desert." *Weavings* IX, no. 2 (March–April 1994): 6–14.

Bonhoeffer, Dietrich. *Ethics.* New York: Simon & Schuster, 1995.

Borg, Marcus. *Meeting Jesus Again for the First Time: The Historical Jesus & the Heart of Contemporary Faith.* San Francisco: HarperSanFrancisco, 1994.

Boring, M. Eugene. "Matthew: Introduction, Commentary, and Reflections." In *The New Interpreter's Bible.* Nashville: Abingdon Press, 1995.

Bouwsma, William J. *John Calvin: A Sixteenth-Century Portrait.* New York: Oxford University Press, 1988.

Brock, Rita Nakashima. *Journeys by Heart: A Christology of Erotic Power.* New York: Crossroad, 1996.

Brown, Warren S., Nancey Murphy, and H. Newton Malony, eds. *Whatever Happened to the Soul? Scientific and Theological Portraits of Human Nature.* Minneapolis: Fortress Press, 1998.

Brueggemann, Walter. "Foreword." In *Psalms of Lament,* by Ann Weems. Louisville, Ky.: Westminster John Knox Press, 1995.

————. *Genesis*. In the series *Interpretation: A Bible Commentary for Teaching and Preaching*. Atlanta: John Knox Press, 1982.

Bruner, Jerome. "Life As Narrative." *Social Research* 54, no. 1 (spring 1987): 11–32.

Brunner, Emil. *The Christian Doctrine of Creation and Redemption, Dogmatics*. Vol. II. Trans. Olive Wyon. Philadelphia: The Westminster Press, 1952.

————. *Revelation and Reason: The Christian Doctrine of Faith and Knowledge*. Trans. Olive Wyon. Philadelphia: The Westminster Press, 1946.

Budiansky, Stephen. *If a Lion Could Talk: Animal Intelligence and the Evolution of Consciousness*. New York: The Free Press, 1998.

Buss, A. H. *The Psychology of Aggression*. New York: Wiley, 1961.

Callahan, Sidney. *In Good Conscience: Reason and Emotion in Moral Decision Making*. San Francisco: Harper/Collins, 1991.

Calvin, John. *Commentaries on the Last Four Books of Moses Arranged in the Form of a Harmony*. Grand Rapids: William B. Eerdmans Publishing Company, 1950.

————. *Institutes of the Christian Religion*. Vol. 1. Translated by Henry Beveridge. Grand Rapids: William B. Eerdmans Publishing Company, 1953.

Campbell, Alastair V. *The Gospel of Anger*. London: SPCK, 1986.

Cardena, Etzel, Steven Jay Lynn, and Stanley Krippner. *Varieties of Anomalous Experience: Examining the Scientific Evidence*. Washington, D.C.: American Psychological Association, 2000.

Cassian, John. *The Institutes*. Translated and annotated by Boniface Ramsay, O.P. New York: The Newman Press, 2000.

————. *The Monastic Institutes, Consisting of On the Training of a Monk and The Eight Deadly Sins*. Eighth Book. Translated by Father Jerome Bertram. London: The Saint Austin Press, 1999.

Cates, Diana Fritz. "Taking Women's Experience Seriously: Thomas Aquinas and Audre Lorde on Anger." In *Aquinas and Empowerment: Classical Ethics for Ordinary Lives*. Edited by G. Simon Harak, S.J. Washington, D.C.:, Georgetown University Press, 1996.

Chambers, Sarah. *A Biblical Theology of Godly Human Anger*. Ph.D. diss., Trinity Evangelical Divinity School, 1996.

Charry, Ellen T. *By the Renewing of Your Minds: The Pastoral Function of Christian Doctrine*. New York: Oxford University Press, 1997.

Childs, Brian, and David W. Waanders. *The Treasure of Earthen Vessels: Explorations in Theological Anthropology*. Louisville, Ky.: Westminster/John Knox Press, 1994.

Christianson, S. A., ed. *The Handbook of Emotion and Memory: Research and Theory*. Hillsdale, N.J.: Lawrence Erlbaum, 1992.

Climacus, John. *The Ladder of Divine Ascent*. In *The Classics of Western Spirituality Series*. Translated by Colm Luibheid and Norman Victor Russell. New York: Paulist Press, 1982.

Collins, Kenneth J. *A Real Christian: The Life of John Wesley*. Nashville: Abingdon Press, 1999.

Cone, James H. *A Black Theology of Liberation*. New York: J. B. Lippincott Company, 1970.

————. *Speaking the Truth: Ecumenism, Liberation, and Black Theology*. Grand Rapids: William B. Eerdmans Publishing Company, 1986.

Cooper, John M. *Reason and Emotion: Essays on Ancient Moral Psychology and Ethical Theory*. Princeton, N.J.: Princeton University Press, 1999.

Cosgrove, Mark P. *Counseling for Anger. Resources for Christian Counseling Series*. Vol. 16. Dallas, Texas: Word Books, 1988.

Crenshaw, James L. *A Whirlpool of Torment: Israelite Traditions of God as an Oppressive Presence*. Philadelphia: Fortress Press, 1984.

Crites, Stephen. "The Narrative Quality of Experience." *Journal of the American Academy of Religion* 39, no. 3 (September 1971): 39–65.

Dalgleish, Tim, and Mick J. Power., ed. *Handbook of Cognition and Emotion*. Chichester, U.K.: John Wiley & Sons, 1999.

Daly, Mary. *Pure Lust: Elemental Feminist Philosophy*. Boston: Beacon Press, 1984.

Damasio, Antonio R. *Descartes' Error: Emotion, Reason, and the Human Brain*. New York: G. P. Putnam's Sons, 1994.

———. *The Feeling of What Happens: Body and Emotion in the Making of Consciousness*. New York: Harcourt Brace & Company, 1999.

Darwin, Charles. *The Expression of the Emotions in Man and Animals*. Chicago: The University of Chicago Press, 1965.

Davidson, Richard J. "Neuropsychological Perspectives on Affective Styles and Their Cognitive Consequences." In *Handbook of Cognition and Emotion*. Edited by Tim Dalgleish and Mick J. Power. Chichester, U.K.: John Wiley & Sons, 1999.

Davis, Stephen T., ed. *Encountering Evil: Live Options in Theodicy*. Atlanta: John Knox, 1981.

De Rivera, Joseph, and Theodore R. Sarbin, ed. *Believed-In Imaginings: The Narrative Construction of Reality*. Washington, D.C.: American Psychological Association, 1998.

De Shazer, S. *Putting Differences to Work*. New York: W. W. Norton, 1991.

Dictionary of Pastoral Care and Counseling. General Editor, Rodney Hunter. Nashville: Abingdon Press, 1990.

Dodd, C. H. *The Epistle of Paul to the Romans*. New York: Harper and Brothers Publishers, 1932.

Dollard, J., N. E. Miller, O. Hobart Mowrer, G. H. Sears, and R. R. Sears. *Frustration and Aggression*. New Haven: Yale University Press, 1939.

Donelson, Lewis R. "The Vice Lists of Pastoral Epistles." *The Catholic Biblical Quarterly* 36, no. 2 (April 1974): 203–19.

Dunlap, Susan J. *Counseling Depressed Women*. Louisville, Ky.: Westminster John Knox Press, 1997.

Dunn, James D. G. *The Theology of Paul the Apostle*. Grand Rapids: William B. Eerdmans Publishing Company, 1998.

Easton, Burton Scott. "New Testament Ethical Lists." *Journal of Biblical Literature* 51 (1932): 1–12.

Edwards, Jonathan. *Religious Affections*. Edited by John E. Smith. New Haven: Yale University Press, 1959.

Ekman, Paul. "An Argument for Basic Emotions." *Cognition and Emotion* 6, nos. 3–4 (May–July 1992): 169–200.

Ekman, Paul, and Richard J. Davidson, ed. *The Nature of Emotion: Fundamental Questions*. New York: Oxford University Press, 1995.

Ellis, Albert. *How to Live With—and Without—Anger*. New York: Thomas Y. Crowell Company, 1977.

Ellwood, Gracia Fay. *Batter My Heart*. Wallingford, Pa.: Pendle Hill Pamphlets, 1988.

Evagrius. *The Philokalia*. Vol. 1. Translated by G. E. H. Palmer, Philip Sherrard, and Kallistos Ware. London: Faber and Faber, 1979.

———. *The Praktikos: Chapters on Prayer*. Translated, with an introduction and notes by John Eudes Bamberger. Spencer: Cisterian Publications, 1970.

Fairlie, Henry. *The Seven Deadly Sins Today*. Washington, D.C.: New Republic Books, 1978.

Farley, Wendy. *Tragic Vision and Divine Compassion: A Contemporary Theodicy.* Louisville, Ky.: Westminster/John Knox Press, 1990.

Fitzgerald, John T. "Virtue/Vice Lists." In *The Anchor Bible Dictionary.* Vol. 6. Edited by David N. Freedman. New York: Doubleday, 1992.

Frank, Arthur W. *The Wounded Storyteller.* Chicago: University of Chicago Press, 1997.

Frank, Robert H. *Passions within Reason: The Strategic Role of the Emotions.* New York: W. W. Norton & Company, 1988.

Freedman, Jill, and Gene Combs. *Narrative Therapy: The Social Construction of Preferred Realities.* New York: W. W. Norton & Company, 1996.

Fromm, Erich. *The Anatomy of Human Destructiveness.* New York: Holt, Rinehart and Winston, 1973.

Furnish, Victor Paul. *Theology and Ethics in Paul.* Nashville: Abingdon Press, 1968.

Gadamer, Hans-Georg. *Truth and Method.* Translated by Garrett Barden and John Cumming. New York: Seabury Press, 1975.

Gaylin, Willard. *The Rage Within: Anger in Modern Life.* New York: Penguin Books, 1989.

Gergen, Kenneth. "The Social Constructionist Movement in Modern Psychology." *American Psychologist* 40, no. 3 (March 1985): 266–75.

———. "Toward a Postmodern Psychology." In *Psychology and Postmodernism.* Edited by S. Kvale. Newbury Park, Calif.: Sage, 1992.

Gergen, Kenneth, and J. Kaye. "Beyond Narrative in the Negotiation of Therapeutic Meaning." In *Therapy as Social Construction.* Edited by S. McNamee & Kenneth Gergen. Newbury Park, Calif.: Sage, 1992.

Gergen, Mary M., and Kenneth J. Gergen. "The Social Construction of Narrative Accounts." In *Historical Social Psychology.* Edited by Kenneth J. Gergen and Mary M. Gergen. Hillsdale, N.J.: Lawrence Eribaum Associates, 1984.

Gildea, Joseph. *Source Book of Self-Discipline: A Synthesis of "Moralia in Job" by Gregory the Great: A Translation of Peter of Waltham's "Remediarium Conversorum."* New York: Peter Lang Publishers, 1991.

Giles, Charles Scot. "The Practical Theology of Martin Luther." *Religious Humanism* 18, no. 1 (1984): 16–25.

Gilman, James E. "Reenfranchising the Heart: Narrative Emotions and Contemporary Theology." *Journal of Religion* 74, no. 2 (April 1994): 218–39.

Goleman, Daniel. *Emotional Intelligence.* New York: Bantam Books, 1995.

Gossip, Arthur. *The Interpreter's Bible.* Vol. 8. General Editor, George Arthur Buttrick. New York: Abingdon-Cokesbury Press, 1952.

Gratsch, Edward J. *Aquinas' Summa: An Introduction and Interpretation.* New York: Society of St. Paul, Alba House, 1985.

Gregory of Nyssa, Saint. "On the Soul and the Resurrection." In *Ascetical Works.* Translated by Virginia Woods Callahan. Vol. 28 of *The Fathers of the Church.* Washington, D.C.: The Catholic University of America Press, 1967.

Greider, Kathleen J. *Reckoning with Aggression: Theology, Violence, and Vitality.* Louisville, Ky.: Westminster John Knox Press, 1997.

———. " 'Too Militant'? Aggression, Gender, and the Construction of Justice." In *Through the Eyes of Women: Insights for Pastoral Care.* Edited by Jeanne Stevenson Moessner. Minneapolis: Augsburg Fortress, 1996.

Grenz, Stanley J. *A Primer on Postmodernism.* Grand Rapids: William B. Eerdmans Publishing Company, 1996.

———. *The Social God and the Relational Self: A Trinitarian Theology of the* Imago Dei. Louisville, Ky.: Westminster John Knox Press, 2001.

Haney, Eleanor H. *The Great Commandment: A Theology of Resistance and Transformation.* Cleveland: The Pilgrim Press, 1998.

Hansen, G. Walter. "The Emotions of Jesus." *Christianity Today* 41 (3 February 1997): 42–46.

Hanson, Anthony. *The Wrath of the Lamb*. London: SPCK, 1957.

Harris, William V. *Restraining Rage: The Idea of Anger Control in Classical Antiquity*. Cambridge, Mass.: Harvard University Press, 2001.

Harrison, Beverly Wildung. "The Place of Anger in the Works of Love." In *Making the Connections: Essays in Feminist Social Ethics*. Edited by Carol S. Robb. Boston: Beacon Press, 1985.

Hart, Archibald. *Christian Counseling Connection*. Issue 1. Forest, Va: Christian Counseling Resources, 2000.

Hart, Tobin, Peter L. Nelson, and Kaisa Puhakka, eds. *Transpersonal Knowing: Exploring the Horizon of Consciousness*. New York: State University of New York Press, 2000.

Hauck, Paul. *Overcoming Frustration and Anger*. Philadelphia: Westminster Press, 1974.

———. "Story and Theology." *Religion in Life* 45, no. 3 (autumn 1976): 339–50.

———. "Whose Conscience? Whose Emotion?" In *Hastings Center Report*. January–February 1992.

Henry, Carl F. H. *Christian Personal Ethics*. Grand Rapids: William B. Eerdmans Publishing Company, 1957.

Heschel, Abraham J. *The Prophets*. New York: Harper & Row, 1962.

Hillman, James. *Emotions: A Comprehensive Phenomenology of Theories and Their Meanings for Therapy*. Evanston, Ill.: Northwestern University Press, 1992.

Hirschman, Axel O. "The Search for Paradigms as a Hindrance to Understanding." In *Interpretive Social Science: A Second Look*. Edited by Paul Rabinow and William M. Sullivan. Berkeley: University of California Press, 1987.

Hodgson, Peter C. *Winds of the Spirit: A Constructive Christian Theology*. Louisville, Ky.: Westminster/John Knox Press, 1994.

Hohenstein, Herbert E. "Oh Blessed Rage." *Currents in Theology and Mission* 10, no. 3 (June 1983): 162–68.

Howard, G. S. "Cultural Tales: A Narrative Approach to Thinking, Cross Cultural Psychology and Psychotherapy." *American Psychologist* 46, no. 3 (March 1991): 187–97.

———. *A Tale of Two Stories: Excursions into a Narrative Approach to Psychology*. Notre Dame, Ind.: Academic Publications, 1989.

The Interpreter's Dictionary of the Bible: An Illustrated Encyclopedia. Nashville: Abingdon Press, 1962.

Janov, A. *The Primal Scream*. New York: Perigee Books, 1970.

Johnson, Luke T. *Faith's Freedom: A Classic Spirituality for Contemporary Christians*. Minneapolis: Fortress Press, 1990.

Journal of Pastoral Theology. Dayton: Ohio: Society for Pastoral Theology, 1991–current editions.

Jung, Patricia Beattie. "Emotion." In *Dictionary of Feminist Theologies*. Edited by Letty M. Russell and J. Shannon Clarkson. Louisville, Ky.: Westminister John Knox Press, 1996.

Kassinove, Howard, ed. *Anger Disorders: Definition, Diagnosis, and Treatment*. Washington, D.C.: Taylor and Francis, 1995.

Keeling, L. Bryant. "Feeling as a Metaphysical Category: Hartshorne from an Analytical View." In *Process Studies* 6, no. 1 (spring 1976): 51–66.

Kidd, Sue Monk. *Dance of the Dissident Daughter: A Woman's Journey from Christian Tradition to the Sacred Feminine*. San Francisco: Harper Collins, 1996.

Kierkegaard, Søren. *The Concept of Anxiety*. Edited and translated with introduction and notes by Reidar Thomte in collaboration with Albert B. Anderson. Princeton, N.J.: Princeton University Press, 1980.

———. *Purity of Heart Is to Will One Thing: Spiritual Preparation for the Office of Confession.* Translated by Douglas V. Steere. New York: Harper, 1948.

Killen, Patricia O'Connell. *Finding Our Voices: Women, Wisdom, and Faith.* New York: Crossroad, 1997.

Kitchen, Martin. *Ephesians.* London: Routledge, 1994.

Küng, Hans. *On Being a Christian.* Translated by Edward Quinn. Garden City, N.Y.: Doubleday & Company, Inc., 1968.

Kushner, Harold. *Why Bad Things Happen to Good People.* New York: Schocken Books, 1981.

Lane, Belden C. *The Solace of Fierce Landscapes: Exploring Desert and Mountain Spirituality.* New York: Oxford University Press, 1998.

Latvus, Kari. *God, Anger and Ideology.* In *The Journal for the Study of the Old Testament* Supplement Series. Sheffield, England: Sheffield Academic Press, 1998.

Lauritzen, Paul. "Emotions and Religious Ethics." *Journal of Religious Ethics* 16, no. 2 (fall 1988): 307–24.

LeDoux, Joseph. *The Emotional Brain: The Mysterious Underpinnings of Emotional Life.* New York: Simon & Schuster Inc., 1996.

Leithart, Peter J. "Stoic Elements in Calvin's Doctrine of the Christian Life." *Westminster Theological Journal* 55 (spring 1993): 31–54.

Lerner, Harriet. *The Dance of Anger: A Woman's Guide to Changing the Patterns of Intimate Relationships.* New York: Perennial Library, 1986.

Lester, Andrew D. *Coping with Your Anger: A Christian Guide.* Philadelphia: Westminster Press, 1983.

———. *Hope in Pastoral Care and Counseling.* Louisville, Ky.: Westminster John Knox Press, 1995.

Lester, Andrew, and Judith Lester. *It Takes Two: The Joy of Intimate Marriage.* Louisville, Ky.: Westminster John Knox Press, 1998.

Lewis, C. S. *Letters to Malcolm.* New York: Harcourt Brace Jovanich, 1963.

Lewis, Paul Allen. "Rethinking Emotions and the Moral Life in Light of Thomas Aquinas and Jonathan Edwards." Ph.D. diss., Duke University, 1991.

Lidz, Theodore. *The Person.* New York: Basic Books, Inc., 1968.

Lindhardt, Jan. *Martin Luther: Knowledge and Mediation in the Renaissance.* Lewiston, N.Y.: The Edwin Mellen Press, 1986.

Lorenz, Konrad. *On Aggression.* Translated by Marjorie Kerr Wilson. New York: Harcourt, Brace & World, Inc., 1966.

Luther, Martin. *Lectures on Romans.* In *Luther's Works.* Vol. 25. St. Louis: Concordia Publishing House, 1972.

———. *What Luther Says: An Anthology.* Compiled by Ewald M. Plass. St. Louis: Concordia Publishing House, 1959.

MacIntyre, Alasdair. *After Virtue: A Study in Moral Theory.* 2d ed. Notre Dame, Ind.: University of Notre Dame Press, 1984.

Macquarrie, John. *Existentialism.* Philadelphia: Westminster Press, 1972.

———. "Pilgrimage in Theology." *Epworth Review* VII, no. 1 (January 1980): 47–52.

———. *Principles of Christian Theology.* New York: Charles Scribner's Sons, 1966.

———. *In Search of Humanity: A Theological and Philosophical Approach.* New York: Crossroads, 1989.

Mair, M. *Between Psychology and Psychotherapy.* London: Routledge & Kegan Paul, 1988.

Malatesta, Carol Zander, and Caroll E. Izard, eds. *Emotion in Adult Development.* Beverly Hills, Calif.: Sage Publishers, 1984.

Mangina, Joseph Layton. "The Practical Voice of Dogmatic Theology: Karl Barth on the Christian Life." Ph.D. diss., Yale University, 1994.

May, William F. *A Catalogue of Sins: A Contemporary Examination of Christian Conscience.* New York: Holt, Rinehart and Winston, 1967.

McAdams, Don P. *The Stories We Live By: Personal Myths and the Making of the Self.* New York: William Morrow and Company, Inc., 1993.

McCabe, A., and C. Peterson. *Developing Narrative Structure.* Hillsdale, N.J.: Erlbaum, 1991.

McCandless, J. Bardarah. "Christian Commitment and a 'Docetic' View of Human Emotions." *Journal of Religion and Health* 23, no. 2 (summer 1984): 125–37.

McCann, J. Clinton. *A Theological Introduction to the Book of Psalms.* Nashville: Abingdon Press, 1993.

McCasland, Vernon. *The Interpreter's Bible.* Vol. 7. General Editor, George Arthur Buttrick. New York: Abingdon Press, 1951.

McCosh, James. *The Emotions.* New York: Charles Scribner's Sons, 1880.

McGinnis, James. "Mercy in Hard Times and Places." Weavings XV, no. 5 (September/October, 2000): 24–29.

McNamee, Sheila, and Kenneth J. Gergin, eds. *Therapy as Social Construction.* London: SAGE Publications, 1992.

McNeill, Donald P., Douglas A. Morrison, Henri J. M. Nouwen. *Compassion: A Reflection on the Christian Life.* Garden City, N.Y.: Doubleday & Company, Inc., 1982.

Meichenbaum, Donald, and D. Fitzpatrick. "A Constructivist Narrative Perspective of Stress and Coping." In *Handbook of Stress.* Edited by L. Goldberger and S. Breznitz. New York: Free Press, 1992.

Meichenbaum, Donald, and Geoffrey T. Fong. "How Individuals Control Their Own Minds: A Constructive Narrative Perspective." In *Handbook of Mental Control.* Edited by Daniel N. Wegner and James W. Pennebaker. Englewood Cliffs, N.J.: Prentice Hall, 1993.

Mesle, C. Robert. *Process Theology: A Basic Introduction.* St. Louis: Chalice Press, 1993.

Metzger, Bruce. *A Textual Commentary on the Greek New Testament.* New York: United Bible Societies, 1971.

Meyerson, Debra E. *Tempered Radicals.* Boston: Harvard Business School Press, 2001.

Mills, Watson E., and Richard F. Wilson, eds. *Mercer Commentary on the Bible.* Macon, Ga.: Mercer University Press, 1995.

Minirth, Frank, and Paul Meier. *Happiness Is a Choice.* Grand Rapids: Baker Book House, 1994.

Moessner, Jeanne Stevenson. "A New Pastoral Paradigm and Practice." In *Women in Travail and Transition.* Minneapolis: Fortress Press, 1991.

Monk, Gerald, John Winslade, Kathie Crocket, David Epston, eds. *Narrative Therapy in Practice: The Archaeology of Hope.* San Francisco: Jossey-Bass Publishers, 1997.

Moo, Douglas J. *The Letter of James.* Grand Rapids: William B. Eerdmans Publishing Company, 2000.

Morris, Desmond. *The Human Zoo.* New York: McGraw-Hill, 1969.

———. *The Naked Ape: A Zoologist's Study of the Human Animal.* New York: McGraw-Hill, 1967.

Morris, Robert C. "Enlightening Annoyances: Jesus' Teachings as a Spur to Spiritual Growth." *Weavings* XVI, no. 5 (September/October 2001): 38–45.

Mozley, J. K. *The Impassibility of God: A Survey of Christian Thought.* Cambridge, England: The University Press, 1926.

Muddiman, John. *A Commentary on the Epistle to the Ephesians.* London: Continuum, 2001.

Muller, Richard A. "Fides and Cognitio in Relation to the Problem of Intellect and

Will in the Theology of John Calvin." *Calvin Theological Journal* 25, no. 2 (November 1990): 207–39.

Murphy, Jeffrie G., and Jean Hampton. *Forgiveness and Mercy*. New York: Cambridge University Press, 1988.

Murphy, Roland E. *The Tree of Life: An Exploration of Biblical Wisdom Literature*. 3d ed. Grand Rapids: William B. Eerdmans Publishing Company, 2002.

Navone, John. *Toward a Theology of Story*. Slough, England: St. Paul Publications, 1977.

Neimeyer, R., and G. Feixas. "Constructivist Contributions to Psychotherapy Integration." *Journal of Integrative and Eclectic Psychotherapy* 9, no. 1 (1990): 4–20.

Newberg, Andrew, Eugene d'Aquili, and Vince Rause. *Why God Won't Go Away: Brain Science and the Biology of Belief*. New York: Ballantine Books, 2001.

The New Dictionary of Pastoral Studies. Edited by Wesley Carr. Grand Rapids: William B. Eerdmans Publishing Company, 2002.

The New English Bible. 2d ed. Oxford: Oxford University Press, 1970.

Niebuhr, Reinhold. *The Nature and Destiny of Man: A Christian Interpretation*. Vols. 1 and 2. New York: Charles Scribner's Sons, 1941 and 1943.

———. *The Self and the Dramas of History*. New York: Charles Scribner's Sons, 1955.

Niebuhr, Richard. "Dread and Joyfulness: The View of Man as Affectional Being." *Religion in Life: A Christian Quarterly of Opinion and Discussion*, no. 3 (summer 1962): 443–64.

———. *Experiential Religion*. New York: Harper & Row Publishers, 1972.

Norris, Kathleen. *Amazing Grace: A Vocabulary of Faith*. New York: Riverhead Books, 1998.

Nussbaum, Martha. *Love's Knowledge: Essays on Philosophy and Literature*. New York: Oxford University Press, 1990.

Nydam, Ronald J. *Adoptees Come of Age*. Louisville, Ky.: Westminster John Knox Press, 1999.

Oatley, K., and J. M. Jenkins. *Understanding Emotions*. Cambridge, Mass.: Blackwell, 1996.

O'Brien, Peter. *The Letter to the Ephesians*. Grand Rapids: William B. Eerdmans Publishing Company, 1999.

O'Donohue, John. *Eternal Echoes: Exploring Our Hunger to Belong*. London: Bantam Press, 1998.

Oliver, Gary, and H. Norman Wright. *When Anger Hits Home*. Chicago: Moody Press, 1994.

Ortony, Andrew, Gerald Close, and Allen Collins. *The Cognitive Structure of Emotions*. New York: Cambridge University Press, 1988.

Osiek, Carolyn. *Beyond Anger: On Being a Feminist in the Church*. New York: Paulist Press, 1986.

The Oxford Dictionary of Saints. 4th ed. Edited by David Hugh Farmer. Oxford: Oxford University Press, 1997.

Ozment, Steven E. *Homo Spiritualis: A Comparative Study of the Anthropology of Johannes Tauler, Jean Gerson and Martin Luther (1509–16) in the Context of Their Theological Thought*. Leiden: E. J. Brill, 1969.

Palmer, Parker J. *To Know as We Are Known: A Spirituality of Education*. San Francisco: Harper & Row, Publishers, 1983.

Panksepp, Jaak. *Affective Neuroscience: The Foundations of Human and Animal Emotions*. New York: Oxford University Press, 1998.

Pannenberg, Wolfhart. *Anthropology in Theological Perspective*. Translated by Matthew J. O'Connell. Philadelphia: The Westminster Press, 1985.

Pepper, Stephen. *World Hypotheses*. Berkeley: University of California Press, 1942.

Perdue, Leo. *Wisdom and Creation: The Theology of Wisdom Literature*. Nashville: Abingdon Press, 1994.

Peterson, Eugene H. "A Pastor's Quarrel with God." *The Princeton Seminary Bulletin* XI, no. 3 (1990): 270–75.

Polkinghorne, D. P. *Narrative Psychology*. Albany, New York: SUNY Press, 1988.

Procter-Smith, Marjorie. "Our Job Is to Stay Angry." *The Living Pulpit* 2, no. 4 (October/December 1993): 16.

Quinones, Ricardo J. *The Changes of Cain: Violence and the Lost Brothers in Cain and Abel Literature*. Princeton, N.J.: Princeton University Press, 1991.

Ramsay, Nancy J. "Compassionate Resistance: An Ethic for Pastoral Care and Counseling." *The Journal of Pastoral Care* 52, no. 3 (fall 1998): 217–26.

Ratey, John J. *A User's Guide to the Brain*. New York: Pantheon Books, 2001.

Reid, John Patrick. Introduction to *Summa Theologiae*, vol. 21, *Fear and Anger*, by Thomas Aquinas. London: Blackfriars, 1965.

Richards, Jeffrey. *Consul of God: The Life and Times of Gregory the Great*. Boston: Routledge & Kegan Paul, 1980.

Ricoeur, Paul. *The Symbolism of Evil*. Translated by Emerson Buchanan. Boston: Beacon Press, 1969.

Riordan, Brendan P. *Anger: Issues of Emotional Living in an Age of Stress for Clergy and Religious*. Whitinsville, Mass.: Affirmation Books, 1985.

Rogers, Lesley J. *Minds of Their Own: Thinking and Awareness in Animals*. Boulder, Col.: Westview Press, 1997.

Rohrer, Norman, and S. Philip Sutherland. *Facing Anger*. Minneapolis: Augsburg Publishing House, 1981.

Rosenau, Pauline Marie. *Post-Modernism and the Social Sciences: Insights, Inroads, and Intrusions*. Princeton, N.J.: Princeton University Press, 1992.

Rosenthal, David M. "Emotions and the Self." In *Emotion: Philosophical Studies*. Edited by Gerald E. Myers and K. D. Irani. New York: Haven Publications, 1983.

Rossi, Ernest Lawerence. *The Psychobiology of Mind-Body Healing: New Concepts of Therapeutic Hypnosis*. Rev. ed. New York: W. W. Norton & Company, Inc., 1993.

Rothchild, Babette. *The Body Remembers: The Psychophysiology of Trauma and Trauma Treatment*. New York: W. W. Norton & Company, 2000.

Ruether, Rosemary Radford. "Anger and Liberating Grace." *The Living Pulpit* 2, no. 4 (October/December 1993): 7.

———. *Sexism and God-Talk: Toward a Feminist Theology*. Boston: Beacon Press, 1983.

Ryken, Leland, James C. Wilhoit, Tremper Longman III, gen. eds. *Dictionary of Biblical Imagery*. Downers Grove, Ill.: InterVarsity Press, 1998.

Sarbin, Theodore R. "The Narrative as a Root Metaphor for Psychology." In *Narrative Psychology: The Storied Nature of Human Conduct*. Edited by Theodore R. Sarbin. New York: Prager, 1986.

Sartre, Jean-Paul. *The Emotions: Outline of a Theory*. Translated by Bernard Frechtman. New York: Philosophical Library, 1948.

———. *Existentialism and Human Emotions*. New York: The Wisdom Library, 1957.

———. *Sketch for a Theory of the Emotions*. Translated by Philip Mairet. London: Methuen & Co. Ltd., 1962.

Saussy, Carroll. *The Gift of Anger: A Call to Faithful Action*. Louisville, Ky.: Westminster John Knox Press, 1995.

Schneiders, Sandra M. "'Because of Women's Testimony . . .': Reexamining the Issue of Authorship in the Fourth Gospel." *New Testament Studies* 44, no. 4 (October 1998): 513–35.

Seneca. *De Ira*. In *Seneca: Moral Essays*. Vol. 1. Translated by John W. Basore. Cambridge, Mass.: Harvard University Press, 1963.
———. "Epistle CXVI on Self-Control." In *Seneca: Moral Essays*. Translated by John W. Basore. London: William Heinemann Ltd., 1935.
Shotter, J. *Conversational Realities: Constructing Life through Language*. London: Sage, 1993.
Smith, John E. Introduction to *Works of Jonathan Edwards*. Vol. 2, *Religious Affections*. New Haven: Yale University Press, 1959.
Soelle, Dorothee. *Suffering*. Philadelphia: Fortress, 1975.
Soelle, Dorothee, and Fulbert Steffensky. *Not Just Yes and Amen: Christians with a Cause*. Philadelphia: Fortress Press, 1985.
Solomon, Robert. *The Passions: The Myth and Nature of Human Emotions*. Notre Dame, Ind.: University of Notre Dame Press, 1983.
Song, C. S. *The Living Pulpit* 2, no. 4 (October/December 1993): 5.
Sorabji, Richard. *Emotion and Peace of Mind: From Stoic Agitation to Christian Temptation*. New York: Oxford University Press, 2000.
Speed, Bebe. "How Really Real Is Real?" *Family Process* 23, no. 4 (December 1984): 511–20.
———. "Reality Exists, OK? An Argument Against Constructivism and Social Constructionism." *Journal of Family Therapy* 13, no. 4 (November 1991): 395–410.
Spence, Donald P. *Narrative Truth and Historical Truth: Meaning and Interpretation in Psychoanalysis*. New York: W. W. Norton, 1982.
Stott, John R. W. *God's New Society: The Message of Ephesians*. Downers Grove, Ill.: InterVarsity Press, 1979.
Strongman, K., editor. *International Reviews of Emotion Research*. 2 vols. Chichester, U.K.: John Wiley & Sons, 1991–92.
Suchocki, Marjorie. "Anxiety and Trust in Feminist Experience." *The Journal of Religion* 60, no. 4 (October 1980): 459–71.
Suggs, Jack M. "The Christian Two Ways Tradition: Its Antiquity, Form and Function." In *Studies in New Testament and Early Christian Literature*. Leiden: E. J. Brill, 1972.
Sullivan, Dwight Matthew. *An Anthropology of Anger: A Possible Dialogue Between Sigmund Freud and the Bible*. Rel.D. diss., School of Theology at Claremont, 1974.
Taylor, Graeme J., R. Michael Bagby, and James D. A. Parker. *Disorders of Affect Regulation: Alexithymia in Medical and Psychiatric Illness*. New York: Cambridge University Press, 1997.
Thistlewaite, Susan Brooks. *Sex, Race, and God: Christian Feminism in Black and White*. New York: Crossroad, 1991.
Tice, Dianne, and Roy F. Baumeister. "Controlling Anger: Self-Induced Emotion Change." In *Handbook of Mental Control*. Edited by Daniel N. Wegner and James W. Pennebaker. Englewood Cliffs, N.J.: Prentice Hall, 1993.
Tillich, Paul. *The Courage to Be*. New Haven: Yale University Press, 1952.
———. *Love, Power and Justice: Ontological Analyses and Ethical Applications*. London: Oxford University Press, 1954.
———. *Systematic Theology*. Vols. 1–3. Chicago: University of Chicago Press, 1951, 1959, and 1963.
Trible, Phyllis. *God and the Rhetoric of Sexuality*. Philadelphia: Fortress, 1978.
Unger, Roberto. *Passions: An Essay on Personality*. New York: Free Press, 1984.
Valzelli, L. *Psychobiology of Aggression and Violence*. New York: Raven Press, 1981.
Van Wolde, Ellen. *Words Become Worlds: Semantic Studies of Genesis 1–11*. Leiden: E. J. Brill, 1994.

Vaught, Carl G. *The Sermon on the Mount: A Theological Investigation*. Rev. ed. Waco, Tex.: Baylor University Press, 2001.

Vine, W. E. *Vine's Expository Dictionary of Old and New Testament Words*. Old Tappan, N.J.: Fleming H. Revell Company, 1981.

Von Foerster, Heinz. "On Constructing a Reality." In T*he Invented Reality*. Edited by Paul Watzlawick. New York: W. W. Norton, 1984.

Von Glasersfeld, Ernst. "An Introduction to Radical Constructivism." In *The Invented Reality*. Edited by Paul Watzlawick. New York: W. W. Norton, 1984.

Wainwright, William J. *Reason and the Heart: A Prolegomenon to a Critique of Passional Reason*. Ithaca, N.Y.: Cornell University Press, 1995.

Wallace, Daniel B. "ὈΡΓΊΖΕΣΘΕ in Ephesians 4:26: Command or Condition?" In *Criswell Theological Review* 3, no. 2 (spring 1989): 353–72.

Walter, John L., and Jane E. Peller. "Rethinking Our Assumptions: Assuming Anew in a Postmodern World." In *Handbook of Solution-Focused Brief Therapy*. Edited by Scott D. Miller, Mark A. Hubble, and Barry L. Duncan. San Francisco: Jossey-Bass Publishers, 1996.

Watzlawick, P. *The Invented Reality: How Do We Know What We Believe We Know? Contributions to Constructivism*. New York: W. W. Norton, 1984.

Waugh, Barbara. *The Soul in the Computer: The Story of a Corporate Revolutionary*. Makawao, Maui, Hawaii: Inner Ocean, 2001.

Webster's Third New International Dictionary, Unabridged. Springfield, Mass.: Merriam-Webster Inc., 1986.

Weems, Renita J. *Battered Love: Marriage, Sex, and Violence in the Hebrew Prophets*. Minneapolis: Fortress Press, 1995.

Wegner, Daniel N., and James W. Pennebaker, eds. *Handbook of Mental Control*. Englewood Cliffs, N.J.: Prentice Hall, 1993.

Wesley, John. *The Works of John Wesley*. Grand Rapids: Zondervan Publishing House, 1958.

———. *The Works of John Wesley*. Edited by Albert C. Outler. Nashville: Abingdon Press, 1985.

West, Cornel. *Race Matters*. Boston: Beacon Press, 1993.

The Westminster Dictionary of Church History. Edited by Jerald C. Brauer. Philadelphia: The Westminster Press, 1971.

White, Michael M., and David Epston. *Narrative Means to Therapeutic Ends*. New York: Norton, 1990.

Whitehead, Alfred North. *Process and Reality: An Essay in Cosmology*. Corrected ed. Edited by David Ray Griffin and Donald W. Sherburne. New York: The Free Press, 1978.

Whitehead, James D., and Evelyn Eaton Whitehead. *Shadows of the Heart: A Spirituality of the Negative Emotions*. New York: Crossroad Publishing Company, 1994.

Williams, Charles B. *The New Testament in the Language of the People*. Nashville: Holman Bible Publishers, 1937.

Williams, Redford, and Virginia Williams. *Anger Kills*. New York: HarperCollins, 1993.

Wink, Walter. *Engaging the Powers: Discernment and Resistance in a World of Domination*. Minneapolis: Fortress Press, 1992.

———. *The Powers That Be: Theology for a New Millennium*. New York: Doubleday, 1998.

Wolf, George. "The Place of the Brain in an Ocean of Feelings." In *Existence and Actuality: Conversations with Charles Hartshorne*. Edited by John B. Cobb Jr. and Franklin I. Gamwell. Chicago: The University of Chicago Press, 1984.

Worth, Roland H. Jr. *The Sermon on the Mount: Its Old Testament Roots.* New York: Paulist Press, 1997.

Zillman, Dolf. *Hostility and Aggression.* Hillsdale, N.J.: Lawrence Erlbaum Associates, Publishers, 1979.

———. "Mental Control of Angry Aggression." In *Handbook of Mental Control.* Edited by Daniel N. Wegner and James W. Pennebaker. Englewood Cliffs, N.J.: Prentice Hall, 1993.

Scripture Index

Author Index

Subject Index